Collected Papers of
Clarence Irving Lewis

Collected Papers of
Clarence Irving Lewis

Edited by John D. Goheen and
John L. Mothershead, Jr.

Stanford University Press, Stanford, California   1970

The editors wish to express their thanks for permission to republish the following selections: to George Allen & Unwin Ltd. and Russell & Russell for "Logic and Pragmatism"; to the Regents of the University of California for "Bergson and Contemporary Thought," "German Idealism and Its War Critics," "The Pragmatic Element in Knowledge," and "Naturalism and Idealism" ("Professor Santayana and Idealism"); to *Philosophical Review* for "A Comment on 'The Verification Theory of Meaning' by Everett J. Nelson," "Experience and Meaning," "The Given Element in Empirical Knowledge," "Realism or Phenomenalism?" and "Types of Order and the System Σ"; to *Philosophy and Phenomenological Research* for "The Modes of Meaning"; to the Liberal Arts Division of the Bobbs-Merrill Company for "Notes on the Logic of Intension"; to the Open Court Publishing Company for "Alternative Systems of Logic" and "The Categories of Natural Knowledge"; and to *Mind* for "Implication and the Algebra of Logic." No part of any of the above selections may be reproduced in any way without the written permission of the copyright holders.

Stanford University Press, Stanford, California
© 1970 by the Board of Trustees of the Leland Stanford Junior University
Printed in the United States of America
ISBN 0-8047-0717-0   LC 73-97913

Preface

In 1962, two years before his death, Clarence Irving Lewis drew up a plan for a collection of his published and unpublished papers and reviews.[1] Evidently he did not find time to perfect the plan, for nine of the 23 unpublished items listed were left with question marks or double question marks, and the ten unpublished papers bore the heading "All doubtful or worse." The remaining published papers were listed without notation, which suggests that he had intended to include them in his final version.

In making his tentative list of 33 papers, Lewis was highly selective. He chose to include only five of his published papers on logic and only ten of his lectures on ethics, along with two published papers on ethics, "The Rational Imperatives" (1951) and "The Meaning of Liberty" (1953). The most surprising omission is that of his important study of Whitehead's early writings, "The Categories of Natural Knowledge." With the exception of the four Wesleyan Lectures, "Foundations of Ethics" (1959), Lewis listed nothing written after 1955, and he omitted a number of his unpublished lectures on ethics given before that year. He may have considered some of these early lectures inferior to his later works. Indeed, he had ambivalent feelings about his unpublished work in general. In a letter of April 14, 1956, to Professor E. M. Adams concerning the preparation of the bibliography for P. A. Schilpp's volume *The Philosophy of C. I. Lewis*, he had questioned the advisability of referring to any of it at all.

In preparing this collection, we made two substantial modifications in Lewis's original plan and several minor modifications. First, although all the papers except the unpublished ethics lectures were arranged in chronological order on Lewis's list, we decided to divide the material into four categories: "Criticism and Commentary," "Value Theory and Ethics," "Epistemology and Metaphysics," and "Logic and the Philosophy of Logic." We followed chronological order within each of these categories, with one exception: we placed the essay "Logic and Pragmatism" at the beginning of the volume because of its interesting autobiographical content. We began the book with the "Criticism and Com-

---

[1] The plan is among the literary remains received by Stanford University in 1966. Those of Lewis's papers and manuscripts that were in his possession at the time of his death are preserved in the Stanford University Library.

mentary" section for this reason. We ordered the sections on ethics, epistemology, and logic to reflect Lewis's view that ethics is the crown-ing discipline on which logic and epistemology, being also normative in character, are ultimately grounded.

The other deviation from Lewis's plan concerns the papers on ethics. In addition to "The Meaning of Liberty" and "The Rational Impera-tives," the original list contained the following unpublished lectures: "Turning Points in Ethics" (Machette Lectures, Wesleyan University, 1952), "The Empirical Basis of Value Judgments" (Yale University, 1950), "Practical and Moral Imperatives" (Swarthmore College, 1949), "Turning Points of Ethical Theory" (Harvard University, 1954), and "Foundations of Ethics" (Wesleyan Lectures, Wesleyan University, 1959). We felt that the Machette Lectures would be out of place in this volume, simplified as they were for an undergraduate audi-ence, and we saw no reason to include "Foundations of Ethics," "Prac-tical and Moral Imperatives," "The Meaning of Liberty," or "The Ra-tional Imperatives," in view of their recent publication in a separate volume edited by John Lange.[2] Consequently, our ethics section in-cludes only "The Empirical Basis of Value Judgments" and "Turning Points of Ethical Theory" from Lewis's original list. To these we have added four unpublished lectures: "Judgments of Value and Judgments of Fact" (Harvard University, 1936), "The Objectivity of Value Judg-ments" (Brown University, 1941), and "Subjective Right and Objec-tive Right" and "The Individual and the Social Order," prepared by Lewis for his proseminar on ethics at Harvard in 1952.

We have added one unpublished paper that did not appear on Lew-is's list, "Logical Positivism and Pragmatism," and one paper from the Schilpp volume on Whitehead, "The Categories of Natural Knowl-edge." We have omitted the short paper "Santayana at Harvard" be-cause of its special nature (Lewis listed it with double question marks). Two published pieces have been added to the section "Epistemology and Metaphysics": "Professor Chisholm and Empiricism" and "A Comment on 'The Verification Theory of Meaning.' " One unpublished paper, "Verification and the Types of Truth," and a note, "A Paradox of Nominalism," were added as well. Finally, on the advice of several consultants, we included the published paper "Implication and the Al-gebra of Logic" and Lewis's review of the second edition of *Principia Mathematica*.

In the course of preparing this collection, we reviewed much other

[2] Clarence Irving Lewis, *Values and Imperatives: Studies in Ethics*, edited by John Lange (Stanford, Calif.: Stanford University Press, 1969).

manuscript material, including lectures and papers written prior to 1956, and some chapters for a book on ethics, written between 1956 and 1964. Since it is possible that these late ethics manuscripts will be shaped into a book at some future time, we did not include any of them here. With respect to the other materials, we were guided in our selection by our judgment of the intrinsic interest of each paper and the value of each as a complement to the papers that Lewis himself had singled out. Except for standard editorial corrections and changes, the published essays are presented here as originally printed. We transcribed the unpublished papers as faithfully as possible from the original manuscripts; editorial interpolations appear in square brackets throughout.

The inclusion of the unpublished papers in this collection was made possible by the permission of Professor Lewis's son and literary executor, Andrew Lewis. Our thanks are due to Sidney Hook for "Some Suggestions Concerning Metaphysics of Logic"; to the Mathematical Association of America for permission to reprint Lewis's review of *Principia Mathematica*; and to *The Journal of Philosophy* for the review of Dewey's *The Quest for Certainty*, "Facts, Systems, and the Unity of the World," "Meaning and Action," "A Pragmatic Conception of the *A Priori*," "Pragmatism and Current Thought," "Professor Chisholm and Empiricism," "Realism and Subjectivism," "Some Logical Considerations Concerning the Mental," and "The Structure of Logic and Its Relation to Other Systems." We were given valuable advice on the selection of the papers on logic by Professor Krister Segerberg of the University of California at Los Angeles, and Professors Georg Kreisel and Jaakko Hintikka of Stanford University. David Woodruff Smith verified the texts of the logic papers chosen, and Harold Hayes was helpful in transcribing previously unpublished papers from manuscript to typescript. We are grateful to Professor Roderick Chisholm of Brown University, who reviewed the collection for Stanford University Press, and to the editorial staff of the Press, especially Paul Gilchrist, who assisted us with the many details of publication. Our deepest gratitude is due to George Cattermole, our editorial assistant: whatever sins of omission or commission on our part this volume may disclose would have been greatly multiplied without his devotion and judgment.

J. G.
J. M.

Contents

Part I. Criticism and Commentary

1. Logic and Pragmatism

The most powerful single influence in my intellectual development was an old lady whom I met when I was fifteen. A year or two earlier I had begun a period of the most intense and furious thinking I shall ever experience. The combination of native scepticism and an orthodox upbringing had proved to be an explosive mixture: I had been plunged into doubts and questions which went on and on until I faced the universe with something of the wonder of the first man. The old lady, with compassionate understanding, confessed that she too was a heretic, and after establishing our agreements we went on to the much more enticing matter of our disagreements. Our discussions continued, at intervals, over a period of about two years, at the end of which time I had worked out my own answers to the puzzles which beset me. Some of these, I am sure, must have startled and amused my mentor, but she always agreed solemnly to consider them.

As yet no book on philosophy had even fallen under my eye; but about this time someone must have said the right word, because I remember reading a short history of Greek philosophy (Marshall's, I think), and then, following the references, looking into Ueberweg and the Zeller books. My chagrin was enormous. Much of my philosophy had been anticipated by two gentlemen named Heraclitus and Anaxagoras, and the rest could be fairly duplicated by a judicious eclecticism amongst the other pre-Socratics. It was my first professional disappointment, and quite the most grievous. I read Spencer's *First Principles* also, and found there much of stimulus and much which broadened my horizons—so much, in fact, that I cannot now recall any sense of bewilderment or failure to understand. Very likely I did not comprehend enough of it even to be properly puzzled.

Nothing comparable in importance happened after that until I became acquainted with Kant. I was now safely under academic auspices, and thinking was no longer a lone adventure. Kant compelled me. He had, so I felt, followed scepticism to its inevitable last stage, and laid his foundations where they could not be disturbed. I was then, and have continued to be, impatient of those who seem not to face the sceptical doubt seriously. Kant attracted me also by his intellectual integrity and by the massiveness and articulation of his structure. The evidence of

Reprinted by permission from G. P. Adams and W. P. Montague, eds., *Contemporary American Philosophy* (New York, 1930), Vol. II, pp. 31–50.

Kant in my thinking ever since is unmistakable, however little I may achieve the excellences which aroused my youthful admiration.

Of my teachers at Harvard, Royce impressed me most. His ponderous cogency kept my steady attention, even though I never followed to his metaphysical conclusions. James, I thought, had a swift way of being right, but how he reached his conclusions was his own secret. Royce was, in fact, my paradigm of a philosopher, and I was prone to minimize the difference from him of such convictions as I had. It was Royce himself, finally, with my doctor's thesis before him, who pointed out the extent of these differences. He concluded by saying, with his usual dry humor, "I thought you were principally influenced by Perry, but I find he thinks you are principally influenced by me. Between us, we agreed that perhaps this is original."

Royce was also responsible for my interest in logic, or at least for the direction which it took. In 1910–11 I was his assistant in two courses in that subject, and he put into my hands one of the first copies of *Principia Mathematica*, Volume I, which came to Cambridge. It is difficult now to appreciate what a novelty this work then was to all of us. Its logistic method was so decidedly an advance upon Schröder and Peano. The principles of mathematics were here deduced from definitions alone, without other assumptions than those of logic. I spent the better part of a year upon it.

However, I was troubled from the first by the presence in the logic of *Principia* of the theorems peculiar to material implication, such as "A false proposition implies any proposition," and "A true proposition is implied by any." The theorems themselves, of course, were familiar; they went back to Peirce and Schröder. But in spite of Peirce's remarks on the topic, I had never taken them seriously, because of their obvious historical origin.

The investigations to which I was moved by this relatively small matter grew in scope and occupied such leisure as I had for the next six years. Moreover, my thinking on other philosophic topics has been much influenced by these researches, so that I must present, as briefly as possible, the gist of this problem.

Those logicians who were earliest interested in an exact calculus of logic had, all of them, turned first to the relations of concepts or classes. This necessitates a choice—as may be discovered by their mistakes—between the logic of intension and the logic of extension. The relations of class-names in intension are meagre in certain ways, and hardly afford a calculus. Boole founded the algebra of logic, where Leibniz and his Continental successors had failed, principally because Boole interpreted logical relations exclusively in extension. This is no particular merit of Boole's; it seems, rather, to result from the fact that he was born in Great Britain, and knew nothing about his Continental predecessors. British logicians, when really original, have always thought in terms of extension; Continental ones in terms of intension. (Some psychologist with an eye for history ought to investigate this.) So Boole took the universal proposition, "All *a* is *b*," to mean, "The class of things *a* is included in the class *b*," instead of "The concept *a* includes or implies the concept *b*," as a Continental would have done. This extensional point of view requires the special case that if there are no members of the class *a*, then "All *a* is *b*" will hold, regardless of the connotations of *a* and *b*. If Boole had any misgivings about this paradox, the arithmetical analogies which he followed in constructing his algebra would have compelled it in any case. The null-class is contained in every class just as $0 < x$, for any positive number x. The converse principle, that any class is contained in the class of "everything," is obvious.

The effect of these limiting cases is to restrict the interpretation of the algebra as a logic of class-terms to the relations of extension. If there are no centaurs, then all the centaurs there are will be Greeks; this is true regardless of the connotation or intension of "centaur" and "Greek." It does not follow that if there *were* any centaurs they *would be* Greeks.

Now Boole discovered a second application of his algebra to propositions (more correctly, to propositional functions). For this, he let the symbols *a, b, c, . . .* represent the times when the propositions *A, B, C, . . .* are true. Here the analogue of "All *a* is *b*" is, "Whenever *A* is true, *B* is true," or "*A* implies *B*." If the algebra is to have this second application, the properties of implication must be point for point analogous to those of classes in extension. Hence if $A = 0$—that is, if *A* is always false—then *A* must imply any proposition *B* whatever. And if *B* is always true—that is, if $B = 1$—then *B* must be implied by every proposition. Boole's principal successors, Peirce and Schröder, observed that a proposition, as distinguished from a propositional function, if once true is always true. Hence as applied to propositions, $A = 0$ may be interpreted simply as "*A* is false," and $B = 1$ as "*B* is true."

Thus the application of the algebra to propositions requires these two principles, "A false proposition implies anything" and "A true proposition is implied by any." In the sense of "implies," which figures in the algebra, "*A* implies *B*" will hold if *A* is false or if *B* is true, and will fail only when *A* is true and *B* is false.

As the analogy with classes shows, this is the case only because the algebra must be restricted to relations of extension. The relation here designated by "implies" is such that a false proposition implies anything, but that throws no light on what it *would* imply if it *were true*.

A meaning of "implies" which is such that the implications of a proposition depend upon its truth or falsity is certainly not the usual one. And the peculiar properties of it are neither important logical discoveries nor absurdities; they are merely the inevitable consequences of a novel denotation for an old and familiar word, long used in common parlance in a different meaning. Thus the calculus of propositions which is historically continuous with Boole is not a calculus of implications, such as those with which logic and deduction generally have always been concerned. This new meaning of "implies" (now called "material implication") should be submitted to some examination before its laws are accepted as a canon of deduction. Such examination was lacking in *Principia*.

Two sorts of problems were before me. First and most obviously: Is there an exact logic, comparable to this extensional calculus, which will exhibit the analogous relations in intension? And is the intensional analogue of material implication the relation upon which deductive inference is usually founded? Second, there were larger and vaguer questions: Could there be different exact logics? If I should find my calculus of intension, it and material implication would be incompatible, on some points, when applied to inference. In that case, in what sense would there be a question of validity or truth to be determined between them? And what criteria could determine the validity of logic, since logic itself provides the criteria of validity used elsewhere, and the application of these to logic itself would be *petitio principii*?

Even the two questions of the first sort could not really be determined in separation from these more general problems. Yet I chose to begin with them. It seemed more promising to argue from exactly determined facts of the behavior of symbolic systems to conclusions on more general problems than to attempt to reverse this procedure. Logicians who argue from "first principles" to the validity or invalidity of logistic developments find themselves in a weak position, since they dogmatize about a matter which they either have not investigated or have approached with an initial prejudice which commits the *petitio principii* just pointed out.

Leaving, then, the larger questions, I turned to the logistic development of the logic of intension. The results of this investigation may be briefly summarized, since it has been outlined in Chapter V of the *Survey of Symbolic Logic*.[1]

The intensional implication relation (or "strict implication" as I called it) gives rise to a calculus as exact as the older logistic systems. It is also more inclusive: when the extensional relations are introduced by definition, it includes the calculus of propositions, as previously developed, as a sub-system. While there are ambiguities about the usual meaning of "implies," and the final issues are such as have seldom been faced at all, on the whole accepted deductive procedures and ordinary logical intuitions accord with strict implication and do not accord with material implication where it diverges.

The only implication relation upon which inference is likely to be based is this intensional or strict implication, for reasons which are fairly obvious. "The proposition A materially implies the proposition B" means precisely, "It is not the case that A is true and B false." This is necessary to ordinary deduction, since otherwise false conclusions could be derived from true premises, but it is not sufficient. To see this, let us inquire how this relation might be verified as holding. In a particular case, it could be verified simply by finding A to be false; but that would mean finding our premise false, so that the conclusion B would ordinarily not be drawn. Sometimes, however, we are interested to draw the inferences from false assumptions. But we should not do this on the basis of material implication, precisely because a false premise materially implies anything and everything. That A materially implies B, *because A is false*, throws no light on the question what A *would* imply if it *were true*.

We might also verify "*A* materially implies B" in a concrete instance by finding B to be true. But this would mean finding our conclusion to be true. Most frequently in such cases we should not "make the infer-

---

[1] A note should be added concerning the mistaken postulate which I there assumed for the system of strict implication. This was later pointed out by Dr. E. L. Post, and corrected by me in a note in the *Journal of Philosophy*. ["Strict Implication— an Emendation." Vol. XVII (1920), No. 11, pp. 300–302.] In developing the system, I had worked for a month to avoid this principle, which later turned out to be false. Then, finding no reason to think it false, I sacrificed economy and put it in. It was because it thus entered the system so late in its development that I was able, when the mistake was discovered, to correct it in brief space. The system of strict implication, as printed, contained no postulate logistically incompatible with a material interpretation, such as $\Sigma p : -p . - (p < -p)$. To include this would have required a fundamental complication, undesirable in a book addressed to beginning students. I am lately in receipt of a proof, made by a Polish student, M. Wajsberg, that the principle $p < . q < p$ is independent of the amended postulates. This covers the same point.

ence" because it would be superfluous. Sometimes, however, we are interested to discover what implies some known fact and what does not—for example, in the testing of hypotheses. But a known fact is *materially* implied by *any* hypothesis. Amongst known facts, the material implications of all hypotheses whatever are identical.

Consequently no use can be made of material implication in drawing valid inferences, except in those cases in which the implication can be known to hold for some other reason than that the premise is false or that the conclusion is true. When we inquire how we can know that it is not the case that A is true and B false, without knowing that A is false and without knowing that B is true, the only answer is: By knowing that if A *were* true, B *must be* true; by knowing that the truth of A is inconsistent with the falsity of B; by knowing that the situation in which A should be true and B false is an impossible situation. That is to say, the only case in which any inference could be based on a material implication is precisely the case in which it should coincide (and *be known* to coincide) with the intensional or strict implication of B by A. This amounts to saying that the real basis of the inference is the strict implication. "A strictly implies B" mean exactly "The truth of A is inconsistent with the falsity of B."

The so-called "formal implication," "For every x, ϕx materially implies ψx," would coincide, in its general deductive significance, with strict implication provided "For every x" be interpreted to mean "For every possible or conceivable x." It will be obvious that "For every conceivable x, it is not the case that ϕx is true and ψx false," is a strict implication, differently phrased. But if "For every x" means "For every x that *exists*," then this formal implication represents the ordinary relation of classes, "Every existent thing having the property ϕ has also the property ψ." In *Principia* it is this second interpretation of formal implication which is chosen.

Various technical problems which came to light in the course of these investigations may be omitted here as probably of small interest to the general reader. However, there is one such matter which must be mentioned because it influenced the direction of my thinking outside the field of exact logic. Early in the course of these researches I formed the conviction that all valid inference, being a matter of intension, rests upon the analysis of meaning. The reasons for this will probably be evident from the foregoing. But the symbolic relations I was dealing with proved to have properties which I had not anticipated, and some of these gave me pause. In particular, while it would not be true, in the system of strict implication, that a merely false proposition implied anything and everything and a merely true proposition is implied by any, it *would* hold that a "necessary" proposition (defined as one which is implied by its own denial) is implied by any, and that a self-contradictory proposition (one which implies its own denial) implies anything.

Had I made a mistake in my assumptions so that the system was out of accord with the properties of analytic inference? Or did the implication relation of ordinary inference have these properties? The latter proved to be the true alternative. There was no way to avoid the principles stated by these unexpected theorems without giving up so many generally accepted laws as to leave it dubious that we could have any formal logic at all.

There were many corroborations. The simplest to set down is as follows: Suppose that a proposition A (say, "Today is Monday") implies another, B ("Tomorrow is Tuesday"). Then the premise A, together with any additional proposition, C (say, "Mars is not inhabited"), will likewise imply B—that is, "Today is Monday, and Mars is not inhabited" implies "Tomorrow is Tuesday." According to another general principle, if two premises give a conclusion, but that conclusion is false while one of the premises is true, the other premise must be false. "All men are mortal" and "Socrates is a man" together imply "Socrates is mortal." Hence if all men are mortal, but Socrates is not mortal, then it follows that Socrates is not a man—that is, we have the rule: If "A and C" implies B, then "A but not B" implies "not C." Applying this rule to our first example, we have: "Today is Monday and Mars is not inhabited" implies "Tomorrow is Tuesday"; hence "Today is Monday, but tomorrow is not Tuesday" implies "Mars is inhabited." In this illustration, the last-mentioned proposition might have been anything you please without altering anything else. Thus ordinary logical conceptions require that the affirmation of a premise, together with the denial of its consequence (a case of contradiction), will imply anything and everything.

If, then, I had made no mistake, the line of division which marks off that class of propositions which are capable of corroboration by logic alone (necessary propositions) from merely empirical truths, and marks off the impossible or absurd, which can be refuted by logic alone, from merely empirical falsehood, is a division of major importance. Possible and impossible, contingent and necessary, consistent and inconsistent—such categories of intension are independent of material truth, and their distinct nature is founded in logic itself. Moreover, as is easily obvious, all the propositions of logic are truths of intension, and therefore certifiable without reference to the merely factual or empirical.

But I had further doubts. In particular it was not clear that if one should, by inadvertence, set out with incompatible assumptions, there would be no conclusion whatever which one might not draw from them by analytic inference. Nor was it clear that all necessary propositions are analytically derivable from any assumption you please. The facts of the symbolic system were inescapable, and ordinary practice corroborated them; but what did these facts mean?

In part, the answer was a simple one which should have been anticipated. These unexpected properties of implication did not mean that all necessary propositions are analytically derivable from any arbitrarily chosen assumptions whatever; they did represent the fact that implication is not a property of isolated propositions as such, but of systems. Necessary truths are all of them principles of logic, or such as can be certified on grounds of logic alone. Without logic, nothing is derivable from anything; the logic of it is implicit in every deductive system. All necessary propositions are thus, explicitly or tacitly, present in every system, and indeed in every assertion conceived as having logical consequences. Inference is analytic of the system rather than of its separate and bare constituents. If there is any exact logic which is capable of representing inference as analytic in any other sense, I have never been able to discover a clue to it. I should but be dumbfounded to learn of such tomorrow, but I have followed every lead that has occurred to me, always with negative results.

If inference is analytic of systems, not of propositions in isolation, does this mean that logic compels the acceptance of a coherence theory of truth or the acceptance of that kind of unity of the world which is maintained by logicians of the "modern" or Hegelian school? I turned briefly to the consideration of this possibility—though, I must admit, without any conviction of the necessity of so doing—because while it had become apparent to me that logic required the existence of necessary propositions, it was not so apparent that it required the existence of any truth which is *not* necessary. That the distinction of necessary and contingent must finally fail and all truth reveal itself as necessary, because inference depends on systematic unity, is just what the modern logicians claim. The conclusions which I reached are outlined in a little paper, "Facts, Systems, and the Unity of the World."[2] The thesis that all truths are necessary, and none independent of any other, is hopelessly implausible in the light of certain facts of mathematical systems concerning which nobody (unless it be the modern logicians them-

[2] See pp. 383–93 below.—Eds.

selves) has ever entertained a doubt. The whole development of modern geometry, for example, must be somehow invalid if they are right.

The most general and important issue was still before me. I had set out to determine a question of truth between two symbolic systems—material implication and a logic of intensional implication. This had raised the further question what kind of an issue of truth there could be in such a case, and what criteria could determine it. I had found, in commonly accepted practices and principles, corroboration of the characterizing features of strict implication—the distinction of necessary from contingent truth, the classification of logical principles themselves as necessary, and, as a consequence, the status of logic as self-affirming or self-critical, its principles being implied by their own denial. Could such necessity or self-affirmation be accepted as a final criterion of truth in logic?

There was unmistakable evidence that such was not the case. In the first place, both material implication and strict implication had this character, yet both could not be accepted as stating the truth about what can validly be inferred from what—the truth of logic. Also I found that other and somewhat similar systems could be devised, each of which would have the same general kind of mathematical precision and methodological integrity. These might be called "pseudo-logics" or "metalogics." Though I made no systematic investigation, it became evident that the number of such would be limited only by some criterion of "logistic system" or of the principles of derivation which should be allowed. Such a criterion would itself be an antecedent principle limiting "logical" truth. That such a system might be totally unacceptable as a "true logic" and yet be entirely consistent, and even self-affirming, in its own terms is due to the curious involution which is peculiar and inevitable to logical truth. "Consistency" is the absence of an "implication": two propositions are consistent when neither implies the negation of the other. Hence if the meaning of "implies"—and consequently the methods of derivation—be allowed to vary, a "queer" logic may be "consistent" or "self-critical" in its own "queer" way.

Thus we revert to the previous question, which now assumes a somewhat complicated form. If formal logic is capable of any exact development at all, then we are confronted with the task of deciding which, amongst various possible and actual logistic systems, is such that its principles state the truth about valid inference. Internal consistency and "self-criticism" are not sufficient criteria to determine a truth which is independent of initial assumptions which are themselves logical in nature. Thus logic cannot test itself—or rather, such test does not prove truth in logic.

It was clear that such a problem has no solution in logic; I was carried beyond logic into the field of epistemology. Many other strands, not mentioned here, were, of course, already woven into my thinking. In particular it had been impressed upon me that it is possible to take symbolic procedures both too seriously and too lightly. To paraphrase Hobbes: Symbols are our counters; they are the money of fools. But on the other hand, the behavior of symbolic systems is nothing more or less than the behavior of the human mind, using its most characteristic instrument: there is nothing in them which we have not put in ourselves, but they teach us inexorably what our commitments mean.

Also, at just this time it became my duty and privilege to turn over the numerous unpublished papers of Charles Peirce. Though I was not specially conscious of it, this was perhaps the means of stirring up old thoughts of the time when I had listened to James, and reminding me also of what Royce used to call his "absolute pragmatism." Again, I had long been attracted to certain theses of Dewey's logic—if only he would not miscall "logic" what is rightly a much wider thing, the analysis of the constructive thought-process! The study of exact logic itself had revealed unmistakably that in every process of reasoning there must be an extra-logical element. This cannot but be so, since from any premise or set of premises whatever an infinite number of valid inferences can be drawn. (This is an immediate consequence of Poretsky's laws.) What is called " *the* conclusion" must be selected from this infinity by psychological obviousness or by some purpose or interest; certainly logic does not dictate it. The *direction* of thought inevitably belongs, then, to such an extra-logical factor. Finally, Peirce's "conceptual pragmatism," turning as it does upon the instrumental and empirical significance of concepts rather than upon any non-absolute character of truth, was at some points consonant with my own reflections where James and Dewey were not.

Whatever it was that turned my thoughts in this direction, at any rate I began to see that the principles of logic will answer to criteria of the general sort which may be termed pragmatic, and that where empirical verification is not in point, and logical "necessity" itself is not sufficient, no other kind of criterion can in any sense be final.

It had become apparent from my little experiments with strange "logics" that two minds which followed different systems in their modes of inference need not be unintelligible to one another—that, in fact, they might be so related that when their premises were common neither (outside of logic itself) would ever reach a conclusion which the other must repudiate as false. But, as between two such, the road from premise to conclusion would be more or less direct, more or less impeded. Fundamental psychological bent might here dictate a choice. Or again, if the general course of experience were other than it is—if, for example, all processes in nature should be reversible—then, although no different choice of modes of inference would be dictated, a different "logic" would apply with more facility. Thus the ultimate ground of accepted logical principles, as against other self-consistent modes, might be criteria of convenience (a poor word, but the best I can think of), somewhat like those which Poincaré suggested as determining our choice of Euclidean geometry.

This thesis, by itself, seems implausible and highly paradoxical : the stronghold of pragmatism supposedly lies in the empirical ; logic is the citadel of rationalism. Nevertheless I became more and more convinced that this was right. Pragmatism, as ordinarily understood, seems to take things wrong end on ; it is the element which mind contributes, in truth and knowledge, which may be pragmatic ; the empirical brute fact of the given is absolute datum. Logic contains no material truth ; it is independent of the given precisely because it dictates nothing whatever with regard to the content of experience, but determines only the mind's mode of dealing with it. This thought suggested others, which soon came to keep it company and mitigate the paradoxical air which it exhibited in isolation.

A variety of other problems, mainly in the theory of knowledge, had been in my mind for the past few years. Some of them were closely related to those already suggested as growing out of logic. I now sat down (this was in 1921) to the first draft of something concerning these, which I projected as "Studies in Logic and Epistemology." These will never see the light. They grew from one box to two, and then to several. But the yeast of the newly awakened pragmatic conceptions was working too strongly. My thought changed and widened as I attempted to formulate it, and the result, instead of moving toward some unity of subject and literary coherence, spread in widening circles through the whole field of philosophy. It was a most satisfactory period to me personally, because in the course of it I squared my account with many problems and brought them into touch with one another. What I shall venture to call "conceptualistic pragmatism" proved to be, for me, the key that opened many doors. But my notes I put away, except for a relatively small portion, and concentrated upon certain closely related topics which I found myself particularly interested to develop further.

The attempt to outline some of these is the remaining task of this paper.

Logic, and that which is certifiable on logical grounds alone, constitutes the *a priori* element in knowledge. The Kantian cross-classification, by which *synthetic* judgments *a priori* become the foundations of science, has more and more clearly been proved to be without foundation, as mathematics and exact science have developed. Mathematics has been shown to be capable of purely logical development, by analysis alone, and without recourse to any synthetic element, such as geometric constructions, which represent an appeal from pure conception to intuition. *Principia Mathematica* represents the final stage of the movement in this direction: we see here the deductive development of mathematics merely from the logical analysis (definition) of the mathematical concepts. There is and must be a synthetic element in judgment about the *applications* of mathematics, about real space, or about concrete collections of things. At the same time that mathematics becomes purely logical and analytic, it becomes abstract. Which of the various abstract geometries applies to space becomes a separate and extra-mathematical question, and, as Poincaré and relativity have shown, one which is to be determined either upon empirical grounds—in which case the answer is probable only—or by some pragmatic choice, or by some interplay between these two.

Hume was right in his somewhat wavering conviction that the truths of mathematics represent necessary connections of ideas, and likewise right that this by itself does not prove any necessary connection of matters of fact. The line between the *a priori* and the *a posteriori* coincides with the division between conceptual and empirical; and it likewise coincides with the distinction between what mind itself contributes or determines and what is given as datum of sense.

A priori truth is independent of experience because it is purely analytic of our conceptual meanings, and dictates nothing to the given. Logic, mathematics, and in general whatever has structure and order and system may be developed in abstraction from all consideration of the empirical by purely logical analysis. It depends upon nothing but its own conceptual integrity for that kind of truth which is possible to abstract systems.

Such *a priori* truth is not assertive of material fact, but definitive. This is the clue to many problems. In the first place, it exhibits clearly the sense in which we can make stipulations applicable to experience but independent of its content. In the absence of definitive criteria, experience would be unintelligible; these are prerequisite to truth and knowledge, though not to mere givenness. The definitive principle is "necessary" truth: it cannot be false; it is prerequisite to intelligibility; it must be taken in advance of the particular experience; it dictates nothing as to the content of the experience.

In the second place, this solves the problem of the criterion between what mind contributes in truth and knowledge and what is independent of the mind. How should we know what mind does, if mind could do no different? I discover what I do solely by the difference in what ensues when I refuse to do, or do differently. If there should be immutable and "ungetoverable" modes of intuition or of thought, the mind could never discover that these belonged to itself and were not characters of the independent real; they would be absolute data, flatly given in experience, and the individual would find them as he finds his ears.

There must, then, in some sense or other, be conceivable alternatives to what is *a priori*. In those modes of our own intellectual activity which are exhibited in the criteria supplied by definitive principles, there are such alternatives. A definition may be laid down in one or another way; we classify and order and understand as we ourselves determine. Once our exact concepts are taken, the unfolding of them is an absolute truth: there is no alternative about that (unless we ascend to some higher choice of alternative modes of deductive order itself). But what concepts we shall formulate, and what we shall apply, admits of choice. The mind approaches the chaos of experience with its own intellectual instruments, which are independent of the given as the given is of them. Truth and knowledge represent the meeting of these two. That the particular truth and knowledge may reflect, in some part, a choice of such instruments, that the net of understanding may be stretched across the given in terms of one or another reference system of conceptual order, is a matter which might well be illustrated at some length, but will probably be evident without such exemplification. And the sense in which the truths of experience will be, on one side, determined by the presence of such definitive conceptual order, though the content of the given is not thus determined, will likewise be clear. The whole trend of exact science serves strongly to enforce the fact of this presence, throughout all knowledge, of an *a priori* element which enters through the simple fact that experience never supplies its own conceptual interpretation, but that conceptual systems, amongst which there may be possible choice, serve as criteria of such interpretation, without imposing any limit on the empirical content. That in the presence of such alternative systems of order, pragmatic criteria, which may reflect on the one side human bent and interest, and on the other a facility determined by the general character of what is presented, will have their place in fixing the truths of experience, needs no special demonstration.

If, however, all truth which can be certain in advance of the experience to which it applies is of this purely analytic and definitive sort, then we might be led to remark that such abstract *a priori* truth tells us nothing of the nature of reality beyond our own minds, and is significant only of our own consistency of thought. This conclusion would be a mistaken one; paradoxical as it may sound, we can predict the nature of reality without prescribing the character of future experience. What the mind meets in experience is not independent *reality*, but an independent *given*; the given is not, without further ado, the real, but contains all the content of dream, illusion, and deceitful appearance.

In fact, the criteria of reality represent a peculiarly illuminating example of the *a priori*. The word "real" has a meaning, and represents a definite conception which, when applied to the content of experience, leads to the interpretation of this content sometimes as "real," sometimes as "unreal." The formulation of the criteria of the real constitutes a merely analytic or definitive statement, representing our interpretative attitude. Such criteria of reality can neither be supplied by experience (since direct generalization from an unsorted experience, not already classified as real, would not serve) nor can experience invalidate them. Whatever in experience does not conform to the criteria of reality is automatically thrown out of court.

We can and must prescribe the nature of reality. We cannot prescribe the nature of the given. The paradox of this is mitigated somewhat when we observe that the word "real" is systematically ambiguous. "Reality" is of different sorts, physical, mental, mathematical—the easily named categories do not cover the easily recognized distinctions. A mirror-image, for example, is its own particular kind of reality, neither "physical" nor "mental," as is also a mirage and "appearances" in general. Each category of reality has its own peculiar criteria, and what is unreal in one sense will be real in some other. *Any* content of given experience will be real in some category or other—will be that kind of reality which is ascribed to it when it is "correctly understood." The categories are neither a Procrustean bed into which experience is thrust nor concepts whose applicability depends on some pre-established harmony between the given and the mind. Rather they are like the reference system which the mathematician stretches through all space and with respect to which whatever positions and motions are there to be described will inevitably be describable. Categorial criteria are neither insignificant and verbal tautologies nor empirical prophecies, but exhibit definitive criteria of intelligent classification and interpretation.

The content of a properly conceived metaphysics is the analytic truths which exhibit the fundamental criteria and major classifications of the real; it is definitive of "real"-ity, not descriptive of the universe *in extenso*. In fact, all philosophy has for its task such analytic depiction of the *a priori*—to define the good, the right, the true, the valid, and the real.

It will be evident that the absoluteness of such *a priori* principles, whenever and wherever they are held, is entirely compatible with their historical alteration, just as modes of classification or alternative reference systems, expressible in definitive principles or initial prescriptions, would be absolute while adhered to, but might be subject to considerations of usefulness and to historical change. The assurance of perpetuity for our categories is no greater than the assurance that our basic human nature and the broad outlines of experience will never alter. There is an eternal truth about our abstract concepts—the given is absolute datum; but the chosen conceptual systems applied to the interpretation of the given are subject to possible change. In the field of metaphysical concepts particularly, such change would seem to be a fact—as the history of such concepts as "matter," "mind," and "cause" bears witness.

The categories differ in no wise from concepts in general except in degree of comprehensiveness and fundamental character. Every concept whatever exhibits criteria of its own little kind of reality. In so far as experience is intelligible and expressible only when grasped in some framework of conceptual interpretation, this *a priori* element of the definitive is all-pervasive.

It is the conceptual order of experience alone which is communicable or expressible. The given, apart from such conceptual interpretation, is ineffable. If, so to speak, one sensory quality could be lifted out of the network of relations in which it stands and replaced by another, the esthetic character of experience might be altered, but everything which has to do with knowledge and with action would remain precisely as before. Community of thought and knowledge requires community of concept or of relational pattern, but if there should be idiosyncrasies of sense which do not affect discrimination and relation, these would be immaterial to our common understanding and cooperation. In fact, in the face of all those *verifiable* differences of sense which are evidenced by our different powers of discrimination, we possess a common understanding and a common reality through the social achievement of common categories and concepts. When the vast and impressive institution of human education—in its wider sense—is remarked, the assumption that such community is simply native or ready-made is seen to be superfluous. My world is my intellectual achievement; our common world, a social one. The frequent objection of the sceptic, that knowledge is implausible in view of the subjectivity of sense, is an *ignoratio elenchi*.

Knowledge grasps conceptual structure or order alone. It was Berkeley who, almost without noting it himself, first phrased this nature of our knowledge. One idea is "sign of" another in the order of nature. If it be a reliable sign—that is, if it bear constant and orderly relationships—one empirical *quale* is as good as another to serve this function of cognition. Knowledge of the external world consists of relations between one item of experience and another, not in the content of experience somehow matching the quality of an external real. Such qualitative coincidence of idea and object—if the notion means anything—would be extraneous to knowledge. This conclusion is quite independent of idealism.

There are not two kinds of knowledge—one of principles or relations, expressible in propositions, and another which we have by mere presentation of the object. The conceptual interpretation of the given is the implicit prediction of other possible experience. As Mr. Whitehead has pointed out, no object can be known without reference to some temporal spread. My knowledge of the object is not the mere having of this presentation, but the implicit prediction of the eventuation of other experience continuous with this. What is thus predicted is not at the moment verified, but it must be verifiable if the interpretative concept is veridically applicable. The mere naming of this thing I see as "desk" predicts eventualities of a specific sort, which, if they should fail to be realized, would lead to the repudiation of the concept "desk" (or perhaps even of "physical reality") as inapplicable to this which I see. The knowledge of any object transcends its given presentation and grasps a structure of experience. Without order, there can be no *thing*, no experience of *reality*. This, in brief, is the deduction of the categories.

That *if* this be a desk it *will be* thus and so, is an analytic consequence of the concept "desk," not subject to any falsification by experience. That any given "this" is really a desk is theoretically not completely certain. Thus there is an *a priori* element which is all-pervasive in knowledge and prescriptive of reality. Yet all empirical truth, without exception, is probable only.

One further note I should like to make in closing. As the word "knowledge" has been used above, it is narrowed somewhat from its usual meaning. It comprises what have sometimes been called the "truths of description" which, as it is here conceived, depend exclusively upon conceptual order. It excludes "truths of appreciation," the esthetic quality of the given, and all that depends upon sympathy and upon that communion of minds which requires coincidence of immediate experience. Evaluation can hardly be indifferent to the quality of the given. Nor can the basis of ethics be laid without reference to the felt character of experience in another mind. And the religious sense, if it is to take reality as the matrix of human values, will likewise transcend the interests of knowledge in this restricted sense. There is, then, a line of division between such interests and cognition of the type of science. And it is suggested that the foundation of these, not being found in knowledge alone, may rest upon some postulate.

2. Naturalism and Idealism

Idealism is a general term applicable to a fairly wide range of philosophic doctrine. Berkeley holds that "to be is to be perceived." The position of Plato may perhaps be summarized in the statement that "to be is to be *con*ceived; the flux of sense perception is deceitful, and the real is transcendent of experience." For Kant, the object of knowledge must be both perceived and conceived: conception without perception is empty; percepts without concepts are blind. Fichte asserts that the real is the valuable; Hegel, that the real is rational and the rational is real. These campaign banners can hardly be got to march all in the same procession. It results from this divergence of doctrines that one may possibly refute Idealism with a capital "I" without hurting the feelings or damaging the arguments of anybody in particular. Whoever attacks Berkeley's position may be hailed as a comrade in arms by those who follow the Platonic tradition; while he who assails Plato's abstract ideas will do a real service to Neo-Kantians and Hegelians. But one who determines to annihilate Idealism in general is likely to waste his ammunition on a straw man, while his real opponents are outflanking him right and left.

This stalking Idealism in effigy has latterly become a favorite pastime. Certain philosophic writers in this country find it easier to play at refuting Idealism than seriously to attempt a construction of their own.

Professor Santayana, however, has not been one of this number. The spirit of his opposition is somewhat different—not directed so much against any particular thesis which he supposes all idealists to hold in common, but aimed rather at the general trend of idealistic thinking. You remember the Athenian who voted to banish Aristides because he was tired of hearing him called "the Just." Professor Santayana casts his vote against Idealism because he is wearied of its gentility. His poetic soul is sated with its eternal validities, and its protagonism of higher values. He finds its ethics "conventional and verbal," its morals "trivial and sanctimonious—based on authority instead of human na-

A lecture given before the Philosophical Union of the University of California. Reprinted by permission from the *University of California Chronicle*, Vol. XIV (1912), No. 8, pp. 192-211. Lewis suggested that the above title was more appropriate than the original, "Professor Santayana and Idealism."—Eds.

ture, with salvation rather than happiness for their goal." It provides a cloak for superstition and allies itself with myth-making theologies. The separate charges in this arraignment cannot, we hope, be substantiated. Indeed they constitute an expression of sentiment rather than assertions to be proved or disproved. But this feeling that Idealism has become infected with the germ of respectability, has even prospered too much and waxes effete and enervating, is probably not confined to Professor Santayana, though he has put it rather strongly. The fundamental insights of philosophy, like those of religion, ever require new and more vital forms of expression. There is, perhaps, this much of justice in Professor Santayana's attitude—that Idealism stands today just a little in need of fresh and vigorous restatement, shorn of all obsolete phraseology, and fully abreast of the best scientific and religious thinking of our time.

Such restatement is not, however, altogether wanting; and even if it were, that would constitute no excuse for denying the validity of the idealistic position. It is significant that Professor Santayana does not hold that the fundamental tenets of Idealism—unless it be Berkeley's—are false. On the contrary, transcendentalism is "true but trivial." I quote from the first volume of the *Life of Reason*: "It was a thing taken for granted in ancient and scholastic philosophy that a being dwelling, like man, in the immediate, whose moments are in flux, needed constructive reason to interpret his experience and paint in his unstable consciousness some symbolic picture of the world. To have reverted to this constructive process and studied its stages is an interesting achievement (he refers, of course, to Kant) ; but that construction is already made by common sense and science, and it was visionary insolence in the Germans to propose to make that construction otherwise. In the heat of scientific theorizing or dialectical argument, it is sometimes salutary to be reminded that we are men thinking; but, after all, it is no news."

This sounds persuasive; but if one conceive that there is anything really at stake, it is hardly convincing. It is not at once obvious why it is insolent to state explicitly what is already implied in science and common sense. One might suppose this to be the function of philosophy. If Kant's fundamental insight—which the passage quoted burlesques just a bit—is "no news," why treat Kantian doctrine as a view opposed to one's own? That one is bored by trivial truths is no excuse for serious disagreement. Moreover, it seems pertinent to ask how, if the primary principle of Idealism is true, the Naturalism which it controverts can be also true. The fact is that Idealism draws from this main premise certain consequences which Naturalism finds it convenient to omit. If we need constructive reason to interpret our experience, then at least experience needs interpretation, and the only interpretation possible is that which is made in the light of constructive reason. The conditions, further, which reason in its constructions imposes upon the object of thought must apply to all reality which is intelligible. And so on:—I hesitate to bore you further with the consequences of this "trivial truth," especially since they are already familiar.

Naturalism is not primarily a positive but a negative doctrine. It does not seek to expand our knowledge of realities so much as to correct certain errors and to limit the field of significant truth and our method of attaining it. For Naturalism, the limits of knowledge are the (ideal!) limits of natural science, and the realm of knowable reality is bounded by causal and mathematical explanation. Anything further would be myth and superstition—or mere verbiage. The only laws of reality are those of mechanics and mathematics, with their derivatives. The laws of constructive reason, you observe, are forgotten in this enumeration. The naturalist may be a materialist and reduce the cosmos, life, mind, thoughts, purposes, and ideals to a concatenation of atoms and molecules, distributed according to the laws of motion. Or he may feel that the hypothesis of molecular matter smacks of metaphysics, and prefer to remain agnostic with respect to the substrate of reality. He seems then to be confined to the assertion that the world is full of a number of things; for further particulars consult the encyclopedias of natural science. His philosophy seems reduced to the aphoristic type, a series of wise observations about life.

Idealism, on the other hand, does not deny the validity or importance of scientific description. Instead, it insists upon it. Idealism does not even deny the reality of matter, the popular supposition to the contrary notwithstanding. Of course, if one mean by "matter" a something-I-know-not-what which is totally indescribable save as that in which qualities inhere, we must deny it. But science has no interest in such a supposititious substance, because it would explain nothing. The matter of science may be represented under a variety of forms, some of which are possibly true hypotheses while others are merely ideal constructions for convenience of treatment. The three dimensional continuum of mass points is of the latter type. The physicist no more supposes that force can be exerted upon a single mass point than he supposes that the weight of a lever can be concentrated at its center of gravity. The mass point is merely a convenient symbolism which simplifies the procedure of mechanics. The question whether mass points actually exist, or how space can be filled by indivisible and non-extended entities would, consequently, be meaningless. With atoms and molecules the case is different. There is no reason, except some advanced by scientists themselves, why a single molecule or atom may not be as real as an alum crystal or a drop of water. That no one can have any direct experience of a single molecule is no objection to their reality; the same may be said of the other side of the moon. To be sure, the scientist himself is likely to regard atoms and molecules either as merely ideal constructs, like mass points, or as at least hypothetical and doubtfully real. The reason is not, however, that no one has directly experienced them, but rather that not all the phenomena of which physics and chemistry treat are readily explanable on this hypothesis alone, and that, in any case, other possibilities are equally conceivable. But if we were once sure that no other hypothesis would explain all the facts, while this one would, both science and idealistic philosophy would confidently assert that atoms and molecules are real. Reality must be through and through intelligible—that is a fundamental thesis of Idealism. If physical and chemical phenomena were inexplicable save on one hypothesis, then that hypothesis must be true. Idealism stands ready to insist upon the existence of matter, if by matter is meant anything which is *itself intelligible* and is required for the truth of science.

This digression with reference to the matter of science has been necessary in order to avoid misunderstanding. For I now have to say that Idealism would deny the existence and the possibility of that "matter" which figures in Professor Santayana's philosophy. The term "matter," he tells us, has two meanings. One, the scientific, you are familiar with. The other, which he calls the "literary or philosophic" meaning, is the sense in which he uses the term. When he styles himself a materialist, he intends no reference to atoms and molecules, mass points, or ions or electrons. The matter in question is a modification of Aristotle's ὕλη or stuff. It can neither be described nor adequately characterized, for reasons which will appear. But its function, as Professor Santayana represents it, is clear.

There is a difference between the idea or definition or essence of a thing (Aristotle's "form") and that thing's existence. This difference is one with respect to matter. Some essences are materialized; others are not. This is *not* the difference between thought and external reality, with which it might easily be confused. For a thought, too, is materialized when some one has it or thinks it. The distinction is, rather, that which holds between actuality and mere possibility—between the third dimension and the fourth, between you and your twin brother, between the thought which somebody thinks and one which somebody *might* think. The merely possible lacks *matter*; the actual has it or is constituted by means of it. The actual is, then, the conceivable or merely possible—the essence—plus matter.

The distinction thus indicated between essences and existences is, of course, a valid distinction. The question why some things exist, while others which are equally conceivable do not, is one which it is permitted anybody to raise—and answer if he can. But the problem is not solved, or even rendered intelligible, by saying "matter." "Matter" then becomes only another name for the problem.

The difficulty with this matter is that it can never be pried loose from the essences in union with which it exists. This is the more troublesome because the essences can readily be separated from matter. The merely possible—e.g., a piece of furniture you would like to have made—is still conceivable or definable. It has a definite nature. You know what you mean, though you do not find it in experience. This desk is the union of its essence with matter. We can separate out in thought its essence—as it was for the person who planned it—from its existence. But when the essence is abstracted from its existence, the matter of it seems utterly to disappear. Do I hear some one murmur "planks"? No, the planks from which the desk was made, or the kindling wood into which it might be converted, are different from the desk. They are not the matter of the desk, but instead, the union of a different essence with matter. When we divide in thought the essence from the matter of the desk, we cannot conceive or describe the matter. It seems utterly to have lapsed. Essences by themselves are conceivable; matter by itself is not. Not only is this matter nowhere to be discovered out of combination with some essence, it cannot even be imagined. Unlike the matter of science it has no particular nature or properties, has no place in space or time, and is totally incomprehensible. Necessarily so, since to describe it or define it would be to give it an essence—a definition or idea—which *qua* matter it cannot have. Matter is the universal dough which lends itself to every shape, but has no shape itself. It is the great Nothing-in-particular.

It looks a little as if Professor Santayana intended us to think that he has solved the problem of existence by conceiving the inconceivable. As a fact, he has only given us a name which names nothing and has no meaning. His "matter" neither explains anything nor can be itself explained. He has indulged a little in that mythology which he attributes to Idealism, has called attention to a problem—probably an insoluble one—and then escaped into the realm of poetic fancies. We admit the problem, but we cannot seriously follow him. The possibility of such an incomprehensible substance as he offers us is automatically ruled out by that trivial truth of transcendentalism—that we can and must interpret experience in the light of constructive reason: that it is meaningless to call anything real whose nature we can never understand.

This discussion of Matter as it appears in Professor Santayana's doctrine lies somewhat aside from our main theme. His materialism is *sui generis*, and its difficulties are not those of ordinary materialism, which intends to assert that all reality is made up of atoms and molecules, or energy—the matter of science. With reference to this doctrine, the attitude of Idealism is clear. The idealist may grant and even insist that matter is real, but he emphatically denies that the real is matter. There are other elements and phases of existence. We disagree with the materialist because he would restrict unduly and falsely the realm of the real and the true. It is the same objection which we would bring against Naturalism in general. Indeed, the materialist differs from other naturalists only in his understanding of science itself. For him, the elements in terms of which phenomena are explained by science are the fundamentally real things; for other naturalists it is the phenomena explained, rather than the elements into which they are analyzed, which are ultimately real.

So long as the naturalist is merely enunciating scientific truth, or even scientific hypotheses, Idealism has no quarrel with him. He is seeking to render some department of experience intelligible and to control nature in the interest of humanity. In this, the idealist, like every other sane person, should be his well-wisher and co-worker. It must be admitted that an idealist here and there has sometimes failed in this respect to be true to his principles, and some have even sought to make capital out of the difficulties of science in its attempt to formulate self-consistent and sufficient hypotheses. Such an attitude is not only captious but subversive of the interests of philosophy in general and of Idealism in particular. We have nothing to gain by taunting the scientist with mistakes and difficulties within the field of science itself.

This statement must not, however, be taken as an admission that philosophy has not the right to call attention to the limitations of science. Natural science inevitably imposes certain restrictions upon itself. It confines its problems; consequently its solutions are equally circumscribed. Its business is to describe and to analyze; consequently its truths are such as can be discovered by analysis or set forth in descriptive generalizations. Science cannot take the place of philosophic thinking. The anatomical analysis of Nature into configurations of atoms, or the generalization of its metamorphoses in the laws of motion, is not the whole truth of Nature. Nor can the description of a brain process in physiological terms be the whole story of thinking or of the will act. There still remains the truth as to the validity of the idea, the rationality or irrationality of the will act—the truth of evaluation, of purposes and ideals. There still remains that truth which interests one who would take an appropriate attitude toward nature in general—its submission to or subversion of human interests, its kinship with our ideals or the opposite. If one choose to use a much misunderstood term, one may say that there is a truth of final causes, over and above—though never contradictory of—the truth of the efficient causes with which natural science deals. The scientist sometimes fears, I think, that final causes are intended as a substitute for further scientific investigation and description. This is natural; the word final suggests that the evidence is all in and the account closed. He suspects that because science leaves the development of the egg into the complete organism somewhat miraculous, we intend to explain it by saying that Nature is seeking to reproduce a certain form. If the term ever had such a meaning—and of this there is some doubt—at least it can have it no longer. The right of description belongs wholly to science. The facts which it is able to furnish us may leave much still uncomprehended. But that which is not yet causally understood can never be made intelligible by merely verbal explanation, or by the mere attribution of "purposes" to Nature.

Suppose, however, the entire process in question were adequately described and reduced to natural law. It is still miraculous, is it not, in the sense that it is wonderful. It is wonderful that the laws of development are what they are. It would be equally wonderful if they were otherwise and worked out different results. It is wonderful that Nature obeys laws at all—that it is uniform in such fashion as to enable science to describe and predict. That Nature seems to have in general that trend which we call upward, because we find that it more and more approximates to our ideals, is in this sense miraculous. If the world were continually defeating human ends in greater number and more grievously, science could still go about its business of describing phenomena and discovering laws—unless, of course, the cosmos began to slough off its uniformities and become chaotic. It would then defeat the ends of science.

The whole truth about Nature is not told until it has been evaluated, measured by the standard of purposes and ideals. That it should have one value rather than another, that progress should be real instead of retroversion, that life is worth living or is not—these are significant truths not contained among the descriptive formulations of science. That there is no corner of the universe whose phenomena are not ultimately reducible to law, that the logical consequences of observed facts will themselves be observable facts, that the inductive method will continue to find itself validated by the processes of external reality—this conformity of the universe to the ideals of *science* is something which science itself can never demonstrate. It must take this conformity for granted before it can set up in business. These are the presuppositions which represent the faith of the scientist—his belief in the validity of his own thought processes and of his rational values.

That there is a truth of final causes means no more than this: reality can be completely understood only when it is viewed in the light of some end or goal—in other words, only in terms of values and ideals. This does not limit the nature of truth so as to exclude any even possible scientific account, because scientific thinking is itself one of the ways in which we seek to realize ideal ends and to control Nature in purposive ways. This is its only excuse for being. Science is engaged in converting the unintelligible into the intelligible and conquering our somewhat chaotic experience in the name of Reason. Science finds its beginning and end in ideals. Its truth is significant because it is valuable. The truth of values includes the truth of description; the truth of description does not include the truth of values. Hence Idealism includes Naturalism so far as Naturalism means the positive assertion of scientific truth, and parts company with Naturalism when that doctrine denies that there is any *other* truth.

But the naturalist here raises objection. He, too, deals with ideas and values; only his method, instead of being transcendental and verbal, is scientific. Thought processes are phenomena as much as chemical reactions; social institutions and ideals are as much the product of discoverable causes as are the phases of the moon. They have their laws, and are more or less predictable. Barring their somewhat greater complexity, there is no more difficulty in explaining mental and moral facts than there is in a problem of mechanics. Indeed, the mental and moral will probably some day be shown to be merely mechanical.

Here again it is necessary to guard against misunderstanding. Idealism does not deny that mental and moral phenomena can be causally explained. It is sometimes said that natural science cannot account for conscience, or for morality, or for our artistic sense, or our civic ideals. With reference at least to morality, even Huxley, otherwise a consistent naturalist, has taken this position. But such a statement is misleading, on account of its ambiguity, and should be avoided. Science can perfectly well account for the *appearance* of our moral and social sentiments and for their *development* along with other phases of civilization.

The division of labor is a means to efficient dealing with environment. It enables the same energy to produce a larger result—more food, better clothing, deadlier weapons, and so on. The group which adopts it will, when brought into competition with a group which does not, or with isolated individuals, be bound to win. It will be wealthier, able to support larger families, will thus become the larger group and overcome the other by sheer force of numbers if in no more direct fashion. And the division of labor is only one among many practical advantages of social solidarity. Organized society means, however, just that abstention from certain kinds of competition—illegal and unsocial acts—which Huxley and some others take to be a controversion of natural processes. But the existence of the successfully integrated social group is possible only through the moral conduct of its members, and the natural processes which bring it about are quite analogous—though more complex—to those by which crystals are formed in a solution. Moral conduct is produced by natural processes in the same way as stronger bodies, better organized brains, and keener sensibilities.

One may object that the processes of Nature can indeed produce more appropriate reactions on the part of the organism, conduct which looks like and works like morality, but not necessarily moral feelings or a conscience. These are still unaccounted for. But the answer is obvious. A hen that liked the feeling of its head under water or had an insuperable aversion to pecking grain would never transmit these characteristics to any progeny, while fowls which felt better with a full crop would naturally flourish. Just so, if the advantages of organized society be granted, Nature will select those individuals and strains whose sentiments are compatible with group order and efficiency. Specific feelings are uniformly conjoined with certain stimuli and certain reactions, or perhaps with the coordination of the two. Whatever accounts for the organism's reactions also accounts for its feelings, in the sense that it discovers their uniform antecedents and accompaniments.

Science—anthropological and biological—offers the only possible explanation of the fact that those reactions which we call moral or artistic or logical are increasingly present in surviving human organisms. And the business of tracing the causal antecedents and physical accompaniments of moral sentiments and intentions, or of artistic perceptions, or logical decisions, belongs solely to the physiological psychologist. It may be true that, so far, psychology has had but indifferent success in its attempt to reduce the phenomena of will and judgment to law. But with those who would deny the possibility of causal explanation in this field and make its facts entirely miraculous, Idealism has no more sympathy than has Naturalism. These objectors, if there be any such, are merely trying to turn back the wheels of progress and substitute mythology for science.

The attitude of modern Idealism on this point is unambiguous. It faces, with Kant, the problem of discovering what validity can attach to moral and religious values, consistently with the entire truth of science in the realm of phenomena. It cannot retract or qualify its assertion that all facts are to be understood. The time is long past when one may rationally suppose that the realm of phenomena contains odd corners to which science can never penetrate, or that the natural sequence of events is interrupted every now and again for the intrusion of a miracle. The divine can no longer be simply interpolated in the natural, the ideal artificially grafted upon the phenomenal. Or, if this is an error, and the natural is shot through and infected with the miraculous and scientifically incomprehensible, then the idealistic interpretation of reality is as much beside the mark as that of Naturalism. Both demand that the category of causality be applicable to whatever appears in space and time, applicable without exception. Neither would argue that the phenomena of religion or morality or art must be incomprehensible to science.

Since Naturalism can at once incorporate in its programme the results of natural science, the difficulty of Naturalism is not to account for the *appearance* of mental or social phenomena; it is to account for their *validity* that gives the scientist pause. That I should have the idea that I see an audience, or that the audience should feel uneasy in their present predicament, or that any other mental phenomena should occur in conjunction with particular brains, the psychologist may explain. Given sufficient data as to the nervous systems concerned and the stimuli impinging upon them, he should be able to predict these facts. But that the idea should be *true* or the feeling *justified* is an entirely different matter. Strictly, the scientist can offer no explanation of the validity of ideas or feelings simply because it is not his business. When he has shown how the thing comes about, has demonstrated that it occurs according to the laws of his particular science, he is done with it. Veridical perceptions and hallucinations, humane sentiments and moral perversions, poetic fancies and insane obsessions—all these he explains by the same laws and shows that they supervene with equal necessity upon their causal antecedents or physical accompaniments.

That one mental operation is knowledge, another error, or that one motor impulse ends in right action, another in crime, does not in the least concern the psychologist, except as they reveal different conditions of nervous tissues or different stimuli. The truth or falsity of an idea, the rightness or wrongness of an intent, are, in the last analysis, judgments of value. That one is better and another worse, the descriptive scientist, merely as such, has no right to decide. As a *man*, he *must*; but that would signify nothing if it merely betrayed the workings of *his* nervous system. Anyone may decide that his own brain mediates a judgment antagonistic to another's, but that does not discover any right or wrong, better or worse, except from the purely personal or subjective point of view. It discovers merely that one likes something or believes something. The objective validity of judgments and evaluations remains entirely problematic.

It is equally true of the sage, the insane person, and the pig that they have their beliefs and preferences. Who shall deny to the pig that raw potato is an end in itself and infinitely more valuable than wisdom? Why labor with the patient's delusions when one only pits one's own nervous system and its workings against another? This is a very old string I am harping on, but the argument is still as sound as when Plato directed it against the Naturalism of his day. Whoever would tell us that the *only* pertinent account of ideas and feelings is description in causal terms places himself at strange disadvantage. For one may reply: "I admit your contention, for the moment, and accept your argument and conclusion at the value which you yourself put upon them. Your brain—save the mark—is different from mine, or else subject to very different stimuli. I now understand why you hold such a strange philosophy. You inherited that kink in your gray matter—or it may be due to something you ate for dinner. Have you ever tried whiskey for it? That sometimes produces a new set of ideas and values." Or one may say, "The air waves from your vocal organs produce in my nervous system a disagreement with you. That is the whole truth of the matter." If validity is a matter of causation, all ideas and evaluations are equally valid, since all are equally caused.

The naturalist seeks to evade this issue. He points out that since man and Nature have evolved together, man finds himself—his nervous system, his beliefs and values—such as harmonize with the cosmos which has produced him. If it were otherwise, he would be quickly cut off, and his particular brand of truth would have no representatives. But while this is true on the whole, it admits of continual exception. No individual organism finds itself in perfect adjustment to environment. (We may remark in passing that the very idea of adjustment involves categories of value; every organism is equally a fact when and where it exists, and while it remains, all forces involved are equal and opposite. Again, values aside, why should evolution mean the survival of the *fittest*?) In any case, maladjustment persists along with adjustment; and the individual mind will, on that showing, always be a curious mingling of truth and error. This, you say, is no vital objection, since it is an obvious fact. Admittedly; but it points out nevertheless that objective validity is not secured to an idea because evolution has produced it. Moreover, each separate nervous system has equally been evolved by the processes of Nature, and accordingly, if the argument proves anything, it proves that all brains are equally good truth producers. Any attempt to escape this consequence will inevitably appeal, in the end, to some judgment of values. And the objective validity of these values will be presupposed. The naturalistic account must appeal to that which Naturalism can never account for. The naturalist, if he explicitly states what his doctrine implies, becomes an idealist.

In this day and age, however, the naturalist further amends his position. Since all ideas are merely somebody's beliefs, and all evaluations somebody's preferences, he recognizes the impossibility of any absolute objective standard. He even prides himself a little upon this catholic point of view, and reviles the dogmatist in proportion. The truth is at best a name for the hypothesis that works. He sets up his ideas alongside Nature and contents himself with observing how Nature treats them. Perhaps he is even willing to set up *this* truth which he has just announced and observe what happens to it. We all have spells of wondering if Pragmatism will work.

But the naturalist, now turned pragmatist, is deceived by the vagueness of his own terminology. Even he is sometimes worried to know just what happens to an idea when it gets verified. It meets an experience which satisfies it, perhaps. But this phraseology is more blind than the first. The whole problem is to know how and in what sense experience can satisfy or refuse to satisfy an idea. The problem is real; the pragmatist does not solve it but only leads up to it and says, "Tag; you're it." The really important question is to know what is meant by an idea or a hypothesis "working." Attention will disclose that the pragmatist uses this word in a variety of meanings. A hypothesis in religion works when it makes you feel good. The idea of an all-seeing power that makes for righteousness works when it leaves you free to take moral holidays. So far it is true. A physical hypothesis works when you can deduce facts from it. Logic says that the hypothesis is thus rendered more or less *probable*, and reminds us that the truth may often be deduced from false premises. But Pragmatism asserts that if the hypothesis gives you the facts, it is so far true. Truth is only probability. Even the laws of probability are only probably true. Or more accurately, *probably* the laws of probability are only probable. It is probably best not to pursue this line of thought too far.

In general, an idea or hypothesis may be said to "work" when it is useful. This is the really important point. But usefulness is obviously a predication of value. The idea works if it is found to be valuable. However, it is just the objective criterion of value which the naturalist has failed to produce. By this excursion into Pragmatism he has only got himself into a vicious circle. In order to prove that our privately owned ideas and ideals have any value, it is necessary to secure their objective validity and truth. To the question "Has the idea which is simply the necessary result of a brain process any value?" the naturalist answers—as everyone must—"Yes, if it is true." But to the further question, "Is it true?" he now answers, "Yes, if it is valuable." If we simply assert the identity of truth with the valuable, we must remember that the account of the valuable from which the naturalist starts is that somebody likes it. And he has not got any further. Finding that he cannot bring subjective feelings and ideas up to any standard of objective truth, he now calls upon us to bring the standard down to the feelings.

He has, it is true, another method of dealing with ideas and ideals. We are social beings, and find ourselves more or less in agreement. Our beliefs and sentiments are not merely subjective, because they are shared by others. Indeed, it is just the error of idealistic ethics that it is based on authority rather than that agreement which we find among men because of their community of feeling. Right and wrong, good and bad, must be decided by counting noses. Charity and head hunting are equally right in the communities which sanction them. The idea is not new: the Sophists invented it.

The real difficulty with Naturalism is not that it is too catholic and democratic, but that it is not enough so. If it would arrive at an objective truth and an objective standard of values, it must seek it in the very roots of human nature. Idealism appeals to authority, but it finds that authority is an agreement which leaves *no* nose uncounted—in the common rationality of mankind. Its initial premises are merely that the real is intelligible and that the truth is free from contradictions. In Ethics, its arch principle is only the law that there shall be law; that right conduct must be rational conduct, and that good wills can never find themselves really at cross purposes. One must so act that he can will the principle of his action as a universal law of conduct. One must seek his happiness by means which do not contradict the possibility of happiness for all. One must so think that the logical consequences of his idea do not contradict the idea itself.

These are no merely subjective standards, though they appeal to no external criteria which are not found in the subject of thought and action himself. They are ideals to be realized in the process of becoming what one means to be and attempts to become in every rational thought and action. Yet the realization of this goal is an infinite task—the vocation of humanity. The truth and objective value of these standards is revealed in the fact that to deny them or refuse them is to contradict one's self, and make life a meaningless muddle.

My task tonight is a rather limited one. If I should attempt further to reinstate Idealism, I should inevitably trespass in fields that belong to the further discussions for the year. Perhaps I have done so already. But I should like, in closing, to say just a little about the general method of Idealism. We are often accused of being dialectical and attempting to catch the adversary in purely verbal contradictions. But, after all, if we are to have any philosophy at all, it ought to be able to state itself without saying what it doesn't mean. Common sense is a good enough formulation of near truths to worry along with. To be sure, even this common stock is the accumulated wisdom of ages. It must have begun as a hard won truth which gradually seeped through the social medium. Common sense is inherited philosophy. Our present business must be to remove contradictions which remain, and state explicitly, if we can, that which is implied in common thought and action.

Because he has this faith in the common rationality of mankind, and believes that every thought and deed means to be intelligent, your idealist is the most presumptuous of men. He supposes that if you let any view develop its own implication and discover its own presuppositions, it will, in the end, assert that the real is rational—that the laws of constructive reason are the universal determinants and the framework of all that is knowable. It will find itself, after all, in agreement with the main thought of Idealism. Either that, or it will fall into contradictions which it cannot solve. Hence he favors letting every view have its say. Its truth will remain, while its errors will hang themselves in contradiction. Like Socrates of old, he is discouraged only when the opponent refuses to take himself seriously and avoids argument by calling names.

If it be natural science that is in question, he finds that the idealistic premises are inevitably presupposed. Science affirms the sovereignty of

Intelligence over Nature, and is itself a process by which Reason takes possession of its realm. When science supplements itself with the statement of what it implies, and what it seriously means to do and be, it becomes Idealism.

Every doctrine must finally assume an absolute truth and an objective standard of values, simply because every view means to be *itself* absolutely true and universally worthwhile. These trivial truths are in themselves the only answer necessary to that Pragmatism which would reduce truth to probability. They constitute a sufficient refutation of that Naturalism which takes the significance of ideas and ideals to be exhausted by description and causal explanation.

3. Realism and Subjectivism

Idealists have so generally united in insisting upon a few important theses that their real and radical differences have been somewhat neglected. Perhaps there is something in the idealistic temper itself which leads to emphasis upon agreements. Since all views have their bit of meaning in the life of history, the idealist has been fonder of including than of controverting them. Hence, whoever holds to the non-existence of any alogical real, to the priority of epistemology, and the precedence of "truths of appreciation" over "truths of description" has been regarded as fundamentally right-minded and trusted to approximate the logical corollaries—one's own—of these principles. But whatever other result the present active criticism may have, it seems bound to break in upon the idealistic love feast. Nothing is more distressing than to be looked upon as discredited when it is one's neighbor, or the remains of one's ancestors, to whom this honor is due. One dislikes to hear of "idealism" when it is a subjectivistic epistemology which is under discussion—provided, of course, one's own view has no "taint of subjectivism."

That the attack of the realists has been upon a subjectivistic theory of knowledge we have their assurance. That all idealists are thereby called upon to feel aggrieved may or may not be the case. Almost every idealism holds as important certain considerations about the predicament of the knower. But they need not be those which Professor Perry has exhibited in his paper on "The Egocentric Predicament,"[1] or the similar ones which figure in the introduction to *The New Realism*.[2]

The idealist is there represented as arguing that all reals must be known, or that knowing is constitutive of reality, because no real can ever be discovered out of relation to a knower. The writer, for one, admits the invalidity of any such argument. It would prove—if it proved anything—altogether too much. For "known" here means "completely and explicitly possessed as content of consciousness," the identity of the object with present experience. At least it is this meaning which

---

Reprinted by permission from *The Journal of Philosophy, Psychology, and Scientific Methods*, Vol. X (1913), No. 2, pp. 43–49.

[1] This journal, Vol. VIII (1911), pp. 5ff. See also *Present Philosophical Tendencies* (New York, 1912), pp. 128ff.

[2] (New York, 1912), pp. 11–12.

the realist seems to have in mind. The identification of reality with that which is present to someone's experience, or with the sum total of present experiences, carries sinister implications. For the whole problem of knowledge, as idealism sees it, turns upon the fact that the knowing experience means or intends something beyond itself, something which just now it *is not*. Otherwise, the experience might have any affective or esthetic value which it happened to possess, but it would not be knowledge. It is characteristic of knowing, as a human activity, that its meaning is not satisfied by the self-evident presence of its own experience or content of consciousness. Hence the part played in idealistic theory by "immediacy and mediation," and the recognition of the "inevitably fragmentary character of human knowing." Thus the history of idealistic epistemology in the last century might be summed up as the history of the recipe for *getting out of* the egocentric predicament. The recognition that nothing can be known except present content of consciousness would be fatal to the idealist's program, for it would dismiss his problem without a hope of solution. The subjectivist's dogma —that to be is to be perceived, or otherwise given in consciousness— is as distressing to idealism as to realism.

To be sure, the idealist often makes use of the conception of an ideal or limiting case of knowledge—the toilless knowledge of an absolute mind—for which knowing would mean just that detailed and explicit identity of thought and object which subjectivism maintains for knowing in general. But the idealistic theory of knowledge can get on very comfortably without hypothecating the *existence* of such a case of knowing, provided only its validity as an ideal be allowed.[8] As an event among other events, no such case of knowing can occur anywhere at any time. The epistemological interest in the absolute is the interest in the validity of an ideal. Idealism must explicitly deny that the total reality is identical with the experience of any finite knower. Hence it is, in general, more accurate to represent idealism as maintaining the essentially know*able* character of reality than to take it as holding that all reals are known.

The knower's predicament is, then, this: all that ever is and ever can be explicitly possessed by a mind which attempts to know will be a present experience, while the sure possession of this experience can never satisfy the interests of knowledge. To glorify the immediate data of consciousness with the adjective "independent" will not help the situation in the least. The present content is there; it is experienced;

[8] Some idealists would disagree with this statement. But the following sentence would, I think, satisfy all but the out-and-out subjectivists.

its "cash value" is already ours. If one has bitten an apple, one is certain of the taste in one's mouth. It matters not whether it be an independent taste or no. What knowledge requires is that a "credit" attach to the taste. It must be significant of the quality of the apple or of another taste; it must intend something which it is not. What knowledge signifies is its meaning; and meaning always reaches beyond the present experience. The problem of the validity of this meaning is the problem of knowledge, as idealism—since Kant—conceives it.

The idealistic interest in the egocentric predicament is to point [out] this problem, and to call attention to the fact that unless it is solved by proving some necessary relation of reality to our ways of knowing, we have only the alternatives of scepticism or various unproved and unprovable dogmas which can neither refute one another nor establish a constructive case.

We may state the problem in realistic terms. "Realism does not deny that when *a* enters into a relation, such as knowledge, of which it is independent, *a* now acquires that relation, and is accordingly different *by so much*; but denies only that this added relation is necessary to *a* as already constituted. Thus when *a* is known, it is *a* itself, as constituted without knowledge, which is independent of that circumstance. The new complex *known-a* is of course dependent on knowledge as one of its parts."[4] To restate the egocentric predicament: All the *a*'s and *x*'s which anybody can ever hope to know will be *known-a*'s and *known-x*'s, and as such dependent on knowledge, while it is the *a*'s and *x*'s as constituted without knowledge that are independent. The *known-a*'s and *known-x*'s will differ from these independently real *a*'s and *x*'s "by so much"—that is, by as much as they are affected by entering into relation to a knower.

All this is trivial enough until we remember that it is exactly the fundamental tenet of all scepticism, and the *bête noire* of every dogmatism. The critical question is: By *how* much does *known-a* differ from *a*?

To avoid misunderstanding, one possible objection based on this difference may be ruled out as negligible. *Known-a* differs from *a* as a relative from an absolute term, or as *a* unqualified from *a* modified by "known." *Known-a* is a complex or one end of a relation, while *a* may be simple and unrelated. This difference is something like that between "truth" and "unpleasant truth," or that between *x*-which-is-greater-than-*y* and *x*-which-is-less-than-*z*. The logical realism of Plato was troubled to make clear how the greater could be also less. Similarly, it might trouble the new realism to make clear how independent *a* can

[4] Perry, *The New Realism*, p. 118.

be identical with an *a* which is known, when *known-a* is *not* independent. The difficulty is to explain identity in difference when relations are external, to explain how *known-a* is still the same *a* and yet different by being related. But any objection which turned upon this difficulty which strict logical realism has with identities would be likely to seem rather thin. Such logical puzzles suggest a *solvitur ambulando*. It is considerations of a quite different nature which have proved historically important for idealism.

It seems useless to deny that knowing is, in some sense or other, a kind of acting. That knowing is acting would seem to argue some effect in that upon which the activity is directed. Hence *known-a* seems likely to differ from real *a* by so much as the knower's activity affects it when it enters the knowledge relation. This will hold true whether the knower is an organism which functions in definite ways of its own, a nervous arc, or merely an unbiologized mind.

Knowing might be a transforming activity of a nervous receptor, so that real *a*'s might be apprehended as upside-down *a*'s or real substances known as complexes of colors and pitches and other "qualities," while the independent substances were not even imaginable. The divergence of real *a* and *known-a* might be as great as that between immaterial essences and space-filling bodies. The possibilities for persuasive dogmatism here are wide.

Or knowing might be, not a transforming, but only a selecting activity. In that event, *known-a* might differ from real *a* as a continuously flowing whole from a cinematograph picture of it, or as a valuable collection from a junk heap, or as an ordered array from a chaos. Knowing might be selecting so as to satisfy certain practical interests. Our Euclidean space might be just such a prejudiced selection from an *n*-dimensional or undimensional reality. And so on, for the other characters of our world as we know it. If knowing is such an activity, dominated by interests, all the reality we can ever hope to know will be relative to those interests. If knowing is acting according to certain principles, then the world of our possible knowledge will reflect the legislation of those principles.

To revert to the predicament in which the knower finds himself: he seems to be confined to the experience of such realities as are, by their nature, capable of entering the knowledge relation—if knowing is passive—or which are transformed or selected according to certain principles—if knowing is a way of acting. If knowledge transforms or interestedly selects, or if some reals are by nature unfitted to the knowledge relation, then known reality will so far fail to indicate the character of reality as it exists independently of knowledge. That independent reality is neither transformed nor otherwise misrepresented by *known-a*'s, the knower can not, from the nature of his predicament, ever know, while the seemingly active character of knowing lends color to the supposition that "knowledge" misrepresents the independently real.

The assertion even that there is such an independent reality must remain a sheer assumption. The realist may point out the fallacy of arguing from the fact that all *known* reals are known. And the subjectivist may retort that if there be any unknown real, it is an identical proposition that nobody knows it. That reality is not transformed when brought into the knowledge relation is a similar assumption. The proof of it would require the impossible comparison of *known-a* with *unknown-a*. That an independent reality has this or that character must remain an unwarranted assertion, when all the *a*'s which can be known will be *known-a*'s.

When the number and variety of activistic theories of knowledge is remembered, it seems a hardy dogmatism which opposes to them all the necessarily unproved thesis that the real is independent of knowledge; and then adds that this independent reality is already so finely divided that no analysis can ever be carried so far as to violate its nature, but that all the relations and all the organization which mind can "legitimately" think are also already there—in particular, that these independent reals maintain all the logical relations; and, finally, that any of these reals or any complex of them may enter into the knowledge relation—a notable case of a relation not already there—without being transformed. Such a happy conjunction of miracles reminds one of Leibniz's pre-established harmony. But this latter-day best-of-all-possible-worlds appeals to no sufficient reason.

Whoever takes the principles of knowledge to be legislative for whatever can properly be called real, and holds reality to be so far dependent on knowledge, will be assured—if he makes out his case—that *known-a*'s and real *a*'s are not of essentially different character, and that knowledge is objectively valid. But the person who recognizes his egocentric predicament, and at the same time insists that reality is independent of knowledge and its conditions, is confined within the circle of his experience, whose relation to reality beyond he can not know. Hence, from the idealistic point of view a subjectivist is not one who takes reality to be essentially relative to knowledge, but one who takes it to be independent. Subjectivism and dogmatism are twins.

If reality is independent, while the knower can not jump out of the circle of his own experience, then we have the alternatives of scepticism—for the critically minded—or any one of a presumably infinite number of dogmatisms. None of these will be able to *prove* that reality is independent of knowledge, because such a proof would require the discovery of not-known reals and their comparison with those known. And none of these dogmatisms will be able to prove that independent reality has the character attributed to it, because the only reals which are, beyond doubt, independent can not be investigated. Thus whatever is constructive in such a theory will necessarily remain indemonstrable. The utmost that can be proved is that some other theorist's argument—e.g., the subjectivist's argument from the egocentric predicament—does not prove his case. The subjectivist's *view*, as a dogma, can not be proven false; it can only be proven not proved. And every dogmatism can perform this service for every other.

If the foregoing is correct, it is no accident that the realistic doctrine is largely negative. Rather, it is inevitably the case that every such view should contain two parts : the more important consisting of proofs that the proofs—not the views—of other theories are unsound, the other portion made up of unproven assertions about an independent reality. It is a psychological defect that flesh is heir to that we are sometimes led to believe a doctrine because arguments for an opposing theory are invalid. The realist surely means to take no advantage of us in this respect. If realists have disproved certain arguments for the dependence of reality upon knowledge, they have not thereby established the independence of reality. If the realist be right, and idealism essentially subjectivistic, it must, to be sure, renounce its claim to a critical foundation. But it would still remain a consistent dogma, and as good as any other.

If it is taken to be the case that realism has undermined the idealist's *proofs* that the logical relations hold among reals because reality is relative to a legislative reason, still the idealistic contention is as probable as any. The realist can not disprove the assertion. He can never catch a reality out of relation to human reason, in order to discover if it still maintains its conformity to logical principles. That the logical relations are found among things does not make realism any more probable. For if to be real means to conform to certain categorical modes of thinking, then it will be an identical proposition which asserts that these principles state the relations of real things. The realist can only set up his own counter assertion and return to the business of demolishing the opponent's proofs. Thus we might conceivably be presented with dogmatic idealism and dogmatic realism as equally consistent and equally unproved doctrines; and the choice between them might, then, turn upon pragmatic considerations of workability or temperamental preferences.

If the realist can advance no direct proof that reality not only may be, but *is* independent of knowledge; that the independently real not only might not be, but *is not* altered when it enters the knowledge relation; that reality not only may be, but *is* so finely divided that analysis can never misrepresent it—and so on for his other contentions—then his arguments must necessarily be confined to the refutation of the proofs of other theories. In that event his case can prosper only if he turns philosophy into a Donnybrook Fair and hits every non-realistic head that shows. Even so, he will not prove his case, but only establish its possible truth—the impossibility of proving the opposite. If this is the utmost that can be hoped from a philosophic theory, it is well that we should recognize it, and pay our respects to Hume.

4. Bergson and Contemporary Thought

It is difficult or impossible to say anything new about the philosophy of Bergson. Especially in this company, which has listened to the very able discussions of Professor Lovejoy, I should be in despair if I thought it necessary to attempt any original contribution to the subject. My purpose will be, rather, to give such exposition as I can of the most significant aspects of this new philosophy. The attempt to criticize will be deferred.

In spite of the fact that all of you have heard much and read much about Bergson, I feel sure that you will forgive this return to the simpler task of stating the content of his system. We frequently find in current literature discussions which in our particular cases are beside the mark. What we most need is to know what it is all about. We are presented with esoteric disquisitions on Feminism or Eugenics or the Montessori method which drive over our heads, because we have no clear idea of what Feminism stands for, or what the caption "Eugenics" means to anyone not on the staff of a funny paper, or how the Montessori method differs from plain spoiling the child. The unfortunate part of it is that such subjects—and the philosophy of Bergson is one—may become so generally discussed that pleading ignorance amounts to bad taste; and we may be drawn into pretending a comprehension we do not possess. When this happens the subject in question can properly be called a fad.

Bergson has become a fad in this country. That is unfortunate both for him and for us, because his philosophy is genuinely of wider appeal than the usual academic system and worthy of sober attention. With the possible exception of William James, no philosopher of our time has issued so vigorous a challenge to his contemporaries or given a new direction to the thinking of so many serious people. Bergson has executed a flank movement on contemporary philosophy; he has called in question the entire procedure and result of science; he has attacked the intellectuals in all departments of culture; and by his defense of the inner life has opened new vistas to many religious minds. Any sufficiently radical person might do all these things; but Bergson has done

An address given before the Philosophical Union of the University of California, January 16, 1914. Reprinted by permission from the *University of California Chronicle*, Vol. XVI (1914), No. 2, pp. 181–97.

them in such wise as to command respect, even when the respect is qualified by antipathy. To have done with Bergson too easily is not a compliment to one's own mentality.

In his own country, I am told, he has less honor than in England and America. As my informant, a Frenchman, phrased it, "He is not popular in France; no, he is popular only with American young ladies." The reason for this—that he is less popular in France—may be due in part to the fact that his philosophy has been taken up by various not too popular movements. Factions as different in temper as the Catholic Modernists and the Syndicalists have hailed him as their prophet. He appeals to the Modernists because he defends the inner authority against all externalism, at the same time offering religion a secure precedence over science. He appeals to the Syndicalists (the I. W. W. here) somewhat accidentally because they too oppose the "intellectuals" who would subordinate practice to a set of preformed principles. The I. W. W. wishes to make its ethics as it goes along, and this, Bergson says, is a characteristic of all living organisms.

In this country, the influence of Bergson is traceable, in no small part, to the friendship of William James. James "discovered" Bergson for us twenty years ago, before *Matter and Memory* and *Creative Evolution* had been written. He was always urging his students to read *Les données immédiates de la conscience*, now translated under the title *Time and Free Will*; he spoke of Bergson in terms of high praise in several of his public lectures, and finally in the volume entitled *A Pluralistic Universe*, James published an essay on Bergson. This essay (the sixth in the volume) presents one side of Bergson's philosophy with that simple clearness and captivating eloquence which only James could bring to such a subject. No more auspicious introduction to American readers could have been devised.

But I am in danger of forgetting my subject amid these gossipy details. Being involved in partisan conflicts on the continent may militate against popularity, and an introduction by a great and much loved reader will make for it, but what are the elements in the philosophy of Bergson which can hold the attention once caught and be worth our continued consideration?

The defense of the inner life has already been mentioned as one of these. Many influences in our present civilization make for emphasis upon externals. We hear much of the materialism of our times. Wellbeing is measured in terms of houses and clothes and money. To regard these as the outward and visible signs of an inward and spiritual prosperity would be pharisaical if it were not comic. The externals are considered ends in themselves, not valued as signs of or means toward something else. In the midst of intellectual and cultural poverty, these constitute the greatness of America. We are rich and grow richer; therefore we are great. This is our materialism in its crudest form— and perhaps I have exaggerated in making the point. The man becomes measured by his possessions. He *is* what he has accomplished, what he can show for himself.

This externalism or emphasis on the outer life has, also, subtler and less objectionable forms. We come more and more to realize that no man lives to himself alone. One might almost say that the world had to wait for twentieth century science, its sociological studies, its political theories, and its preventive medicine before the significance of that saying could be realized. The diseased individual has ceased to be an entity and become a symptom, the symptom of unsanitary community habits. The criminal is no longer an inherently vicious man; he is the characteristic by-product of a bad economic situation, or points the lesson for the teacher of eugenics. If we do not so readily translate spiritual graces and intellectual attainment into the terms of our community life, that is only because we are always most attentive to the loose screw and the broken shaft. We have not yet felt the need for understanding these unobjectionable phenomena in the light of our new insight. Very surely we are growing away from that individualistic temper which framed the Declaration of Independence. We no longer fear that society will encroach upon the individual, who must be protected in his inalienable rights. Rather we understand the danger that the individual will encroach upon society. We see that the integrity of the individual consists not in keeping his fences intact but in preserving mutually satisfactory relations with his neighbors and the state.

Now when we consider the criminal as a symptom and not inherently bad, we identify him with what is external to his inner life—his old-fashioned soul—just as surely as when we measure the successful man by what he can show. We even go further in this case. We *translate* the inner life of the criminal into something external to it; we identify his criminal tendency with something inherited from his bad ancestry or borrowed from his debauching environment. We minify him as a free moral agent and magnify him as an event appearing in a context of explanatory events. The emphasis upon relations—with things, events, and other people—must everywhere be at some expense of emphasis upon the inner life, the life which is hid, self-contained, and self-explanatory.

I hope you will not understand me to argue for or against the criminal, for or against any sociological or economic theory; I intend only to state a fact about contemporary tendencies of thought. That many influences at present make for emphasis upon the external as opposed to the inner life, I think there can be little doubt. Yet there are large and important interests which make the other way. Noteworthy reactions against the prevalent materialism have appeared in our time, and a certain religious temper—one is tempted to say *the* religious temper —will always stand sternly opposed to anything which should tend to magnify the outer as against the inner life. In the extreme case this temper sets the exact antithesis and translates all externals into negligible accidents or mere evidences of the inner and spiritual reality.

To all who stand thus in opposition to externalism in its various forms—to the mystic in religion, to the individualist who is frightened or confused by our socialistic tendencies, to him who fears our materialism, and to those who think our sociological and economic theories "o'erleap themselves and fall on the other side"—the philosophy of Bergson may come as a new gospel. For in its very essence this doctrine insists upon the necessity of grasping the inner life as such, upon its self-explanatory character, upon the fact that it develops by growth and not by external accretion, and upon the fact that other things may be interpreted in terms of this inner life but not *vice versa*. It is not a thread whose character and direction are determined by surrounding warp and woof. Rather it is like the spider which makes its own web.

These agreements of various thinkers or temperaments with Bergson may be superficial; and I fear you will think I have traveled far to disclose a few trivialities. But whether these agreements are superficial or vital, whether the *reasons* for these conclusions are the same in the two cases or not, it still remains true that Bergson has furnished many with a new rationale for their temperamental inclinations, has phrased extraordinarily well their own convictions, and, by attacking the common enemy, has furnished them with new weapons of offense and defense. And just this fact, if I am not mistaken, explains in large measure the popularity of Bergson. He has never had any considerable number of disciples who studied his philosophy closely and cherished it in all its detail, but he has gathered a large following of those who like his main conclusions and delight in the confusion of the enemy.

In a somewhat similar way Bergson appeals to those who may be called, for lack of a better name, the "anti-intellectuals." We are so given to using "intellect" as the synonym for mentality in general that the issue here might easily be confused. One might take "anti-intellectual" to mean a person who worshipped physical being or was opposed to education or something of the sort, but this would, of course, be a mistake. No one can deny that intellect or reasoning power is only one of the faculties or functions of mind. We have also instincts and feelings; and perhaps will, too, should be distinguished. We might, then, characterize as an "intellectual" anyone who maintained the logical or analytical function of mind to be the highest, and held that ideally all conduct should be guided by the reasoning power.

Taking the term in this sense, we have various kinds of anti-intellectuals. In art and literature for instance, we should have as the intellectuals those who insist upon the fundamental importance of the canons of art, and maintain that there are intelligible principles which no artist may violate without thereby injuring his work. There are also the anti-intellectuals, or romanticists, who insist that the great artist makes his own rules, that the greatness of his art lies in the greatness of his inspiration, in the power and fineness of his esthetic intuition. The romanticist is likely also to insist that what is portrayed need not be a real or even a possible object; the artist is engaged in transferring to the canvas or marble his unique inspiration or feeling. Right feeling, not right understanding, makes great art. The artist's intellect should be in abeyance or engaged merely in such things as selecting brushes and tubes; the result, if good, will spring from the fineness of his feeling. Similarly the just appreciation of art must depend upon the cultivation of right feeling, not upon the understanding of principles.

Few of us are artists, however, and not so many have felt the necessity of taking sides for or against the futurists. If the distinction of intellectualism and anti-intellectualism had no wider application, it would be negligible to our discussion. But all of us feel the necessity, in one department or another, of assessing the value of the logical faculty and taking sides with intellect or with feeling. Cold reason and passionate longing, the analytic dissection of the situation and the intuitive apprehension of it in the whole—these are bound to run counter sooner or later. In religion, shall we be guided by the dictates of reason, proceeding to what seems certain or most probable, or shall we put our faith and hope in the sublime intuition of the moment when doubt—and reasons—fled away? In the important affairs of life, in the great decisions, in love, and in the presence of death, shall we trust reason and pause where its guidance ceases, or shall we look for another sort of guidance and discard reason when it falters? Shall we face the facts as intellect dissects them from the tangled web of life and marshals them in orderly array; or shall we seek a larger kind of comprehension of the web itself, and assign reason to some humbler office? Put in these terms, the issue is a vital one. And I think you will see that the romanticist—if we use that name for the partisans of feeling and intuition—are a numerous body, often an organized body with vested interests in the world of culture. They are also a much set-upon party and are sometimes hard put to it, especially because their kind of comprehension is inarticulate and does not easily give account of itself.

In Bergson the romanticists have found a powerful ally. Life and its creatures are not to be grasped by intellect, he says. The analytic understanding is merely one outgrowth or fulmination of life, created for the humbler and limited tasks of daily practice. Instinct is an equally efficient and accurate comprehension, though poorly developed in the human species. Instinct even has a superiority over intellect in that it grasps life on the inside and is one with the vital impulse of it. If only instinct could be made to give account of itself, it is here that we might seek the solution of our difficulties. Intellect, being analytic, readily portrays its findings, but just because it is analytic and pulls things to pieces, it comprehends only pieces and cannot understand the great wholes of life. The typical mode of operation for intellect is dissecting and piecing together. It works as if everything were spatial and could be grasped in space terms. The typical product of intellect is machinery. But life doesn't run by machinery, and the particular go of it is not found in any of its parts nor in the way they can be patched together. The secret of life is its unity, its integrity, and this can never be discovered by the analytic judgment which immediately externalizes life and treats it as a spatial thing.

These are hard sayings, but the tenor of them is grateful to the partisans of feeling and intuition. Life has a meaning forever hid from the coldly logical mind. Its secret lies open only to those who, discarding reason, face the mystery with instinctive or intuitive insight. And this will be true likewise of those spiritual realities in which life speaks directly to life—in art, in literature, in religion. One understands these things as one would understand a friend—that is, by intuitively identifying one's self with the friend, and thus grasping the true import of the friend's inner life. One comprehends them as a little child who gives his sympathetic attention but does not analyze. Art, poetry, nature itself as the external upthrust of the great life—these reveal their true significance only as we go out wholeheartedly to them and bring their meaning home to our own inner being.

I fear my colleagues in the department will think I am overstating the case and making Bergson out to be the defender of pretty nearly everything dear to the human heart. But again I remind you that the agreement between Bergson and his admirers may be fairly superficial. There is much that one may desire to save from the cold grip of logic and science, but one might not care to save it in just the fashion that Bergson does. Nevertheless one would discover in Bergson's writings much that one would sympathetically appreciate and find inspiring. One might also discover a host of new arguments to replace the old ones, some of which might be getting threadbare.

Something like this, I think, has happened. Many who would not go the whole road with our author find him a most pleasant companion for the while and gather courage from his company. Whatever in him they find not true is at least interesting and suggestive. It is the case, moreover, that the majority of present-day tendencies make the other way. Other contemporary *isms* show a leaning toward logic and science. Other philosophies seem to become more cold and analytic as time goes on, and the life of them more and more squeezed out to make room for technicalities. Thus Bergson is the more congenial to the romanticist who seemed in the way to be lonesome by-and-by.

Just here, in the conflict of many of life's large interests with the science of our day, is another prime source of the vogue which Bergsonism has acquired. Or perhaps we should say that this is the most important case of the more general conflict between the inner life and the external view of it, between the feelings and the analytic judgment. As science has pressed farther and farther into the inner nature of man—in biology, politics, economics, sociology, psychology—this conflict has become sharper, until it seems as if we must carry our science in one pocket and our "higher interests" in the other. Somewhere between his laboratory and his home the scientist puts away his cause and effect explanations and takes out his intuitions and sympathetic comprehension. Somewhere between his home and his settlement work the clergyman pockets his free moral agency doctrine and takes out his cause and effect sociology. Neither statement is wholly just, but they may serve to hit off the situation. Science perennially runs counter to the romantic interests, most of all when we use it to help them to success.

Phrasing the matter loosely: the higher interests are inevitably personal. Science is interested in things; religion and art are interested in the experience of things. Science intends to discover what *is there*; religion and art ask how it feels to dwell *in the presence of* such things. The different attitude of the practical man and beauty lover toward Niagara or Hetch-Hetchy will serve to illustrate. The one sees a natural reservoir or so many foot-pounds pressure; the other is filled with the glow of a sublime spectacle. For religion and art, Nature is the matrix of experience; for science it is the concourse of events in causal sequence.

These two divergent tempers or tendencies may dwell amicably side by side. It is difficult to see with the eye of the scientist and of the poet at the same time; but one may now observe with the impersonality of science, now appreciate with the passion of the artist or the mystic. The two moods may not overlap, yet they need not contradict one another. They are, nevertheless, opposite in direction, and may easily run into contradiction. The higher interests translate facts into terms of spiritual life; science tends to translate spiritual life into cold facts. If now, the scientist maintains that science must claim the right in the end to explain everything, and that when science shall have had her say no other explanation is valuable or significant, then we have an emphasis upon one point of view which renders all others superfluous. Something like this claim is occasionally made, and the tendency to take it for granted without explicitly making it characterizes a great many. On the other hand, the protagonists of religion and ethics do not make a similarly sweeping claim, but they do sometimes assert that no explanation of any fact has meaning except an explanation ultimately in terms of the significance which that fact may have for human life. This claim does not invalidate science, but it makes science distinctly subservient to the higher interests. "I will show you cause and effect for your moral conduct and your esthetic appreciation," says the scientist. "I will evaluate the method and results of your scientific explanation," retorts the defender of the spiritual life. This exchange of compliments presages warfare.

In our time, the thick of this fray has always gathered about the standard of evolution. Professor Lovejoy has analyzed this situation and shown the relation of Bergson's doctrine to past and present biological theory so brilliantly that I ought not to touch upon it. But I suspect that some of you may be—like myself—rank amateurs in biology, and may relish a statement of the issue in simple—even falsely simple— form. Darwin's great hypothesis supposes that the explanation of the forms of life can be given completely in terms of material environment and the principles of heredity and selection. Even the inheritance of acquired characteristics—the privilege of passing on to our children the qualities we develop in ourselves, which Darwin did not deny— was soon supplanted by a sterner doctrine. After Weissmann had cut off the tails of twenty generations of rats and observed that the twenty-first were still born with tails, the evolutionists declared that any modification of life forms not rigidly determined by heredity in the germ plasm must be accredited to spontaneous variation. The temper of this new biology was distasteful to the tender-minded. It seemed to rob life of a meaning and dignity which it had previously enjoyed. In the early part of the last century, Agassiz suggested that flowers had brilliant colors in order that they might attract the bees. The beautiful love for life which animated Nature and governed her decrees for Agassiz was now turned topsy-turvy. Beautiful flowers, wonderfully designed organisms, man with his spiritual interests—these forms of life did not spring from Nature through any love or Providence; they grew upon the face of an unappreciative Nature because they were able to stick there. Whereas an earlier account might interpret Nature as that which led up to and won its significance in life and spiritual values, life and its values were now translated into terms of environment and simple staying power.

And when the evolutionist had bethought himself to annex politics, psychology, and ethics, the direct clash was inevitable. Man and his institutions, his ethics, his art, his religion—these are but incidents of the struggle for survival. Man, without protective coloring, without any hard shell to retreat into, or any noteworthy agility in escaping his enemies, has survived largely because of the complexity of his nervous system and his herd-loving instinct. His herd-loving instinct becomes conscious and is perpetuated by the formulation of principles for keeping the herd together—that is his ethics. The complexity of his nervous system complicates and prolongs the connection between perception and reaction in a thousand ways—that is, in general, his inner life.

This, you say, is an old, old story, and this controversy died of inanition long ago. And, moreover, no biologist today holds such an evolution theory as has been described. But has the antagonism between the diverse points of view ceased with the controversy? If I am not mistaken, the opposition between those who would view Nature in the light of life and its values and those who would look upon life from the point of view of naturalism is just as real and significant as ever. What has happened is something as follows: the protagonists of the higher interests have for the most part been unable to follow the growing complexity of biological theory. It has gone over their heads, leaving them with a feeling that the opposition was still there but in terms they no longer understood. Thus they have been left with the crude conception of the controversy which I have outlined, silenced by the realization of its inadequacy, but unconvinced that *any* such theory can be just to the true nature of life. Nor is their understanding of the matter so inaccurate after all. For there are, in general, only two ways in which the original evolution theory could be modified. It might be altered by supposing that the principles which govern life are more numerous and more complex in their working, but still lie completely within the field of that which can be analyzed and exactly predicted by science. Or the theory might be altered by supposing that the study of life processes must forever find an irreducible residuum of facts which are essentially unpredictable and must be accredited to the vital principle—to the very essence of life itself.

Let us consider these two kinds of modification. The first characterizes the great majority of current biological theories. Those who hold them admit the inadequacy of Darwin's and of Weissmann's hypotheses, but they still insist that the finally correct explanation must be an explanation in just such terms. Any admission of an irreducible residuum or of a vital principle which produced the unpredictable is, they say, unscientific and unthinkable. But this leaves the opposition of science and the higher interests in exactly the same shape as before. The terms may be new but the intent is the same. The scientist still reads spiritual values in the light of naturalism. There is no comfort for the tender-minded in any such account.

With a modification of the second type, which credits life with producing something which is new out of its own hidden sources, the spiritually sensitive might be satisfied. For such a theory, life and the values which it cherishes might be a factor in determining the future; life might be in part arbiter of its own destiny and view Nature genuinely as its instrument and not its master. Such a theory, especially if simply put and ably defended, would appeal to many as the solution of their problem.

And this is one important significance of Bergson. Life, he says, is just that irreducible and unanalyzable impulse which continually produces the unpredictable. Modified forms, new organs, and new species are not the result of external forces and natural selection. They represent rather the eternal upthrust of life itself, surmounting its barrier and transmuting obstacles into instruments of its own development. The real evolution is a creation unceasingly renewed. At the root of life there is an effort to engraft on the necessity of physical forces the largest possible amount of *indetermination*. Science can never understand life, for life is more than mechanism, while mechanism of some kind or other is the only thing which science can comprehend. In aiming at complete prediction, the sciences of life merely create more and more complex mechanisms which misrepresent the very nature of what they attempt to portray.

In such a view as this of Bergson's—so many will think—life regains its lost dignity. The spirit is more than matter and life is more than mechanism. The inner forces of life are superior to its external circumstances and may dominate them. To such minds, Bergson appears as the new and vigorous champion of the higher interests—of ethics, of art, and of religion. He flourishes the sword of the spirit, and mechanical science is banished to the realm of inanimate matter.

I suggested in the beginning that, in dealing with such a subject as Bergson's philosophy, it might be well to see what it was all about. What has preceded represents the attempt to cover that aspect of the topic. If Bergson had not made connection with vital issues of our own day, he might have suffered that neglect which has been the portion of many excellent philosophers. Mere correctness gets us nowhere in these stirring times. But Bergson has brought his philosophy into direct relation with some of the universal interests of mankind and has taken sides on some of the most deeply felt of current issues. He has, moreover, championed that party which gives its sympathy and admiration most readily. He has defended the interests of ethics and religion and art against the mechanistic interpretation of science; he has championed esthetic comprehension and the mystic's intuition as against cold-blooded logical analysis. He has placed the emphasis upon the inner life and protected it from all forms of externalism and materialism. And he has done this—so it may seem—not testily, not hastily, but coolly and with nice deliberation—and in elegant French.

Bergson takes this defense of feeling, of intuition and the inner life, most seriously. The title of his first book is itself suggestive, *Les données immédiates de la conscience*—the data of immediate experience. The title under which the English translation later appeared, *Time and Free Will*, gives the other half of its message. Bergson named it from the thought presented in its early chapters; the translator was more impressed with its conclusions. In this book Bergson bids us to go back behind science, behind our philosophies, behind the very *things* with which our daily life seems to deal. We are to uncover the very stuff these are made of—the data of immediate experience. We must recover for the time from the distractions of practical activity and retire into ourselves. And what shall we find? Why just *this*!—this moment, this felt significance, this pulse of life, forever growing out of itself with no line between old and new! "We are such stuff as dreams are made on"; mayhap, but surely we are the vital reality. Where else should any *thing* or circumstance arise, but just in this immediate experience? Where else shall you find any bit of reality? What else is there for science or art or religion to interpret but just these felt significances? The moment—that is reality; the moment forever burgeoning from within itself and growing into the new; the moment, slipping into eternity and carrying eternity with it; the eternally present *now* of reality, which is no invisible demarcation line between dead past and future yet to be, but the very substance duration itself—living, vital time, the soul of being.

This real duration, which we are, is activity itself—time and free will. But what shall we be active about, what shall the moment do? What but interpret itself, understand itself, act out its own meaning. Upon this point, our author is a little regretful. For when the moment —or when *we* begin to "understand" that content of immediate experience which we are, the perverse tendency to forget the initial unity of being breaks in upon us. We pay attention, we single out, we select. We emphasize this phrase and that bit; we set up boundaries and make distinctions. We break the unity of pure duration into the multiplicity of things; we project them into space; we disjoin and relate; we create science—and the devil is upon us. For science does not stand above this multiplicity and distinction—as we do when we take thought of ourselves. Science is governed by our practical activity and serves it. Science proceeds by way of these disjunctions and relatings which it is the business of the selective act and the analytic understanding to set up. Without space, as the medium of division, without multiplicity, without the machine-like concatenation of things, there is no science. And just for this reason, science can never see beyond these mechanical relations and spatial division of things. It can never penetrate back to its source and stand in the presence of life, its creator. To comprehend that true reality, we must reverse the process by which science arises. We must translate the distinctions of science back into the pulsing moment which created them. We must return to the inner life and be at home with ourselves. Which then, in these terms, is the higher point of view, and the truer—the science which interprets life in terms of things or the intuition which translates things in terms of life? Which is the medium of genuine comprehension—the analytic reason which dissects wholes into parts and then arranges the fragments in imitation of the whole again, or that sympathetic insight which grasps at once felt wholes and does not seek to analyze?

The same antithesis persists and is elaborated in Bergson's later writings. We have the same insistence that science and logic are merely the useful instruments of our practical activity, never the means whereby true knowledge of reality can be gained. And we have the same intent to replace this fragmentary analytic view with the intuitive grasp which belongs to the inner life itself. Not a world of things creating eventually life; but Life itself is to appear, finally, as the master and creator.

5. German Idealism and Its War Critics

If there be any hour in history when the fundamental and vital importance of philosophy should be apparent, that hour has come. At this moment we are engaged in a war more terrible, more destructive, in some respects more subversive of human interests and more ruthless than the world has ever seen. And we must realize, if we are at all observant, that were it not for certain ideals that have been set up, certain conceptions of the state and of the relation of the individual to the state which have been entertained, a certain attitude toward life which has characterized some classes at least of the German people, this war could not have been. Other causes have contributed, without doubt— fear of encroachment by other peoples, the desire for unhampered economic expansion, mutual fear and suspicion, the intrigues of a secret diplomacy. But, giving these causes their proper weight and place, it still remains true that were it not for a certain philosophy, certain ways of thinking and feeling about the distinction of German and alien and about a nation's moral obligation to other peoples, the more materialistic considerations would hardly have sufficed to precipitate this crisis. The most potent issues do not concern merely material aims but incompatible doctrines of right and of the state—opposing ideals.

Philosophy—German philosophy at least—is not a negligible affair; it is capable of wrecking nations, of setting the world afire, of renouncing national obligations upon which international assurance depends, of providing apologetic for inhumanities more barbarous than the world had thought to see again. For the rest of the world, the comprehension of this philosophy is no luxury; it may be a matter of life and death.

It is for such reasons, no doubt, that so large a portion of current literature is philosophical in tenor and that so much of it is concerned with the evaluation of German thought. It is a little surprising, however, that these discussions of German philosophy have been so largely occupied with Kant and his successors in the idealistic tradition—a movement whose prestige in Germany suffered notable eclipse in the latter half of the nineteenth century, while during that same period it became the dominant philosophic influence in England and America.

Read before the Philosophical Union of the University of California, September 28, 1917. Reprinted by permission from the *University of California Chronicle*, Vol. XX (1918), No. 1, pp. 1–15.

The presumption would seem to be against any intimate connection between this philosophy and the present state of the German mind. Yet a majority of those who have discussed the subject in print have inclined to consider just this idealistic movement as expressing the principles which underlie the most sinister aspects of the present temper of Germany—its egotism, its subjectivism, and its idealization of the German state, ignoring the rights of individuals and of other states.

Professor Dewey, in the series of lectures entitled "German Philosophy and Politics," has traced what seems to him the connection between this movement and certain obliquities of the present German attitude—between, for example, Kant and Bernhardi. Mr. Santayana's "Egotism in German Philosophy," though written in somewhat different vein, still emphasizes much the same thought—the great defect of the German genius is its subjectivism, its other-worldliness, its glorification of the internally willed, as against the external and palpable fact. This egotism finds its philosophic expression in German idealism, its expression in deeds in the present war. M. Félix Sartiaux, writing under the title *Morale Kantienne et morale humaine*, is concerned to show that the ethical principles of Kant are destitute of all generosity and every esthetic charm, lacking any true sense of the individual, of liberty and of humanity. And J. M. de Dampierre, in *German Imperialism and International Law*, has said: "It was German philosophy which constituted the essential originality of Germanism. . . . The origin of that remarkable mentality which characterizes actual Germanism—a mentality of which so-called Pan-Germanism is only a brutal and premature expression—is to be found in the teachings of the German philosophers of the later eighteenth century. Tannenberg or Bernhardi are descendants in the direct line from Hegel, Fichte, or Kant, by way of Treitschke, Lasson, or Ostwald."[1]

This temper of the more competent critics is reflected also in the unguarded and extravagant statements of writers less well equipped, until the bloodguiltiness of German Idealism threatens to become a platitude.[2] And so far no voice has been raised in protest, although the stric-

[1] (New York, 1917), pp. 22–23.

[2] For example, the following paragraph from a popular periodical: "The philosophical basis for the defense of war, imperfectly expressed throughout the ages, was finally crystallized by Kant in his harmful political philosophy. That gentle and ascetic old person, who pondered and wrote in an age when any philosophy, not scientific inquiry, was the basis of thought, worked it out that a state has a soul apart from the individual souls which compose it. The duty of citizenship is to advance the state without regard to the interests of the individuals in that state. If, by a given movement, like a war, the interests of the state are advanced, it matters not whether every person in the state is rendered poorer and unhappier. The glory of the state has been achieved and the highest duty is fulfilled."

tures of the lesser critics have, some of them, amounted to libel against the dead. Surely it will be well to mention Kant's *Perpetual Peace*, to examine the political and cultural background of Fichte's nationalism, and to note that Neo-Kantians and Neo-Hegelians are counted amongst the most liberal thinkers in recent political and legal theory. To allow an impression so one-sided to gain currency will work a double injury; it will prejudice discussion of the philosophic issues between idealism and various rival views by interjecting inapposite considerations, and it will blind us to other, and probably more potent sources, of the present German temper.

One searches in vain through this critical literature for references or quotations from the writings of Kant and Fichte which deal specifically with war and with the state—Kant's *Perpetual Peace* and *Ideas for a Universal History of Mankind* and *Principles of Political Right*, or Fichte's work of the untranslatable title, *Der geschlossene Handelsstaat.* Professor Dewey says that it is difficult to make quotations from Kant which will be intelligible without command of his technical vocabulary. But surely he is not thinking of any of the treatises just mentioned. For these will be sufficiently clear to the most unlearned, and the proposals set forth in *Perpetual Peace* are summarized in six theses:

Preliminary Articles of a Perpetual Peace Between States

1. No conclusion of peace shall be held to be valid as such if it is made with the secret reservation of material for a future war.
2. No state having a separate existence—whether it be large or small—shall be acquired by another state by inheritance, exchange, purchase, or donation.
3. Standing armies shall be entirely abolished in course of time.
4. No national debts shall be contracted in connection with the external affairs of the state . . . [since] a credit system when used by the powers as an instrument of offense against one another . . . is a dangerous money power.
5. No state shall interfere by force with the constitution or government of another state.
6. No state at war with another shall adopt such modes of hostility as would necessarily render mutual confidence impossible in a future peace, such as the employment of assassins or poisoners, the violations of terms of surrender, the instigation of treason, and such like.

The Definitive Articles of a Perpetual Peace Between States

1. The civil constitution of every state shall be republican [i.e., shall provide for a representative form of government].
2. The Right of Nations shall be founded on a Federation of Free States.

Nor are these isolated passages which have been chosen to give a favorable impression. Examination of the context and comparison with the other political treatises will show that they are typical and that, did space permit, much more could be quoted to the same effect.

As for Kant's attitude toward the problem of the individual and society we need only remind ourselves that his most fundamental principle of morality is stated thus: "So act as to treat humanity, whether in thine own person or in that of any other, in every case as an end withal, never as means only"; and as a corollary to this, where *public* right is in question: "All actions affecting the rights of other men are wrong actions if the maxims from which they follow are inconsistent with publicity."

So this is the harmful political philosophy which contains the seed of Pan-Germanism or worse, and of which Bernhardi is a lineal descendant: the doctrine, namely, that the ultimate goal of political organization is a federation of free states for the sake of perpetual peace, and that to this end every state should have a representative government—since peace cannot be hoped for, so long as the glory of a ruler "consists in the fact that without his requiring to encounter any danger himself thousands stand ready to be sacrificed at his command for a cause which may be no concern of theirs"—that standing armies shall be abolished, that no state shall interfere violently with another, and that none, great or small, shall be made subject to another. One is surprised that those who discover a connection between Kant and Bernhardi do not go a step further and find the taint of Pan-Germanism in President Wilson's War Message and the Bryce Report.

How is it, then, that our critics have been so misled about Kant? One cannot say. But it is possible that the presumption of continuity between his philosophy and that of Fichte and Hegel has contributed to their error. This continuity has been in all respects exaggerated, and in just this matter of political philosophy it is not a continuity at all. Kant's cosmopolitanism and humanism belong to the Germany of the *Aufklärung*, of Lessing, Goethe and Beethoven, not to the new nationalized Germany which the Napoleonic wars were to produce and the political acumen of Bismarck to cement.

When Fichte made his stirring "Addresses to the German Nation," in 1807, this new movement was already under way. At the moment the German states were disunited and well nigh prostrate before the conqueror; public sentiment was lukewarm; many of the intellectuals, hypnotized by his power and personality, were secret or open partisans of Napoleon; the brother of the invader himself governor-general in Berlin. It was at such a time that the new Germany had its birth, a Germany which was to forget now that cosmopolitanism for which

Kant had stood and to become keenly conscious of its own peculiar genius and its need for national self-consciousness. There is much which challenges reflection in this picture.

And yet withal this new Germany is a spiritual Germany. It formulated its new consciousness in the project of the Kingdom of the Air, the conception of a moral and intellectual realm in which the native genius of the German peoples should find expression. Jean Paul Richter said in derision that since the French ruled the earth and the British the seas there was nothing left for Germans but the air. The implied challenge of such sceptics—for Jean Paul was not the only carping critic—was accepted; the University of Berlin was founded as the first concrete expression of the new spirit and as a point from which Germany should begin its spiritual conquest, first of itself and then of the European world. The Kingdom of the Air is to be realized, in part, through a new system of national education, a system which shall have as its aim the cultivation of the moral nature of the individual and the binding together of all individuals in the life of the nation. Fichte is one of the prime movers of this enterprise and its chief spokesman. In the peroration of his "Addresses" he had said:

The memory of your forefathers speaks to you. Think that with my voice are mingled the voices of your ancestors from the far-off ages of gray antiquity, of those who stemmed with their bodies the tide of Roman domination over the world, who vindicated with their blood the independence of these mountains, plains and streams which you have suffered to fall a prey to the stranger. They call to you: "Be ye our defenders! Hand down our memory to future ages, honorable and spotless as it has come down to you, as you have gloried in it and in your descent from us. . . . But as matters now are with you, seek not to conquer with bodily weapons, but stand firm and erect before them in spiritual dignity. Yours is the greater destiny—to found an empire of Mind and Reason, to destroy the dominion of rude physical power as the ruler of the world. Do this, and ye shall be worthy of your descent from us!"

Fichte had promulgated the doctrine of the Spirit in History, the conception of the development of the life of humanity upon earth as the unfolding of the Divine Reason itself. Thus he invests each epoch, each racial and national contribution, with peculiar significance, and he sees in the threatened disintegration of the German people a menace to the life of humanity itself. "Even the stranger in foreign lands," he says, "pleads with you, in so far as he understands himself and knows aright his own true interest. . . . If ye sink, Humanity sinks with you without hope of restoration."

In this appeal, and in its accompanying appraisal of the peculiar and indispensable contribution of Germany to human history, there is much of that national egotism and lack of perspective which we now associate with the Pan-Germanist delusion. In fact, one could make out a much better case than any of the critics has done by pointing out the correspondence of these two. There is, indeed, this much of real connection : Pan-Germanists, such as Treitschke, love to quote Fichte, and while exaggerating this aspect of his writing conveniently to forget the rest—a procedure characteristic of demagogues and sophists in all lands. But it is only fair to Fichte that we remark the difference between emphasizing the peculiar and indispensable genius of the Germans, in Berlin in 1807, with agents of the French government present in the hall, and the nation addressed so apathetic that the French governor-general did not feel it worth while to suppress the lectures—between this and the expression of similar sentiments in Berlin in 1907. Such considerations do not absolve Fichte from the charge of narrow-minded nationalism, but certainly they enable us better to understand the patriotic zeal which inspired his utterances. And it is abundantly clear that nothing was further from his thought than that such sentiments as his should ever lend themselves to any project of Pan-Germanism. It is sufficient demonstration of the folly of any dream of universal empire, so he had said, that it could only be realized at the cost of national individuality.

In the early years of Fichte's public life he was accounted a dangerous radical and leader of the democrats, so that at one time he was refused freedom of speech and even residence in Saxony and other German states, and was accorded these only in Prussia. He never recanted his democratic principles. The monarch he speaks of in his later writings is but the agent of the state, a citizen—so he explicitly says—like every other ; and none, in a state which has progressed to rational organization, can be a subject.

So far as his attitude toward war is concerned, he regarded its eventual abolition as the natural result of rational state organization. The only true state, he tells us, is one in which each shall be compelled to respect the security of every other, and by the establishment of such a state the possibility of foreign war, at least with other such states, is cut off. But he regards war as inevitable among states which have not reached this level of development. Nor was he in favor of peace at any price. In his "Idea of a Just War"—lectures delivered in 1813 when Prussia was preparing for the final struggle for freedom—he voiced a powerful plea for unity against the enemy ; and there is not lack of emphasis upon the potency of war as a purifier of the national consciousness. It is here that the passage occurs : "A nation becomes a nation through war and a common struggle. Who shares not in this present war can by no decree be made a member of the German nation." This sentiment we today can understand.

Fichte's relation to the temper of present-day Germany is, then, quite different from that of Kant. Fichte contributed largely to the development of the nationalistic spirit, and in making this contribution he exaggerated the peculiar gifts of the German people. But his ideal for Germany was still a spiritual ideal, and he never contemplated political domination or the imposition of German culture by force of arms. If the Pan-Germanists have thought to find aid and comfort in Fichte's words—well, we have the best of authority that a writer is not responsible for those who quote him.

A first-hand acquaintance with Hegel further enforces the thought that we here deal with distinct ethical and political theories, not with any "idealistic movement." The personality of Hegel, like his politics, stands almost in antithesis to Fichte. Fichte, fiery and impetuous, always a radical and frequently in difficulties with the constituted authority, still burned with such ardor to serve his country and the cause of righteousness as he conceived it, that he was capable of subordinating his dream of a state where every man should eat his bread in the sweat of his brow to the ideal of a Germany freed from foreign domination and united in the development of its national genius. Hegel, cool and astute, finished his *Phenomenology* almost within sound of the guns which dealt to Germany the staggering defeat of Jena; and he hailed the victorious Napoleon as "the World-Spirit on horseback." At no time were his published doctrines unacceptable to the constituted authorities, though he was capable of setting forth what was in reality a radical or heterodox view in sonorous and edifying phrases of apparent orthodoxy. It is consonant with his doctrine of morality that the really good man must be effectively good, and he never jeopardized his effectiveness as a public teacher by espousing any cause foredoomed to failure. Hegel's philosophy has sometimes been criticized as romantic: though it has its romantic side, still, regarding it as a whole, I get quite an opposite impression and am tempted to adapt a familiar characterization and call his view *Real-Philosophie*. Whatever is is right in Hegel's eyes, provided that this which *is* does not carry within itself the seeds of dissolution. Permanent success is the perfect test of righteousness. Kant had pondered upon the fact that we must somehow believe that only the cause of righteousness can permanently triumph, but he had pointed out the paradox that he who essays righteousness for the sake of any sort of loaves and fishes is not a righteous man. Thus those who maintain the identity of the moral life and the prudent one are still divisible into two opposing classes: there are those who find in the justice of the cause the prophecy of its eventual success, and those who find in success the justification of the cause. Hegel impresses me as belonging to the second group. As someone has put it: Leibnitz wrote a Theodicy in which he justified the works of God; Hegel, a Demonodicy justifying the works of the Devil. War is one of these works, and it is characteristic that Hegel finds for war an indispensable place in the realization of the Divine Idea.

But this characterization will be wholly unjust if we do not view more widely the place of evil—of "negativity"—in Hegel's system. His attitude is quite accurately expressed in the biblical account of evil: "It must needs be that offenses come, but woe unto him by whom the offense cometh." And it is in this sense that he justifies war, amongst other human ills. Hegel advances the notion of poetic justice seriously as the actual basis of our perpetual progress to the Divine Idea. "They that live by the sword shall perish by the sword"; it is the function of evil in the world to become its own worst punishment. The function of evil in the life of man is to drive him beyond himself, to cure the ills of egotism by revealing the tragic inadequacy of the isolated will to find its own satisfaction. The life of man, to be rational, must be social, must be consciously obedient to that greater will which expresses itself in the corporate life of mankind; and the spur to this obedience comes through the disclosure of all those ills which are implicit in the strife of merely private, and therefore capricious, plans and purposes. War but realizes the evil which already inheres in the opposition of divided interests. It is the glory of war that if it is an evil its evil is purgative— it cures. By its very inevitability it displays the necessarily vicious character of aims which are divisive and self-willed. Hegel's attitude toward war is something like the attitude he takes toward death in a passage in the *Phenomenology*: The slave may learn a needed lesson from the whip of the master; but the master, how shall he be humbled of his false self-assertion? How, but by Death? In the midst of his prideful career shall come the realization of his vanity, for Death is master of us all. Whoso cuts himself off from the life of our common humanity, he in very truth shall die.

I would not conceal that side of Hegel which is intolerable to most of us; in fact, the friends of Hegel will think that I have over-emphasized it. But if Hegel extols war, still we find here no apology for the national pursuit of military power—quite the opposite. If he extols war, it is precisely because and in so far as war represents the self-destruction of the materialistic and egotistic attitude, and is a means to the triumph of the spiritual and universal. This is hardly the spirit which is attributed to the Junker, though the doctrine that strife is a prime essential to the spiritual salvation of peoples is itself sinister enough.

A more objectionable feature of Hegel's philosophy is his conception of the state. In spite of the fact that his theory of the relation of the individual or family to the state applies point for point equally well to the relation of states within what should be the corporate life of humanity, Hegel everywhere speaks of the state as absolute and as capable of realizing completely within itself the ends of human organization. And the state which he thus idealizes is what he calls a "constitutional monarchy," with a separate military class which is politically dominant —in other words, it is the Prussian state. Just why Hegel neglects the implications of his own principles for this theory of the absolute state one can only conjecture: it represents not only a lack of moral and political insight but a defect in the logical structure of his system. How different his political theory might otherwise have been may be seen in the writings of the English Hegelians, T. H. Green and Bernard Bosanquet. That Hegel committed himself to such a doctrine must represent some lack of philosophic acumen, or else it is a sin against the light; in either case it justly arouses suspicion with reference to his whole philosophy. But a candid and fair-minded examination will compel the admission that this particular doctrine is not representative of his system and that its inadequacies do not, therefore, indicate the general temper of his writings or the main influence which they may be supposed to have exercised.

I am in no sense an admirer of Hegel, but I see no just hope of subtracting from the esteem in which he is held by tracing any notable connection between him and the present war. It simply does not exist. Less than fifteen years after the death of Hegel, in 1831, German thinkers very generally repudiated him and all his works. And those who did not so reinterpreted his doctrines as to make them, from our present perspective, hardly recognizable. The idealistic movement thus came to a somewhat abrupt termination, so far as Germany is concerned, and it is a commonplace that the materialism which then replaced it is more characteristic of the present German temper.

This materialistic movement, represented in the field of political philosophy by Feuerbach and Stirner and Marx, influenced popular thinking in Germany much more powerfully than idealism ever did. And the indications of its present prestige are both numerous and notable. The idea that material forces ultimately dominate in the molding of history, that customary morality and law are no more than the expediency of the dominant will, the doctrine that might is the only right which commands or deserves to command respect—these are prominent in this materialistic movement, as is also a certain pragmatic attitude: the consciously formulated principle that different peoples and different times demand a different truth, that one can essay no truth that shall be universal, valid for all periods and all nations. As Marx expressed it: "The same men who establish social relations in conformity with their material production [as all men do] also create principles, ideas and categories in conformity with their social relations. . . . All such ideas and categories are therefore historical and transitory products."[3] In many ways Germany today exhibits this materialism and this pragmatism. In its diplomatic dealing with other nations Wilhelmstrasse seems to have taken the pragmatic oath: "We swear to tell what is expedient, the whole of what is expedient, and nothing but what is expedient, so help us future experience." In the effrontery with which it has pursued wholly private and material aims under the name of the welfare of humanity, in its unblushing substitution of "military necessity" for the universal principles of justice and decency, and in the deliberate search for "truths" which will justify themselves by being credited and by contributing to German success, Germany seems to exhibit belief in a truth and a morality which are relative simply to German needs and German expediency. One may describe this attitude in the words with which Josiah Royce once characterized the pragmatic revolt against intellectualism:

There is no absolute truth. There is only the truth that you need. Enter into the possession of your spiritual right. Borrow Nietzsche's phraseology. Call the truth of ordinary intellectualism mere *Sklavenwahrheit*. It pretends to be absolute; but only the slaves believe in it. "Henceforth," so some Zarathustra of a new theory of truth may say, "I teach you *Herrenwahrheit*." Credit what you choose to credit. . . . When, apart from the constraints of present verification, and apart from mere convention, I say: "This opinion of mine is true," I mean simply: "To my mind, lord over its own needs, this assertion now appears expedient." Whenever my expediency changes, my truth will change.[4]

Mr. Santayana and Professor Dewey have rightly characterized the philosophic sin of present Germany as subjectivism—as the egotism which would elevate a deliberately limited point of view and a private interest to the position of universal truth and moral principle. What

---

[3] Preface to the *Communist Manifesto*.
[4] *William James and Other Essays* (New York, 1912), p. 230.

they fail to discern is that not idealism but materialism and pragmatism are the essentially subjectivistic philosophic doctrines.

One might, indeed, following out and illustrating the thoughts suggested above, make out an excellent case for the connection between pragmatism and the present German attitude, or materialism and *Realpolitik*. But all such argument is essentially sophistical. It ignores, on the one hand, the complexity of modern national life, and it exaggerates, on the other, the possible connection between nationality and philosophic doctrine. German Idealism is no more peculiarily German than English Evolutionism is peculiarly English or Comtean Positivism is peculiarly French. In fact, the influence of evolutionism and positivism in Germany since 1860 have far exceeded the influence of idealism of the "absolute" type, while in England and America, from 1875 to 1900, exactly this idealism represents the dominant philosophic influence. The critics mentioned represent philosophic movements which have arisen in the last twenty years to combat this previously dominant idealism, and it is to its influence in England and America, and not at all to its influence in Germany, that we are indebted for this critical literature. In Germany this idealism has not for forty years been sufficiently prominent to warrant much critical consideration.

Under these circumstances, it seems absurd to trace any noteworthy connection between German Idealism and the present crisis. If we are concerned about the issues between idealism and pragmatism or idealism and materialism, why drag in the war? And if we are concerned about the war, we shall not need to find its important causes in any philosophic movement of a century ago. The present period already presents a sorry enough chapter in the history of critical discussion. Let us leave the confusion of war prejudices with intellectual concerns to the ninety-three German professors.[5]

---

[5] A reference to a manifesto in defense of the German invasion of Belgium, signed by ninety-three German intellectuals. This document is given in English translation in R. H. Lutz, ed., *Fall of the German Empire, 1914–1918* (Stanford, Calif.: Stanford University Press, 1932), Vol. 1, pp. 74–78.—Eds.

6. Review of John Dewey's *The Quest for Certainty*

The Quest for Certainty: A Study of the Relation of Knowledge and Action. JOHN DEWEY (New York: Gifford Lectures, 1929).

It is not necessary to characterize a book which we shall all read, but one can not lay down Professor Dewey's Gifford Lectures without yielding to the temptation. This is a completer and better-rounded statement of the author's point of view than any which has preceded it, and on some points it is a clearer one. It is also a contribution to literature. It begins, one feels, where the author himself begins; the directing intent is laid down in the opening pages; and it moves forward with uninterrupted sweep to that which, one is persuaded, constitutes the personal goal of his thinking. The concluding chapter especially is impressive; it contains passages which will always be quoted.

In its simplest terms, the theme is not new, but is that in which the West has always announced itself as against the East, the modern world against the ancient: Man may not reach the goal of his quest for security by any flight to another world—neither to that other world of the religious mystic, nor to that realm of transcendent ideas and eternal values which is its philosophical counterpart. Salvation is through work, through experimental effort, intelligently directed to an actual human future.

The development of this theme is, of course, peculiarly Professor Dewey's own. Man must recognize his continuity with nature, and he must read that continuity both ways. Nature in general is not a completed and independent reality prior to his action. Nor are the objectives of his quest legitimately or safely determined in complete abstraction from that experience in which environment is met and moulded. The world is not a "block-universe" and finished; its growing reality is in part for us to create. But the sense of this is not conveyed in the simple and bold terms of a Jamesian "absolute chance" and "will to believe," which either did or did not appeal to the reader's prior inclination; it comes by way of an examination of the relation between knowledge and action, and of the nature of "the valuable" as the object of an activity which, though intelligently directed, is never cast in final form or loses its character as experimental and hypothetical.

Reprinted by permission from *The Journal of Philosophy*, Vol. XXVII (1930), No. I, pp. 14–25.

The persistent fallacy of epistemology has been the conception that the norm of knowledge is some antecedent reality. In their opposite ways, both rationalists and sensational empiricists are in error by their common assumption that reflection—thought involving inference—is reproductive, and that ideas are tested by some comparison with an object which has prior existence. For rationalism, this object is a reality already informed by transcendent and constitutive reason. For sensational empiricism, sensory qualities as merely given are the antecedent models with which ideas must agree if they are to be sound or "proved." But objects are not finalities which "call for thought only in the way of definition, classification, . . . subsumption in syllogisms, etc." (99, 112). Sense qualities are something *to be* known; they set the problem to be solved instead of supplying the answer which knowledge seeks. The model of true knowledge is to be found in the experimental investigations of science. The principal traits of such inquiry are three: "The first is the obvious one that all experimentation involves *overt* doing, the making of definite changes in the environment or in our relation to it. The second is that experiment is not a random activity, but is directed by ideas which have to meet the conditions set by the need of the problem inducing the active inquiry. The third and concluding feature, in which the other two receive their full measure of meaning, is that the outcome of the directed activity is the construction of a new empirical situation in which objects are differently related to one another, and such that the *consequences* of directed operations form the objects that have the property of being *known*" (86–87). The concepts which direct such experimental inquiry comprise or prescribe a set of operations by which the presence of the character conceived is tested (111). Thus "ideas have an empirical origin and status. But it is that of acts performed . . . not reception of sensations forced on us from without" (112). As directly given, objects are not the terminus and test of knowledge, but the occasion of it; experimental procedure reduces them to the status of data. "This resolution is required because the objects in their first mode of experience are perplexing, obscure, fragmentary; in some way they fail to answer a need. Given data which locate the nature of the problem, there is evoked the thought of the operation which if put into execution may eventuate in a situation in which the trouble or doubt which evoked inquiry will be resolved" (123). "Ideas that are plans of operations to be performed are integral factors in actions which change the face of the world. . . . A genuine idealism and one compatible with science will emerge as soon as philosophy accepts the teaching of science that ideas are statements not of what is or has been but of acts to be performed" (138). "Henceforth the quest for certainty becomes the search for methods of control; ... theoretical certitude is assimilated to practical certainty; to *security*, trustworthiness of instrumental operations" (128).

The important consequences of this theory of knowledge, for Professor Dewey's further thesis, is suggested by the last two quotations. Knowledge here takes its place in a world which is in part its own creation. A knower, as such, is a doer, not a passive spectator of a ready-made world. The terms in which reality is defined, for our cognition, are terms into which our own activity, directed by this knowing, has already entered. Knowing is prediction of the result of our own intelligently directed ways of acting—if I do thus and so, the result will be such and such. "If we persist in the traditional conception, according to which the thing to be known is something which exists prior to and wholly apart from the act of knowing, then discovery of the fact that the act of observation, necessary to existential knowing, modifies that pre-existent something, is proof that the act of knowing gets in its own way.... If knowing is a form of doing and is to be judged like other modes by its eventual issue, this tragic conclusion is not forced upon us" (205).[1]

In the pages from which these excerpts are taken, the principles set down are illuminated and enforced by consideration of physical science, past and present, which constitutes an analysis and critique of scientific procedure which is worth reading quite apart from its bearing on the issue. In the omission of this here, much which gives significance and support to the conclusions must inevitably fail to be suggested.

With the main theses of this conception—the continuity of knowing and acting, the function of empirical concepts as prescription of operations to be performed, the significance of knowing as prediction of a future into which our action enters—the present writer is so fully in accord as to have no comment save applause. And I believe that nothing which a just theory of knowledge can contribute to other problems, theoretical and practical, is more important than this realization that reality can not be an alien and imposed somewhat, or a net of tight-bound circumstances in which we are caught, because the only reality there can be for us is one delimited in concepts of the results of our own ways of acting.

Yet I conceive that the proponents of the various "spectator" theories of knowledge may feel aggrieved by this account. If it is difficult

[1] The context is especially concerned with certain implications of physical relativity.

to deny what Professor Dewey positively says, it is nevertheless possible to feel that something has been left unsaid which is important. In particular, it may be remarked that the author is preoccupied with the forward-looking function of knowledge to the neglect of its backward-looking ground or premises. It seems evident that Professor Dewey dislikes abstractions, and views with suspicion any attempt to separate factors or interrelated problems. Always his emphasis is upon the living integrality of process. Traditional conceptions, by contrast, have often formulated their problems and found their solutions by just such abstraction and separation of factors. One such problem—historically it overshadows and colors all the others—is this question of the ground, basis, validity of knowledge: How do we know? How is science possible? What justifies our cognitive assurance? To this question, we can not return the answer, "The dénouement of future experience will tell us," because the future is what we never catch up with. If knowledge is knowledge only as it directs action into the future it predicts, and this future is the test of its validity, the no knowledge is assured until it is dead and its function has ceased. Knowledge, on these terms, will be foresight—and the only assured foresight will be hindsight. Nor is it possible to escape the point by the observation that knowledge is hypothetical. "Hypothetical" is here ambiguous: if what is meant is that the *content* of knowledge is a *hypothetical proposition* —"If I should do thus and so, the results would be such and such"— then it is to be observed that it is not the hypothesis of this proposition which wants assurance: it is the judgment as a whole, and particularly the prediction contained in its consequent clause, whose ground and validity are in question. The only sense of "hypothetical" which is pertinent to the present issue is that of "tentative" or "probable." But if what is meant is that empirical knowledge is probable, then the question merely recurs in another form: What makes it probable? What justifies the judgment as a knowledge of probabilities?

By his predominant interest in the *function* of knowledge, Professor Dewey almost identifies knowing with *finding out*;[2] traditional theories mostly exhibit an opposite preoccupation and insist that the discussion of knowledge properly refers to the cognitive state which follows upon finding out, not that which leads up to it. If reference is taken to such experimental processes as characterize scientific investigation, it may be urged that the knowledge which directs and controls the experiment

[2] For example, "Taking what is already known or pointing to it is no more a case of knowledge than taking a chisel out of a tool-box is the making of a tool" (188).

should not be confused with the knowledge which results from it. An experimenter already knows something, and in the light of this tries to find out something else. If he succeeds, he then knows two things (perhaps connected) : what he knew before and what the experiment has just revealed. But the first of these items of knowledge is presumably independent of the experimental findings ; it relates to something antecedently determined. And the second item becomes knowledge only when the experiment is concluded and its result, therefore, acquires the status of antecedent fact.

If I read Professor Dewey correctly, he would object to such analysis as artificial, because he would take the typical situation in knowing, and especially in scientific experiment, to be one in which activity is guided by an hypothesis tentatively held, which the result of this experimental activity will confirm or falsify. The guiding idea is itself prediction of consequences to be reached by certain operations it prescribes. But does this manner of reading the cognitive situation abrogate the distinction between the *ground* of knowledge and the *content* of knowledge as matters requiring separate examination ? Let us accept, as typical of cognition, the case of hypothesis and experimental verification. Let us further agree that the significance of the hypothesis is the prediction of certain results to be reached by operations it prescribes. At the initiation of the experiment, when the hypothesis exercises its instrumental function of prescribing operations, is this hypothesis knowledge ? The answer, in the typical case, will be that it has a certain probability. If the experiment confirms it, it will then have a higher probability (or perhaps certainty). But the question, "Why is it probable (or certain) ?" will, at either moment, have to be answered, not in the light of what is, for that moment, future, but of what is present and past. The content of the hypothesis—its prediction of a result of action—relates to the future ; and we may agree that the significance of cognition generally lies in such leading and in such prediction. But at every moment, the validity of it as knowledge depends upon the past.

So far as I can see, there is nothing here which would deny to knowledge its significance as an instrument of action, nor the author's further point that reality as an object of knowledge is something into which our own activity enters as a partial determinant. These points relate to the *content* and *function* of knowledge : the content of a cognition may be the prediction of the future and of a future as conditioned by action, although the just ground of such prediction, or warrant for our knowledge, is something antecedent. However, if we grant that a practical belief has a just ground only in the light of what is past, we then make connection with traditional issues in their traditional form. Warranted beliefs, hypotheses justifiably held, are possible only if something learned from the past is pertinent to the future. The possibility of knowledge argues some continuing stability which extends through past and future both. It is such transtemporal stabilities, or the basis of them in reality, which constitute the object of the traditional quest for certainty. The elevation of such transtemporalities to the status of the transcendent, as eternal objects of a constitutive reason, or even their abstraction from that temporal process in which human action may make a difference, is—we may agree with Professor Dewey—an illicit procedure and the source of further errors. But in some terms or other, some such background, in the more-than-particular, will be required for empirical beliefs if the problem of their validity is to be solved.

Moreover, the presentations of sense-experience must exercise some other function than that of setting problems if empirical knowledge is to be possible. That presentation which is the occasion of the cognitive process must serve as clue to, or a sign of, what our practical belief predicts as the eventuation of a certain mode of action. Acts do not produce their empirical consequences regardless of the situation into which they enter. What that situation is, we must rely upon such given data of sense to disclose, even though they portray it only in fragmentary and inconclusive fashion. They constitute such ground as we may have that, in this circumstance or on this occasion, a particular mode of action will yield a predictable result. Furthermore, such ground of our prediction must reflect some generalization—that on such occasions as this, a particular act will result thus and so—and the only possible basis of this generalization is something prior, even though the generalization be a tentative one, subject to correction in the light of further experience. It can only be thus corrected when such further experience has itself become antecedent fact.

I do not suppose that there is anything here set down (unless in detail) with which Professor Dewey would disagree, since this does little more than emphasize the obvious : that if knowledge is to be other than a random leap in the dark, a belief must have some ground or warrant; and that what is future to it can not, in the nature of the case, provide such warrant. But perhaps these trivialities justify the observation that knowing has its retrospective as well as its prospective significance. Its content as prediction and its function as guide to action look toward the future; its warrant, or validity as belief, looks back to something prior. We may suspect that one reason for Professor Dewey's preponderant, and almost exclusive, emphasis upon the forward-looking aspect of content and instrumental function is that the traditional problems of validity do not greatly interest him. In any case, nothing which might be here at issue touches the point—important for the sequel—that the reality we know is conditioned by our action, not something preformed, and contemplated by a passive spectator.

The other outstanding thesis of this theory of knowledge, which is carried forward to the consideration of further problems, is that the end of knowledge is not in knowing but is in doing—the subservience of the cognitive activity to further interests, which are to have authority over it. This may seem to be merely the definitive intent of "instrumentalism"; but that word has two quite different meanings. Plato, for example, is an instrumentalist in the sense of holding that the essence of a thing is the "good" of it. The axe is defined in terms of its cutting function. And no empirical axe is fully real just because no lump of metal ideally subserves that function. The bridle is an instrument for controlling a horse without injuring his mouth; and it is a transcendent idea because no such thing can be more than approximated to. Plato as much as Professor Dewey takes the correct apprehension of an axe to lie in a concept of which it might be said that it prescribes certain operations and forecasts their result. And for Plato likewise it is true that, in the case of particular empirical axes, this forecast is hypothetical and probable only. But for Plato it is the intellectual apprehension of this essence which is the aim of the cognitive process; the advance of knowledge is toward better and more precise concepts. For Professor Dewey, this advance is to be tested by a better accomplishment of the world's work: "Ideas are worthless except as they pass into actions which rearrange and reconstruct in some way, be it little or large, the world in which we live. To magnify thought and ideas for their own sake apart from what they do . . . is to reject the idealism which involves responsibility" (138). Thus the two points of view are in agreement that the good of the axe is in the woodpile, and that a just concept must so take it; Plato and Professor Dewey are both instrumentalists in holding a functional theory of the concept. But Professor Dewey would also maintain that the good of *knowing* or understanding the axe is in the woodpile, and thus is an instrumentalist in a further sense. It is this transfer of "the seat of intellectual authority" to the arts of practical guidance and control which is the underlying thesis of the book.

The issue here revealed becomes poignant whenever the interests of precision and finality of conception run counter to the practical applicability of knowledge and direct scientific endeavor away from those complex and unprecise affairs which are proximate to human interests. The subversive results of holding intellectual apprehension to be an end in itself are numerous and subtle. The hypostatization of Platonic ideas, and the consequent other-worldliness and contempt for the practical, is only an extreme example. It likewise leads to disrespect for sensibly observed material in science (88), to a turning away from change to the changeless (84), to relegation of the problematic and the individual to the "subjective" (233), and to the elevation of abstract "standardized" things, such as the entities of physical science, to the position of a higher, more fundamental kind of reality (237ff). It also results in an invidious designation of the abstract disciplines as more truly "science," in contrast to those departments of knowledge more directly pertinent to concrete and involved human affairs. Hence as a further effect, the social sciences may be misled, through an attempt to be more "scientific," to give over the effort at instrumentally valuable formulations in favor of empty abstractions and sterile classifications (199, 220ff). It may even, through the false dichotomy of intellectual and practical, result in false ideals of education; in "devotion to training in technical and mechanical skills on one hand and to laying in a store of abstract information on the other"—both in contrast to the "development of intelligence as a method of action" (252).

The real nature and legitimate intent of abstract scientific procedures is clearly set forth. Such remoteness from the concrete is necessary for "arriving at statements which hold for all experiencers and observers under all possible varying individual circumstances" (218). The operations and relations implicit in our dealings with the concrete become explicit and generalized and are then symbolically dealt with. "All that was required for the development of mathematics as a science and for the growth of a logic of ideas, that is, of implications of operations with respect one to another, was that some men should appear upon the scene who were interested in the operations on their own account, as operations, and not as means to specified particular uses" (156). The relative perfection of conclusions is connected with the strict limitation of problems. *"Artificial simplification or abstraction is a necessary precondition of securing ability to deal with affairs which are complex, in which there are many more variables and where strict isolation destroys the special characteristics of the subject-matter....* [But] objection comes in, and comes in with warranted force, when the results of an abstractive operation are given a standing which belongs only to the total situation from which they have been selected" (217). "The abstractions of mathematics and physics represent the common denomi-

nators in all things experienceable. . . . Erected into complete statements of reality as such, they become hallucinatory obsessions" (218).
To make a transcript of this rational structure [of nature] in mathematical formulae "gives great delight to those who have the required
ability. But it *does* nothing, it makes no difference in nature" (211).

The underlying issue here is not so much metaphysical as ethical;
or it is metaphysical because it is first ethical. Ontological subordination of the "abstract" to the "concrete" is the corollary of the ethical
principle that the (intellectual) activity which leads to abstract objects
should not *terminate* in them, but should be instrumental to something
further and practical. It is the counterpart of the repudiation of the
ancient ideal of contemplative insight in favor of absorption in the
world's work. The assignment of exclusive or preeminent reality to
the entities of exact science, as against those of everyday experience,
is certainly a metaphysical blunder, and merits the vigorous criticism
here accorded it. But surely the "common denominators of all experience" have their own kind of reality; they are not fictions. And in view
of the author's earlier point, that real objects in general are the termini
of intelligently directed activity, it becomes evident that "concreteness"
does not connote mere givenness, but implies some sort of intellectual
delimitation, abstraction, or construction. Otherwise we should conclude in favor of the exclusive reality of sensations. This being so, it
does not appear in what sense the metaphysical preeminence of every-
day objects over the scientific is more warranted than its opposite. Perhaps the author does not intend to assign such preeminence. In any
case, the ethical thesis of instrumentalism should stand on its own feet.

With respect to this ethical issue, probably we shall all agree that
Professor Dewey's emphasis upon practical doing falls in the right
place, though some may feel that his enthusiasm for the strenuous life
leads him to overstate the case, and smacks of rigorism. To "make a
difference in nature" is not the whole end of man. Perhaps he will allow
us moral holidays, for the celebration of scientific insight as an end in
itself.

A further motive for emphasis upon the desirable continuity of science and practical affairs becomes evident in the ensuing chapters: it
is to the end that something of the method learned in science may be
carried over to the problems of concrete human ends. "The problem of
restoring integration and cooperation between man's beliefs about the
world in which he lives and his beliefs about the values and purposes
that should direct his conduct is the deepest problem of modern life. It
is the problem of any philosophy which is not isolated from that life"

(255). As a result of the lack of continuity with natural science, beliefs about values are "pretty much in the position in which beliefs about nature were before the scientific revolution. There is either a basic distrust of the capacity of experience to develop its own regulative standards, and an appeal to what philosophers call eternal values, in order to ensure regulation of belief and action; or there is an acceptance of enjoyments actually experienced irrespective of the method or operation by which they are brought into existence" (256). What is needed is an extension of the experimental method to the construction of human good. This would mean, on the one hand, the repudiation of transcendent "values," known by reason or divinely revealed, and, in consequence, of that subjectivism which throws the emphasis upon change in ourselves instead of the world in which we live. Standards would no longer be accepted as something antecedent and fixed: "All tenets and creeds about good and goods, would be recognized to be hypotheses" (277). The more exacting test of consequences would be substituted for fixed general rules (278). On the other hand, the experimental method will deny any final significance to the mere fact of casual desire or given enjoyment. "The fact that something is desired only raises the *question* of its desirability" (260). "A *feeling* of good or excellence is as far removed from goodness in fact as a feeling that objects are intellectually thus and so is removed from their being actually so" (265).

"Where will regulation come from if we surrender traditionally prized values as our directive standards? Very largely from the findings of the natural sciences" (273)—when the effects of the separation of knowledge from action have been removed. *"Judgments about values are judgments about the conditions and the results of experienced objects; judgments about that which should regulate the formation of our desires, affections and enjoyments"* (265).

Many readers will, I think, find this part of Professor Dewey's doctrine puzzling to a degree in which the rest is not. The sense in which "experience can develop its own regulative standards" is not clear. It is to be observed, of course, that "experience" does not here mean something merely given; for Professor Dewey, the experiencer and his attitudes and acts are in the experience. Further, we shall all admit that what is good has to be learned; that in part the achievement of the valuable must come through our own more just evaluations, and that this learning is not a process of merely rational reflection, but is empirical, including observation of the consequences of acts and of the connections of things. But is it not the case that we must ourselves bring to experience the ultimate criterion and touchstone of the good; that otherwise experience could no more teach us what is good than it can teach the blind man what things are red? Experience—and experience alone—can teach us what is good, if by that we mean what situations, things, events are good; that is, only the wisdom of experience can show us where goodness is to be found. Hence if we mean by "ideals" such concrete aims as democracy or wealth or the comity of nations, then experience must develop its own ideals—though whether it can be *trusted to* is, perhaps, another matter. But can experience determine the nature, essence, criteria of goodness? Before one embarks upon the practical and empirical problem of realizing the valuable or constructing the good, is it not essential that one should be able to recognize it when disclosed; that one should know, not what objects or what concrete situations, but what quality of life—whether pleasure or self-mastery, activity in accordance with virtue or the intellectual love of God—it is which is to be realized or constructed? Toward this problem, we can hardly take hypothetical attitudes, leaving the just answer for the social and historical process to determine, because the question whether human history is progress or decadence will depend upon it.

Professor Dewey has, I think, declined to separate these two questions of the essence or criteria of the good and of its locus in experience and reality. And by so doing, he omits the former altogether. It is precisely this problem of the nature or definition of the good to which traditional theories have been principally directed. Hence no issue is really joined. In spite of this, however, it seems to me that Professor Dewey's strictures upon traditional conceptions are wholly just and that the corrective which he urges is most salutary. With respect to the second problem, of concretely realizing the good, traditional doctrines have almost universally done one or other of two things: either they have, broadly speaking, assumed that moral science is concluded with the delimitation of the *summum bonum*; or they have proceeded as if he who apprehends this nature of the good can forthwith produce it or find it, with no more equipment than mother-wit provides. As examination of their "illustrations" will show, they go straight from basic principle to the most intricate and difficult of personal and social problems, with no intermediaries. This is as if one could proceed from the definition of "beauty" to the production of a symphony or to the criticism of Renaissance architecture. Quite clearly, either in or added to the traditional type of value-theory and ethics, there is needed just that continuity with a humanized science, just that learning of the connections and consequences of things, and just that experimental method and attitude of mind in behalf of which Professor Dewey speaks. This is just that connection between an understanding of the world we live in and our beliefs about our purposes and values which might bridge the present chasm between theoretical apprehension and the art of the good life. This is the goal of the quest for certainty and security.

With respect to values, there is a third question which philosophy has sought to answer: So far as these transcend man's power to achieve, how do they stand related to things in general? There is something which bears upon this in the concluding chapter of the book. But that chapter will be omitted here. Perhaps it is a matter peculiarly between Professor Dewey and his readers. I should not wish to underscore any part of it by quotation, or to mar it by marginal annotations.

7. Pragmatism and Current Thought

It is somewhat difficult in the case of pragmatism to determine what are its essential and distinctive theses. That there should be thirteen distinguishable pragmatisms, however, is not a peculiarity: these could be set alongside the thirty-seven idealisms and fifty-one realisms. William James is reported to have said that he was pleased to find that pragmatism had this wealth of meaning; he accepted all thirteen. In any case, such variety merely marks the fact that pragmatism is a movement, not a system. Its beginnings are attributable to Charles Peirce. But Peirce has something the quality of a legendary figure in American philosophy. His originality and the wealth of his thinking are not fully evident in his published writings. Apart from a few persons—amongst whom were James and Royce—some of his most important conceptions can have had little influence, because they have never been printed: and the coincidence of these doctrines with the views of later pragmatists is distinctly limited. James's enthusiasm for them must in part be set down to that catholicity of appreciation which was so notable a part of his character. James called himself a "radical empiricist" as well as a pragmatist, and the connection, or lack of it, between these two aspects of, or strands in, his philosophy has been a matter of some question. We must, of course, look to Professor Dewey's writings for the integration and systematic elaboration of pragmatism. But no one could have exercised the quite unparalleled influence which he has had upon American thought without giving rise to a wealth of resultant views which is a little confusing when one tries to grasp their coincidence or central meaning. Hence it is not a matter for surprise if those most deeply influenced by him show a tendency to drop the term, lest a too extended agreement with one another be suggested, and that those of us who still have ventured to use it are doubtful of our right to the designation.

If, then, I venture to suggest what is the core of pragmatism, and what I think may be the chief significance of it, both in philosophy and for other branches, I hope it will be understood that I do not take myself too seriously in the matter. This view is presented to those who will best know how to correct my mistakes.

Reprinted by permission from *The Journal of Philosophy*, Vol. XXVII (1930), No. 9, pp. 238–46.

Pragmatism is, as James indicated, not a doctrine but a method: viewed logically, it can be regarded as the consequence of a single principle of procedure. But this principle, though by itself it says nothing material in the field of metaphysics or epistemology, and though its application is by no means confined to philosophy, has nevertheless a wealth of philosophic consequences. It implies at least the outline of a theory of knowledge; and if it dictates no metaphysical theses, at least it rules out a good deal which has been put forward under that caption, and it operates as a principle of orientation in the search for positive conclusions.

I refer, of course, to the pragmatic test of significance. James stated it as follows: "What difference would it practically make to anyone if this notion rather than that notion were true? If no practical difference whatever can be traced, then the alternatives mean practically the same thing, and all dispute is idle."[1] Peirce formulated it with respect to substantive concepts rather than propositional notions—though the two come to the same thing: "Our idea of anything *is* our idea of its sensible effects. . . . Consider what effects that might conceivably have practical bearings, we conceive the object of our conception to have. Then, our conception of these effects is the whole of our conception of the object."[2] It is one importance of this pragmatic test that it is so obviously valid and final: once it has been formulated, there can be no going back on it later without conscious obscurantism. Any consequence of it, therefore, shares in this imperative and binding character. Peirce's dictum draws our attention to the fact that there is a kind of empiricism which is implicit in the pragmatic test: What can you point to in experience which would indicate whether this concept of yours is applicable or inapplicable in a given instance? What practically would be the test whether your conception is correct? If there are no such empirical items which would be decisive, then your concept is *not* a concept, but a verbalism.

If one does not find in Professor Dewey's writings any terse formulation which is exactly parallel (and of that I am not sure), this is only

---

[1] *Pragmatism: A New Name for Some Old Ways of Thinking* (New York, 1925), p. 45.

[2] "How to Make Our Ideas Clear," *Chance, Love and Logic* (London, 1923), p. 45. Compare: "Since obviously nothing that might not result from experiment can have any direct bearing on conduct, if one can define accurately all the conceivable experimental phenomena which the affirmation or denial of a concept could imply, one will have therein a complete definition of the concept, and *there is nothing more in it*. For this doctrine he [the writer, Peirce] invented the name pragmatism" ("What Pragmatism Is," *Monist*, Vol. 15, 1905, pp. 162–63).

because here the pragmatic test is clothed with its consequences; it pervades the whole, and is writ large in the functional theory of the concept. Ideas are plans of action; concepts are prescriptions of certain operations whose empirical consequences determine their significance. This connotation of action is not, of course, a new note; it appears in Peirce's emphasis upon conduct and experiment, and in James's doctrine of the "leading" character of ideas. Is this functional theory of the concept implicit, like empiricism, in the pragmatic test?

So far as Professor Dewey himself is concerned, it would appear that this doctrine antedates his explicit pragmatism, and may have been the root of it. (Perhaps he will tell us.) It appears in his paper on "The Reflex Arc Concept in Psychology," the first important document for "functional psychology," published in 1896.[3] He there criticizes current psychological theory as not having sufficiently avoided the fictitious abstractions of sensationalism. "The sensation or conscious stimulus is not a thing or existence by itself; it is a phase of a coordination." "[A coordination is an] organization of means with reference to a comprehensive end." "The stimulus is that phase of the forming coordination which represents the conditions which have to be met in bringing it to a successful issue; the response is that phase of one and the same forming coordination which gives the key to meeting these conditions, which serves as instrument in effecting the successful coordination. ... The stimulus is something to be discovered. ... It is the motor response which assists in discovering and constituting the stimulus." Substitute "sensation" or "sense data" for "stimulus," "operation" or "action" for "motor response," and what is here quoted will be found occupying a central place in all Professor Dewey's subsequent expositions of his pragmatic doctrine. Three years later, he wrote: "I conceive that states of consciousness ... have no existence as such ... before the psychologist gets to work." "Knowing, willing, feeling, name states of consciousness not in themselves, but in terms of results reached, the sorts of value that are brought into experience."[4]

If, then, I am right in the derivation here assigned, Professor Dewey's functional theory of knowledge is the necessary consequence of a methodological principle applied to psychology; namely, that concepts used should designate something concretely identifiable in experience, not abstractions apart from that which serves for their empirical dis-

---

[3] *Psychological Review*, Vol. III, No. 1 (1896), pp. 357–70.

[4] "Psychology and Philosophic Method" [*University of California Chronicle*, Vol. II (1899), pp. 159–79]. It is interesting to remember that in the preceding year, James presented the first statement of *his* pragmatism, "Philosophical Conceptions and Practical Results," under the same auspices.

covery. Sensations, or sense data, are condemned as not thus identifiable apart from the responses to which they lead and the ends such action serves.

The functional theory of the concept has, as I have tried to show elsewhere, other grounds, of a more purely logical sort. Viewed in this way, however, and apart from psychological considerations, it is not, I think, a simple consequence of the pragmatic test, but has a conceivable alternative, namely, immediatism or the presentation-theory of knowledge. By this logical approach, one has to adduce reasons for repudiating the conception that empirical knowledge—or *some* empirical knowledge— is immediately given, in order to reach the conception that activity and its issue are indispensable and characterizing factors in empirical cognition. The theory that meanings connote action and truth connotes prediction is implicit in the notion that truth and meanings are something *to be tested*; hence, that they do *not* bring their own warrant in being simply given.

I believe we here arrive at a turning-point in pragmatic theory. On the one side, the pragmatic principle seems to stress the directly empirical. Put enough emphasis on that, and one might conceivably— though not validly, I think—arrive at a highly subjectivistic theory of knowledge as immediate. On the other side, it stresses the limitation of meaning to what makes a verifiable difference, and of truth to what can be objectively tested. Follow out the consequences of *that*, and of the functional theory of knowledge which it implies, and I believe one is inevitably led to the doctrine that concepts are abstractions, in which the immediate is precisely that element which must be left out. To this point, I should like to adduce certain illustrations, drawn from contemporary science.

The new physics is, in good part, based upon certain applications of the pragmatic test. And to these physicists the validity of this methodological principle and the functional interpretation of conceptual meanings seem to be simply synonymous. One main premise of physical relativity is, of course, the impossibility of deciding which of two bodies in relative motion is at rest with respect to an absolute space. (We may remind ourselves that James's illustration of the pragmatic test—the man and the squirrel—is simply an example of the relativity of motion to frames of reference.) In elaborating the consequences of this relativity of motion, it became necessary to repudiate other absolutes, such as length, time, simultaneity, etc.; and this was done by identifying these with the actual modes by which they can be tested—the pragmatic test once more. The resultant methodology may be generalized in what Bridgman calls "the operational character of concepts."

"We evidently know what we mean by a length if we can tell what the length of any and every object is, and for the physicist nothing more is required. To find the length of an object we have to perform certain physical operations. The concept of length is therefore fixed when the operations by which length is measured are fixed: that is, the concept of length involves as much as and nothing more than the set of operations by which length is determined. In general we mean by any concept nothing more than a set of operations; *the concept is synonymous with the corresponding set of operations.*"[5]

Why does the physicist thus identify his concepts with operations of testing? Is it because the properties he is concerned with are peculiarly those which are difficult or impossible of immediate apprehension? Not at all. Suppose a critic to observe: "But of course your concept of length goes back to an immediately given somewhat. You test the relation of a particular length to the yardstick, but unless your yardstick were an immediate so-longness, directly apprehended, your concept of length would be entirely empty." He will reply that this immediate so-longness has nothing to do with physics, because it can not be tested. The *yardstick* can be tested; as it happens, the measurement of it will differ for different relative motions. But any immediate so-longness of it is something which makes no difference to physics: if it had one so-longness to A and another for B, that would be unverifiable and ineffable. It is the significance of the operational character of concepts to extrude such ineffables from physics. Subjectively it may be that A and B both seem to themselves at rest in the center of the universe, directly apprehending certain so-longnesses, so-heavinesses, felt endurances of things, and what not. But physical position and motion are simply relations to a frame of reference, physical time a relation to clocks; physical properties in general consist in those operations and relations by which they are assigned and tested. The standards are absolutely standards—that is, arbitrary—but they are not absolute in any other sense. The standard yardstick, or clock, or whatever, has its length or the measure of its seconds, etc., in an entirely similar and verifiable set of relations to other things, and only so. Any immediate content of the concept is extruded by the principle of the pragmatic test. If your hours, as felt, are twice as long as mine, your pounds twice as heavy, that makes no difference, which can be tested, in our assignment of physical properties to things. If it *should* thus make a difference in our predication of properties, we should at once decide that one of us must be mistaken. Such decision would reveal our implicit recog-

---

[5] *The Logic of Modern Physics* (New York, 1927), p. 5; italics are in the text.

nition that our concept of the predicated property excludes this subjective element, and includes only the objectively verifiable relations.

The physical concepts are not, by this extrusion of the immediate, emptied of meaning. Their meaning is, as Bridgman says, in the operations of verification and their results; it is contained in that complex network of relationships which constitute the laws and equations and physical predications of which the science consists. The concept is, thus, merely a sort of configuration or relational pattern. Whatever the immediate and ineffable content which is caught in that net may be—for John Jones or Mary Doe or anybody—it does not enter into the science of physics. The resultant conception of the content of the science is admirably expressed by Eddington: "We take as building material *relations* and *relata*. The relations unite the relata; the relata are the meeting points of the relations."[6] The conceptual in knowledge is the element of pure structure or operational construction.

Thus the pragmatic test becomes a kind of law of intellectual parsimony, and leads, in science, to what might be called "the flight from the subjective." Physics is by no means an isolated example: the parallel thing has happened, or will happen, in every science, because it is simply the extrusion of what the science can not finally and conclusively test. Mathematics, being the oldest science, did it first. Geometry begins with rope-stretching and ends as the deductive elaboration of purely abstract concepts, the problem of the nature of space being handed over to physics and philosophy. Arithmetic begins with counting empirical things and ends in the logical structure of *Principia Mathematica*, for which the existence of the number 8 (for a certain type) requires an extraneous assumption. Just now mathematics threatens to go further and restrict itself to systems of operations upon marks. Psychology first got rid of the ineffable soul; a pragmatic psychologist then asked, "Does consciousness [as distinct from its content] exist?"; and now we have behaviorism, based on the methodological principle of restriction to what is objectively verifiable. If some of these movements go beyond what is necessary or valid, at least they exhibit the tendency, and the ground of it.

Professor Dewey seems to view such abstractionism in science as a sort of defect—sometimes necessary but always regrettable; an inadequacy of it to the fullness of experience. In various ways, it seems to him to threaten the relations between knowledge and life. Professor Eddington's book suggests that a doubt on this point besets him too when, as physical scientist, he finds himself also constrained to assess

[6] *The Nature of the Physical World* (Cambridge, 1929), p. 230.

philosophical significances. That the world as experienced and life as lived are not going to be thrown out of the window goes without saying. Particularly for Professor Dewey, it seems to me that this apprehensiveness is misplaced, because he has himself indicated the main considerations essential for the solution of the problem which results— the problem of the relation of abstract concepts to the concrete and directly empirical. Time does not permit attention to all the pertinent considerations. But I wish to suggest one which is important, by a final illustration, drawn once more from physics.

As an eventual result of subatomic and quantum phenomena, the new physics has abolished imaginable matter. Analysis of the physical emerges finally in something like Schrödinger's Ψ-functions, in mathematical expressions of probability, concrete representation of which can only be approached in terms of an admittedly fictitious sub-ether of variable dimensions. Immediately apprehensible matter dissolves into mathematics. Two other expressions of this same abstractness of the physically ultimate occur in Eddington's later chapters: one is that statement about relations and relata, already referred to; the other is to the effect that physics reduces the concrete object to pointer-readings.[7] The elephant sliding down the grass slope is at once an immense flock of Ψ-functions getting integrated, and a set of pointer-readings. The two interpretations do not seem interchangeable. Let us fasten on the pointer-readings. Why reduce the elephant to pointer-readings? In the first place, because physics can not deal with the elephant as a whole. It comprehends a good many—perhaps most—of the elephant's properties, but that he is, for example, a wonderful fine fellow and very intelligent must be omitted from physical consideration. Let us call that organization of properties which physics *can* deal with "the physicist's elephant." Why is the physicist's elephant reduced to pointer-readings? First, because, with the apparatus oriented upon the elephant, the elephant *determines* the pointer-readings. Second, because such pointer-readings are a conveniently hybrid sort of reality: the apparatus and pointers being physical, their readings correlate with the properties of the elephant; and the readings being numerical, they translate those properties into mathematical values. The significance of the pointer-readings is merely for the purpose of such translation. The last state of the physicist's elephant, like the last state of the electron, is in mathematical functions. But this last stage for the *physicist* is merely an intermediate stage of operations with respect to the elephant. The numerical values given by the pointer-readings are substituted for the

[7] *Ibid.*, pp. 251ff.

variables in some mathematical equation expressing physical law. They thus determine a numerical value of some other mathematical function. This last can be translated back into something of the order of pointer-readings, and hence back into some other and previously undetermined property of the elephant—with the eventual result, perhaps, that we get the elephant safely into a box-car. Such eventual result is the reason for being of the whole set of operations. If it be asked, then, "Why reduce the elephant to mathematical functions?" the answer is that this is the best way known to man for getting him into the box-car.

The physicist's elephant is an abstraction, but a rather palpable sort of abstraction. All of him that the physicist finally deals with is what is common to the elephant and the pointer-readings; namely, a more abstract, a *very* abstract, configuration of relationships. This structure of relations is what, in general terms, the mathematical equations of physics express.

Thus if the last conceptual stage of the elephant—and of the physical in general—is in mathematics, or a set of relations of relata, it is not necessary to try to follow this transmogrification of the elephant, or of matter, with the imagination. Nor is it appropriate to cry shame upon the physicist for leaving the world of palpable elephants in favor of such unimaginable abstractions. The physicist's concept represents simply an intermediate stage in a process which begins and ends with elephants and such—not with the physicist's elephant even, but the one which slid down the bank and got put in the box-car.

As Professor Dewey points out, the physicist and mathematician simply take this intermediate stage off by itself and deal with it on its own account.[8] Thus if we reflect upon the functional theory of knowledge, I think we may come to the conclusion that there is no implication of it which is incompatible with the notion that concepts in general are abstractions—are even very thin abstractions. Because the function of concepts is not to *photograph* elephants but to get them into box-cars. Concepts represent simply that operational function of cognition by which it transforms the something given, with which it begins, into the something anticipated or something done, with which it ends. That they may have lost, or discarded as irrelevant, those elements of the concrete and immediate which characterize direct perception and imagination, is nothing to the point. Goodness in a concept is not the degree of its verisimilitude to the given, but the degree of its effectiveness as an instrument of control. Perhaps Professor Dewey might even, with entire consistency, find less occasion to regret that

[8] See *The Quest for Certainty* (New York, 1930), pp. 156ff.

the relatively undeveloped sciences of human affairs show a tendency to imitate this abstractness. When the social sciences attain that degree of abstractness, and consequent precision, which already characterizes physics and mathematics, perhaps they will have less trouble getting their social elephants into their social box-cars. Economics is the best developed of the social sciences, and a fair illustration.

To conclude: the fact that the pragmatic test seems, on the one hand, to demand that all meaning be found eventually in the empirical, and on the other, seems to induce a flight from the immediate and directly apprehensible into abstractions, is not, in reality, any contradiction or any difficulty. In one sense—that of connotation—a concept strictly comprises nothing but an abstract configuration of relations. In another sense—its denotation or empirical application—this meaning is vested in a process which characteristically begins with something given and ends with something done—in the operation which translates a presented datum into an instrument of prediction and control.

DEWEY'S REPLY: I find myself in such sympathy with the article of Mr. Lewis that I shall confine my comment upon it to one minor point. He says, "Professor Dewey seems to view such abstractionism in science as a sort of defect—something necessary, but always regrettable; an inadequacy of it to the fullness of experience." I fear that on occasion I may so have written as to give this impression. I am glad, therefore, to have the opportunity of saying that this is not my actual position. Abstraction is the heart of thought; there is no way—other than accident—to control and enrich concrete experience except through an intermediate flight of thought with conceptions, relations, abstracta. What I regret is the tendency to erect the abstractions into complete and self-subsistent things, or into a kind of superior Being. I wish to agree also with Mr. Lewis that the need of the social sciences at present is precisely such abstractions as will get their unwieldy elephants into box-cars that will move on rails arrived at by other abstractions. What is to be regretted is, to my mind, the tendency of many inquirers in the field of human affairs to be over-awed by the abstractions of the physical sciences and hence to fail to develop the conceptions or abstractions appropriate to their own subject-matter.[9]

[9] Reprinted by permission from *The Journal of Philosophy*, Vol. XXVII (1930), No. 10, pp. 276–77.

8. Meaning and Action

To say anything new and important about Dewey's logic would be, I suspect, beyond my powers. I shall not attempt it but, instead, wish to offer here brief comment on one conception of his, which I take to be central for his logic and for his point of view in general, and which I believe to be both correct and important: the conception, namely, that meaning and action are essentially connected.

Dewey does not write by the method of theorem and corollary; and one does not find any single statement into which the full significance of this thesis has been compressed and from which all its implications can be drawn. But what is here in question is no platitude, to the effect that since humans are active beings their meanings are likely to reflect their interests and their practice. Nor does it merely serve to point an emphasis, characteristic of the theory in which it appears but setting it in opposition to no other which could plausibly be maintained. Rather, it is the distinctive conception, incompatible with most views, that the cognitive or meaning situation does not admit of bifurcation into an activity of the knower and a preformed object which is contemplated; that knowing or meaning is integral with other activities which shape the objects to which they are addressed; that meanings themselves serve to frame the situations of action into which they enter, and exercise an operational force upon what they serve to formulate. It is implied that an idea or a meaning, apart from some possible action and the reality in which it should eventuate, is a fictitious entity not found in human thinking. And conversely, it is implied that the objects of knowledge, without reference to meanings and the actions to which they may lead, are equally fictitious. From this conception there issues a sharp challenge to those views—comprising the greater number—which would portray the reality known as "antecedent" to the activity of knowing, and to "spectator" theories of knowledge which would represent the knower as a disinterested contemplator of a ready-made world which *qua* knower he does not affect.

So far from being a commonplace, this thesis, when fully grasped, has something of the aspect of a hard saying. Almost it is as if Dewey had claimed that all meanings and all inquiry are subject to a kind of

Contribution to a Symposium of Reviews of John Dewey's *Logic: The Theory of Inquiry* (New York, 1938). Reprinted by permission from *The Journal of Philosophy*, Vol. XXXVI (1939), No. 21, pp. 572–76.

indeterminacy principle. Thought itself displaces or transforms that which it means or inquires about: but if it thus affects the object concerned, how can inquiry disclose what it sets out to reveal? One can not suppose that this thesis has met with that acquiescence which the relative absence of discussion would suggest. Its force has been insufficiently felt. This conception has not been generally accepted by philosophic readers; but it has been answered mainly by neglect.

Yet however contrary to prevailing views, or even paradoxical, this conception may be, the considerations which would enforce it are fairly obvious. That thinking, meaning, knowing are other than—as Dewey claims—activities performed at need is *prima facie* implausible. But if they are thus instigated, an effect of them upon that to which they are directed is implied. That the activity of the knower is itself a part of the world-process and a factor in determining its events could not easily be denied. But if it is such, then plainly the conception that objects of inquiry are merely given to a contemplative knower must be fundamentally erroneous.

For example, empirical knowledge, on almost any view, will be admitted to have the aspect or the pervasive implication of prediction. Any report of empirical fact, and any generalization such as a law of natural science, leads either to categorical predictions of future events or to hypothetical predictions that such and such will take place under certain specifiable circumstances. And that the main if not the exclusive motive of science and empirical knowledge in general is found in the possibility of such predictions will be denied by no one. Yet if the world-process were that kind of antecedently determined enchainment of events which it is often supposed that science must take it to be, in order that such prediction may be possible and valid, then precisely in being thus predictable reality must be inaccessible to and unalterable by any activity of the knower. In that case, what boots it to know this completely inevitable futurity? It requires no initiative on our part— cognitive or of any other sort—to "avoid the impossible and cooperate with the inevitable."

Such considerations might perhaps meet with the reply that our aim in knowing what is predetermined lies in something else; that we wish to know whether it will rain, not in order to affect the weather, but in order to know whether to carry an umbrella. But if this way of meeting the difficulty—suggested by the common-sense answer in our trivial example—were to be taken as a satisfactory kind of analysis of situations in which knowledge and action are involved, it would lead to difficulties which are serious if not insuperable, because it would seem to assume that there are two sorts of futurities: those which are predetermined for our inquiry and about which alone unconditional predictions can be made—"it will rain"—and those which are not thus antecedently determined—"I shall get wet"—which depend on what we do in the light of this knowledge. The former class are inaccessible to our action; the latter are not cognitions of objective reality but matters of decision. By implication, the world-process must be viewed as divisible into those events which are unconditionally predictable and about which we can do nothing, and those our activity can affect but which are not the objects of any cognitive inquiry. Fully carried out, this would lead to the conclusion that knowledge—or at least knowledge as having implications for the future—is exclusively of the inevitable; but that this knowledge is of practical value exclusively for its bearing on what is unpredictable.

The point is not so much that one who should elevate the attitude suggested to the status of philosophical analysis would stand in danger of violating his own systematic presuppositions—though that is a fact. It is not consistently possible to carry out such a double-aspect view of the world: to think of it as if one could, *qua* knower, view it as made up of predetermined and unbreakable chains of events, with one's self outside and looking on; and then, having through such passive receptivity acquired knowledge, could step out of one's contemplative role and take a hand in shaping the future thus predicted. One can not in this fashion place the subject, who both knows and acts and whose knowing is integral with and for the sake of his acting, both in and out of the process of events to which his knowing and his acting are addressed. But I say that this is hardly the point: probably that "universal determinism" sometimes supposed to be an essential presupposition of science is not something to be judged false or true but merely a pedantic fable, such that even if admitted in words it could find no application to any actual situation in which a human investigator has a real purpose in prosecuting an inquiry.

The more important point is one which concerns the meaning of our predictions themselves—and so far as empirical knowledge is implicitly predictive, the meaning of what we know in general. Such meaning can not exclude but must include the significance of the knower's activity, because the validity of a genuinely cognitive meaning must be capable of verification. That a substantive meaning applies or does not apply, that a proposition is true or false, must be capable of test. And what tests are pertinent must be implicit in the meanings themselves. Whoever speaks of X but does not know it could be determined whether a presented thing is X or not means nothing by his term: whoever asserts P but could not specify how the truth or falsity of P should be determined makes no genuinely meaningful statement. So much of the pragmatic conception of meaning is quite generally accepted, and could not well be denied, though hairs may be split in the interpretation of it.

The meaning of a prediction, or of a cognition implying predictions, must be found in some future possible experience or experiences which would confirm its truth. *But there are no such verifying or confirming experiences which can be predicted without reference to the activity of the subject.* There are no future experiences which, concretely enough specified, are inevitable. There could be no experience of ours genuinely foreseeable but such that literally we could do nothing about it. In fact, precisely the point of foreseeing what is called "inevitable"— and it is seldom the experience itself which is so called—is that at least we may blunt the poignant painfulness of what is anticipated, or sharpen and clarify its satisfying quality, by our foresight. And in the case of most predictable eventualities, we can do something more than merely to modify their character as experienced by going forward to meet them in an altered attitude.

Furthermore, there is no dichotomy between categorically predictable eventualities—"It will rain"—and hypothetical and avoidable ones —"I shall get wet." All verifications, all predictable confirming experiences belong in the second classification. The fact of rain is verifiable only by some manner of experiencing it: by getting wet, or by seeing it, or hearing it, or . . . . But we shall not get wet if we protect ourselves; and there would be some manner or another of avoiding any one of these verifying experiences. We might refuse altogether to put our statement to the test. Each such possible verification turns out, on examination, to be some eventuality which will accrue or not accrue according as we adopt or refuse to adopt some attitude or course of action. And beyond such future possible experiences which would verify it, "It will rain" means nothing. Put in general terms, the meaning of any "fixed" or "objective" fact which could be believed in or asserted has, as the final terms of its analysis, some set of hypothetical propositions, the hypotheses in which concern some mode of action. In this nature of our empirical meanings lies the connection between knowing and doing, and the explanation of the fact that knowledge of that reality which "is what it is independently of being known" has application to our practice.

There would not be space here for comment on the consequences of this point concerning meanings. And, obviously, my discussion has been inadequate to the point itself. It is the less necessary to elaborate these implications because so many of them have been made clear in Dewey's writings.

9. Logical Positivism and Pragmatism

The attempt to characterize any philosophic movement is a somewhat dubious enterprise, and the comparison of two such is doubly dubious. A movement is to an extent a fiction: there are only the individual thinkers agreeing in certain respects, presumably fundamental, and disagreeing in others; and to say anything important about their agreements without continual qualifying references to their divergences is almost inevitably to be inaccurate in some degree. Particularly this is true of pragmatism. To mention only its outstanding figures, Peirce and James and Dewey are all of them notable for the creative character of their thinking and the individuality of their genius. While to remark their influences upon one another is to comment on the obvious, it is equally obvious, both historically and by the internal evidence of their writings, that no one of them was primarily determined by such influence. Moreover, while James and Dewey, if not Peirce, have had great influence upon other philosophic thinkers in America, this influence has been notable for the breadth and variety of its effects rather than for its concentration into any definitely marked tradition. And again, although it is hardly justified to say that pragmatism is a method and not a theory, still the theses central to pragmatism do not cover the whole field of philosophy. Of Peirce in particular it is true that pragmatism is only one strand which entered into the complex pattern of his thought.

Logical positivism is less subject to this difficulty, on account of its origin in the Vienna Circle and the continuing intent of its proponents to cooperate. But one here encounters another: the vitality of this movement is evidenced by a habit of revision; from time to time its expositors move on to better judged positions in details and to more judicious formulations—or indubitably, to somewhat different ones. And however admirable this tendency, it makes it necessary for one who would mark them out to aim at a moving target, and be correspondingly doubtful of his accuracy.

Finally, I suffer the personal handicap that any comparison I may attempt between these two movements must be suspect on the ground of partisan sympathy and conviction.

Originally prepared for publication in *Revue Internationale de Philosophie*; not published because of German invasion of Belgium, 1940. This version was completed by Lewis in 1941.—Eds.

I do not attempt to avoid these difficulties; they must be taken as limitations of what I shall have to say. Even within them, I must hope, there may be interest in comparison between views which approximate to one another at points which are important but diverge at others which are no less significant. I must assume my capacity—though the reader need not—to elicit fundamental agreements in pragmatism; exegesis of doctrines of the individual pragmatists and defense of one's interpretations would be a topic by itself. And I shall attempt to mitigate the difficulty which an outsider must encounter with respect to logical positivism by having particularly in mind certain recent writings of Professor Carnap.[1] The comparison will be held to four topics: empiricism, the scope of science, the significance of metaphysics, and the status of evaluative and moral judgments—and of necessity, to the simpler and more manageable considerations falling under these heads.

I

Both movements present themselves as forms of empiricism; and for both, the crucial consideration in such empiricism is a conception of empirical meaning or 'sense.' Both would repudiate as lacking such meaning any statement which cannot be verified, or confirmed, by reference, ultimately, to specifiable empirical eventuations. Statements not having such empirical meaning need not be meaningless, in the ordinary sense; they may, for example, be analytic statements of logic or of pure mathematics. But a synthetic statement, affirming a matter of objective fact or state of affairs, either has such empirical meaning or it makes no genuine assertion.

Amongst pragmatists, the distinction of empirical meaning from the significance of analytic statements for the most part passes unremarked. Excepting Peirce, they have not much concerned themselves with what are here called 'analytic statements.' And it is doubtful whether Dewey would recognize such analytic statements as occurring in actual human thinking or discourse. But setting aside this topic of analytic statements, there would be a fundamental approximation of pragmatists and logical positivists in such a conception of empirical meaning as is suggested above. This is also the point of clearest agreement amongst pragmatists themselves, indicated by James's 'pragmatic test' and by Dewey's conception of meaning as exhibited in the outcome of a pro-

---

[1] *Philosophy and Logical Syntax* (London, 1935), *The Unity of Science* (London, 1934), and the paper "Testability and Meaning," in *Philosophy of Science*, Vol. 3, pp. 419–71 and Vol. 4, pp. 1–40.

cess of inquiry in which a problem is resolved, and identified by Peirce with his intended signification of the term 'pragmatism.'[2]

One notes that there are here in the pragmatic conception other elements than the emphasis upon empirical eventuations in which the meaning in question would be satisfied: there is also the emphasis upon conduct, upon experiment as an activity—borne out by the ever-recurring term 'practical' in pragmatic literature—and there is the qualification 'conceivable' which Peirce at least characteristically inserts when the set of phenomena pertinent to a meaning are referred to. These two adjectives 'practical' and 'conceivable' might be thought to be opposed in their significance here. But that is not the sense of the term 'practical' which is characteristic of pragmatism; its intended connotation is of *interests of action*, not of the practicable as opposed to what may be impracticable under existing conditions; the intended restriction is one of relevance, not of possibility. Thus pragmatism would regard meaning as limited by reference to what could make a difference for some active intent, but would regard any conceivable eventuality having such relevance—and not merely those which conditions allow to be realized—as comprehended under the meaning in question.

The pragmatic emphasis upon relevance to some active intent is largely or wholly omitted in logical positivism. But that point is, perhaps, of secondary interest in the present connection. Generally speaking, logical positivists resolve the other question—whether meaning concerns all conceivable empirical eventualities which if they could occur would be relevant, or only such as existing conditions allow—in the same way as do pragmatists: that is, in favor of the former alternative.[3]

The pragmatic conception of empirical meaning can, thus, be suggested by saying that, in the field of statements of objective matters of fact, and of terms intended to have application to them, whatever is, in the last analysis, non-sensuous is nonsensical. An empirical term has

[2] "... since obviously nothing that might not result from experiment can have any direct bearing upon conduct, if one can define accurately all the conceivable experimental phenomena which the affirmation or denial of a concept could imply, one will have therein a complete definition of the concept, and *there is nothing more in it*. For this doctrine he [the writer, Peirce] invented the name 'pragmatism.'" (*Monist*, Vol. 15, 1905, pp. 162–63.)

[3] It would not be possible here to take account of complexities in Carnap's painstaking analysis of 'confirmable' and 'testable' in "Testability and Meaning." I attempt, however, to avoid any statement which would be misleading on account of such omission. The concept of 'realizable' there introduced would be pertinent to comparison with pragmatic instrumentalism or activism.

meaning only if a determination of its applicability can be specified in terms of sense-presentation or of what is imaginable; an objective statement is significant only so far as empirical confrontations which would attest its credibility can be specified. Terms and statements so intended but for which no such determination of their applicability or their credibility can be formulated are meaningless. And this conception is a point of approximation to the logical-positivistic conception of 'sense.'

However, there is a point of difference between the two, and one which does not have to do with refinements of theory, but rather with the fundamental fashion in which meaning is to be determined. The logical positivists show a tendency to substitute for the question, "What empirical confrontations would confirm this statement?" the different question, "What observation-sentences are consequences of this sentence?"; and to substitute for the question, "What criteria attest the applicability of this term?" the different question, "To what class of observable predicates is this term reducible?"; and for the question, "What is the empirical meaning or content of this term?" the question, "What other terms are synonymous with this one?" The content of a sentence is identified with a class of its non-valid consequences (its consequences which would not equally be consequences of *any* sentence); and two expressions are said to be synonymous if the content of any sentence containing one of them is not changed if we replace that expression by the other.[4] Such substitutions are regarded as desirable in the interest of confining questions of meaning to questions of *logical* sense, and avoiding what is psychological and likely to be vague. Any question of the sensuous signification of a sentence or an expression is thus excluded. "Sometimes by 'sense' is meant the kind of thoughts and images that are connected with a given sentence. But in this case the question is a psychological one and has to be examined by the experimental method of psychology. In logical (syntactic) analysis we are not concerned with such questions."[5] "But [in characterizing a language] is it not also necessary in order to understand the 'sense' of the sentences, to indicate the 'meaning' of the words? No; the demand thereby made in the material mode is satisfied by specifying the formal rules which constitute its syntax."[6]

---

[4] See Carnap, *Philosophy and Logical Syntax*, pp. 57–58; and *Logical Syntax of Language* (London, 1937), p. 42.

[5] Carnap, *Philosophy and Logical Syntax*, p. 57.

[6] Carnap, *The Unity of Science*, p. 39. I believe that Carnap would now modify this statement, but am not sure.

No pragmatist could be satisfied with such a conception; it must result in specification of meaning in which precisely what a pragmatist would take to be the empirical meaning is omitted. Specifying the observation-sentences which are consequences of a given sentence indicates, or helps to indicate, the meaning of the given sentence only if the observation-sentences themselves have such meaning, and that meaning is already understood. Indicating the observation-predicates or perception-predicates to which a term is reducible indicates the empirical meaning of that term only if these observation-predicates already have an understood reference to specific qualities of experience. No reference to the *logical* relations between sentences or between terms can ever, by itself, convey the empirical meaning of anything. However unlikely it may be, it is theoretically possible that a person should know completely the formation rules and transformation rules of a language—the syntax of it and all synonyms in the dictionary of it—and yet be completely ignorant of the empirical signification of any term or sentence in that language. Such empirical meaning consists precisely in what Carnap here excludes, the associated imagery or the criterion in terms of sense by which what is meant is recognized when presented in experience. Words and sentences without such associated imagery are marks or noises without significance. Without associated imagery, strings of marks or of noises are not even words and sentences—are not even nonsense. The logical-positivistic theory fails to distinguish between syntactic or linguistic meaning—a relation of one verbal expression to other verbal expressions—and empirical meaning, which concerns the relation of expressions to what may be given in experience.

This difference between the logical-positivistic and the pragmatic mode of approach to questions of meaning runs very deep, eventually, because this attempt to logicize all problems, and to regard them as correctly and unambiguously statable only in 'the formal mode'—in terms of syntax of language—is connected with the logical-positivistic conception that philosophy has no legitimate business except that of logical analysis, and that philosophic questions which are characteristically stated in 'the material mode,' and which, *e.g.*, concern the relation between something stated and given experience, or between experience and real objects, are 'pseudo-problems.'

One point of special importance in this connection concerns the possible confirmation of statements—the validity of empirical cognition. Pragmatists and logical positivists would agree that such confirmation ultimately concerns what would be stated in 'observation-sentences' or in what were earlier called (in *The Unity of Science*) 'protocol sentences.' But where pragmatism would characteristically speak of 'the content of experience,' logical positivism characteristically speaks of 'the protocol' or 'the observation-sentence,' thus confining statement of the problem to 'the formal mode' and the philosophical account of it to logical analysis. A pragmatist must regard such restriction to the formal mode as inevitably resulting in failure to deal with the problem of confirmation at all, and as ruling out the possibility of a genuinely empiricistic account of knowledge. This issue is worthy of careful attention, because it indicates a critical difference between the pragmatic and the logical-positivistic interpretation of empiricism.

The signification of 'observation-sentence' in more recent writings of the logical positivists is not identical with that of 'protocol sentence' in the earlier account. 'Protocols' are what would ordinarily be termed 'reports of experience' or 'statements of what is given,' although the meaning of such protocols is held to be 'interpersonal.' An 'observation-sentence' or the attribution of an 'observable predicate' is characterized as one with respect to which a person "is able under suitable circumstances to come to a decision with the help of a few observations." "There is no sharp line between observable and non-observable predicates because a person will be more or less able to decide a certain sentence quickly, *i.e.* he will be inclined after a certain period of observation to accept the sentence."[7] However, the issues in question can be indicated without regard to such differences of formulation. A first point here is that when a certain statement which is not itself an observation-statement (whether 'protocol' or 'observation-sentence') is to be confirmed, question of that confirmation—it is agreed—eventually reduces to question of certain observation-statements. Affirmative decision with respect to such an observation-statement will be a decision that the statement to be confirmed is actually so confirmed (though presumably in part or in degree only). This connection between the statement to be confirmed and the observation-statement— it is agreed—is one which is established by an analysis of meaning (in some appropriate signification of the word 'meaning'). But it is not this relation to the observation-statement which confirms the statement so related to it—if it is actually confirmed—and it is not the observation-statement itself which confirms it; what confirms the statement to be confirmed is what determines 'acceptance' of the observation-statement as true or as credible. And what is that? Logical positivists perhaps regard the answer as one which goes without saying. We might agree; but in philosophic analysis it is sometimes well to state the obvi-

---

[7] "Testability and Meaning," in *Philosophy of Science*, Vol. 3, p. 455.

ous. What determines the observation-statement to be true or credible, and thus confirms (partially) the statement to be confirmed, can be nothing but the content of an empirical presentation. The observation-statement is found 'acceptable' if the empirical presentation accords with what that 'observation-statement' asserts. It is no logical relation to any other statement which is here in question; it is a relation between a criterion of recognition in terms of sense or imagery (the empirical meaning of the observation-statement) and what is given in experience, or fails to be so given. An analysis of confirmation cannot be given in statements in the formal mode alone, because confirmation does not end in what observation-statements *mean* but in the determination of them as *true* or *credible*, by experience. To leave that obvious fact out of a supposedly empiricistic theory of verification or confirmation is to give us Hamlet without the Prince.

There is a further point which concerns this relation between protocols or observation-sentences and what determines them to be true or credible. A report of observation can have either of two intended meanings, and can be construed in either of two ways: (1) as formulation of an immediately presented content of experience or empirical confrontation, or (2) as an assertion of objective fact. An example of the former would be "This looks red" or "Red now"; of the latter, "This object has the color red." The alternatives in question are mutually exclusive; these two statements are of quite different import; the former can be true when the latter is false, and the latter can be true when the former is false. Statements of the former type may be called, for lack of a more appropriate term, 'subjective reports'; those of the latter type, 'objective reports.' Any report of observation will have one of these two meanings or the other. And except by an ambiguity which would require to be dispelled, no report could have both these meanings. We seldom have occasion to express subjective reports, and ordinary language is in consequence unsuited to unambiguous formulation of them; but we have occasion to apprehend what they express as often as we determine any empirical truth or credibility, since these are determinable ultimately only by reference to given experience. In the nature of the case, the truth of a subjective report is certain for the maker of it—unless he deliberately tells a lie in making it. But by contrast, an objective report is *not* certain. No statement of objective fact, such as the actual color of a seen object, is made certain by any single observation, nor indeed more than highly credible ('practically certain') by any finite set of observations. What an objective report affirms may be partially verified by what is presently given in experience—and what would be formulated by the corresponding subjective report—but it is in all cases something capable of and calling for further verification, and such that methods of such further verification could be specified by anyone who understands what it means. By the same token, no even partial confirmation of *any* statement can *terminate* in objective reports, since these themselves require further confirmation.

In logical positivism, 'observation-sentences' are so characterized as not to be identifiable unambiguously either with subjective reports or with objective reports. Use of this expression thus serves to obscure issues which are critical for any empiricistic theory of knowledge. Indeed I think we must find it extraordinary that when we come precisely to that point where a confirmation is supposed to be finally assured, what we are told about the manner of this assurance is that a person "is able under suitable circumstances to come to a decision with the help of a few observations."[8] And it is only by failing to meet the issues here involved that the logical positivists are able to formulate their account of confirmation exclusively in terms of statements in the formal mode—statements about the relations of linguistic expressions—and to avoid discussion of the relation between statements and presented experience, between statements and objects, and between experience and the objective facts it evidences. "These pseudo-questions," they tell us, "are automatically eliminated by using the formal mode."[9] The question is whether they are eliminated or merely ignored.

That others who incline to the pragmatic point of view would make precisely these objections to logical positivism, I cannot of course say. But I am sure that they concern fundamental points with respect to which the pragmatic conception of verification and of the significance of 'truth' and of 'knowledge' differ from that of logical positivism.[10]

II

Both pragmatism and logical positivism represent generalization of attitudes which might be regarded as derived from natural science and as looking to science as the exemplar of knowledge in general. But pragmatism has never stood for that physicalistic pan-scientism which is a distinctive feature of positivism, nor indeed for pan-scientism in any sense which would exclude the equal significance of other types of

[8] *Ibid.*

[9] *The Unity of Science*, p. 83.

[10] There are further implications, besides those suggested, which would likewise be important. In particular, the whole account of probability-judgment must be profoundly affected by such issues; and the question whether there are any ultimate certainties upon which the credibility of statements which are less than certain can come to rest, or whether credibility finally depends upon some such mutual relationship of less-than-certain statements as is put forward in rationalistic theories of the 'coherence' type.

formulation than the 'scientific.' It is one thing to say that scientific formulation is always pertinent and possible; it is a quite different thing to say that no other than scientific formulation is meaningful.

Moreover, what 'science' preponderantly connotes is different in the two cases. With logical positivism it is the *content* of science as exact formulation in physical terms upon which emphasis falls; with pragmatism, it is the *method* of science and its experimental and instrumental point of view—its attitude of regarding all accepted findings as in some degree provisional, and as attesting themselves by their value as working hypotheses and their usefulness in application—which is emphasized.

In the days when James's pragmatism was first put forward, the off-hand comment that it represented merely a generalization of the actual procedures of science was frequently made; and James evidences, in the chapter, "What Pragmatism Means,"[11] his acceptance of this as fundamentally correct. The same would hardly be said of Dewey: his conceptions derive in larger measure from critical consideration of the nature and significance of scientific truth, rather than from generalization of what could be thought of as taken over from science without being first subjected to such critique. But it is even more evident in the case of Dewey than it is with James that pragmatism means experimentalism and instrumentalism. And nothing could be more alien to either of them than recognition of physicalistic conceptions as the exclusively significant vehicles of truth. In the chapter above referred to, James has said:

"When the first mathematical, logical, and natural uniformities, the first *laws*, were discovered, men were so carried away by the clearness, beauty and simplification that resulted, that they believed themselves to have deciphered authentically the eternal thoughts of the Almighty.

"But as the sciences have developed further, the notion has gained ground that most, perhaps all, of our laws are only approximations. . . . Investigators have become accustomed to the notion that no theory is absolutely a transcript of reality, but that any one of them may from some point of view be useful. . . . They are only a man-made language, a conceptual short-hand, as some one calls them, in which we write our reports of nature; and languages, as is well known, tolerate much choice of expression and many dialects."[12]

And of pan-scientism, he overwrote specifically:

[11] In *Pragmatism: A New Name for Some Old Ways of Thinking* (New York, 1907), pp. 43–81.
[12] *Ibid.*, pp. 56–57.

"Certain of our positivists keep chiming to us, that, amid the wreck of every other god and idol, one divinity still stands upright,—that his name is Scientific Truth. . . . These most conscientious gentlemen think they have jumped off their own feet,—emancipated their mental operations from the control of their subjective propensities at large and *in toto*. But they are deluded. They have simply chosen from among the entire set of propensities at their command those that were certain to construct, out of the materials given, the leanest, lowest, aridest result. . . .

"The knights of the razor [Occam's razor] will never form among us more than a sect; but when I see their fraternity increasing in numbers, and, what is worse, when I see their negations acquiring almost as much prestige and authority as their affirmations legitimately claim over the minds of a docile public, I feel as if the influences working in the direction of our mental barbarization were beginning to be rather strong, and needed some positive counteraction."[13]

It is in point that this essay was written in 1881: the positivists referred to are not of course the logical positivists but that earlier school from whom they distinguish themselves—those who would reduce reality, in James's language, "to the bare molecular world." In how far he might have regarded such strictures as justifiable in the case of those who maintain instead that all states of affairs are expressible in physical language, one cannot say. To be sure, Carnap has said: "Our approach has often been termed 'Positivist'; it might equally well be termed 'Materialist.' No objection can be made to such a title provided that the distinction between the older form of Materialism and methodological Materialism—the same theory in a purified form—is not neglected."[14] And there are sure to be some who will think such a statement more revealing than the complicated theory of physicalistic interpretation. However, it is clear that James's objection is to 'negations,' and would lie against the claim of *exclusive* truth for the scientific interpretation of reality and experience rather than against the supposition that all matters of observable fact are capable of such interpretation.

Apart from the repudiation of metaphysics and normative ethics—which, of course, itself sets signal issues—I do not find that the logical positivists have clearly declared themselves upon the question whether there are significant statements about 'states of affairs' which are *not*

[13] "Reflex Action and Theism," in *The Will to Believe and Other Essays* (New York, 1897), pp. 131–33.
[14] *The Unity of Science*, pp. 94–95.

in the universal language of physics, and not reducible to that language. In the earlier formulation, in the *Unity of Science*, Carnap states the physicalist thesis in the form: "Our thesis now makes the extended assertion that the physical language is a universal language, *i.e.* that every statement can be translated into it (every state of affairs can be expressed in it)."[15] In the later discussion, in "Testability and Meaning," he says: "The so-called thesis of *Physicalism* asserts that every term of the language of science ... is reducible to terms of the physical language. ... We may assert reducibility of the terms, but not —as was done in our former publications—definability of the terms and hence translatability of the sentences. In former explanations of physicalism we used to refer to the physical language as the basis of the whole language of science. It now seems to me that what we really had in mind as such a basis was rather the thing-language, or, even more narrowly, the observable predicates of the thing-language."

And he expresses preference for the formulation: "Every descriptive predicate of the language of science is confirmable on the basis of observable thing-predicates."[16] The revisions here are critical for the question whose answer we are attempting to determine. The earlier formulation asserts that the *physical language* (identified with a language of physics) is sufficient for expression of whatever is expressed in *any* significant statement. The revision says that the language of *observable thing-predicates* is sufficient to express the confirmations of all scientific predications. One may assume that it is still intended to affirm that all significant statements are reducible to statements of science; but that is not said. And if it were said, that would not mean— in terms of the revision—that all significant statements can be reduced to statements of physics; it would mean only *that they are such as would be confirmable by observation.*

I think that not only pragmatists but all empiricists who would object to the notion that all significant statements are reducible to terms of physics must be gratified by this revision; because although the term 'physicalism' is retained, the doctrine with which it appears to be identified here is merely to the effect that all statements of scientific matters of fact (and perhaps all formulations of states of affairs) are such as would be confirmable by observation. This paper "Testability and Meaning" is a notable contribution to empiricistic analysis. But so far

---

15 *Ibid.*, p. 55.
16 *Philosophy of Science*, pp. 467–68. 'Thing-language' is identified with "that language which we use in every-day life in speaking about the perceptible things surrounding us." See *ibid.*, p. 466.

as physicalism is concerned, it would appear to mark the withdrawal of any thesis for which that name would be peculiarly appropriate, in favor of a doctrine which, in its general tenor and apart from details, must be acceptable to adherents of almost any empiricistic theory of knowledge.

James, and pragmatists in general, would certainly not be willing to be identified with any such doctrine as physicalism in the form in which it was announced in *The Unity of Science* and in earlier writings of the logical positivists. On this point, question of approximation of the two movements would depend upon the extent to which the radical nature of the revision which I seem to find in "Testability and Meaning" really characterizes the present position of the logical positivists.

If there is any 'translation' or 'reduction' of synthetic statements in general of which pragmatists would approve, it would not be into the language of physics but into the language of experience. If the pragmatic position were to be expressed in a fashion comparable to the logical-positivistic account, it might, I think, be roughly indicated as follows:

(1) The universal language, to terms of which all meaningful statements of matters of fact are reducible, is the language of direct experience, of actual and possible empirical confrontations.

(2) The reduction of any physical statements, or of any assertion of objective fact, to terms of experience would be given by the formulation of its possible confirmations.

(3) Single constituents of this reduction of statements of objective fact to terms of experience would, in general, be hypothetical in form, because (*a*) the *conditions* of a possible confirmation may not exist when the statement is made or entertained, and in particular (*b*) possible confirmations characteristically depend upon an activity of the subject, as is suggested by such words as 'experiment' and 'test,' commonly applicable to instances of confirmation.

It is by reference to some such thought as is suggested in (*b*) that pragmatism is an activistic, instrumentalist conception. It would also be in point that, as has been indicated in Part I, there would be question whether what might figure as 'language of direct experience' in a pragmatic account would coincide with what is intended by 'observation-sentences' in logical positivism.

Pragmatism would not favor the imposition upon significant statements in general of those restrictions which particular sciences impose upon themselves—and commendably so—in the interests of economy. The term 'science' can be, and often has been, given the wide meaning in which it signifies merely what is verifiable and thus coincides with 'empirical knowledge' in general. Since pragmatists tend to identify what is significantly assertable as objective fact with that for which some conceivable verification could be specified, they can be numbered amongst those who hold all that is objectively factual as belonging to the field of science in this wide sense of the word. But if 'science' be restricted to a narrow meaning, connoting some special technique of investigation, or some special mode of formulation such as 'physical language' or 'quantitative determination of a coefficient of physical state,' then as the quotation from James serves to indicate, they would not admit such universality of science. Rather, they would regard science in any such narrow sense as one mode of interpretation amongst many which are equally valid and equally faithful to that content and character of experience which, in the last analysis, all statement of objective fact must concern. And if they recognize that science represents a peculiarly desirable form of knowledge, such recognition would be on the ground of human interests which are felt to be especially frequent or exigent, such as the interests in prediction and in control of the environment. And they would also be likely to emphasize, as James does, that however important the interests served by science, there are also other interests which are comparable in importance; and they would deny exclusive significance, or perhaps even preeminence, to the scientific formulation of truth.

III

We have so far said nothing concerning the special question whether metaphysical statements are meaningful. It is plain without discussion that pragmatists and logical positivists would not be in agreement on this point. Peirce identified himself with a metaphysical position which is a form of pan-psychism or objective idealism. James criticized absolute idealism not as meaningless but as false; and argued not only for realism and pluralism but also for the significance and possible truth of various more speculative metaphysical assertions—as in "The Will to Believe" and "The Energies of Men." If Dewey ordinarily eschews metaphysical questions and exhibits toward certain metaphysical theses —such as those of Platonism—an attitude somewhat approximating to that of the logical positivists, at least he is definitely a realist, and could not plausibly be interpreted as denying significance to all metaphysical issues.

It is questionable how far the contention that metaphysical statements are without significance is capable of profitable discussion, in view of the vagueness and ambiguity of the term 'metaphysics.' We can, perhaps, roughly distinguish two meanings of that term which are exemplified in common usage. First, it is used to cover statements about reality or nature or experience which have a high degree of generality and whose credibility is supposed to be capable of determination mainly or wholly by reflection and without recourse to any particular and singular statements of fact which would serve as verification or confirmation of them. Second, it has been used to cover statements regarded as altogether incapable of proof or of disproof by empirical findings, and likewise indeterminable by logical analysis. An example of the first sort would be "There are causal laws governing natural events"; of the second, "There is another life beyond this."

Those who have made use of the title 'metaphysics' in the first sense would differ greatly amongst themselves as to the manner in which they suppose such theses to be capable of support. Some would conceive that such questions are capable of solution mainly or exclusively by analysis of the meanings of terms: for example, that the assertion of causal law could be established by logical principles once we should become sufficiently clear what is approximately meant by 'cause' and by 'event in nature,' or that any further premises, beyond logical principles, which would then be needed for support of this statement would be such as can be taken without proof, such as "There are events after one another in time" or "We have experience of objects." One variant of such conception—still sticking to our example—would be a position like that of Kant, who takes the premise of events in time to be synthetic but *a priori*, and the premise of our experience of objects as setting a condition within which alone there would be problems to discuss. Another variant of this general conception would be the notion that whatever assumptions are requisite to such metaphysical assertion are pragmatically compelled. This position would be exemplified by those who regard an assumption called "the uniformity of nature" as requisite to the assertion of causal law, and as a synthetic and indemonstrable statement in the absence of which science would be impossible. Still another variant, of course, would be the position of the skeptic, who regards such statements as significant and even highly important but altogether indemonstrable.

Still others who maintain theses which are metaphysical in this first sense would regard them frankly as hypotheses which, better than any alternative assumption, explain and are confirmed by empirical findings in general. The critical realists exemplify this position.

An objective examination of theses of this sort labeled 'metaphysical,' and of positions taken with regard to them, would, I think, reveal that the presumption that they can be established completely *a priori* has been relatively infrequent; appeal to experience in some sense is usually implicit if not explicit. But a reasonable justification of the distinction of 'metaphysical' from 'physical' or from 'scientific' theses would here be found in the consideration that, with respect to such theses, appeal to single experiment or observation, or even to any set of them which a scientist might perform, would be pointless—either because what is in question is something which, so far as it is empirically ascertainable, is sufficiently evident to everybody; or because induction from a few instances would be futile for a question of such magnitude; or for both of these reasons.

Some meaning of the general sort suggested would, I believe, be found to be the best justified by history of use of the term 'metaphysics' in philosophic discussion. And it is sufficiently evident that no one who discusses the general problems of knowledge or of science can avoid such questions. Consonantly, I think the most appropriate form of the assertion intended by "Metaphysical statements are significant" would be "There are questions with respect to which some decision must be made in the interest of any theory of science or of knowledge in general, or of the character of experience in general, with respect to which any limited set of experiments or observations, such as those of the natural sciences, is either unnecessary or is futile or is both." In that sense, metaphysics is an unavoidable problem of human reflection; and it is obvious that the logical positivists do not avoid it—for example, in the physicalistic assertion, in its earlier form at least, and in the assumption of causal law. Perhaps it would be just to observe that the precise nature of the kind of corroboration they would offer for such theses is left a little obscure in their discussions, and that further elucidation of that matter by them would be appreciated by many readers.

It is a reasonable supposition that not all the problems labeled 'metaphysical' in some meaning of the sort suggested are of the same type. Some of them may have the character which the logical positivists suggest: that of false problems created by inappropriate modes of thought and of language. Time out of mind, some metaphysicians have accused others of such verbalism, and it would be surprising if where there has been so much smoke there should be no fire. But would it not be equally or more surprising if all such problems are solely created by such misconception? Even the thesis of logical positivism—that all legitimate problems of the sort labeled 'philosophical' are capable of solution by logical analysis alone—wants defending, and is a thesis of just the sort which is in question. Obviously this statement itself is not one which can be established by logical analysis. There is some implicit reference here to 'all that is to be met with,' if not to 'all reality,' which seems to set the conditions for determining the truth of this thesis.

A different type of statement commonly classified as 'metaphysical' is that which is also commonly characterized as 'speculative.' Some of these—for example, those made by physical determinists, by vitalists, and by emergent evolutionists regarding the phenomena of life—are of a sort which seek to anticipate what the future development of science would alone be sufficient to determine. While labels are relatively unimportant, probably we should agree that it is confusing and undesirable to call such statements 'metaphysical,' since that would be incompatible with any valid distinction between metaphysics and the special sciences. Another kind of such speculative statements, however, are distinguished by the fact that they are incapable of proof or disproof by scientific methods. Notable examples are the assertion of another life beyond this, of a power determining the direction of natural evolution toward the humanly desirable, of the existence of consciousness without physical embodiment. To deny that such statements have meaning would be a position too egregious to be taken by anyone. One remembers that Schlick has said that the question of immortality is an empirical question—hence significant.[17] The sense in which it is empirically verifiable, if true, is obvious. And the sense in which it is unverifiable and therefore speculative is equally obvious. But the sense in which it is unverifiable plainly precludes it from the field of any of the natural sciences. It happens that, with the notable exception of James, pragmatists, like logical positivists, have not been much given to discussion of such questions. But if these are recognized to be significant, then it seems required to remark the existence of a class of statements, commonly labeled 'metaphysical,' which have meaning but are nevertheless not verifiable under human conditions, and do not belong to the field of science.

IV

It is with respect to problems of evaluation and of ethics that the contrast between logical positivism and pragmatism is strongest. The repudiation by logical positivists of normative ethics does not forthwith mark such a contrast; whether it does so or not would depend

---

[17] See "Meaning and Verification," in *Philosophical Review*, Vol. XLV, pp. 356–57.

upon what is here meant by 'normative.' Pragmatism is not a doctrine of ethics, and there is no reason to assume agreement amongst pragmatists on all points of ethical theory. But if 'normative ethics' should apply exclusively to the conception that moral standards are determinable *a priori* and without reference to empirical matters of fact, then since pragmatists are empiricists, there is ground for presumption that they would agree in repudiating such conception. Rather, the point of contrast would be with respect to the relation conceived to hold between judgments of value and judgments of fact. Pragmatism is an activistic, an instrumentalist conception; it could be characterized as the doctrine that all problems are at bottom problems of conduct, that all judgments are, implicitly, judgments of value, and that, as there can be ultimately no valid distinction of theoretical from practical, so there can be no final separation of questions of truth of any kind from questions of the justifiable ends of action.

While James wrote little directly upon the topics usually comprised in theoretical ethics, the whole body of his writing is colored throughout by a sense of the human problems of the good life and the validity of ideals. And concerning development of his own conceptions, Dewey has written:

"I became more and more troubled by the intellectual scandal that seemed to me involved in the current (and traditional) dualism in logical standpoint and method between something called 'science' on the one hand and something called 'morals' on the other. I have long felt that the construction of a logic, that is, a method of effective inquiry, which would apply without abrupt breach of continuity to the fields designated by both these words, is at once our needed theoretical solvent and the supply of our greatest practical want. This belief has had much more to do with the development of what I termed, for lack of a better word, 'instrumentalism,' than have most of the reasons that have been assigned."[18]

In contrast to this, Carnap has written:

"The word 'Ethics' is used in two different senses. Sometimes a certain empirical investigation is called 'Ethics,' *viz.* psychological and sociological investigations about the actions of human beings, especially regarding the origin of these actions from feelings and volitions and their effects upon other people. Ethics in this sense is an empirical, scientific investigation; it belongs to empirical sicence rather than to philosophy. Fundamentally different from this is ethics in the second

[18] *Contemporary American Philosophy* (New York, 1930), Vol. 2, p. 23.

sense, as the philosophy of moral values and moral norms, which one can designate normative ethics. This is not an investigation of facts, but a pretended investigation of what is good and what is evil, what it is right to do and what it is wrong to do.

"A norm or rule has an imperative form, for instance: 'Do not kill!' The corresponding value judgment would be: 'Killing is evil.' . . . But the value statement, 'Killing is evil,' although, like the rule, it is merely an expression of a certain wish, has the grammatical form of an assertive proposition . . . and must be either true or false. Therefore they give reasons for their own value statements and try to disprove those of their opponents. But actually a value statement is nothing else than a command in a misleading grammatical form. . . . It does not assert anything and can neither be proved nor disproved."[19]

In the longer statement by Schlick, in his *Problems of Ethics*, the terms 'norm' and 'normative' are used in a different way; nevertheless there is substantial—though not verbal—agreement in the conclusions: "When I recommend an action to someone as being 'good,' I express the fact that I *desire* it" (p. 12). A rule or norm, correctly considered, "gives us only the conditions under which an act or disposition or character is actually called 'good' " (p. 15). The questions, "When is a person judged to be good?" "Why is he judged to be good?" admit of factual and scientific answer. But the questions, characteristic of normative ethics as often conceived since Kant, "With *what right* is that person judged to be good?" "What is valuable?" "What should be valued?" are not similarly meaningful (see p. 17). "On the other hand, the question what actually is desired for its own sake is of course quite sensible, and ethics is actually concerned only with answering this question" (p. 19).[20]

The conception that value-statements are, along with metaphysical statements, merely expressive and neither true nor false, and on the other hand, the conception that they are capable of some *a priori* justification, by no means exhaust the possibilities. An omitted alternative is the essentially empiricistic conception that value-judgments are verifiable in the same general manner as are judgments of other qualities. From this third point of view it would be recognized that the ultimate reference of judgments of value is to value-qualities given, or capable of being found, in direct experience, just as the ultimate reference of predications of non-value properties is likewise to the qualities given

[19] *Philosophy and Logical Syntax* (London, 1935), pp. 23–24.
[20] David Rynin, trans. (New York, 1939).

or capable of being found in direct experience. But recognition that the final test of the correctness of a value-judgment is thus empirical, and not *a priori*, no more impugns their objective significance than does the similar recognition that the final test of physical statements is by reference to data of direct experience impugn the objectivity of physics. Nor does this third and empiricistic point of view imply that generalizations concerning values are merely psychological or sociological—unless physics is equally a branch of psychology or of sociology. At an earlier date, Carnap himself indicated the possibility of such empiricistic conception:

"Die Konstitution der Werte aus gewissen Erlebnissen, den '*Werterlebnissen*,' zeigt in mehrfacher Hinsicht eine Analogie zur Konstitution der physichen Dinge aus den 'Wahrnehmungserlebnissen' (genauer: aus den Sinnesqualitäten).... Das bedeutet keine *Psychologisierung der Werte*, so wenig wie die Konstitution der physischen Gegenstände aus Sinnesqualitäten etwa eine Psychologisierung des Physischen bedeutet."[21]

Nor does such an empiricistic conception of the status of value-judgments remove the difference between the determination of what is valuable and the (psychological or sociological) determination of what in fact is valued or of what is experienced with felt satisfaction. It may be admitted that the ultimate test of correctness of a value-judgment is by reference to the quality with which the thing in question is, or could be, experienced, without in the least implying a subjective or merely 'expressive' character of value-statements. The analogy to objective predication of other properties than value is, on this point, obvious. The statement that something is large, or is red, can have no other test of its correctness than, finally, by reference to the manner in which it is or may be experienced; to the observable quality characters with which it is presented. But the judgment that a thing is large, or is red, is nevertheless true or false; and the determination of such truth or falsity is not a problem of psychology or of sociology—unless, as has been said, all problems of truth or falsity are such. That a thing is valuable or desirable, no more means, from the empiricistic point of view suggested, that it is now valued by someone, or is felt with satisfaction by someone, than does the statement that a thing is red mean that someone now judges it to be red or sees it as red. We cannot quarrel with the immediate observation of what is presented—with the report of felt satisfaction or of seen redness—but that fact in no wise removes the question whether the thing observed has the color

21 *Der Logische Aufbau der Welt* (Berlin-Schlachtensee, 1928), pp. 203–04.

red, as could be further verified; nor the question whether it has the property of being 'valuable.'

Questions of *moral* evaluation—of acts, characters, persons—are admittedly of another and more complex kind. With respect to these, pragmatists would be likely to agree with Schlick that the validation of standards or norms is secondary to, and derivative from, an antededent determination of goodness in that toward which conduct is directed; that is, they would be likely to agree that the indicated test of any principle or standard of conduct is by reference, eventually, to the consequences of conduct conforming to that standard, and in terms of actual or possible felt satisfactions. But again, that admission does not remove the question of the validity of such norms. Correspondingly, the standards of correct procedure in making a physical determination have reference, eventually, to the consequences of laboratory conduct conforming to these standards, and to whether these consequences are good or bad. But that fact, so far from making the question of the correctness of scientific procedure one about the psychology of scientists, or about their social connections, is precisely what distinguishes this question from any which is psychological or sociological and makes it objective.

Objective truth of *any* sort has imperative significance for conduct: crudely put, the significance that those who act upon it will prosper, and those who do not will wish that they had. And if it should be observed that such imperative significance, implicit in statements of fact, is hypothetical only (not categorical), then it should be further observed that a hypothetical imperative becomes categorical whenever the hypothesis of it is satisfied, and that one the hypothesis of which never is or could be satisfied is indeed non-significant.

Norms are, or should be conceived to be, standards or principles of correctness. All correctness and incorrectness has to do with actions, and with consequences of actions, and with some species of value of these consequences. The conception that determinations of correctness and incorrectness are subjective, and statement of them merely 'expressive,' or that they fall exclusively within the province of psychological and sociological description, is inadmissible, because such admission would erase the distinction between valid and invalid, and eventually between truth and untruth. When we determine truth, we determine that which it is correct to believe and that upon which it is desirable (not merely desired) to act. There is correctness and incorrectness of belief because believing is itself a decision, and one whose significance is found in the control by it of other modes of action. And whoever should say, "When I speak of something as correct to believe and act upon, I express merely my wish that you and others should believe it and act upon it," would adopt an attitude which releases others from taking him seriously—except as an obstacle to the business in hand.

For the pragmatist, there can be no final division between 'normative' and 'descriptive.' The validity of any standard of correctness has reference to some order of 'descriptive facts'; and every determination of fact reflects some judgment of values and constitutes an imperative for conduct. The validity of cognition itself is inseparable from that final test of it which consists in some valuable result of the action which it serves to guide. Knowledge—so the pragmatist conceives—is for the sake of action; and action is directed to realization of what is valuable. If there should be no valid judgments of value, then action would be pointless or merely capricious, and cognition would be altogether lacking in significance.

10. The Categories of Natural Knowledge

In accepting our editor's invitation to undertake an additional essay for this collection of studies on the philosophy of Whitehead, I am aware of my temerity. Already the volume is complete and balanced in the scope of its topics and admirable in detail: attempted addition is likely to be mere intrusion, trespassing on ground already covered. And in addressing myself to Whitehead's base-concepts for the philosophy of nature, I see in advance that I can satisfy none of the usual desiderata. This reformulation of the categories, set forth in *An Enquiry Concerning the Principles of Natural Knowledge, The Concept of Nature,* and *The Principle of Relativity*[1] is such as defies any effort to summarize, being already succinct to that point beyond which further compression must be mere omission. Nor can one readily facilitate the reader's comprehension or render any point more clear by alternative formulation. To attempt that is to risk falling into those errors of common misconception and unguarded expression which are precisely what the author is engaged in pointing out and avoiding. And if one be minded to bring perspective upon the conceptions presented, by comparison of them with others which are outstanding in the history of philosophic thought, then one finds that Whitehead has already done that too, either in the pages we study or in later writings, and in a fashion discouraging of all attempts to imitate. My one excuse for this choice of subject must be that these three books represent that part of Whitehead's thought to which I have oftenest been drawn back for further study and reflection. And with respect to this topic, I cannot expound, save fragmentarily, nor can I elucidate unless at some sacrifice of adequacy and of precision. What I can justly do is simply to call attention, hoping by some characterization to emphasize what I take to be the radical novelty and the permanent significance of this

Reprinted by permission from P. A. Schilpp, ed., *The Philosophy of Alfred North Whitehead* (2d ed.: New York, 1951), pp. 703–44.

[1] Alfred North Whitehead, *An Enquiry Concerning the Principles of Natural Knowledge* (Cambridge, 1919) ; *The Concept of Nature* (Cambridge, 1920) ; *The Principle of Relativity with Applications to Physical Science* (Cambridge, 1922). These three books will hereafter be cited by the principal word in the title, i.e., as *Knowledge, Nature,* and *Relativity,* respectively.

philosophy of natural knowledge. But if I can in any measure perform that office then I shall not be withheld by any foresight of unavoidable limitations in so doing.

The three books mentioned have a common subject-matter and intent, with respect to which they are mutually supplementary statements. It is in *The Principles of Natural Knowledge* that their common project is most comprehensively surveyed and the new and precise concepts on which Whitehead builds are so introduced that their place in the whole scheme may be most clearly seen. *The Concept of Nature* might, in comparison, be taken to emphasize the enforced transition from older but still dominant conceptions—in terms of which the gap between common understanding and current physical science has now become so difficult to bridge—to categories of thought which will allow the world of our everyday knowledge to be viewed once more as that same world of which contemporary science also gives account. That project requires the profoundest philosophic re-examination of those terms in which common sense, inheriting as it does from the whole stream of western philosophy from Plato down, has come to think of the world of nature. It likewise and at the same time requires attention to those challenging features of the new physics which accentuate this necessary revolution in our thinking. The two sides of this project, and their essential connection, are stressed in the opening chapter of *The Principle of Relativity*:

To expect to reorganize our ideas of Time, Space, and Measurement without some discussion which must be ranked as philosophical is to neglect the teaching of history and the inherent probabilities of the subject. On the other hand no reorganization of these ideas can command confidence unless it supplies science with added power in the analysis of phenomena. The evidence is twofold, and is fatally weakened if the two parts are disjoined.[2]

In this third book Whitehead also makes evident his conviction that relativity physics, in the prevailing form, calls for certain amendments of its basic procedures, rendering them less paradoxical to common sense and less divergent from the older physics. And after summary statement of premises already presented in the earlier books he here proceeds to the fundamental equations for mathematical physics in that form which he would give to this subject.

Let it be said at once, however, that I must here disjoin what Whitehead has said should not be put asunder. Both my own preponderant interest—perhaps the reader's also—and my illiteracy in the mathematical language of relativity physics dictate restriction to what con-

[2] *Relativity*, p. 4.

cerns revision of the categories of antecedent philosophies and prevailing common sense, leaving aside that corroboration of the value of the revised concepts which comes from the demonstrated adequacy of them for the new physics. That any set of philosophic concepts should be submitted to a test so stringent, and indeed developed with that as one end in view, is unprecedented in the history of thought; and we shall do well to pause in appreciation of that fact. But the categorial conceptions whose importance is thus strikingly signalized are bound to have a wider significance, independent of this technical import of them, however impressive that may be. And plainly that accords with Whitehead's own conception and intent. What he here presents to us is in no sense a set of concepts and principles devised for the sake of a physical theory, as one may devise definitions and postulates for a predetermined mathematical system. The validity and power of this philosophy is attested by its adequacy to technical use; but the adequacy derives from the validity, not the validity from the adequacy. Even if the orientation toward physics should be supposed to dominate, there would still be a pertinent remark which we can extract from his own writings: "The . . . philosophic generalization will, if derived from physics, find applications in fields of experience beyond physics. It will enlighten observation in those remote fields, so that general principles can be discerned as in process of illustration. . . . In other words, some synoptic vision has been gained."[3] It is to Whitehead's synoptic envisagement of the world of nature, as expressed in these three books, that attention will be directed here.

We can, however, begin with that generality which most closely relates to what is technical and connects with the discussion of physical theory; namely, with space-time as the general structure of events. That topic is basic; it runs through the whole discussion, affecting every other aspect of this conception of nature. The form which the account of space-time eventually assumes is highly complex. But the root of the matter is in something which is more simple—and may be more readily grasped. That is, it may be so grasped if we understand at the beginning what it is which is to be achieved by such a theory, and those requirements which, as Whitehead conceives it, are to be met by any concept validly introduced in any systematic account of natural knowledge or in any scientific theory. He demands that every such concept shall be validated by identification of what it denotes in terms of factors of observable fact. It is sense-awareness which discloses such fact, and the factors so disclosed are entities for thought.

[3] *Process and Reality* (New York, 1929), p. 8.

Thus there are three components in our knowledge of nature, namely, fact, factors, and entities. Fact is the undifferentiated terminus of sense-aware-ness; factors are termini of sense-awareness, differentiated as elements of fact; entities are factors in their function as termini of thought.... Evi-dently the relations holding between natural entities are themselves natural entities, namely, they are also factors of fact, there for sense-awareness.[4]

These are slightly cryptic sayings, not to be fully grasped without some further understanding of Whitehead's procedures. Let us first illustrate:

Instantaneousness is a complex logical concept.... For example we con-ceive of the distribution of matter in space at an instant. This is a very useful concept in science especially in applied mathematics; but it is a very complex idea so far as concerns its connexions with the immediate facts of sense-awareness. There is no such thing as nature at an instant posited by sense-awareness. [The least that we perceive involves always some dura-tion.] What sense-awareness delivers over for knowledge is nature through a period. Accordingly nature at an instant, since it is not itself a natural en-tity, must be defined in terms of genuine natural entities. Unless we do so, our science, which employs the concept of instantaneous nature, must aban-don all claim to be founded upon observation.[5]

What this complex logical concept of the instantaneous is, does not so far appear. Whitehead is, in fact, preparing here to introduce it; and we shall likewise mention it later. But the present point is that even a concept of a property or character which does not present itself to sense—is not 'posited by sense-awareness'—must be definable in terms of factors of what does present itself to sense, if its introduction in a scientific account of nature is to be justified. Even the instants of time and the points of applied geometry, as well as the point-particles of kinematics, the molecules and electrons of physical science and all other entities which are not to be identified in our perception of the macroscopic, must be conceptually reducible to terms, ultimately, of what can be disclosed in sense-presentation. Otherwise the concepts in question will be empty and require abandonment of all claim that the science which uses them is founded on observed fact. "The construc-tions of science are merely expositions of the characters of things per-ceived."[6] This is what I shall call Whitehead's radical empiricism.

We shall do well to pause briefly upon the character of this empiri-cism, because it is like no other in history, and the confusion of it with that of Locke, Berkeley and Hume, or with that empiricism for which

[4] *Nature*, p. 13f.
[5] *Ibid.*, pp. 56–57.
[6] *Ibid.*, p. 148.

objects are Kantian appearances in a mind, would mislead us no end. In the first place, although Whitehead is not a naturalist in the sense of regarding nature as the whole of reality, but tells us instead that nature is an abstraction from something more concrete, he confines himself in these three books to the discussion of nature. And he defines nature in terms of sense-awareness. "Nature is that which we observe in perception through the senses."[7]

Second, the deliverances of sense are not for Whitehead findings of subjective immediacy in a mind which cognizes the world only mediately and through inference. The observer is one enduring entity and the object is another enduring entity; but perception is a relation between a percipient *event* and another event in which the object is situated. The percipient event is itself in nature, being merely the relevant state of the observing organism. Hence perception is a natural relation between entities in nature. The bifurcation of nature into a phenomenal appearance in mind and an object which is inferred as the cause of it, or constructed from immediate data by the necessities of mind in thinking an object, is wholly unacceptable to Whitehead. In the first place, the attempt to explain knowledge as the interplay between a mind which is outside of or above the world of objects in nature and a stuff which never enters mind but appears to it only through a surrogate and with 'psychic additions'—this attempt at 'metaphysical' explication of the fact of knowledge is no part of the business of natural philosophy, which legitimately concerns itself only with the relations of factors *within* knowledge. And in the second place, admitting the problem, this manner of explanation by dividing nature into two kinds, one apparent but ineffective and the other causal of the appearance but only inferable by the mind which knows it, must fail by its inability to explain our way of knowing about these two parts into which reality is so partitioned. Though Whitehead does not in so many words acknowledge it, he repudiates the whole problem of knowledge in that form which attempts a Cartesian defense against skepticism in view of the predicament of a mind which has no direct contact with the natural world except through the pineal gland. And that problem, posed by 'bifurcation,' dominates the history of theory of knowledge from Descartes to Kant, if not down to the present day. A good part of our difficulty in understanding Whitehead arises, I think, from our being historically conditioned to revert to that problem in almost every philosophic context, and to confront every answer to every philosophic ques-

[7] *Ibid.*, p. 3.

tion with the challenge, "But how do you know that?" So far as it is our knowledge of nature which is in question Whitehead is, so to say, prepared to rebut this skeptically motivated challenge with the answer: "You know it by observation—finally, by the deliverances of sense-awareness." When the sensibly disclosed is no longer subject to suspicion by interpretation of it as mere datum in a mind shut off from every immediate contact with reality, this skeptical approach has lost its point. This is Whitehead's realism; it is even, if you please, that form of realism commonly called 'naive'—though a word less appropriate to Whitehead's thinking, it would be hard to find; and he by no means repudiates or ignores the problems set by delusive apprehension and the other relativities of perceptual knowledge. That we shall see later on.

For similar reasons, he repudiates as invalid that watered-down form of bifurcation-theory which would interpret the scientific realities of points and instants, point-particles, electrons, molecules, and so on, as useful fictions, or merely logical constructions which, instead of being definable in terms of actual and perceptible entities of nature, enter as 'mathematical models,' or are introduced by stipulation, or though not in terms of actual entities of nature and apprehended fact, are supposed justified by intellectual convenience *à la* Poincaré, or otherwise savor of the pragmatic in the bad sense of pseudo and as-if.

The current answer to these objections [made by Whitehead to this attenuated form of bifurcation-theory] is that, though atoms are merely conceptual, yet they are an interesting and picturesque way of saying something else which is true of nature. But surely if it is something else that you mean, for heaven's sake say it.[8]

To 'say it' in terms that are traced back to the deliverances of sense-awareness is a highly complex business; but Whitehead will not settle for less.

In a highly subtle way, it is just this repudiation of concepts by stipulation and principles by convention which prevents Whitehead's full acceptance of the Einstein conception of space-time; though he always acknowledges his indebtedness to, and his deep respect for, the innovations of Einstein and Minkowski. He objects to the Einstein 'signal theory' of light, which is introduced by the stipulation (defining simultaneity of events at a distance) that, *e.g.*, if lightning strikes the railroad track at two places, the two strokes are simultaneous just in case an observer situated midway between the two places and provided with

8 *Ibid.*, p. 45.

mirrors for observing both at once would observe these two strokes simultaneously.[9] Whitehead does not object to, but accepts, simultaneity of observation as the primitive criterion for, *e.g.*, barking both shins at once. And of course he does not object to defining simultaneity for distant events in a manner dependent on such simultaneity here and now. He does, however, object to the favored position so accorded to deliverances of one sense; and when, in his own equations, he introduces the constant c, characteristic of special relativity theory, he does so with the remark: "There is however this difference that the critical velocity c has [here] no reference to light, and merely expresses the fact that a lapse of time and a stretch of spatial route can be congruent to each other."[10]

He also objects to interpreting the component measurements, in that expression of a field of force which is constant for all frames of reference, as indicating a curvature of the space-manifold. "I do not allow that physical phenomena are due to oddities of space."[11]

His most fundamental objection, however, is that the Einstein account contains no 'antecedent theory of measurement'—a lack which Whitehead would make good by his theory of congruence. "Einstein, in my opinion, leaves the whole antecedent theory of measurement in confusion, when it is confronted by the actual conditions of our perceptual knowledge. . . . Measurement on his theory lacks systematic uniformity and requires a knowledge of the actual contingent physical field before it is possible."[12] It is this objection which, if we can grasp the import of it, may lead to understanding of the fundamental connection between Whitehead's interpretation of space-time and the basic position he assigns to the category of events. Why should the theory of measurement be 'antecedent'; and antecedent to what? The answer is: antecedent to the application of measurement to any dimension of physical objects or physical properties, and to any phenomenon it is the business of physical science to investigate. And antecedent because, unless some basis of measurement is so involved in the structure of nature as to be independent of the contingent properties of physical objects investigated and measured, there will be a circle in the very conception and definition of such measures.

All physical things are in process and any physical property of them may become altered. And all such properties of objects which physical

[9] See Albert Einstein, *The Meaning of Relativity* (London, 1922), p. 27f.
[10] *Relativity*, p. 76.
[11] *Nature*, p. 184.
[12] *Relativity*, p. 83.

science would determine are contingent properties which are indeterminable save by observation and experiment. If, then, measurements are *defined* by stipulated operations with yardsticks and clocks and other physical instruments, then our yardstick may turn out too rubbery or shorten if it is moved (and shorten with respect to what?) ; our clocks may run slow or fast or be affected by a magnetic field. And if we determine the simultaneity of distant events by means of observations in a mirror at the midpoint between them, then mirrors, or *this* mirror, could have physical peculiarities affecting the matter. And in spite of what Einstein says to the contrary—in the context above referred to— our determination of simultaneity, so made, must either assume that the velocity of light is uniform in opposite directions, or this operation will be utterly unsuited to any disclosure of a property significantly correlated with the occurrence of other properties as found in nature. Concepts arising by stipulation must be forever at the mercy of contingent natural facts for any status other than that of triviality. Defining our concepts for the discovery of order amongst contingent facts in terms of contingent characteristics of the same general kind as those to be determined, is like defining elasticity by reference to an elastic standard of the rigid.

For physical science, and indeed for any knowledge of the physical, the basic presumption is that the spatio-temporal characteristics of physical things are contingent properties of them; no physical object, or kind of object, has its particular and discoverable spatio-temporal properties *a priori*. But if all physical description and determinations of physical properties are not to become relative in a sense which philosophy and science have so far spared us, then there must be *something* which stands fast and provides a norm not itself subject to the contingencies of fact we would unravel.

The point here is not to avoid such assumptions as that something or other is a sufficiently rigid body, or a sufficiently reliable clock, to serve as an instrument of measurement; the point is to avoid circularity in the very conception of the various spatial and temporal equivalences (spatio-temporal congruences) which constitute our measures; to escape, for example, the absurdity of saying that because, by stipulation or convention, the platinum bar in Washington is the standard yardstick, it could not by any physical contingency become elongated or shortened, and so fail to be, at one place and time, congruent with itself at another place and time. At the very least it will be granted that it is desirable to avoid, if that can be managed, this manner of confusion between space-time itself and the contingent space-time properties of physical objects which it is the business of science to determine.

I have presented this point in my own way, and perhaps in a manner which Whitehead would not approve. But it is to this kind of problem that his conception of 'event' and of space-time as the general structure of events is addressed. The fundamental consideration here is that events, and the relations of events, unlike physical objects and their contingent relationships, are not subject to change. Space-time as the comprehensive order of events can provide a kind of ultimate frame of reference for the processes of physically changing things precisely because an event, unlike a material object, is inalterably just what it is and related to other events just as it is.

This contrast between event and object, and the precise significance of this category of 'events,' can at first be puzzling; especially since, *e.g.*, Mr. Blank throughout his lifetime is both a complex object and a complex event. But the basic distinction between an event which we may apprehend and an object which we may at the same time be perceiving is one which is at bottom simple and is capable of clear statement in common-sense terms. An event is a happening; it happens just when it does and where it does; and the notion of just this event as happening elsewhere or at another time is simply a contradiction in terms. By contrast, an object may be in one place at one time and in another place at another time. It is the kind of entity which endures, and by that fact may become altered.

Events have always some spatio-temporal spread. They 'occupy' time and space, because that manner of speaking is merely an inaccurate way of saying that spatio-temporal order is an abstraction from the comprehensive relations of events to one another. One event 'extends over' (includes as a proper part) any other event which can be marked off within it. The event of the clock striking three extends over the events of the separate strokes, and extends over them as parts having just that relationship to the whole event and to one another which they do. Mr. Blank eating breakfast at seven-thirty and Mr. Blank running for the train at eight are likewise events, and both are extended over by the event which is the life of Mr. Blank from seven to nine. If we see Mr. Blank at eight o'clock, we may recognize the object Mr. Blank, but what is directly delivered to our sense-awareness is the happening, Mr. Blank running for the train. This is a particular space-time piece out of nature in its passage, delineated as what takes place then and there within our observation. But what is so observed, Whitehead takes to be, not a subjective phenomenon 'within our minds,'

but just this event now happening, and happening in relation to a percipient event which is our seeing Mr. Blank run. Also, these two events
stand in their specific spatio-temporal relations as parts of the more
comprehensive event which is the neighborhood of the railroad station
from seven-fifty to eight-ten.

We describe events as 'in' space and time, that is, by indicating their
spatial and temporal bounds, or we describe them by reference to objects like Mr. Blank which are ingredient in them, or we use both
methods at once in specifying what event is spoken of. But it is neither
the space and time which the events are said to occupy, nor the objects
ingredient in them, which are the primordial constituents of nature.
These ultimate constituents are the events themselves. "There is time
because there are happenings, and apart from happenings there is
nothing."[13] It could likewise be said that there is space because there
are happenings, because events have separate parts related as one here
and one simultaneously there. As for objects, that is a story we shall
come to shortly.

First, however, let us pause to observe those distinctive features of
this conception of space-time as the structure of events by reason of
which it avoids that confusion of spatio-temporal relationships with
the contingent physical properties of changeable physical objects, and
to note, in most general terms, the possibility so afforded for the introduction of concepts requisite to measurement in a manner which is
free of the difficulty mentioned above.

In spite of the multiplicity and variety of theories of space and time,
historical conceptions exhibit three general patterns. There is the primitive notion of space and time as 'absolute'; of space as the 'empty
bowl,' partially or wholly occupied by bits of matter, but in which, and
independently of what occupies and moves in it, there are absolute positions, directions, and the characters of measurable extent. With this
goes the notion of time as the equable flow of nothing whatever or of
everything in general, which is independent of and provides the basis
for measuring the particular rates of motion of things which move and
the rate of change of other processes.

This conception of space and time as absolute never really satisfied
anybody. Even amongst the ancients who first recorded it we likewise
find record of the unanswerable objection to it: this view ascribes a
kind of being to that which is not, and assigns to this nothing a character antecedent to all characters, fixing the measures of things. The no-

[13] *Nature*, p. 66.

tion of the ether as the physically ultimate frame of reference is the last relic of this theory, and with the Michelson-Morley experiment it passed into history.

Second, there is the type of theory called 'relative' before the advent of relativity physics made that designation confusing: the conception namely that there are no such entities as space and time apart from what occupies them, that space is constituted by those relations of material objects which are called 'spatial,' and that time is constituted by the order and relations of the processes which objects undergo. In spite of that iconoclastic confinement to the palpable which gives this theory its plausibility, it fails to cover that sense of temporality which is reflected in the eternal flitting away of life and all states of things, even when relationships observed appear most stable. It also arouses some sense of having tucked the spatio-temporal order under things to start with, in order to be able to discover later this *general* order amongst their contingent and particular and unanticipatable relationships to one another. Specifically there is a difficulty here which affects all measurement, by making all measures relative to some contingent and alterable character of some material object or set of objects, or to some particular relationship amongst objects which could change with time. What measures time-lapse must *ipso facto* be accepted as suffering no alteration in that character of it which provides this measure; and what measures space must *ipso facto* be immune to alteration of its spatial characters. But there are no material objects thus immune to alteration of their spatial and temporal properties. Antecedent to physical investigations, involving measurements of the space-time characteristics of objects, there can be no guarantee that any of them will endure unaltered in that respect relied upon to provide a standard applicable to other objects. But until there is such an unchanging standard, physical measurement of changing things cannot proceed.

Unless space and time are in some sense antecedent to and independent of those properties of material objects which are recognized to be contingent and discoverable only by empirical observation and empirical generalization with respect to their spatio-temporal characteristics, then all scientific measurement is, theoretically at least, involved in a vicious circle, even if we refuse, practically, to be frightened lest the stars should change in their courses—thus falling back, in point of fact, on the absolutistic theory we supposedly have repudiated.

The currently fashionable method of cutting this Gordian knot, is by stipulation of operational criteria. This is as much as to say, *e.g.*: "We refuse to recognize any alteration of those material objects which provide our standard measures, in those characteristics of them which constitute this accepted criterion." But either this is justified by antecedent empirical investigations, showing this object, or kind of object, to be reliably correlated with other processes in nature, so that appeal to it will not make chaos of our attempted discovery of some general order and law amongst the processes of things at large—and in that case we are back in our vicious circle once more—or else it is a mere counsel of despair.

The third type of theory, of which Kant is the clearest representative, seeks to recover the antecedent and independent character of spatial and temporal order and its clear distinction from contingent spatial and temporal characters of particular things, by superimposing on the relativistic conception an epistemological distinction of the *a priori* from the empirically learned. For earlier theories which might be classed as of this type, space as the essence of extension may be taken as knowable *a priori* by *reason*. But Kant observes that geometry depends on steps of proof which cannot be justified by rules of logic simply, and the *a priori* status of our knowledge of space and time is attributed to the fact that space and time are forms of intuition, within which alone phenomena can appear to the mind. Taking mathematics (applied geometry, and arithmetic as generated by the time-order of counting) as indubitably valid, he seeks to establish this *a priori* character of them by showing that we know fundamental characters of space and time which could not possibly be learned by any generalizing from particular experiences.

Bergson's theory of space and time might be included as representing a fourth type; and Bergson is supposed to have influenced Whitehead. But Bergson's conception is hardly coordinate with the above three, and it offers nothing pertinent to the point to which I would direct attention here. Whitehead's conception of the 'passage of events' as 'creative advance' suggests Bergson, and there are other recognizable points of approximation. But Whitehead's conception of time in nature as measurable, and of a lapse of time as possibly congruent with some stretch of spatial route, directly contravenes the Bergsonian conception on these same points.

Whitehead's theory of space-time repudiates the absolutistic notion: he takes space-time order to represent an abstraction, though an abstraction of something which is there in nature to be abstracted. He accepts not only the general relativistic conception above but the further relativity involved in the new physics. Also he repudiates any manner of apriorism, making no doubt that we discover this space-time structure of nature in the same general manner that we discover other natural facts—eventually through the deliverances of sense. His theory rejects Kantian phenomenalism and any intuition of form independent of sense-content. But it nevertheless preserves a distinction between the space-time structure of nature and the contingent relations of physical objects. And by preserving this distinction, it makes possible a theory of measurement which avoids that circularity of conception pointed out above. The space-time structure of nature is independent of and 'antecedent' to spatio-temporal characteristics of material objects which, by being involved in the natural process, can undergo some alteration, and whose reliability as possible standards of the measurable must first be attested by some empirical investigation and generalization about the physical properties of these material objects. If I may here use 'necessary' merely as the suggested antonym to 'contingent,' then I may say that on Whitehead's theory the 'geometry' of space-time expresses necessary relationships in the space-time structure of nature. (Whitehead does not use the term 'necessary' in this connection, and he uses 'antecedent' somewhat incidentally—as in the quotation above. The usage of these terms here is mine, though in what I use them to express, I believe that I am accurate to his thought.)

Whitehead's theory of space-time is historically unique because his category of 'events' is historically unique. Space-time is the general structure of *events* in nature. Thus in accepting the relativistic conception, he does so with a difference; and this difference is profoundly important. The relationships which constitute the abstractable space-time structure of nature are not here the contingent relations which material objects exhibit in the course of their adventures in the natural process. Objects have no space-time relationships except through their connection with events. And the relations of events, constitutive of that abstractable structure which is space-time, are 'necessary' in the peculiar sense that they could not be other than in fact they are. This 'necessity,' however, is not one of logic; and in spite of other differences Whitehead is at one with Kant on just this point.

Every event has spatio-temporal extension, and extension in both respects. Every event extends over other events which are its parts, and every event is in turn extended over by others. In terms of 'extending over,' further relations of events are definable. Two events having a common part 'intersect.' Two which do not intersect are 'separated.' In terms of these, other relations are definable. (I omit the further designated relationships and their definitions.) On the basis of relationships so defined, Whitehead proceeds to the 'Method of Extensive Abstraction,' to be mentioned later; and on the basis of concepts so determined he indicates the whole 'geometry' explicative of space-time as the structure of relations of events. In this 'geometry,' the metrical concepts are introduced by his theory of congruence. Durations, moments, time-systems (essential to relativity physics), the various types of spatial entities, motion, and the basic concepts of physics—all receive their consequent explication.

But to return to what belongs in a synoptic view: It will be evident without explanation in detail that just as the when and where of an event are of the essence, and its having any other locus in space-time would be a contradiction, so also its extending over just those events which in fact are parts of it, and its being extended over by just those events in which it is a part, as well as its intersecting or being separated from another event, or its having any other relationship, definable in terms of these, to another event—all these facts of relationship can only be just what they are, and follow from the events so related being just the events that they are. These relations of events are, thus, 'internal.' The whole order of space-time as the structure of events in such relationships, is fixed and 'necessary' in this sense that it could not be otherwise than in fact it is, even though our awareness of what is so contained in nature is highly fragmentary, and in our grasp of its structure, abstractly taken, we could be mistaken in ways which may not reflect any failure of cogency. There is no guarantee of certitude beyond what is implied in this nature of events, and in their universal involvement with others as being parts and as containing parts, and so on.

If now one wishes to know what difference, after all, this makes as to the distinction of the spatio-temporal from the contingent properties of material things, then the answer can be suggested briefly. The practicalities of measurement may be unaffected, and in any case the choice of a metrical unit is arbitrary. But we now have a 'geometry' of space-time, including parallels, though it also allows for different time-systems in accord with the new physics. We have also a developed and precise meaning of 'congruent with.' If we have our yardstick before us, the length of it can be 'projected' throughout the space-time system; and the *meaning* of 'one yard long' is 'congruent in length with the length of this here and now yardstick,' regardless of any vicissitudes which this physical yardstick may undergo in its adventures in time and space. That circularity in the meaning of the metrical concepts which is involved in the definition of spatio-temporal entities by stipulated relation to material objects in process, is thus obviated. Space-time itself is not constituted by the relations of material objects but by reference to events which, by their nature *as* events, can undergo no change. And if under certain physical conditions all material objects should be systematically 'shortened,' the explanation to be sought must be physical, and is not to be found in any attribution of curvature to the space-time manifold.

> This doctrine leads to the rejection of Einstein's interpretation of his formulae, as expressing a casual heterogeneity of spatio-temporal warping, dependent upon contingent adjectives.
>
> The case of the yard-measure illustrates my meaning. It is a contingent adjective of the events where it is situated. Its spatio-temporal properties are entirely derived from the events it qualifies.... The yard-measure is merely a device for making evident obscure relations between those events in which it appears.[14]

Already the reader has been disturbed by the obscurity of referring to objects, in a conception in which it appears that what is ultimate in nature does not include objects but is constituted by unalterable events in an order of relations to one another which is likewise unchanging and intrinsic to them. But that is the fault of my having disarranged the order of Whitehead's exposition in my comments here. Let us now proceed, belatedly, to this topic of the nature of objects and their connections with events.

Objects are derivative and 'adjectival' entities which *are* by being ingredient in events, and are elicited by recognition in or through those same deliverances of sense which are also our direct apprehensions of events. Events happen only once, and are spoken of as 'apprehended'; objects are the kind of entities which can 'be again'; and are said to be 'recognized.' It follows that the same object can be ingredient in, or 'situated' in, more than one event. Apart from events (happenings) there is nothing whatever; but without the recognition of objects in events in which they are situated, we could not discern or mark off the events themselves, within the continuity of space-time. Ingredient objects are thus certain *characters* of the events which are their situations.

The simplest kind of recognition of an object is recognition of some permanence within the specious present, of some ingredient character which characterizes both the before-part and the after-part distinguishable in even the smallest event that we can apprehend. And the simplest objects so recognized are qualia or sense-data: tastes, colors, shape-size, and so on. Whitehead calls these 'sense-objects.' Merely as now presented and situated in the directly apprehended event, such a sense-object is concrete or individual, and it could in no sense share that kind of abstractness which characterizes universals like goodness

[14] *Relativity*, p. 65.

and triangularity. But sense-objects have a kind of duality by being entities for thought as well as for direct awareness. Recognition of an object is significant of it as something recollectable, and the same in more than one event. As such as entity for thought it loses something of the individuality which it has as just this object, ingredient in this event now apprehended, retaining only the individuality of character. It is thus a kind of universal, though Whitehead does not here apply that word.

Both these references are involved in recognition—since that requires cognizance of something both as given now and as being 'again.' The distinction is relative to this duality of the factors in recognition: as characterizing this occasion, the given sense-object shares the individuality of this present sense-awareness; as recognized from one occasion to another, it constitutes an abstractable entity for thought.

For other theories, sense-objects, or sense-data, are assigned their metaphysical home in experience or in the mind, and perhaps are allowed no status as constituents in objective reality, even though recognized as *ratio cognoscendi* of some physical object. But this manner of conception leads to or presupposes the bifurcation of nature which Whitehead will not allow. There are such sense-objects as vague sounds or odors which may be given without apprehension of their situation in any specific event. But apart from such vagrant items, and in those cases in which the sense-awareness finds its place in some full perception of a physical thing, awareness of the sense-object as situated in an event is basic for authenticity of the perception. On this point he says: "The situations of sense-objects form the whole basis of our knowledge of nature, and the whole structure of natural knowledge is founded on the analysis of their relations."[15]

So long as we deal with sense-objects (or sense-data), Whitehead's conception of them as merely adjectival entities characterizing events (or occasions of experience) may not affect our common sense with any feeling of paradox. But when we come to the next category of 'perceptual objects'—the stones, trees, tables and other objects commonly recognized—then I think that the conception of such entities as adjectival and merely permanences of character, characterizing certain passages of events, does arouse some sense of paradox; and we may not be able to follow Whitehead with full understanding unless at this point we exercise our metaphysical imagination a little. We are so wedded to the notion of perceptible physical objects as ultimate realities, and of the world as that big barrel in which the whole collection of them

[15] *Knowledge*, p. 85.

is thrown together, that we have difficulty in envisaging nature as the continuum of happenings in their total relatedness, within which objects present themselves as lesser and included continuities, elicited by their relative preservation of continuing characters, in patterns the interconnections of which constitute their intelligible relationships.

If I may use a distant analogy, events in their all-pervading continuity constitute that ocean of nature in which perceptual and physical objects are waves which we may discern. If there were no recognizable shapes and high-lights (sense-objects) here and there, then the whole ocean would be characterless and could not be marked off into distinguishable parts (separate events). And if there were no waves, recognizable as propagated continuities of these sensible characters, then there would be no relatively permanent objects at all. The permanence of the association of sense-objects *is* the perceptual object which is recognized.[16] My analogy fails most notably in that nature is no ocean all there for apprehension at one time but is the continuum of happenings in their all-pervasive passage and creative advance.

What it is most essential to observe, in turning from sense-objects to the category of perceptual objects, is that sense-awareness by itself does not constitute perception. Normally, however, sense-objects are apprehended as associated in some perceptual object. For example, we seldom see the color of the horse without also 'seeing the horse,' though what we *see*, in the strict sense of the term, is only a shape-size-color complex in a situation. What we do not thus strictly see, or otherwise directly sense, in perceiving an object, is 'conveyed' by the sense-object (or associated sense-objects) given in sense-awareness. This distinction between the sensed element in the perceptual object and the element which is conveyed illustrates the distinction between 'cognition by adjective' and 'cognition by relatedness.' What is cognized by relatedness—the unseen side of the horse, or of the moon, and the closet behind the door—is known by way of the space-time relations of events, in which what is sensed is situated, to other events which are not apprehended by sense at the time in question. What is thus conveyed by what is cognized by adjective is, characteristically, determinate as to locus but relatively vague in other aspects—as *e.g.*, we are a little vague about the color of the other side of the horse. However, without this significance of the conveyed which attaches to the element directly sensed, there would be no distinction of objects as normally perceived from sense-objects—from sense-data merely.

That normally we see houses, trees, and so on, and not merely some

[16] Cf. *ibid.*, p. 88.

patch of color in a situation, Whitehead recognizes by saying that perception is primarily the positing of an object in sense-awareness, rather
than a judgment. But he adds: "Judgments quickly supervene and form
an important ingredient in what may be termed 'completed recognition.' "[17] What such perceptual judgments particularly concern is the
situation of the object perceived in events. When this judgment of situation is correct, the object perceived is not only a perceptual object but
a 'physical object.' When the judgment is incorrect—when what we see
is not there where we see it—the perceptual object as perceived is a
delusion. It is obvious, though Whitehead does not remark it in this
context, that not only perceptual judgment but also the positing of an
object in sense-awareness which does not rise to the level of conscious
judgment may on occasion have this delusive character.

It will also be sure to occur to us in this connection that the possible
validity of perceptual judgment—the possibility that certain disclosures
of sense may *validly* convey physical objects situated in those events to
which perceptual judgment, or the habitual positings of sense-awareness, normally assigns them—depends upon some lawfulness of nature.
The rest of the horse must normally be there on those occasions when
the deliverances of sense, constituting what we strictly see, thus conveys an unseen side. The same will obviously be true for *any* cognition
by relatedness unless what is so cognized should be *completely* vague
except as to its space-time relationship with what is directly sensed.

We shall further observe that the kind of lawfulness of nature which
is so called for is not satisfied by the 'necessary' laws of space-time by
which whatever has a given situation in events must stand related to
something in the space-time relationships of 'continuous with,' 'tem-
porally before' or 'after,' and so on. What is required is some further
and contingent lawfulness: that order of nature by which, in Berkeley's
terms, one deliverance of sense is 'sign of another which is to come'—
e.g., of something we should see if we decided to walk around the horse.
In this connection, let us also remark the importance of that continuity of events and of what characterizes them which Whitehead's
theory prescribes. Whatever is given is given as itself having some
space-time spread, and also as 'necessarily' continuous with *something*
further. Thus the atomic character of Berkeleian ideas and Humean
impressions is avoided, and with it the inevitable debacle of historical
empiricism in the skepticism of Hume. Whitehead's conception of the
'relatedness of nature,' correlative with 'cognition by relatedness,' is

[17] *Ibid.*, p. 89.

integral with his whole doctrine of 'significance.' But plainly the laws expressive of the general space-time structure of events are not enough for this. It is further required that such space-time continuities must exhibit also some more specific type of continuity: some preservation of character, or some relatedness of character, formulatable by some contingent law, if perceptual knowledge and other forms of cognition are to be brought into this account.

There are likewise further problems—not only those set by delusive perception and other forms of error, but such questions as concern the star seen now though it may have exploded two centuries ago, and what is seen as in front of us and behind the mirror, though really located behind us. Whitehead by no means ignores such questions; in fact those here alluded to are the ones he mentions. Consideration of these problems must bring us to topics more complex and difficult than those so far covered; but they are also such as will lead us to our final topic of 'scientific objects' and the nature of science itself.

First, however, let us observe what *kind* of account it is which Whitehead will offer us concerning such matters. He does not attempt to explain the fact of knowledge, or the fact of the phenomena which we observe, by any metaphysical appeal to entities more ultimate in their nature and not themselves discoverable within knowledge and by perception. Any such account of knowledge explains the known by the unknown, and can give no account of *itself*. Thus he refuses that manner of explanation which supposes objective realities, beyond what appears, as causes of the appearances in mind, which appearances are then the bases of mental 'constructions' miraculously corresponding to those objects which operate as the initial causes of these mental phenomena. He likewise repudiates the myth of a transcendent mind confronting an *an-sich* reality, whose appearances it informs by its own modes of receptivity and by imposing relations reflecting its own essential modes of understanding. Any account of knowledge he would attempt must, by his radical empiricism, be in terms of the factors of fact which are knowable as *in* nature, and not in terms of entities which, by being antecedent to natural fact in general, are incapable of being known in that manner of knowledge they are invoked to explain. Nor would he attempt to explain or justify the validity of knowledge in general in that manner which could only be done if, miraculously, we had some premises of fact antecedent to all knowledge, from which the validity of it is deducible. The fact that things exist to be known, and the fact that there is perception and things perceived, are ultimate and incapable of any explanation. The only manner of their explanation to be given is one by reference to the factors of fact *in* nature and the structure of relations of factors in constituting both nature as known and our knowledge of it. In the following he speaks of science, but what he says extends also to natural knowledge generally: "Science is not discussing the causes of knowledge, but the coherence of knowledge. The understanding which is sought by science is an understanding of relations within nature."[18]

First, let us observe that, as is evident already, the fact that there are any perceptible and physical objects at all is the fact of contingent continuities in events. That there is anything identifiable to sense-awareness, and hence anything for our knowledge to be 'about,' lies in the fact of some permanence of character pervading some space-time region and recognizable from moment to moment. Without that manner of continuity there would not even be sense-objects. Second, and connected with this, there is that manner of continuity which holds between the side of the horse which we see and the unseen side. Without this further kind of continuity, there would be for us no perceptual objects as distinct from mere sense-data. Let us also note the fundamental similarity between these two modes of continuity by reason of which events present to us enduring objects, and that kind of temporal continuity of events by which they constitute a causal chain. That kind of continuity of events by which they present to us the same object may in fact be regarded as a particular kind of causal chain: a character of events, so to say, propagating itself, or more accurately, pervading a certain historical route in space-time.

Incidentally, however, and lest we fall into confusion here, let us digress for a moment to observe that it is inaccurate to speak of an object as having parts. It is a consequence of this conception of objects as constituted by the persistence of character in events that, except derivatively and through their relation to events in which they are situated, objects can have no parts. But if this be paradox, then the paradox is mainly linguistic, and the incurring of it is incident to the explanation of certain common-sense facts. The point is that, for example, the *disjecta membra* of a chair do not constitute a chair. The leg of the chair is 'part of the chair' only when and where it adjoins the rest of the chair—that is, only within those events which can be spatially partitioned into one part in which the leg is situated and an adjoining part which is the situation of the rest of the chair. This easily adds up to the common-sense notion that there is a chair only when

[18] *Nature*, p. 41.

and where there is the whole of the chair. The part-whole relation is a space-time relation of events involved in any situation of the chair as a whole. This also illustrates rather well that 'this chair' is an adjectival qualification of events, and designates a certain uniformity of character pervading that particular continuum which is the historical route in space-time presenting the life-history of the chair. The life-history of the leg may be longer in both directions; but while the chair endures—and the leg adjoins the rest—the situation of the leg is part of any situation of the chair. That is precisely what it means to say, "The leg of the chair is part of the chair," and this does not leave open the puzzling question whether the chair, having lost one leg after another, and finally the back, is still the same chair, or whether one leg on the woodpile is still part of the chair. An object is a permanent recognizable character of its various situations.

Let us now return to the considerations which are essential for dealing with those problems of perceptual knowledge which still remain. Another point to note is that an object may be discoverable not only by sensing it directly in its situation but also by other typical manifestations: by characters which 'reflect' its presence in the neighborhood. The cook in the kitchen is typically manifested in the dining room when dinner is before us. And the star's crossing the meridian, as observed from Washington, is typically manifested throughout the United States wherever people hear the time-signal on the radio. Indeed, if we ask here, "How big is a neighborhood?" we already know the answer: "When I drop this chalk I shake the farthest stars"—though beyond a limited region, a particular type of manifestation may be neither detectable nor of any importance. We here stand in the presence of that fact which Whitehead speaks of as the 'relatedness of nature,' that fact by reason of which objects are not merely 'cognizable by adjective' in direct perception, but 'cognizable by relatedness' through their manifestations as modifications of the characters of events distinct from, but spatio-temporally related to, those events within which they are situated for our direct sense-observation. This manner of fact, Whiteheads speaks of as the 'ingression of the object' into an event. An object is said to have this relation of 'ingression into' any event if the character of the event in question typically manifests the existence and character of this object or—in my own language rather than Whitehead's—if the character of the event is evidence of the object: if the event reflects the existence and nature of the object. It is obvious that we may say, in a sense which is intelligible, that the object is present wherever and whenever it manifests itself; and to overlook this fact is to risk committing the 'fallacy of simple location.' Indeed 'situation' is only a special and simpler type of 'ingression,' whose peculiar character is illustrated by the cook who stays in the kitchen though her presence there is made manifest elsewhere.

However, we must not forget here— because 'ingression of the object' suggests the object *doing* something—that even as restricted to its situation, 'the object' is only a character characterizing this and other events, and perhaps then and there observable to sense. If that manifestation of an object which is a modification of the character of an event be thought of as an 'effect' of an object, not situated in this event but in some other, then this modification of character, perhaps observed, is 'really due to' some other *event*: the event whose character the object peculiarly 'is.' "The conditions which determine the nature of events can only be furnished by other events, for there is nothing else in nature."[19] As for the object, its situation, and the variety of its ingressions throughout the rest of nature, we must be reminded of the occasionalists' explanation of Cartesian doctrine: the soul is present throughout the body but peculiarly present in the mid-brain, just as God is present throughout the universe but peculiarly present in the temple of Solomon. The object is somehow present in every event whose character it qualifies—and that includes, in some manner or another, the whole manifold of events in their total relatedness—but it is peculiarly present in that event (if any) in the apprehension of which it may be 'cognized by adjective' in our sense-awareness.

In considering this manner of the relationship of events, and of objects as the characters pervading certain continuities of events in space-time, we are, obviously, considering nature in its 'causal' aspect. The event of the stone dropping into the pond manifests itself in widening circles—eventually throughout the universe. But this 'causally' propagated manifestation is, in contrast to relation of this event to the rest of simultaneous nature, one whose 'direction' determines that dimension of nature which is *time*, and is significant of passage and becoming. As we move outward in space, following this manifestation of the dropped stone, we are coincidentally moving forward in time. And if it were a scientific 'particle' of kinematics, P, instead of a dropped stone, what we should be so concentrating upon would be 'P's kinematic future,' the 'tube of force' associated with it. It is on such a point that we find the closest affinity of Whitehead's doctrine to that of Bergson: the direction of creative advance as the time-dimension, in con-

[19] *Knowledge*, p. 73.

trast to relations with the simultaneously enduring, as spatial dimensions of matter as inert. "There are two sides to nature, as it were, antagonistic the one to the other, and yet each essential. The one side is development in creative advance, the essential becomingness of nature. The other side is the permanence of things, the fact that nature can be recognized."[20]

Just one more point, and then we shall be ready to complete the picture of perceptual knowledge. In that qualification of an event which is the ingression of an object into it, and represents the conditioning of this event by the character of some other, there will be differences in the manner in which this event may so reflect the other event. There will be events so conditioning the one in question that they may, in this relation, be classed as 'active conditioning events.' They qualify or modify or manifest themselves in this event in a manner typical of their own character; as *e.g.*, the cook's cooking in the kitchen later modifies or is manifested in events in the dining room; or as the emission of light from the star modifies the event of the image approaching the cross-hair of the telescope; or as that event in turn modifies the events in which the time-signal is heard. Amongst such active conditioning events of the one in question, we can perhaps select one as the 'generating event' whose character is 'transmitted' as successive modifications through some series of events. (But when I here speak of one event, A, as 'modifying' another event, B, this must be understood as meaning only that the *character* of A manifests itself, in some degree or manner, in the character of B. Events cannot *do* anything to one another.) There will also be events which are passive conditions of the one in question; if they were not there, when and where they are, then the event in question would not be as it is, but they account for no modification of this event which peculiarly reflects their character. Amongst such passive conditioning events, some may be called 'transmitting events'; when the emission of light from the star conditions the event of observation at the telescope, all the events of surrounding nature are also, in some degree and manner, relevant for the final happening—since, owing to the total relatedness of events in nature, if they were not as they are, then this event would be subtly, and perhaps unobservably, different—but the events spatio-temporally intervening in the causal chain between the emission of the light and the observation at the telescope will constitute an obvious illustration of this class of transmitting events. Whitehead hardly supplies any more precise cri-

[20] *Ibid.*, p. 98.

teria for these classifications than are suggested here: it appears likely that he thought of them as suggestive for our contemplation of the different modes of significance grounded in the relatedness of events in nature, and manifested as the cognizable ingressions of objects into events in their constitution of the order of nature itself. These are factors of fact which are there to be elicited for thought. But the total order of events is all there, independently of our thinking: 'nature is closed to mind.'

The broader category of the 'ingression of objects into events,' as contrasted with the narrower category of 'situation,' which is a simpler instance of it, affords possible explanation of certain facts of perception which would otherwise offer difficulty. It is obvious that any perception of an object is an instance of the ingression of the object into the event of perception. Although Whitehead points out the impossibilities of that type of theory which would explain perception as cause-effect relation of stuff inhabiting space to a mind not itself in nature, he nevertheless does bring perception under the rubric of 'ingression,' which category includes—though it is not confined to—various modes of 'causal' relationship. In order to apply this manner of explanation, however, we must observe that the mind thus causally related to an event which is 'external to it,' must be itself some entity in nature, standing in some natural relationship to the event it apprehends. First remarking then, that Whitehead nowhere implies that mind is confined to nature but often explicitly states the contrary, we must remember that it is not mind as thus transcending its implication in the natural, but the percipient event, which figures in the account of perception. And, "The percipient event is the relevant bodily state of the observer."[21]

It thus becomes possible to explain the distinction of veridical from delusive perception, and to deal with otherwise puzzling questions about the situation, in events, of the star seen now though it no longer exists, and with the problem set by the objects perceived in a mirror. Whitehead always speaks of sense-objects as situated when and where they are sensed as being. But perception has, as we have seen, two phases, one as a primary positing in sense-awareness and another when perceptual judgment supervenes in completed recognition. Difficulty could so arise over the situation of perceived objects—seen now, or seen in a mirror—as assigned by the sense-positing of some primitive

[21] *Nature*, p. 152.

savage, let us say, and as assigned in the observation of a scientist. But reference to the various modes of ingression can cover all such facts.

In the first place, we must recognize that perception is not a simple relation of the percipient event to that event in which the object perceived is situated, but is subject to various conditioning by other events, such as those which spatio-temporally intervene and are transmitting events for this relationship. Thus perception represents a polyadic relation of the percipient event to others, variously and complexly conditioning the ingression into the percipient event of that character recognized as the perceptual object.

So far as the distinction of veridical and non-veridical is the question, the criterion can be given as follows:

The definition of delusiveness and non-delusiveness is sufficiently obvious, namely, a perceptual object is non-delusive when it is the apparent character of an event which is itself an active condition for the appearance of that character as perceptible from all percipient events.... The situation of a physical object is its 'generating event.'[22]

Remembering that a physical object is defined as a non-delusive perceptual object, we may note that the above passage specifies two, concurrent, criteria of veridical perception: (1) the situation of a veridically perceived object is an active, generating event for the appearance of it to, or in, the percipient event—*i.e.*, for the ingression of that object in the bodily state of the observer; and (2) a veridically perceived object has the same situation for all percipient events.

Let us further remind ourselves that the awareness of *sense*-objects is simple cognition by adjective, but that perception arises by the addition to this—whether by that positing which is primary and antecedent to judgment, or by a judgment which quickly supervenes—of something conveyed and cognized by relatedness. Looking back now to condition (1) above, of the veridical character of perception, and remembering the various modes of the ingression of objects and the conditioning of events, it seems justified to rewrite that condition as follows: For perception to be veridical, it is essential that the given appearance be ascribed (by positing or by judgment) to an object actually situated in an event which is an active and generating condition of the event of this appearance; where event O is an active condition of event A just in case the character of A typically manifests a character of O; and O

<hr />

[22] *Knowledge*, p. 184.

is a generating condition of A just in case the character of A manifests a character of O transmitted through any series of events intervening between O and A.

I have here been a little more explicit than can fully be warranted from Whitehead's pages. But if this interpretation is correct, then the kind of account to be given of such matters as the star seen now though it no longer exists, and objects viewed in the mirror, is fairly obvious. The image of the star *is* seen now passing the cross-hair of the ocular lens of the telescope. For the further phenomena such as radio time-signals, that event is generative, and the consequent apprehension of the terrestrial time of day is veridical. But for the observer whose object of apprehension is a happening in the heavens (the star emitting the light) and not a happening in the situation of the telescope, the event in the locus of the telescope is a transmitting event, spatio-temporally intervening between the event where the star is and the percipient event. For valid perception of the star, what is cognized by adjective in looking through the telescope is correctly situated in that event which is generative for the whole series terminating in the event of this perception. Some character of the initial event is typically manifested through the series for which it is the generating event, and though typically further modified by the intervening active condition of the event in the telescope, still conditions the event of its perception in a manner constituting a manifestation of it to, or in, the percipient event.

If we should be inclined to rebel against the vocabulary of this type of explication and perhaps to consider explanation by reference to such categories as in some part verbal, then let us ask ourselves if substitution of the ambiguous terminology of causation would suit us better. It is 'causal nature' which is here dealt with in these categories of the relatedness of events in nature: cognition by relatedness, significance, and the ingression of objects into events. At least this Whiteheadian account does not end by confronting us with the debacle of causal knowledge in Humean skepticism, nor with the insoluble puzzle of correspondence between appearances in minds which have no genuine contact with external objects and objects having no actual ingress into minds. Nor does it, as less complex forms of direct realism characteristically do, leave us with no plausible or even possible explanation when confronted with the facts of delusive experience and error. Let us also remind ourselves of the methodological character of this account. It does not attempt—as epistemology since Descartes has persistently attempted—to explain how knowledge is possible by some 'deduction' of the validity of knowledge, starting from no premises of objective fact as given, or allowing itself only such initial premises as are vouchsafed to reason by the natural light. Instead it seeks to elicit those relations of factors of fact which are there to be elicited in the relatedness of nature, and are implicit in the deliverances of sense because the relation of an object perceived to a percipient event is one instance of the general relation objects have to events in general; and because the relation of a percipient event to other events is likewise homologous with relations which events within our apprehension have to one another. There is no 'problem of knowledge' here, because there is no inner experience which is an initial datum but not a datum of fact, and self-consciously may doubt its own status as knowledge. Fact is the terminus of sense-awareness; until there is sense-awareness, there is nothing to be doubted; and there is no better kind of fact to be called knowledge.

There is, however, the distinction of 'causal nature' from 'apparent nature,' as there is the correlative distinction of cognition by relatedness from cognition by adjective.

Natural science peculiarly concerns itself with knowledge by relatedness though, as Whitehead everywhere insists, it has no other data than the data of perception. Specifically, its business is to elicit those connections which obtain between continuities in the apparent character of events—continuities of sensed character, constitutive of objects ingredient in these events—and space-time relationships of the events exhibiting these sensed characters.

This long discussion brings us to the final conclusion that the concrete facts of nature are events exhibiting a certain structure in their mutual relations and certain characters of their own. The aim of science is to express the relations between their characters in terms of the mutual structural relations between the events thus characterized.[23]

Whitehead also phrases this by saying that the project of science is to explain apparent nature in terms of causal nature.

But science has also two further essential characteristics—essential to its going beyond our common and perceptual knowledge. First, it moves in the direction of simplicity and uniformity of the factors of fact which are the terms of its formulations, and toward a corresponding comprehensiveness in the laws expressing their relationships. And second, in this progression to simplicity, it is obliged to discard, as its recognized objects, the vaguely bounded and relatively impermanent

---

[23] *Nature*, pp. 167–68.

physical objects identifiable by their character as apparent, in favor of permanences of character identifiable through the *relationships* of such perceptual objects.

Physical objects fail to satisfy the requirements of science. They lack definiteness and permanence, and are not adequate for the purposes of explanation. Now the characters of their mutual relations disclose further permanences recognizable in events and among these are the scientific objects. . . . If we follow the route of the derivation of knowledge . . . molecules and electrons are the last stage in a series of abstractions. But a fact in nature has nothing to do with the logical derivation of concepts. The concepts represent our abstract intellectual apprehension of certain permanent characters of events, just as our perception of sense-objects is our awareness of qualities of nature resulting from the shifting relations of these characters.[24]

Whitehead is primarily concerned with the objects of *physical* science—quite naturally so since the presentation of fundamental principles of mathematical physics is one objective of this whole account; and what we here review provides the basis of that. The scientific objects here in mind are the physical entities affording approximation to these scientific ideals of the permanence of objects related and the comprehensiveness of laws expressing their relationships. Whitehead speaks of the electron as representing such a scientific object for that stage of science in which he wrote. But the analyses he gives are, characteristically, of scientific objects in an even more elemental sense— such entities as instants and mass-particles.

For the most part, the discussion of scientific objects belongs to that technical part and bearing of the content of the three books which is, perforce, omitted here. And already this essay runs beyond appropriate length. But one topic I shall further mention briefly because it concerns the epistemological question how the scientific formulation of laws in terms of imperceptible scientific objects can escape that status of the fictional and as-if to which Whitehead has objected, saying "If it is something else that you mean, for heaven's sake say it." This point is also the same one raised in another quotation above, in which it is acknowledged that 'nature at an instant' is *not* an entity in nature, but that if this concept is to have standing in a science which acknowledges no other basis than observable fact, it must be *definable in terms of* entities which *are* observable factors of fact and disclosed in deliverances of sense. An additional reason for some brief consideration of this problem is that the general procedure of Whitehead's attack upon

[24] *Knowledge*, pp. 187–88.

it—his Method of Extensive Abstraction—is one of his signal contributions to the theory of scientific knowledge.

Let us try to discover in advance the salient points here, by reference to the notion of instantaneousness already mentioned. The scientific concept of an instant is one which arises through the attempt to achieve a general, and generally adequate, manner of answering any question 'When?' Since such a question may relate to an event which happens anywhere, an appropriate form for the general type of answer will be to locate this event within a duration taken as a temporal slab of all nature. If this is the period of one day, all events so specified will be determined within twenty-four hours; and that degree of precision is adequate for many purposes. But for other purposes, it would be insufficiently precise. A more accurate determination will be to locate the event within a slice of that duration, an hour. As our questions call for greater and greater precision, we can determine progressively more precise answers by specifying a slice within the slice, and then a slice of that, and so on. We can determine the time of an event to the day, to the hour, to the minute, to the second, to the thousandth of a second. . . . But in order to allow for perfect generality, we cannot admit any limit to such progressively further steps in answering questions as to exact time. And if any protagonist of an operational theory of the meaning of concepts tells us that there is a limit nevertheless, set by the necessity of some actual physical operation for determining the answer, then we may reply to him that we (or scientists) are inventive people; and when we find a pressing need for greater precision in time-determination, we shall invent an operation and devise the apparatus to determine it. We shall so indicate that it is the meaningfulness of the question which is antecedent to the operational answer, and not the other way about.

What we so observe, however, is that our concept of 'when' will never be assured of the requisite generality if we stop with any specified degree of precision: with determination of the event as within any time-slice of nature, however small. So we proceed to the limit, with the scientific ideal of an instant—of a time-slice so thin that it has no time-extension. But now we have arrived at a paradox. Our successively specified time-slices, each thinner and included in the preceding ones, are still, however small, actual entities in nature. But the limit proceeded to is no longer an actual slice and is not a natural entity, though definable as just the limit approached by this series of approximations.

This crudely suggests the Method of Extensive Abstraction, by which Whitehead defines, first, entities which figure as elements in the 'geometry' of space-time—its 'levels,' 'rects,' 'puncts,' as well as durations and motions in their relativity to time-systems—and then proceeds to conceptual delimitation of entities more obviously connected with the scientific expression of physical facts in mathematical equations, such as 'event-particles' and 'mass-particles.'

Any adequate account of this Method of Extensive Abstraction could not be included here; that would require another essay of comparable length to this one.[25] Let us here confine ourselves to what directly concerns the epistemological status, in an account like Whitehead's, of those scientific 'idealities' which are thus definable as limits of some series of approximation the members of which are themselves identifiable as natural entities and factors of natural fact. Particularly we shall be interested in what concerns the paradox above, which in one or another form affects the definition of all scientific idealities. It is to resolution of that paradox that the method is addressed.

In understanding this, I think we may help ourselves out by reference to another matter which surely was in Whitehead's mind and could, perhaps, be regarded as a sort of mathematical model of the Method of Extensive Abstraction—namely, Dedekind's conception of the nature of numbers. Let us remind ourselves that, prior to Dedekind, the natural numbers in series, and the rational fractions, definable as pairs of natural numbers (a/b) in the dense or compact order of their fractional values, were recognized as numbers in good standing, intrinsically intelligible to mathematicians. Irrationals, however, did not share this intrinsic intelligibility, but had stood since the time of Pythagoras as a conceptual puzzle and mathematical anomaly. The illuminating discovery of Dedekind, since recognized by mathematicians as dispelling that puzzle, was that the irrationals, like $\sqrt{2}$, can be specified in terms of the series of rational numbers alone. They can be so specified since, for every rational number, there is a corresponding 'cut' in the total series of rationals, i.e., a specifiable manner of dividing the whole series into two segments such that (a) every member of the one segment precedes every member of the other segment,

---

[25] The best succinct outline of it which I know of (outside of Whitehead himself) is that of Professor Nathaniel Lawrence, "Whitehead's Method of Extensive Abstraction," *Philosophy of Science*, Vol. 17 (1950), pp. 142-63. Professor Lawrence there proceeds also to a discussion of matters affecting the point to which attention is directed here.

and (*b*) every member of the series belongs to one segment or the other. For any rational number, *a/b,* the corresponding cut divides the series into a fundamental (earlier) segment comprising all rationals preceding or 'less than' *a/b,* and the segment comprising the remainder of the series. No two such cuts correspond to the same rational number. But there is also such a 'cut' in the series of rationals corresponding to each irrational number—for $\sqrt{2}$, the division into a fundamental segment comprising all rational numbers whose square is less than 2, and a segment comprising all rationals the square of which exceeds 2. This cut, corresponding to $\sqrt{2}$, does not coincide with the cut corresponding to any rational number. For any rational number, *a/b,* there will be members of the fundamental segment approaching *a/b* as a limit which are not members of the series approaching $\sqrt{2}$, or *vice versa.* Each such cut is therefore uniquely determined by the series of rational numbers which approaches the limit specified by the cut. It thereupon becomes possible to *define* the real numbers, in series, as the *series of cuts* in the series of rational numbers. It is obvious that one can, alternatively, define the real numbers as the series of fundamental segments of the series of rationals. The logical structure of the concept is the same, or equivalent on all logical points, whether you speak of the limits approached—and *as* approached by the specified series—or whether you speak of the corresponding series which approaches the limit in question.

The one point to which I would direct attention—and the important point for analogy with Whitehead's method—is that if a series of natural entities (in terms of the analogy, some series of natural numbers) approaches some extra-natural and scientifically ideal entity (in terms of the analogy, an irrational number) as a limit, then you can, in the conception of this 'scientific object,' regard that particular series which approaches or converges to it as a limit as being in some sense logically equivalent to this limit which it so defines in the sense of uniquely determining.

This general mode of logical equivalence—the relation namely which holds between a series which so approaches a limit as to determine it uniquely, and the limit so approached—is one which, perhaps, awaits the attention of logicians and might profitably receive such attention. Whitehead's Method of Extensive Abstraction involves a further specification of this general type of relationship; in fact it involves more than one such further specification of it, as may be seen by examination of his particular applications of the method. If we do not altogether understand its logical character and import, at least the following point, which is the crucial one for Whitehead's theory, seems clear: the concept of the series approaching the limit gives us the concept of the limit, and there is no need to reify the limit itself as anything over and above those entities in terms of which it is so constituted for our thought.

It is in this sense of determining uniquely as a limit, that a series of durations, which are entities in nature, may define an instant, which is no natural entity, as that entity to which they converge.

> I will use the term 'moment' to mean 'all nature at an instant.' A moment . . . has no temporal extension [and hence is no natural entity], and is in this respect to be contrasted with a duration which has such extension. . . . A moment is a limit to which we approach as we confine attention to durations of minimum extension.[26]

In the context just quoted, Whitehead explains the main reason for thus progressing to limits and formulating our laws of mathematical physics in terms of such ideal scientific objects: "Natural relations among the ingredients of a duration gain in complexity as we consider durations of increasing temporal extension. Accordingly there is an approach to ideal simplicity as we approach an ideal diminution of extension."

If Whitehead speaks in conflicting ways about such scientific idealities (and I think he does)—sometimes speaking, as in quotations above, so as to exclude them from nature and natural fact, insisting only that they are definable in terms of natural entities, but sometimes making other statements which imply, if they do not assert, that they are nevertheless factual ingredients in nature—then I think the resolution of the puzzle so set is suggested in the following passage concerning durations and instants:

> It is evident that an abstractive set [of durations] as we pass along it [in the order from including to successively smaller and included] converges to the ideal of all nature with no temporal extension, namely, to the ideal of all nature at an instant. . . . Now the whole point of the procedure [the Method of Extensive Abstraction] is that the quantitative expressions of these natural properties do converge to limits though the abstractive set does not converge to any limiting duration. . . . Thus an abstractive set is effectively the entity meant when we consider an instant of time without temporal extension. . . . The difficulty is to express our meaning in terms of the immediate deliverances of sense-awareness, and I offer the above explanation as a complete solution to the problem.[27]

---

[26] *Nature*, p. 57.
[27] *Ibid.*, pp. 61–62.

That is to say: the set of natural entities (the finite durations considered in their order of diminishing extent) determines and defines and '*is effectively*' the ideal limit (the instant) so determined and defined; although the durations are all of them entities in nature, however small those later in the series may be, whereas the instant is an ideal entity which is nothing in nature.[28] What so determines and defines, is in some sense equivalent to and substitutable for what is determined and defined. (The correlative point may be observed in the 'mathematical model' I have suggested above.) What is scientifically said by speaking of the ideal limit could, in some manner or another (and allowing a sufficiently horrendous complexity of statement), be said in terms of the natural entities forming the abstractive set, in the order considered. And whatever is scientifically said in terms of the limit approximated to determines something correlative which can be said of natural entities in the degree of their approximation to it.

In this manner—which I have attempted to suggest though I have given no full and proper account of it—Whitehead forges the final link in the chain of connection between science and its ideally simple scientific objects on the one hand, and on the other the objects of perceptual knowledge and those deliverances of sense-awareness which are the ultimate and only possible basis of all knowledge of nature. Thus he demonstrates his thesis that the world of our sensible apprehension and common knowledge is likewise that same natural world of which science also gives account. Likewise, and at the same time, he establishes the mutual relevance of his most technical formulations of fundamental principles of physics in tensor equations, and his philosophical prolegomena which we have here reviewed and which provide both the basis for and the rigorously accurate interpretation of such technical and scientific formulations affording confirmation of them.

In conclusion, I should like to say two words concerning the relation between the conceptions set forth in these three books belonging to Whitehead's 'middle-period' and those presented in such later writings as *Process and Reality*. There is, first, that kind of difference which reflects his self-imposed restriction of topic in these earlier writings. He confines himself here to the metaphysics, or 'pan-physics,' of nature; and he defines nature by reference to sense-awareness, in contradistinction to all other modes of apprehension, including the evaluative and

---

[28] The set of durations successively considered do not, of course, literally converge to anything; they merely are what they are, and stand in those natural relations of inclusion in which they do. It is the quantitative measure of them which literally converges to zero as a limit. On this point compare *Nature*, p. 81.

any discernment of that more comprehensive and more concrete reality from which nature is an abstraction. So much, he says explicitly.

There is also, comparing later with earlier, much new vocabulary, making it difficult to determine whether what the earlier categories cover is still there, under some new designation or included in some different classification, or whether the older conceptions have been displaced, in whole or in part. That there is in the later an enrichment of his thinking, goes without saying. For a mind like Whitehead's that must be the case over any lapse of time.

It is, however, my opinion that divergence of his conceptions in these two periods could easily be exaggerated. I venture to think that there is little, if anything, basically important in the earlier, which is merely abandoned in the later. But what I would particularly suggest is that the prominence of conceptions, in *Process and Reality*, which cannot be found explicitly expressed in the three books we study, would hardly substantiate the inference that these later-formulated conceptions were simply not in his mind in the earlier period. There are frequent, though usually brief, references in the three books here discussed which would seem to indicate that it is the restriction of their topic which is the principal consideration affecting this kind of difference of the earlier from the later writings. The following are amongst them:

Nature is nothing else than the deliverance of sense-awareness.[29]

I also take the homogeneity of thought about nature as excluding any reference to moral or aesthetic values whose apprehension is vivid in proportion to self-conscious activity. The values of nature are perhaps the key to the metaphysical synthesis of existence. But such a synthesis is exactly what I am not attempting.[30]

Nature is an abstraction from something more concrete.[31]

Memory is an escape from transience. . . . memory is a disengagement of the mind from the mere passage of nature; for what has passed for nature has not passed for mind. . . . We may speculate, if we like, that this alliance of the passage of mind with the passage of nature arises from their both sharing in some ultimate character of passage which dominates all being.[32]

Finally there are the words with which Whitehead concludes the first of these three books, *The Principles of Natural Knowledge*:

[29] *Nature*, p. 185.
[30] *Ibid.*, p. 5.
[31] *Relativity*, p. 63.
[32] *Nature*, p. 68f.

So far as direct observation is concerned all that we know of the essential relations of life in nature is stated in two short poetic phrases. The obvious aspect by Tennyson,

> Blow, bugle, blow, set the wild echoes flying,
> And answer, echoes, answer, dying, dying, dying.

Namely, Bergson's élan vital and its relapse into matter. And Wordsworth with more depth,

> The music in my heart I bore,
> Long after it was heard no more.

Part II. Value Theory and Ethics

1. Judgments of Value and Judgments of Fact

The intended denotation of the phrase "judgments of value" will probably be clear. It is unlikely that you would choose any example as a judgment of value which would not be within what is here meant by the phrase. It will also be clear in what quarter of the universe of discourse "judgments of fact" are to be found: they are those whose truth or falsity is determinable by reference to some criterion or criteria which can be stated in eventually empirical terms. Any lack of clarity in the phrase will be due to problems as to what are and what are not such empirical criteria of truth and falsity, or problems concerning the application of such criteria. To clear away all such problems would preclude the possibility of going on to any further topic. But one or two comments may be made which have a bearing on what follows.

Questions concerning the relation between what are called "judgments of value" and judgments of fact are particularly in our minds just now because statements of intended normative significance would commonly be classified under judgments of value; and by those who so classify them, it would also quite commonly be held that some sort of truth or validity of normative statements must be possible if judgments of value in general are to have truth or falsity as anything more than psychological assertions about subjective feelings.

Both pragmatists and the adherents of the Vienna Circle are committed to the thesis that meaningful statements must be such as are verifiable, though at the present moment it is none too clear just what "verifiable" is here to mean. We become aware—I take it—that in putting forward this dictum, we bit off quite a sizable chunk, and some chewing will have to be done before it is swallowed. It is clear, however, that something suggested by "theoretical or intrinsic verifiability" rather than something narrower, suggested by "practical verifiability," would properly be in point. In *Language, Truth, and Logic*, Mr. Ayer has suggested the qualification that meaningful statements must be such that something empirically determinable can genuinely affect the *probability* of them. For example, electrons are perhaps not verifiable but their existence is genuinely probable. In a paper titled "Experience and Meaning"[1] I have made somewhat different suggestions toward rendering the criterion of "verifiability" intelligible and acceptable.

Read before the Harvard Philosophy Club, 1936.
[1] Pp. 258–76 below.—Eds.

This problem, however, is of a different order from that which is posed, for those who would accept normative statements as meaningful, by the contention of the Vienna Circle that such pronouncements of the normative have no theoretical but only "emotive" meaning. Protagonists and opponents of the objectivity of norms are in agreement here that if so-called normative statements assert nothing determinable beyond the state of feeling of the assertor, they are philosophically negligible—or at least fail to possess meaning in the fashion which is essential to the place they have been assigned by their defenders. This is, of course, only the current form of a perennial issue. Extreme naturalism or positivism has always maintained that the only significant account of ethics must be at bottom descriptive, psychological, or sociological; and their various opponents have always taken that thesis as a vitally important error.

At once, it should be said, however, that the repudiation of objective truth for normative statement does not, apparently, carry with it the repudiation of truth or falsity for value judgments in general, in the minds of the members of the Vienna Circle. In § 152 of *Logische Aufbau der Welt*, Professor Carnap says: "The constitution [or construction] of values out of certain immediate experiences [*Erlebnisse*], the 'value-experiences,' exhibits in many respects an analogy to the constitution of physical things out of 'perceptive experiences' (more exactly, out of sense-qualities). A few examples of such experiences may suffice as indications. Thus for the constitution of ethical value, we should have (amongst many others) experiences of conscience [*Gewissenserlebnisse*], experiences of duty or of responsibility, and the like." And he further says: "This signifies no psychologizing of values, any more than the constitution of physical objects out of sense qualities signifies a psychologizing of the physical. In realistic language, value is not itself merely experiential [*erlebnishaft*] or psychical, but subsists [*besteht*] independently of being experienced and merely becomes known in the experience (more exactly: in the value-feeling, whose intended object it is), just as the physical thing is not psychical, but subsists independently of perception and merely becomes known in the perception whose intended object it is."[2]

I must confess my inability to interpret this passage in a manner consonant with the general position of the Vienna Circle with respect to the normative—for example, in Schlick's *Problems of Ethics*. A part of the explanation doubtless lies in the next sentence: "Throughout,

[2] R. Carnap, *Der Logische Aufbau der Welt*, Berlin-Schlachtensee, 1928, pp. 203–4.

the constitution-theory does not make use of this realistic language, but is neutral with respect to the metaphysical components of realistic expressions." The whole context of the passage would also be in point; and I must not give the impression that Carnap commits himself here to the objectivity of ethical values. I simply do not know what the passage implies; but quite clearly that there is some truth about values which is not merely psychological, since constitution theory could not well be neutral as between a meaningful formulation and one which would be meaningless; nor construct out of *Erlebnisse* a concept which was empty of empirical denotation. At least it seems meant that values are independent of being felt or experienced in a manner analogous to that in which physical objects are independent of being perceived. It would seem to follow that predications of value are no more psychological or sociological in their genuine import than are predications of physical properties.

It may be thought, however, that the admission of empirical or matter-of-fact meaning for predications of value as a genus does not imply a similar meaning for normative pronouncements as a supposed species within this genus. Protagonists of the normative have, in general, supposed this implication to hold: they have believed that the objective truth or falsity of some normative propositions was essential to there being objective truth or falsity for value judgments of any sort—for their being anything more than statements expressive of subjective feeling, for their being materially equivalent to any proposition which would be true or false other than some empirically descriptive proposition of psychology or sociology.

The last issue very likely is here. But let us first examine some considerations having possible bearing on what are called value-judgments in general. The analogy which Carnap suggests to judgments of perception indicates an analysis of the meaning of value-judgments which seems to me obvious, and which gives to them as definite an empirical content as the judgments of other qualities.

Immediate goods, immediate values, are as directly and simply given in experience as immediate sense-qualities—the beauty of the rose as its form and color, the gratefulness of the summer night as its stillness and its blended shadows, the glory of the symphony as its pitches and its rhythms. In fact, the beauty of the rose *is* its form and color. We are reminded of an old argument of Berkeley's about the pain of the burning fire and the heat of it; we do not perceive two sensations, but one, which is at once its painfulness and its hotness. It is peculiarly evident with respect to the various goods and bads of given experience that they are not separate from the qualities of sense, but only separable by abstraction and construction. Mostly the predominantly "cognitive" interest seizes upon the more colorless elements called "sense," and these more poignant goods and bads are left behind and labeled "feeling" or "subjective." But, as given, the redness of the rose is as much feeling as the beauty of it, and is equally subjective.

As I have elsewhere tried to explain, attempted report of the immediate—whether of sense-quality or of value-quality—has the character sometimes labeled "subjective," partly because there are no words whose meaning is the purely denotative one of pointing to the quality merely as felt. If I say the rose is red, I imply something about the further experience of it; implicitly I predict that this now given character is a more or less permanent possibility for such further experience and also, e.g., that it will alter, with changed illumination, in certain ways and not in others. "Redness" as an objective quality of the rose is a whole complexus or series of given qualities in experience; no single immediate datum is sufficient to determine the presence of this objective quality. It is for this reason—that is, because of this complexity and temporal spread of what the objective predicate "red" as applied to the rose requires—that the assertion "The rose is red" is something verifiable, and requiring verification beyond the immediate given for establishment of its truth.

Because of this meaning of "red" as an asserted predicate, there is no word left to convey the immediate felt quality, no word which will clearly intend just this qualitative character as given without further implications; this is what I have meant by saying that the given is ineffable.

The same point may be put in another way. Language has other uses than this predominant one called "cognitive" by which words denote complexities or possible progressions of experience, and assertions made are implicitly predictive. In particular, language has what may be called its expressive use, where the interest is in felt quality of the immediate experience itself, as perhaps in lyric poetry. In this expressive meaning, the statement that something seen or imagined is red is shorn of its complications and predictive implications, and intends to convey simply the qualitative character of the experience as given. Language is mainly preëmpted to its cognitive, pragmatic, predictive uses; thus poets and other makers of expressive statements suffer the difficulty of speaking in a foreign tongue, and saying what they do not literally mean. Or perhaps—since we shall all recognize that the pragmatic or predictive and the expressive intent are normally present together, and most statements are so understood—it will be more accurate to say that pragmatic and predictive meanings are ordinarily emphasized: that they have been elaborately studied in logic, and made the subject of epistemological theory, while expressive meaning has been relatively neglected, and theories of meaning have been elaborated as if this expressive intent of language did not exist at all.

It should also be observed that the expressive statement—the report of the given as such—is not a judgment in any strict sense, and that it would probably best not be classed as "cognitive." There is no question, for the maker of it, of its truth or falsity: as intended, it either expresses what he knows to be true, or it is a lie and he knows it. Since it has no import beyond the present, it stands in no need of verification. One can say it is immediately verified, or that verification is irrelevant to its truth. But according as one chooses either the first or the second of these alternative statements, it should be noted that one chooses a slightly different meaning of verification. In the one case, it means or includes in its meaning as verification the relation of accord between denotative intent and that which directly meets or satisfies this intent; in the other case verification is confined to that concerning which there could conceivably be doubt or error, and hence does not apply to what is immediately and certainly determined in its truth or falsity, having no further implications.

The words "verification," "judgment," "cognition," "knowledge," as they are commonly used, are all [of] them ambiguous on this point, as to whether they do or do not include the relation between an intention to denote and what immediately and completely satisfies that intention. This ambiguity is responsible for much confusion in theories of knowledge and of meaning at the present time. In what follows, I shall use the words "judgment," "cognition," "knowledge" in the narrower meaning: the apprehension of the immediate is not—by itself and without prediction of anything further—a case of knowledge; the formulation or report of the immediate is not a judgment, since there is nothing which could be in doubt and no possibility of error.

But it would be highly paradoxical to say that such expressive statements are not true or false. And it would be at least unfortunate to use the word "verification" so narrowly as to exclude the assurance of accord between such expressive statements or formulations of the immediate and what satisfies their denotative intent. Obviously this is so, because all verification of any statement must come about eventually through determination of such accord in *some* experience or experiences which will be immediate when such verification takes place. And if the formulations of such accord cannot be true or false, then the ordinary cognitive and predictive judgment must be verified, eventually, by what are not themselves cases of verification. And if "truth" and "falsity" do not apply to formulations of the immediate, then either predictive statements never can be verified or it will be impossible to state what would verify them, because the formulation of what would verify them must consist of statements which will never be either true or false.

I shall, then, speak of expressive statements as true or false, with the meaning indicated—accord between their denotative intent and that which is presented, or the absence of such accord. And I shall include the assurance of such accord in the meaning of "verification," although verifications of this type are such as there could be no doubt about.

It will still be true, of course, that statements spoken of as verifi*able* will ordinarily be such as are predictive and cognitive, and not expressive, since it is rather pointless to speak of anything as verifiable whose truth or falsity is immediately and certainly verified.

If you permit the suggested use of the terms in question, we have then the result that there is a class of apprehensions, obviously empirical and obviously indispensable to any empirical knowledge, which nevertheless are not themselves cases of cognition, and the formulations of them are not statements of any judgment, although, without their use, the meaning of an empirical judgment could not be stated, and they are ultimate constituents in which the explication of all empirically meaningful statements must terminate.

A particular point of this is that, with respect to such considerations, there is no essential difference between the redness of the rose and the beauty of it, between sense-qualities and value-qualities. If it should be thought that value-predications are subjective or ineffable or merely expressive and not meaningful or not verifiable statements for such reasons, it needs to be pointed out that predications of objective sense-properties and other matters of fact have their meaning, and can have meaning only, in terms of constituents which are subject to precisely the same limitations. And if it be supposed that the contrast is between expressive statements and those whose meaning is empirical, it seems clear that a more palpable blunder in analysis would be hard to find.

The analogy between value-qualities and sense-qualities further indicates a transition from merely immediate apprehension and merely expressive formulations to cognitive judgments and verifiable, predictive propositions—in the one case as in the other. When I say the rose is red, I mean more than the report of its immediately given and ineffable sense-quality, because I imply possibilities of further experience, the accrual of which would verify the truth of my assertion. Thus my statement is of an objective property and represents a genuine judgment. Similarly, when I say that the rose is beautiful, I mean more (or may mean more) than the report of its immediately given and ineffable value-quality, because I imply possibilities of further experience, which by having such and such value-aspects or qualia, and not other characters of experience, would verify the truth of my statement. Thus my assertion is of an objective value-property and represents a genuine value-judgment. There is a difference, perhaps, in the statistical incidence of the objective and cognitive meaning, as against the merely expressive meaning, in the case of sense-qualities and value-qualities. Value-predications may be somewhat more frequently intended in the expressive sense rather than the cognitive. But if so, that probably signifies nothing more important than the necessity of preponderant attention in life to sense-qualities, and the regrettably incidental character of our interest in the value-aspect of experience. At least, there is no reason here for denying the possibility of objective meaning in the case of value-predications.

There is a further difference which commonly distinguishes our intent in the two cases. If I address to you some "matter of fact" statement about the redness of the rose, my interests of communication will probably be satisfied by certain results of my statement upon your observable behavior. If when I ask the florist for red roses, he gives me the kind I want, my interest of communication is satisfied, whether red things look to him the way they do to me or whether by some idiosyncrasy of sense apparatus the immediate and ineffable quality he apprehends in red things is quite different from what I see. But if I address to you some statement about the beauty of the rose, my interest of communication will probably not be satisfied by results in terms of your behavior alone. If by some idiosyncrasy you do not find the continuing possibility of that same satisfaction of immediate experience which I intend by "beauty," then although you apply the term to the same general class of things, and although you may smile, applaud, and assume postures of gratification in presence of things I call beautiful, my interest of communication will probably be defeated, and if I think you understand my meaning and share my judgment, I shall be deceived.

This will be the case because the characteristic interest in apprehensions of sense-qualities or "matters of fact" is practical, pragmatic—that is, not an interest in the quality apprehended for its own sake, but an interest in it as an instrument toward something else, and for guiding action to that further end. By contrast, the interest in value-qualities is characteristically for its own sake : in fact, this direct answering to an interest and to purpose is at least one criterion of the classification of any quality as a value-quality.

On account of this difference in characteristic interest in the two cases, it is reasonable to take community of behavior as the criterion of common or intersubjective meaning in the case of the purely pragmatic, the scientific, and so on, because the principal purpose of communication will be cooperation in action. The communication of value-judgments may, oftentimes, be similarly pragmatic in intent and directed primarily to cooperative behavior, since many, perhaps most, values are extrinsic rather than intrinsic. But so far as the value in question is intrinsic and the purpose of communication concerns this quality as intrinsic, the interest in communication concerns some possible coincidence or similarity of immediately felt experiences (or experiences which may be had) for those between whom such communication takes place.

We arrive here at an end-point of reasonable argument. There is no law against defining intersubjective value-meanings by reference to community of behavior. But one who does so is merely talking about something else, and begging a question by a dictum about language. Dogmatism of definition is just a little worse in philosophy than dogmatic metaphysical assertion, though it is much harder to avoid, because it requires not merely logical clarity and precision but precision and clarity about the locus of the really vital issues. So far as the restriction of intersubjective meanings to exclusively behavior significance is based upon a definite theory and not a mere choice of method, I should obviously not have time for any sufficient consideration here.

The connection of this last point with the meaning of normative pronouncements will be obvious. The word "objective" has two quite different meanings, though most frequently these two coincide in the division they effect, of items considered, into "subjective" and "objective." For one of these two meanings, that is "objective" which belongs to or pertains to concrete objects, and that is "subjective" which varies with states of mind. To elicit the precise criteria of subjective and objective in this common meaning is a matter of some complexity. I should be glad to avoid it here, merely suggesting seen red in given experience is subjective as against the red color of the object, which is objective. The former is identified, from one to another experience, by inspection of its qualitative character as given ; the other, by reference to generalizations as to a uniformity of alteration from one to another experience—as red alters in its given quality with changed illumination. The other meaning of "objective" is what Carnap calls "intersubjective"—the same for all persons in question. If the meaning of this last phrase terminates in community or consonance of behavior, then objectivity in the second sense, "intersubjectivity," is a complex instance of objectivity in the first sense, which may be called "first-person objectivity."

I have suggested that the intended meaning of value-predications, taken as valid for, let us say, all rational subjects (I use that phrase merely because its historical connotation will tell you what I mean to denote) is such that the behavior of others is not, by itself, a sufficient criterion of it. To take that as such a sufficient criterion of objective value is to define value so that normative statements become meaningless. But if, when I pronounce a thing to be good, or give it any more specific value-predicate, my intention is such that I should take my pronouncement to be in error if, regardless of the behavior of others, their immediate experience in the presence of the object is not similar to mine in the respect in question (and I assert that to be my meaning, and ask you to verify that it is contained in yours), then the truth of a value-predication requires a statable kind of community in the quality with which the thing in question is experienced, or may be experienced, by the generality of persons.

(It may be noted that it does not require a simple and direct coincidence of immediate experience of the object in its value quality—any more than intersubjective roundness of the penny requires that we all see it alike. It means—let us say for brevity—the possibility of seeing it alike under appropriate conditions.)

If the objectivity of value-predications, in the sense of intersubjectivity, has this meaning which I suggest, then while it is by no means the case that this solves all basic problems about normative pronouncements, it affords plain suggestions for the solution of some of them. Values which are intrinsic or final, and hold good for all subjects, have one requisite character of norms. The predication of such intersubjective value characters has normative significance if it be granted that the intrinsically and intersubjectively valuable ought to be realized. I suggest that this last statement is a tautology, contained in the meaning of the word "ought." If this is true to the meaning of "ought" in use, then clearly questions of oughtness are, so far, questions of objective fact.

It will, perhaps, avoid confusion of issues if we note that the word "normative" as commonly used imports an entirely different problem than this one of the ultimate and interpersonal community of values.

Some values are competitive in their incidence in things; some goods are such that their possession or realization by some persons militates against their possession or like realization by others. The problem of composing this situation precipitates the question "What claim of respect does the possible realization of value for others lay upon my purposes directed to realization of value for myself?" This may be thought to be the distinctive question of ethics. But I hope that it is plausible without discussion that this is a different question from the one toward which the above suggestions are offered—which relates to the problem, or groups of problems, associated with the traditional phrase "the summum bonum."

The first objection likely to be raised to this suggested analysis will—I suppose—be directed against the proposed intersubjective meaning of value-predications. It will be said that this admits of no test, and that value-predications, so intended, must therefore be meaningless. This objection, I must protest, springs from a dogma of definition—a dogmatically taken meaning of meaning, which arbitrarily excludes what I believe to be an essential part of the actual intention of value-predications. Rather little can be put forward toward settling a question of that sort.

But perhaps something can be done. I have elsewhere spoken of such meanings, which include reference to the immediate quality of experience in other minds, as not subject to verification but nevertheless subject to meaningful postulation. The terms of such postulate, I have thought, possess concrete denotation; and that is all which is really essential. It is that which distinguishes the "intrinsically verifiable" (but perhaps not practically verifiable) from the intrinsically unverifiable—and which lends plausibility to the dictum that the meaningful must be verifiable.

But perhaps one need not admit so much. The quality of experience in another mind can be "tested" if one be willing to retreat, as Mr. Ayer has done, to the position that assertions have meaning insofar as their *probability* may be affected by the empirical determining. Mr. Ayer has electrons in mind; and the analogy may be useful. The existence and conceived character of electrons is an hypothesis whose probability is affected by the experiments which verify consequences of it. Evidently Mr. Ayer would not be willing to say that the electron merely *is* or *means* the totality of this verifying and directly observable behavior of molar masses.

In view of the extraordinarily extended and thoroughly verified analogy of humans in other respects, and of the fact that all inductive reasoning is at bottom analogical, perhaps the hypothesis of like immediate experience associated with like behavior is one whose probability is genuinely affected by directly observed facts of behavior. But the experience which is the subject of this hypothesis is not to be *identified* with this behavior any more than the electron is to be identified with the behavior of molar masses observed in the laboratory.

I feel much surer of what I *do* mean when I attempt to communicate judgments of objective value to you than I do about this last point that such meaning can be assimilated to the "verifiable" in the sense of partially verifiable and hence probable hypothesis. I feel sure of what I *do* mean; and if you urge that I ought not to entertain this meaning because it is inconsistent, I might conceivably reply that I can be inconsistent if I want to. Apart from some appeal to the normative, I don't know what you could well do about that, unless you thought it properly subject to corporal punishment. And you would not, of course, attempt to *justify* such punishment. You would be consistent and admit it was only the expression of your feeling of exasperation.

2. The Objectivity of Value Judgments

What I ought to present is a clear thesis on a restricted topic: decisive argument of a sharply defined issue. Instead I have taken a large topic; and what I should like to say about it cannot be put precisely in a short statement. In broad terms it is this: that value-judgments represent a form of empirical knowledge, and that in general they are objective in the same sense, or senses, that other empirical apprehensions are.

This, of course, runs counter to many prevalent conceptions. The value-character of things is often called a tertiary quality. Evaluations are reduced to mere liking and disliking: to personal reactions rather than apprehension of anything objective and factual. Value affirmations are classed as expressive or hortatory, regarded as emotive, and as making no verified or verifiable assertion of any matter of fact whatever.

The mistake I would attribute to such current notions lies not so much in their ascribing subjective significance to some value apprehensions and some value-statements, as in the failure to observe the exactly parallel significance in the case of physical statements and the apprehension of other characters than value. The difference is not between physics and ethics, or between space-time properties and value qualities, but between different types of apprehension and different significances of empirical assertion which may be observed in any field and for any type of subject matter. In order to understand statements about value, it will be necessary to give attention to the main types of empirical affirmations in general.

There are, I take it, three main types of empirical statement: three different meanings which assertions based upon experience may have. First, there are reports of the directly presented, of the immediate and given content of experience—statements of appearances, of what I see or hear or feel, without regard to any question about the real object supposed to cause these appearances or its objectively real properties. We do not often make such statements: there is seldom any need to, since what they would formulate is something directly and indubitably present and needing no verbal surrogate. On the few occasions when we wish to make them, we find it very difficult to do so; language is not devised for that kind of expression, but at once suggests the ob-

Read before the Brown University Philosophy Club, 1941.

jective fact which, in such a case, we do not wish to assert. We have to use locutions—"looks like," "feels like," "seems to be"—in order to indicate an intention to assert only what is given or directly appears. Those who approach the problems of knowledge by way of linguistic analysis might well be discouraged from supposing there are any such *Protokolsätze*. But such linguistic difficulties of formulation have nothing to do with the thing itself which we attempt to formulate. From the point of view of cognition, such direct apprehensions of the given are fundamental: they represent our absolute data, our only unqualified certainties in the realm of the empirical. It is only by them that any basis is provided for empirical belief, and it is only through them that such beliefs can be corroborated. Empirical knowledge is based on experience, and if experience itself is not certain, then all is lost and there is no hope.

Mr. Moore thinks there are *other* empirical certainties over and above those certainties of the merely given—for instance, that here is a sheet of white paper. But I think Mr. Moore is optimistic. If the President of the United States should thrust something like this toward Mr. Moore and offer to bet him the United States Navy for England against an embargo on further export of arms that it isn't a sheet of paper, I think Mr. Moore would want a second look or reach out and feel of it before taking the bet. What is certain is an appearance you and I are now seeing, even though if we try to express just that, we are likely to get it mixed up with an inference we naturally make from what we see.

I shall refer to such formulations of the directly and indubitably given as "expressive statements." What is expressed by them is hardly judgment; what is given need not be judged, and it is doubtful if they ought to be called "knowledge" if we separate them from all inference. But they are true or false—*true* if we are not telling lies.

Second, there are predictions which we make, on the occasion of a given presentation, of some further possible passage of experience. At the present moment I am predicting that when I look back at this, I shall see some more ink-marks on it, and that it won't go pop and disappear in smoke. Otherwise I should behave differently, and I shouldn't call it a piece of paper. Ordinarily such predictions have to be hypothetical in form because there is little or nothing of my future experience which I can predict categorically. In particular, it depends on my action. If I look below where I am just now looking, I shall see the next sentence—I hope. If I shut my eyes, however, I won't. Such predictions of further possibilities of experience, conditional upon action,

I shall call "terminating" judgments. Unlike merely expressive statements of sense-data, they are genuinely judgments because one can be in error about them. And they are "terminating" in the sense that what they affirm is decisively and completely verifiable.

Third, there are ordinary affirmations about objective realities—that so and so exists, that some object has a certain property. Also there are general statements about a class of things, based on these. These affirmations of objective reality are not reducible to any report of the directly observed, as we have seen. Even in the simplest case, they say more. Presumably they say nothing, however, which is not intrinsically verifiable. What they say is testable, theoretically, in further experience—if we act so as to make the test. They *imply*, then, terminating judgments. It is by way of such implications alone that they are verifiable. But *how many* such further testable eventualities of experience do they imply? Obviously, as many as will be true if this objective assertion is true. And that number is unlimited. For one reason, because no matter how many tests of this truth have been made, another test of some sort will always be possible. Thus the statement, for example, that this piece of paper is really rectangular contains in the meaning of it nothing that can't be put to the test; but it is capable of test in so many different ways, and will be testable over so long a period of time, that if we think of all the variety of possible experience which the assertion of it implicitly predicts we shall see that the complete test of all that it implies could never be finished. For this reason, I shall call such ordinary judgments of objective fact "non-terminating judgments." They have a significance which, though exclusively empirical, is empirically inexhaustible. For this same reason also they are, at any given time, theoretically probable only and not certain. Experience to date may have given us reason to believe them, but not 100 per cent assurance of their truth.

If you take the simplest kind of statement which we are likely to make when a thing is presented to us, such as "That is red," "This thing is hard," you may well be put to it to know which one of these three possible significations it is intended to have. Is it intended merely to report a mode of appearance: "That *looks* red to me now," "This *feels* hard"? Or to make prediction of a particular possible experience: "If I place that alongside the first band of the spectrum, the two will look alike," "If I poke that vigorously, it will hurt my finger"? Or does it mean this last kind of thing but also a whole lot more: "If this thing is submitted to all the thousand and one tests which could be made of red-color, or of hardness, in an object, it will satisfy them all"? Ordinarily the question which of these meanings is intended would not be raised or even thought of; but if it should be asked, "What is required in order that the statement be true?" then it would have to be raised, because clearly the answer would be quite different in the three cases. And if the question should be, "Does the statement assert something subjective or something objective?" then also these meanings must be distinguished, and the answer would depend upon which type of meaning is in question.

Now precisely this consideration is the fundamentally important one if it be asked whether what value-predications assert is something subjective or something objective. Because value-statements, like other empirical assertions, may be any one of these three types. There are, first, expressive statements of a value-quality found in the directly experienced. One who says at the concert, "This is good," or makes a similar remark at table, is presumably reporting a directly experienced character of the sensuously presented as such. He is making an expressive statement of a value datum. In that meaning, his statement is of no different import than if he said, "I like this" or "I am enjoying this." But he may, of course, have a quite different intention: he may mean to assert that the musical composition being played has the qualities of counterpoint, harmony, and so on, which make it a permanently valuable contribution to our culture; or to assert that the steak he is engaged with contains a certain combination of protein, mineral salts, etc., and a certain physical structure, characteristic of nourishing meat well-cooked. In this latter case, the immediately experienced value quality or datum—its good tastingness—is very likely the empirical cue to his judgment, but what is judged is not this directly apprehended character of the given—that requires no judgment—but an objective property comparable to the real roundness of his plate. Or in the case of the music, if it be intended to assert its permanently verifiable excellence, then the hearer's immediately experienced enjoyment may be the basis of his judgment, but what is judged is something which will require the verdict of musical history for its full assurance.

Directly experienced goodness, like apparent redness or felt hardness, may be made the matter of report on its own account. A value-predication may thus intend assertion of nothing beyond the apparent quality of what appears. In that case, it is an expressive statement: one which is, for the maker of it, self-verifying, in the only sense in which it could be called "verifiable" at all. Such a statement is true or false (since we can tell lies about our immediate enjoyments and discomforts), but for the maker of it it is subject to no possible error—except linguistic error in the words chosen to express it. The apprehension it expresses is a matter of complete certainty; and by the same token it is not a judgment and hardly to be classed as knowledge in the strict sense of the word.

There are also evaluations which express terminating judgments: the prediction that, under given circumstances, experience of felt goodness (or badness) will accrue. Belief that a certain act will result in enjoyment, or in pain, is such a terminating judgment. Such beliefs may be put to the test by adopting the mode of action in question, and are then decisively and completely verified or decisively found false. Being predictive, and subject to possible error, they represent a form of knowledge.

Finally there is the third and most important type of value-predication, which means the ascription of the objective property of being valuable to an object, event, state of affairs, or other existent entity. Such objective judgments of value are quite complex in meaning. They are also of various types—judgments of aesthetic quality, or of moral worth, or of utility. But they all possess the common character of being what I have called non-terminating judgments. In that respect they are no different from judgments of the real color of a thing, or of shape, or of hardness, or of any other objective property.

Also, it is of first importance to consider the relation of such objective value judgments to value-predications of the terminating sort: to predictions of the possibility of direct experience of felt goodness. As we saw in the case of other objective judgments—for example that an object is red or is rectangular—what it means becomes evident if we consider how the truth of it could be tested, how it would be corroborated. Any possible such confirmation must come down to something discoverable in direct experience, under some specifiable conditions. It must come down to some terminating judgment or other: "If one does so and so, then such and such an eventuation of experience will result." That is the only determinable kind of difference, which anybody can discover, that the truth of any objective statement can make. And there is nothing in the meaning of such an objective empirical statement beyond just such discoverable differences that its being true will make or *could* make, in the experience of somebody. If there should be anything more, then that more would make no conceivably testable difference to anybody, and if the supposition of it should be meaningful, at least it certainly would not be empirical.[1]

Now in the case of objective judgments that a thing has genuine value, what is it that we mean which would thus make a conceivable and testable difference to somebody? It is—Is it not?—that under certain circumstances, this thing would give enjoyment to somebody, would bring felt satisfaction, would result in some goodness found in his direct experience. Or am I wrong; and do we call a thing good although under no thinkable circumstances could anyone ever enjoy it, or find any satisfaction in it, or experience any felt goodness which he might not equally find if it had never existed? Assertion of the objective property of being valuable means—I take it—precisely this: that existence of the thing in question is capable of contributing some directly findable goodness to somebody's experience; and it means nothing more or different from that. The only thing that is finally and absolutely good in itself is that someone should have a satisfactory or gratifying experience or be rid of one which is unsatisfactory or painful. All other things whatever that are good at all are good because they are *good for* that—good because they are capable of contributing positive felt value to somebody's experience of life.

But this—be it noted—is quite different from that Protagorean relativism which consists in saying that that is good which you like or enjoy, and that is bad which you don't. One should remember that Protagoras would also say that a thing is red or rectangular if it *looks* that way to you, and otherwise it isn't. And to say that potentiality in a thing for producing satisfaction in experience is its objective goodness is no more to be confused with such subjectivism than is, for example, the statement that what it means to say that a thing is rectangular is that it will satisfy all the tests we can make of rectangularity in direct experience. No: this is to say only that the assertion that a thing has objective value is one which can be tested; and the kind of result which means a positive result of such test is the disclosure in direct experience of some felt goodness.

One should also observe that this conception of objective value does not mean that the value of a thing consists in its being liked or being

---

[1] Lewis made this notation in the margin of the manuscript: "The totality of such terminating judgments, about possible experience, which an objective statement implies, seems beyond limit, as we have seen. No one of them, or set of them, exhausts its meanings. Nevertheless there is nothing different in kind from these [terminating judgments], which it [an objective statement] signifies."—Eds.

desired. One can like what is bad and dislike what is good, just as one can mistake a trapezoid or rhomboid for a rectangle and think a really rectangular thing is rhomboidal in shape. One can—as we say—*see* a rectangle that way; and equally one can experience a thing in a manner which is deceptive as to its actual value-quality. One can make a mistake in judging that a thing will contribute positively to experience. One can desire a thing, believing it will be productive of felt satisfaction, and find that one has made a bad blunder.

Perhaps we ought also to remark that although what it means to say that a thing has the objective property of goodness is that it possesses potentiality for experience of felt goodness, still this objective property in a thing may be evidenced in other ways—just as one may find evidence that a thing is really red or rectangular in other ways than by seeing it so. For example, I may believe that my neighbor is a good musician on account of the way he persists in playing cadenzas and difficult passages, though this does not contribute to my enjoyment. Or we may confirm the good cutting quality of an edged-tool by the misadventure of cutting ourselves. But it is not this possibility of cutting ourselves which constitutes its goodness: if it could be so devised as to minimize or remove this possibility of mishaps, it would be even better. What makes it good is the possibility of cutting out beautiful or otherwise desirable things with it.

In fact, we can summarize the conception of value here put forward by saying that the only kind of thing having value in the ultimate sense, in and for itself, is the realization of positive good in experience; all else that is valuable at all possesses its value only by being instrumental to or contributory to such realization of immediate goodness. The immediately good and immediately bad are simply found. In the predication of them there can be no possibility of error, because like seen redness or felt hardness, they belong to the realm of appearance. As Santayana would say, they characterize essences; as Prall would say, they belong to the aesthetic surface. With respect to what is thus immediate or apparent or given, there is no distinction between *esse* and *percipi*. To seem to be immediately enjoyable or painful is to be immediately enjoyable or painful. Goodness or badness as an objective property in a thing is quite different; concerning these, we can and frequently do make mistakes. Nevertheless such objective goodness or badness in things is merely utilitarian; the judgment of it is simply the judgment of potentialities in the thing for directly experienced satisfaction or dissatisfaction.

This is the kind of view of the nature of value which has frequently been called subjectivistic. But if that epithet is meant to imply some kind of error, then I should be minded to ask, first of all, whether, subjectivistic or not, it is a correct account of what we mean when we say a thing has value or disvalue. And for the rest, I would point to the extended parallel which obtains between judgments of value, so described, and judgment of other properties. To attribute any property whatever to a thing means—I should suppose—to predicate something which is verifiable. But no ascription whatever is verifiable in any other manner than by *some* eventual finding in direct experience—by reference to something given or to be given, something which appears or is found, some disclosure which is immediate. There is no other kind of corroboration for any empirical statement or belief. Even physical science can find no other basis for its pronouncements nor any other kind of corroboration for what it asserts as true. The basal statements for empirical belief of any sort can be nothing other than expressive statements of the findings of direct apprehension. If such expressive statements are to be repudiated as non-significant, or as lacking some particular and desirable kind of significance, then that will—I feel sure—prove as disastrous in its implications for physics and the importance of statements made by scientists as it will for ethics or for the statements made by aestheticians.

Furthermore, if this conception of the nature of value should seem to suggest that there is no real goodness or badness in things, but that the value ascribed is merely in the beholder or appreciator, then I believe that careful consideration should show that this suggestion is not really borne out. A thing is constituted valuable by relation to actual or possible experience, and the felt goodness or badness of it. But it does not follow from this that the value or disvalue predicated is in the experience, or the subject only, and not in the thing. To draw that inference is merely bad logic. It is also true, for example, that a father is constituted a father only by relation to a child. But it does not follow that the property of fatherhood is not really in the father but in the child. If the objective value of a thing belongs to it only by relation to experience, or possible experience, still this objective value is a property of the object and not of any experience or subject of experience to which it is thus related.

The trouble here is not one peculiar to value-theory but one which affects our conception of empirical knowledge in general. It is a hangover of that form of representationalism characteristic of commonsense dualism; the notion namely that whatever can be labeled 'appearance,' 'sense-datum,' etc., is in the mind and subjective, in a sense which precludes our saying that it is also in the object. In the case of illusion or error, for example, common sense representationalism says that what is apprehended is merely an appearance or idea in the mind, which corresponds to nothing in the object. This is not so much incorrect as pointless. It is merely a way of disposing verbally of a difficulty —a comfortable way because it has become habitual, but one which has no explanatory value whatever. Because, as Berkeley pointed out, the criterion of being correct in our knowledge or being in error which this representationalist conception offers is one that nobody could ever make use of. If we are deceived by an appearance, we can't find that out by comparing the appearance or idea in the mind with an object that never can be inside the mind. We can only compare one idea or presentation with others. And a sensible and useful theory should tell us just how we do that: what the genuinely *discoverable* difference is between knowing a fact or a real object and being deceived by an appearance.

Appearances, sense-data, the content of given experience, are neither subjective nor objective; or they are equally both. We may interpret such given content by viewing it in either of two contexts: we may view it in relation to a stream of consciousness, the history of a mind, a context of associated ideas, or in relations of space-time contiguity. Sometimes the interpretation which views the given content in its mental context is the one which has explanatory value; sometimes the useful explanation is by reference to the space-time context. But all presentations equally have a context of both kinds—even in the case of illusion, though there the peculiarly significant space-time context is likely to be found in the subject's sense organs or nervous system. And as between these two kinds of context, the given is, in its own nature as given, neutral. To call it *either* subjective or objective is an afterthought, an interpretation, and not a reading of its character as appearance.

And in any case, there is nothing here which affects the value-quality of the directly presented differently than any other such as seen redness or felt hardness. There is nothing in any such consideration which implies a subjective nature in the property of being good or bad any more than in the property of being red or hard.

We should also observe that, on this conception, although the objective value of a thing is constituted by its potentialities for realization of immediate felt value, still such objective value is a character which the thing has—if it has it at all—without reference to the question whether this potentiality for directly found goodness is realized in any actual experience or not. A saw, for example, is good only if it is useful for sawing. But if it were made and hung up in a toolshed and destroyed by fire before ever being used, there would be nothing in that to evidence that it wasn't a good saw.

The value of a sunset—to take a different kind of example—would be the beauty of it. And that which holds no potentiality for the immediate gratification of a beholder cannot be beautiful. But the pattern and symphony of colors in a sunset are properties it would have as much if it occurred over the desert of Sahara, with no eye to behold it, as if it occurred over San Francisco Bay and were the cynosure of ten thousand eyes. Its value is as objective as its colors or the shape of its patterns, and is in fact inseparable from these, being an intrinsic quality of the presentation-complex which they constitute. Or again: if some eye comes, at a given moment, to observe this previously unobserved sunset, it does not *become* beautiful at that instant when its potentialities for enjoyment are realized. We correctly say that this beauty of it is merely discovered.

To be sure, we might say that a sunset over San Francisco Bay is better than one over the Sahara, because more people could enjoy it, just as medicine in the house in an emergency is better than medicine in the drug-store. As has been observed, our ways of predicating value to things are really quite complex and various. Value statements of the same or similar verbal form have now one meaning, now a little different one; and it is necessary to be observant of such differences of meaning. The present case is an example. But a correct analysis of what such statements intend would show nothing here which is incompatible with what our common sense would lead us to say. It is better to have the medicine in the house; and it is better for a beautiful sunset to be where people can see it. But the medicine is just as good medicine in the drug-store, even if its being there prevents our using it. And the sunset is just as beautiful if it occurs over the Sahara where there is no eye to behold it.

In all this, however, it may be that I have not touched on that issue which—as it may seem to you—is the most important one of all when the question of objectivity or subjectivity of evaluations is raised. That is the question of community as between different persons. Our immediately felt or found values in the presence of the same things are— you will remind me—notably subject to individual difference. The potentialities for positive value experience to be found in things are very different for you and for me. On that score, you will say, the kind of conception I put forward deliberately accepts the notion that correct evaluation is relative to the individual and hence subjective.

If you so say, then I must at once admit your main premise—individual difference in immediately found value-quality. And that consideration calls for a good deal more to be said about it than there will be time here to say. But I might also call to your attention the fact that if you should make this objection, you are jumping to a conclusion—the conclusion namely that I should be minded to say: A correctly judges a thing to be good if he correctly believes that it contains potentialities for *his own* satisfaction or enjoyment, and incorrectly judges a thing to be good if he so judges on the ground that it contains potentialities for the satisfaction of B and C and D but not for himself. And—I might remind you—I haven't said anything about that important moral issue at all. There is no reason in what precedes why it is not open to one who holds the view I am suggesting to decide that a thing is truly good so far as it holds potentialities for direct satisfaction on the part of *anybody,* or of people in general, and to think that in deciding such a question, the speaker or the one who judges a value should count for no more than anybody else. That question is simply a further question, not so far touched upon.

What would be more directly to the point of the issue in hand would be to observe two things. My time is—or ought to be—about up, and I can only suggest them.

First, I would point out that *whichever* decision should be made about this issue I have called the moral issue, there need be no *misapprehension of fact* about it on the part of anybody. It would be, in one aspect, a merely verbal decision to use the word "good" or "valuable" in the basic sense to mean (1) "good for me" or (2) "good for people in general." It is obvious that, as a matter of fact, everybody does use such terms in *both* senses; and what we have here is—so far—merely an ambiguity of language. It is regrettable that we do not have different words for these two different meanings; and to argue which is the *correct* usage is pointless: both are correct if they are understood as meaning what the speaker intends by using them on any particular occasion. The rest is the moral question how the speaker ought to behave toward what is good for people in general but not good for him. That is a terribly important question; it is not a question of any *fact* with which a correct *understanding* about values is concerned.

Second, perhaps it is worthwhile to call attention to the fact that, on the point in question, the difference between value-quality and other qualities in things is easily exaggerated. Other qualities also are, as directly apprehended, affected by individual differences. Let me choose just one example—weight. You are, let us say, an athlete in good training, and I lack such muscular development and lead a sedentary life. If we both try to lift a cannon ball, the felt heft of it will be quite different to the two of us. Now mass—to which weight is nearly related—is a basic physical property. Weight ought to be a good example of an objective property if statements of physics are objective. And the point is that while lifting things and feeling the drag of them on our muscles is the commonest of all ways of experiencing weight, we don't trust it in making physical statements about weight. Instead we use scales. Why? Because it is so important that we should *agree* about the objective weight of things—about the pound of sugar you sell me for example. For that reason we choose to *define* weight in such wise that what is *called* the weight of a thing will be verifiable in a way which is not affected by our individual differences in *experiencing* weight. And my point here, briefly suggested, is this: if it were primarily important to *agree* upon the *value* of things as it is to agree upon the weight of things, we could easily set up an arbitrary standard of value like the one for weight which is implied in the use of scales and the tests of them according to the Bureau of Standards. There are some people who would like to set up a sort of Bureau of Standards in Washington for our values in general. But some of us do not care for that suggestion, because we think there is something more important here than getting around our individual differences in experience by passing a law. But that again is a moral question. The point is that the difference between the objective property of weight and the subjective property of value—if you choose to call it subjective—is not that experiences of value are affected by individual differences and experiences of weight are not. There is no greater community in the one case than in the other. The main difference, again, is merely verbal—a difference in the way we choose to use the word "weight" and the way we choose to use the word "value." So I would go so far as to suggest that if "objectivity" is to mean "community of judgment," and "subjectivity" the lack of it, then there is nothing in a candid examination of the facts of experience which would bear out the notion that physical qualities of things are any more objective than value-qualities. We merely use physics-words customarily in a more objectivistic sense, value-words with a more subjectivistic connotation. And that fact of verbal usage could be remedied if it were important or desirable to change it.

Furthermore, the *main* point concerning correctness or incorrectness of judgment is the question of verifiability. Community is important as a test of knowledge mainly because we can so often assure or correct our judgments by appeal to the reports of others. But the final test of judgment is prediction and verification. And so far as "objectivity" means verifiability, these questions concerning the community of valuation, or the lack of it, are not the most important ones. In the sense of verifiability at least, value judgments are either correct or incorrect, and as objective as any that we make.

3. The Empirical Basis of Value Judgments

I would like to begin with brief reference to matters which lie outside my topic in order to point out the reasons why, as it seems to me, they are not possible of discussion at one and the same time with questions of the general theory of values. Most discussions of the thesis I have ventured to put forward concerning values—most of those I have seen —turn out to be discussions of basic questions of ethics. I am vitally interested in those questions, but I think that some solution of problems of the general theory of values must be antecedent. And moral goodness is *sui generis*, connoting 'right,' 'imperative,' 'obligatory.'

It is even unfortunate to speak of right acts and right intentions as merely good, because of the quite distinctive criteria according to which moral intentions and moral acts and moral desert must be judged. An act is morally right if it springs from conviction of the doer that he ought to do it. Now somewhere in the world there doubtless is a man who is convinced that he ought to destroy all humanity with atom bombs, because we have sinned in the sight of God and there is no health in us. Let us hope this gentleman is in some institution ; but wherever he is, he is a completely moral man if and only if he is doing his best to conform his behavior to this conviction which he has. I take it that any sound ethics must recognize his moral praiseworthiness if he is thus firmly minded to do the right as it is given him to see the right. But it is, I hope, also permitted us to deplore his judgment of values.

There is this other kind of question about what he feels morally bound to attempt—the question, namely, whether accomplishment of the contemplated action will or would help to make the lives of those affected the kind of lives they will find it satisfying to live. And this second question is one of empirical facts, of cause and effect relationships. The two questions are intimately related because no one can decide what it is that he ought to do without considering the value-effects, to himself and others, of the alternatives of action between which he must decide. I am supposing that the peculiarly *moral* problem does not even arise unless or until one contemplates the value-consequences,

---

Read before the Yale Philosophy Club, 1950.

to himself and others, of whatever act may be in question. But any honest mistake one makes in this judgment of values will be of no effect upon the moral quality of his decision to do or not to do. If, however, having exercised his best judgment on this question of empirical fact, he then chooses that course of conduct which will bring most satisfaction to himself, though its consequences will be devastating to others, and defends himself by advancing egoism as the justified principle of such decision to do or not to do, then we have a question of moral rightness. The foresight of value-consequences does not settle that; and no decision regarding that external problem will make the smallest difference to this other question of what in fact the value-consequences of the proposed course of conduct will be.

I wish to set off these two questions from one another for two reasons: first, because a frequent motive for resisting the conclusion that value-judgments are questions of empirical fact is, I think, preoccupation with goodness in this sense which is peculiar to the moral. Those amongst my critics whose attitude I applaud and whose opinions I respect are most often those who seem to fear that recognizing value-judgments to be judgments of empirical fact will somehow prejudice recognition of the independence of the moral imperative from anything empirical and the autonomy of basic moral principles. If this conception that value-judgments are empirical does in fact have this consequence they seem to fear, then so far as I am concerned, it is this theory of values which must be given up, because the autonomy of moral principle cannot rationally be denied. But second, I would draw this distinction from positive interest in pointing out, that basic moral principles never determine, all by themselves, what concrete acts it is right for a reasonable man to do. The uninformed and foolish may be as moral as possible, but the rest of us may need to be protected from the consequences of their wholly righteous intentions. Or to put the issue in more traditional terms, I would point out, as has often enough been pointed out before, that either the Kantian categorical imperative must, contrary to Kant's own interpretation, appeal to some empirical understanding of what in fact would happen if everybody acted on the maxim one proposes to adopt, or else the Kantian ethics is empty of any determination of any concrete act whatever as either right or wrong. It offers a criterion of right mindedness only, and can do nothing to resolve that practical dilemma of the morally minded man, as to what course of conduct, at just this juncture and in this society and this factual world, is the one whose adoption will be justified by the consequences of it, to himself and others. Good intentions being given

—or morally bad ones—there is still that question of the valuable results which the morally good man wishes to achieve or the disvaluable
ones which the morally bad man is willing to inflict upon those his act
affects.

If the good intentions of moral men generally brought pain and sorrow to their fellows, and the bad intentions of immoral men normally
contributed to the happiness of others, then this world would indeed
be a crazy place to live in; but I suggest that it would be crazy in exactly that way if good intentions were not usually supplemented by a
modicum of good empirical judgment of what is valuable and what
disvaluable.

I wish, therefore, to set these questions of ethics to one side in this
paper—not because they are less important, but mainly because they
concern a quite different matter, and the attempt to discuss two different problems at one and the same time can only result in confusion.
There are value-judgments of the sort required in answer to the question, "Is the hydrogen bomb a good thing or a bad thing?" without
reference to that peculiar question of a very special kind of goodness,
judgment of which is required if the question be, "Is Mr. Blank, who
is urging our production of hydrogen bombs, acting morally in so doing?" I wish to separate them because, for one thing, Mr. Blank may
be a saintly character though the hydrogen bomb is an invention of the
devil, or Mr. Blank may be a political opportunist without a trace of
morals but the hydrogen bomb the only hope for the future of civilization. And leaving aside such questions as Mr. Blank's righteous or
unrighteous motivations, the question about the bomb is a question
of empirical factualities, though factualities which the wisest of men
might find it difficult to determine.

Concerning value-judgments in this sense in which they are independent of moral goodness and badness even though the two are related
we shall still have troubles enough because of the multiplicity of senses
in which value-terms are used, and the corresponding variety of modes
in which values are judged. Many debates about the nature of values
and of value-judgments are relatively pointless for the same reason as
the debate between "the three wise men of Hindustan / to learning
much inclined / who went to see the elephant / though all of them
were blind." As you remember they encountered various parts of the
beast and each insisted on a total characterization of the elephant on
the basis of the part seized upon. We have already tried to rule out
those who characterize good generally by reference to the peculiar
properties of moral goodness. They are like the wise man who, having

grabbed a leg, insisted that the elephant is very like a tree. Value is indeed a wondrous beast with variously modified parts. But the head end of the animal doubtless is 'intrinsic value': the value of that which is valuable for its own sake. This is the head end because, obviously, whatever is said to be valuable, in any *other* sense, is called valuable because of some supposed relationship to what is valuable for its own sake.

Now I hope you will agree that nothing is finally valuable on its own account—for its own sake—except that quality of a life which, if it could be envisaged with utter clarity and veracity, as it is to be or would be, is such that one would wish to live a life having so far as possible that quality. I hope you will not object that there is no general answer to any question of the goodness of a good life. I am not talking about the recipe for a good life, what ingredients to put in, in what proportions, and how to mix them; I am talking of the inescapably found quality of it. How to cook up a good life, out of whatever ingredients, or out of the ingredients to be found in the cupboard, is indeed the practical problem of every man. But it would be an utterly hopeless problem if he did not know what manner of thing he was wishing to achieve; if he had no touchstone of success or failure of this most final of final aims. The good in this ultimate sense is that which if a man possessed it he would ask for nothing more. The proof of a good life would be found in the living. That is what Mill meant to say in observing that there is no proof of the ultimately desirable except that it is desired—though unfortunately it is not what he did say, because he overlooked the fact that nothing concretely aimed at and in fact desired can be guaranteed to turn out as we desire it to be. And it is this finally uncriticizable character of good as found in living which I have intended to express by speaking of my conception of values as naturalistic, though that may have been a blunder in view of the many other things which 'naturalism' is taken to mean, and are such as I could not defend. In particular, 'pleasure' is not an apt name for the ultimate good. And the ancient observation that a pig might find pleasure alone sufficient but a man does not is a completely pertinent and sufficient reason. The point is simply that the quality of goodness in a good life is the quality of complete fulfillment, and that this inevitable and natural aim is subject to no alien criticism of its correctness. If any moralism like Kant's is supposed to show that something we all clearsightedly desire is not desirable, then that moralism is confused or impertinent. To be moral and to do the right is an unqualified imperative; to deny that would be, I think, a self-contradiction. And to be moral frequently means acceptance of a sacrifice of some part of what we should otherwise clearsightedly desire for ourselves. Right there is, indeed, an inescapable problem of ethics. Kant faced that problem, honestly, in distinguishing *das Wohl* from *das Gut* and *das Böse* from *das Übel* and *das Weh*, even if he did blur that distinction over again by calling virtue the supreme (*oberst*) good. He did not becloud but clearly pointed out the fact that the question "Are you a moral man?" is the question "What would you do if you saw it to be your duty to sacrifice, in some part, your claim to that happiness which all men wish?" And he likewise pointed out that a man who does not have to face that question has no moral sense and no moral problem at all. As we all remember, he found no way to satisfy his troubled sense of this matter except by the postulate of God. I could not agree with Kant, but I would not pass this point without pausing to remove my hat to him. Such questions do not, however, belong to the general theory of values.

The ultimate good is the quality of a life found good in the living of it. If we must have some synonym, the Aristotelian term 'happiness' is the least bad choice. What is valuable in any other sense is so derivatively by connotation of essential relationship to such final and directly findable goodness.

The closest of such derivative goods is the momentary goodness of the constituent experiences which are ingredient in, and together constitutive of, a life as lived, and which by the quality of them contribute to or detract from the comprehensive temporal gestalt of a life found good or bad on the whole. Such temporary goods and bads of passing experience do not 'add up to' the goodness or badness in a whole life, which is final, because goodness in a life is consummatory and not additive, and any calculus of contributory goods is wide of the mark. And what temporarily gratifies or grieves is subject to this further critique of its contributory effect upon a whole life. It may be momentarily bad but conducive to good on the whole, or momentarily good but on the whole may make life worse. But the passing experience is not something external to and externally affecting a life on the whole but ingredient in it as well as affecting other such constituents of it. Like the lower left-hand detail in a picture, it both contributes to the whole composition—well or badly—and is a part of the picture. To call its goodness or poorness 'instrumental' would be an inapt use of the term. Shall we say 'contributory'? The goodness or badness of ingredient experiences is both intrinsic and contributory to the goodness or badness of a life, because they are part of it. They have intrinsic goodness or badness as those constituents without which there would be no whole gestalt. And the intrinsic goodness or badness of such ingredient passing experiences, which they have within themselves—like the intrinsic goodness or badness of the whole they constitute—is simply the good or bad quality found in them as experienced.

However, so far as the good of passing experience is not within itself but in the contribution it may make—or the detraction it may effect—in other experience and so in a whole life, the value or disvalue of it is one that has to be judged. It takes some wisdom of life to stop eating or drinking while one still enjoys, or to compose the opportunities of work and recreation, business, family, and social service into the best possible life on the whole. Children find that wisdom hard to learn; it involves a few tough experiences even for the most docile, and there are some who never learn. So far as the goodness of a good life is not found in the immediately realized satisfactoriness or unsatisfactoriness of its temporary and passing experiences but in their relations together and their effects on one another, the evaluation of them is a matter of judgment, which does have to be learned and can be learned only from experience; and it is no less empirical because we can learn some part of it by being told, instead of the hard way, just as physics is no less an empirical and inductive branch of knowledge because we learn most of it from books instead of in the laboratory.

That goodness or badness which a passing experience has within its own boundaries calls for no judgment; it is a datum, in the same sense that the visual quality of apparent redness is a datum. The distinction between this value-datum and the red datum, which it is most important to make, is that the value immediately found in passing experience is *real* value—not subject, as the red datum is, to judgmental decision whether it is objectively real or it is apparent only and not what it seems. Even this difference is one of our point of view, purpose, or verbal usage only. The *experience* of apparent redness, is a real experience, really having this mentioned quality. The subject of the psychological experiment who says, "I see red," when in fact the given visual quality is that of yellowness, tells an untruth. The point is here that the experienced value-quality of a passing experience is an intrinsic value. It is that quality of experience, whether momentarily or in life on the whole, which is that *for the sake* of which any other kind of good or bad thing is either good or bad. By contrast, things that are red, not in the quality with which they appear but objectively, are not red for the sake of being seen as red. Such language would be nonsense. The distinction of 'intrinsic' or 'extrinsic' does not apply to redness, hardness, and the like, or any quality but value.

As soon as we take even one step away from that immediate value found within the momentary experience as such, and judge it as affecting other experience and a life in which it is ingredient, we find at one and the same time that this value which it has as contributory is one which has to be judged, and with respect to which we can be mistaken, and that the called-for judgment requires and has to be learned from the experience of life in general, and is inductive and empirical.

So far, we speak of value as predicable of experience only, whether of passing experience or of a life on the whole, or some stretch of it, such as a week, or a vacation, or our middle years. It is only experience itself which has value for its own sake. And all else that has value is for the sake of it, for the sake of goodness as a quality directly findable in living. If you deny this, I shall not know how to argue for it further—unless perchance I should think I detect some confusion of thought underlying your denial, or see that it turns upon some divergence between us in what the words used are used to mean.

It follows at once that there is no value in objects or in any property of objects which is valuable in any other sense than the sense of being valuable for the sake of something else—ultimately for the sake of a contribution which this object or objective character of it can make to the quality of some experience, its possible contribution of a goodness findable directly in the quality of living.

There are, however, two kinds or modes of such extrinsic value in objective existents. There is the kind of value which characterizes good pictures and good food, which may be called inherent value; and there is the kind of value which a good knife or good spade may have, even though it is not pleasing to look at or enjoyable to use, because it serves a purpose. This we may call instrumental value. An object is *inherently* good or valuable if or insofar as it has a value realizable in the presentation of this object itself—as a good tasting meal is found good in the eating and a beautiful poem is found good in the reading of it. And an object has instrumental value if or insofar as it can be *productive of* an inherent value, findable in the presence of some *other* object but not in this one whose value we presently assess. Tools and raw materials are of course the prime exemplars of objects having such instrumental value. Objects having any worth at all most frequently have *both* an instrumental value and some measure of inherent value, especially since, by the psychological law of association, that which characteristically leads to or conduces to what pleases by its presence to us, thereby becomes an object which it gratifies us to possess and to see about us. A sink for example, is seldom an esthetic object, but we male animals can be surprised at the direct pleasure a good housewife may find in looking at a nice convenient sink.

But whether value in an object is inherent or is instrumental or is both, it is never a value for its own sake, for which the adjective 'intrinsic' is best reserved. That qualification—'intrinsic and for its own sake'—attaches only to the goodness of a good life, or of some constituent or ingredient findable in a good life. An object, or property of an object, or any objective state of affairs can be good only in the sense of being something which may contribute goodness to a good life and *because* it may so contribute.

If you are willing to go with me this far, then it becomes obvious, does it not, that any value which an object has is a quality or character of it which must be discovered empirically, like other properties of things, because the value of an object is some property resident in the nature of it by virtue of which it produces, or is capable of producing, certain effects which impinge upon the quality of human living. And like cause-effect relationships in general and the properties of objects in general, by which they produce certain effects and not others, any quality or character of an object by which it conduces, whether immediately and directly, or mediately and by some causal chain of connection, to a goodness or a badness findable in human living, is something which has to be learned by observation and experiment, and formulated as an inductive generalization. In fact, human learning from experience is largely devoted, in the final significance of it, to discovering what potentialities for good and ill reside in what things, and how, in a world where all that we can do is, finally, to pick something up and put it somewhere else, these value-potentialities things have can best be exploited to our advantage. The correct assessment of values in objects, objective situations, actual states of affairs, and states of affairs which we can bring about is the overarching condition of any manner of success in human doing, and sets the end for which any other kind of human learning is a means only.

I will not say that valuation is an empirical *science*, though it is a kind of knowledge essentially antecedent to any significance to be found in any science; without correct evaluations, all sciences would be useless to us. I will not call this understanding because the correct evaluation of the objective is so largely a matter within the common-sense capacity of men with practical wisdom rather than being a problem which calls for the wide information of an expert or some special training and technique. But I would point out two things. First that the value of any science (apart from the wholly real satisfaction which may be found in knowledge for its own sake) is a value which accrues when scientific learning becomes applied, by the engineer, the technologist, or the craftsman, for the production, devising, or arrangement of things so as to conduce more largely to what men find satisfactory for their living, and the avoidance of what brings grief and sorrow. Correct evaluation is the first and most essential of all learning, and without that any other manner of learning could be of little worth.

And I will further suggest that within this wide area of called-for practical wisdom there are included fields which do require some higher degree of special competence and a wider body of information than it is possible for otherwise busy men to acquire. There should be as many value-sciences as there are major classifications of human needs, and of instruments or types of activity which serve them. These are, or should be, the fields of the social sciences, from which we should be able to learn what things, arrangements, institutions, and modes of social cooperation will conduce most largely to the possible satisfactoriness of human living. We should be able to look to the economist to tell us what manner of organizing the social forces for the production of material goods, and what social arrangements governing the distribution of them, will be productive of the maximum or optimum fulfillment of the kind of needs such goods can meet and the kind of satisfactions they can bring. We should be able to look to the science of jurisprudence not only for learned analyses of various bodies of law and modes of making, interpreting, executing, and enforcing law, but also for expert *evaluation* of these, in their impact upon human life, as contributing to the realizable good of it or detracting from and preventing goods which might be so realized. We should be able to look to the sociologist, the experts on political institutions, and the anthropologist, as we can look to the physician and those engaged in scientific medical research, not merely for the formulation of descriptive scientific facts, but for those value-judgments and prescriptive advice for the realization of human values, for the correctness of which such a background of expert information and command of special technique is, if not absolutely essential, at least most helpful, in the assessment of economic, legal, political, and social values, resident in objective circumstances and things or realizable if we know better in what direction to apply ourselves.

Either within or alongside of each of these sciences which peculiarly deal with phenomena of human life, we need some equally expert and informed appraisal of the particular values with which these phenomena are affected. But as a fact, these expert evaluations which are needed are hardly recognized today as the business of anybody. Medical science would be the only clear exception. It is one aspect of the fact that modern civilization begins to look ridiculous by its scientific topheaviness and we seem as likely to be destroyed by it as to utilize the potentialities so afforded for the betterment of human life. That fact should, I think, strike us as an extraordinary and inexplicable feature of our culture and particularly of our educational programs.

This deplorable state of affairs is itself a highly complex phenomenon, with many strands which have gone into the making of it. One is the fact that so many of our practitioners and teachers of the social sciences are imitating the methods of the older and more exclusively descriptive sciences, or even recognize no finding as scientific unless it is a purely descriptive generalization, and divorced from any interest of appraisal. And another would seem to be that so many social scientists have caught the relativity disease from our neo-Protagoreans, or have revived that great discovery for themselves. All values are relative; and they take that to mean that there are no value-facts for any objective method to discover and formulate. These two tendencies of descriptivism and relativism can lead to cynicism concerning problems of evaluation. The economist may say, "Economic value is merely what a thing will sell for"; the jurist, "Law is simply what the court decides"; the expert in government, "I study the facts and workings of different modes of political organization; moral judgments are out of my line"; and the sociologist, "There are no social values which can be assessed except in relation to the dominant cultural trends of the society in question." Or if this is a caricature which I draw, I fear it is one from which the subject of it could be easily recognized.

I hope you will excuse my feeling that the view I hold of values is correct, and even that it could be of service because of this correctness. I would not accept 'the greatest good of the greatest number' as a satisfactory formulation of any ethical or otherwise valid directive. But it is a useful phrase as a quick approximation to something of major importance. And what it is, amongst any set of alternatives, which would come closest to the greatest good of the greatest number is as hard and fixed and objective and obdurate a fact as the weight of a tank or the velocity of a rifle bullet, though it is something much more complex and difficult to determine; and you won't find it by integrating any statistical curve. What it is which, with respect to any problem, represents the optimum achievable value is an empirical factuality, however difficult of discovery. Perhaps if we could persuade our social scientists of this objective reality concerned by value problems, and of the complete scientific respectability of attempted solution of it, we might help to produce a climate of opinion more conducive to realistic instead of cynical appraisal of existing or projected social institutions, and there would be better hope that science will continue to operate as a servant for the betterment of human life, and less possibility that it might turn out a Frankenstein and destroy the civilization which has produced it. At least, I suppose we are all convinced that the world has become, somewhat abruptly, too small and too humanly complex for the exigent problems of evaluation, and of value-engineering, to be solved without some degree of explicit and careful attention, and some manner of concerted effort.

But let me retreat from my small and presumptuous preachment, back to those questions with respect to which we are supposed to be more competent.

One major impediment to clarity in matters of evaluation and to the recognition that problems so posed may have objective answers is the confusing multiplicity of the types or modes of value-assesment we are called upon to make. Not only are there species of values—economic, esthetic, prudential, moral, instrumental, intrinsic, and any number more—but there are also different ways of assessing these, or many of them, according as the problem is, for example, to assess the contribution which the thing or matter judged may make under the limiting conditions of certain practical premises, or to judge any item or plan in terms of idealities representing an eventual goal to aim at. There is also value to me, value to you, social value to a community, and so on. And the consequence is that one appraisal, oriented in one manner to one problem, may have a result which seems to contradict another appraisal of the same thing which is oriented in another manner or to a different problem. These are amongst the so-called 'relativities' of value. And as a first hasty indication of the direction in which to look for resolution of the puzzle so indicated, let us observe that this kind of relativity—if it is that—is not confined to valuation. There is the weight of a thing in air, its weight in water, its weight in vacuo, its weight on the moon, its weight as determined by a spring scale, and its weight by balances, which under some circumstances may be different, and the physicist resolves this puzzle by finding that each and every such determination of the weight of the thing may be correct, though different: in fact, they would not be correct and manifestations of the objective mass of the object *unless* they were different. He surmounts this relativity by incorporating it: weight is mass × gravity, and there is no constant of gravity except in relational terms which make its measure likewise different for every different relationship to other masses in the system.

We have the great variety of modes of value judgment that we do, principally because value is so preeminently important a characteristic of things. In fact, in the last analysis, value is Mr. Important himself; and other characteristics we are capable of discovering in objects are worth noticing only because certain complexes of them have a determinable correlation with some kind of value as assessed in some specific way.

There is, however, one generic sense of value, of which other types of value and modes of value judgment represent some further qualification or specification. In general terms, the value of an *object* is the potentiality of it for conducing to some *intrinsic* value directly findable in experience. In brief, that has value which makes life better or could do so if the potentiality resident in the nature of it should be utilized.

It is this character of value in things as potentiality, along with the 'relativities' just mentioned, which is mainly responsible for the suspicion that value is not objectively ascribable at all. This is a topic which hardly could be covered adequately in the time that remains; I must try to hit each high spot once.

First, let us remark that potentialities, ascribed by 'disposition predicates,' are not, by being such, unobjective or correctly ascribed only in that relation to other things in which the potentiality becomes actualized. That salt is soluble means that if it be put in water it will dissolve. But a good deal of salt never is put in water (at least within our observation); that has nothing to do with the objective property by virtue of which it *would* dissolve if it *were* in water. And the salt that *is* put in water is soluble *when* it is *not* put in water. In fact, if there be paradox here, the paradox would lie in calling the salt soluble when it *is* dissolved.

So too with the value of an object. This thing either *would* contribute thus and so to realization of direct satisfaction in experience, or if you create the thus and so conditions for attesting a value ascribed, you find that this object does *not* produce the expected satisfaction—and in that case your predication of value to it proves mistaken. But whether the thing in question actually would or actually would not produce this value-effect, under the conditions implicitly understood, is an objective fact about the objective nature of it. You could satisfy your hunger with an egg, or it is a china nest egg and you couldn't. The potentiality for alleviating hunger is in the objective nature of the one and not in the other. And the egg has this character, which is the kind of value eggs have, even if the starving man hoards it against his last necessity, but is rescued and fed, and finally throws it against a rock in celebration. It was a perfectly good egg. That goodness was a potentiality not realized. It objectively possessed this value as potential nourishment.

Second, if it be supposed that value, by being thus a potentiality of objects, differs from other properties in things which, some of them at least, are not potentialities but—what shall I say?—inactive, then we must remark that this is simply an ancient and persistent superstition, all of a piece with, and exemplified by, the outmoded distinction of primary qualities from those secondary qualities which are taken to be relative to the sensory apparatus of the perceiving organism.

There are *no* properties whatever ascribable to objects in any different sense. All properties of things are potentialities and all are equally 'relative' to the particular circumstances and possible manner of observation which must be found implied in a clear concept of the property to be determined. Bridgman has most aptly and forcefully pointed out this fact, though Charles Peirce said it earlier and more succinctly: "Consider what effects, which might conceivably have practical bearings, we conceive the object of our conception to have. Then, our conception of these effects is the whole of our conception of the object."[1] Or in Bridgman's terms (with a little supplementation which is, I think, essential), the concept of any physical property is the concept of certain operations to be performed with the observable result which is accepted as verification of the property in question. The thing has a weight of ten pounds if, being put on the scales, the pointer will be observed to rise to the mark 10. But it weighs just as much—has the same objective property so tested—when it is sitting on the floor, or sitting or floating in water, and if it never is placed in any scale pan. Common-sense concepts of properties are 'relative' to common-sense tests; scientific concepts are relative to prescribed and standard conditions. But theoretically untestable properties are nothing whatever and any ascription of them is gibberish. All are potentialities for producing certain effects under specifiable conditions. They reside in the object in the sense of potentialities for producing their predicted effects. And the ascription of them is no different in kind than the ascription of solubility to salt when it isn't dissolving or the ascription of beauty to the Venus of Milo when no one is looking at it, or utility to one's razor when he is not shaving.

But one says: At least the objective properties are such that there is interpersonal community between those who test and observe; and value fails this test of objectivity. If time permitted, I should try to show, first, that community is *not* essential to objectivity, nor does ob-

---

[1] Cf. Charles S. Peirce, *Chance, Love, and Logic* (New York, 1923), p. 45.

jectivity imply community of this sort. And second, that most of the community so easily assumed is in fact spurious. But I have not time to hit those high spots even once. I think it may be even more illuminating to observe that the actual coincidence or close approximation in observation in matters such as the scientific are only skin-deep affairs. Mainly they are carefully contrived social devices for securing reports which coincide even though the property of the thing in question is very differently experienced by different people.

Weight, once more, makes a good example. The historically earliest tests of weight were undoubtedly to lift the thing or to see how far you could carry it before your ambition evaporated. And individual differences are then the rule. But even before scales, nobody, presumably, was so foolish as to attribute this relativity of experienced weight to the object lifted. By deliberate intention, we get around this relativity of heft by using weighing machines. And the dodge so used becomes quite general for all 'exact' determinations. Don't test the property by A's, B's, C's experience of it. Do it by a standard procedure with standard tools which are affected by any observer as little as possible. Put a pointer on your machine against a numbered scale. Then if observers do not report the same number, make the pointer longer and the divisions on the scale wider until they do. These are extremely useful social devices for social cooperation by eliminating many differences of opinion. By all means stick to them in the interests of community. But each man must then learn his own coefficient of sensitivity and his own fatigue point, and translate this artificial and contrived community back into the idiosyncratic significance of what the pointer readings signify for his experience. Two pounds of beefsteak doesn't mean much until it is translated into half a day's pay, which is relative to income, or enough meat for dinner, which is relative to the children's appetite for steak.

But with respect to values, while we have our devices for community—marginal utility, for example, as the measure of economic worth —we are comparatively less interested in indirect determinations which are relative to machines or to conventions, because we are more interested in the diverse and various manifestations of things valued in terms of individual experience. Otherwise put, we are less interested in value in the generic sense and more interested in highly specific tests and ways of judging.

The two most important general modes of value judgment are of value for a person and social value or value to the community—possibly in the end, to humanity at large.

Determination of value to me is the assessment of the potentiality of the thing for conducing to a goodness realizable in my life; and only as I achieve objective and correct judgments of that sort will there be any possibility that anything that I can do will make that life better than if I had not made that judgment and adopted that mode of action instead of some alternative. What one so judges with respect to an object in question is that if he behaves in this or that manner involving this object or with reference to it, then certain satisfactions or dissatisfactions will accrue to him in result. And what one so judges is a matter of absolute fact, as he is sure to find out if he is wrong and puts his judgment to the test.

Nor is correctness of judgments of value relative to persons confined in the importance of it to judgments that are first-personally so. If we wish to do any other person any good or any harm we shall have to discover the empirical facts which are essential—what kind of stuff, put in his personal soup, will please and nourish him and what kind will make him ill. Even if we be consistent egoists, we shall be under the necessity of giving attention to alio-personal values, if we wish to live happily, because of the prevalent human failing of doing to others as these others do to us.

Judgments of social value obviously represent two things: (1) the attempt to find some core of valuations with respect to which there is community, and (2) to achieve some integrated assessment of the value and disvalue effects of whatever is in question on the whole group of those affected by this thing. Attention would disclose that there are somewhat different modes in which one may guide such attempted integration and determine social values. This topic lies particularly close to ethics, because, for example, the difference between an ethics of principle, like Kant's, and an ethics of consequences, like J. S. Mill's, turns precisely upon the question of what mode of social evaluation is taken to determine what a morally right-minded man should do. On that point, Kant saw his own view correctly. It leaves room for personal persuasion of the ideal state of affairs, whereas the greatest happiness of the greatest number leaves none whatever—except that indeterminacy which reflects our inevitable ignorance and stupidity.

4. Subjective Right and Objective Right

The distinction which I wish to draw under this title is one which comes to our attention most clearly and pointedly in connection with Kant's ethics. And it is to be noted that Kant's ethics is almost exclusively a theory of justice, since he disallows any moral worth attaching to acts done from prudential aims. Let us note in passing, however, that Kant does not deny that value as determined by satisfactions found, or to be found, functions as criterion of what it is right to do; he merely obscures that question. In fact, in the *Metaphysics of Ethics* (not the *Grundlegung*), he says that it is our duty to act from respect for the happiness of others, though he disallows any weight attaching to consideration of our own happiness except in a strange way; we should conserve our own happiness because personal misery will leave us open to temptation, e.g., the starving man will be tempted to steal. Just why, compatibly with the rest of his theory, we should not rather seek misery in order that our moral triumph over such temptations may be the greater, we may be puzzled to see. But the main point here is that he *does* consider it an obligation to act with respect for happiness of others. Indirectly also, he does not rule out value as satisfaction from functioning as criterion of what it is right to do, because the categorical imperative in the form "So act that you could will the maxim of your conduct to be a universal law" does not rule out *any* maxim one could so will—and so does not rule out as the most comprehensive principle of justice, "Act so as to achieve, so far as in you lies, the greatest happiness of the greatest number," if it happens that this is the principle you would will that all men on all occasions act upon. In fact, it neither prescribes nor rules out *any* criterion for determining what particular acts are to be accounted right, just so you could accept that as such a *universal* criterion of the rightness of action. That fact is frequently pointed to as the total failure of Kant's formalism.

But I mention these details of Kant's theory only in order that they may not later impede discussion of another point with which we shall be mainly concerned here.

That point is the distinction between two modes of the assessment of the rightness of acts and, more broadly, rightness of decisions generally. First, we assess decisions according as they conform or fail to

Written for a proseminar on ethics given at Harvard in 1952.

conform to the principles of correctness applying to such decisions. (And may I remind you that up to this point we have indicated different modes of correctness separately—consistency and cogency in decisions as to fact, and prudence and justice in decisions to do—and have given no consideration to the problem of decisions which must be judged in more than one of these ways, at one and the same time, or the possibility that they, as the correlation dictates, might then appear as conflicting. There must be such a problem: most obviously, when the dictate of justice runs counter to the dictate of prudence. We are not yet ready for that kind of problem. We still confine ourselves here to judgment of rightness in these separate ways. And with respect to any one of them, there will be the two modes of assessment mentioned in our title.)

The first of them is the assessment of the decision as conforming or failing to conform to the principles of correctness, e.g., rules of logic. That is what I wish to call a judgment of objective rightness. It is the attempt to answer the question, "What should any right-minded man decide in this case, i.e., in the premises of the problem?" The other mode of such judgment, which I wish to label judgment of subjective rightness, is assessment of the merit or demerit of the agent who decides in taking the decision in question, whether this agent be ourselves or some other person. This mode of judgment is the attempt to answer the question, "Should we approve or disapprove of the agent in his taking of this decision? Is the taking of this decision a fault of the agent or is he blameless in so taking it?"

We may note that the question of subjective right or wrong is a separately important question from the question to be answered in connection with any justification of punishment, and any assessment of desert. It is the question to be decided in any law court called upon to convict or acquit the defendant charged with a crime or misdemeanor, or to assess damages in a case of tort, as distinguished from equity merely. It is also in point in any award of merit, including that most important of awards, good repute amongst our fellows. It is a main consideration in any judgment of good or bad character. It is likewise what is in question in our self-approval or disapproval and in any self-correction of our attitudes, as well as in social correction of an individual's attitudes by others. It is thus a major question of education— one grossly neglected in the most common conceptions of education, i.e. when education is correctly conceived as concerned development of right attitudes and good character and not merely as the acquisition of information and development of skill. But the judgment of subjective right is never directly the judgment of correctness in the decision taken.

To anticipate our conclusion concerning the nature of subjective rightness—because I think that conclusion should be obvious—a decision is subjectively right if and only if, at the time of taking it, the agent believes that it is objectively right. And the main point—which becomes obvious if this conception accords with the rational ground of approving and disapproving of persons, with respect to what they think and do—is the point that if there were no other criterion of the rightness or wrongness of thinking and doing than the criterion of subjective rightness or wrongness, then there would be no determinable rightness or wrongness at all.

It is for the sake of that conclusion that consideration of this distinction between subjective right and objective right is interpolated here: in order that we may see the necessity for recognizing some criterion of right, for any mode of rightness and wrongness, which is independent of the question whether the agent is at fault or not in his decision or in the act he decides to do.

This should, in any case, be obvious, though many men of admirable mind have missed the point. Unless there is something which is as it is and not otherwise, regardless of what anybody thinks about it, there is nothing for any decision to decide, no ascertainable difference between a correct decision and one which is incorrect. And if there is nothing right or wrong to believe and to do, independently of the conviction of any particular agent at any particular time, then all questions of right and wrong, including those of the subjective rightness and wrongness, are pointless and have no answer.

I shall suggest that, in questions of right doing, the fact that there are principles, conformity to which is essential to such rightness and is imperative, does not determine what particular act, amongst alternatives which could be chosen, it is right to do. Such prime imperatives of doing, I have suggested, set the criteria of right and imply some type of value correlative with the manner of rightness which is in question. In the case of prudential action, or the assessment of action as prudent, that final aim is value to one's self in one's whole lifetime, with equal consideration of the distant or the nearer eventualities which may be affected by the contemplated act. But the application of this criterion to the prudential problem in hand—to a contemplated act— is not determined by the principle. That question of what decision the principle dictates is a question of empirical fact. That is obvious: what value for my good life the contemplated act will have is not determined by the prudential dictate so to act as to maximize the value realizable in a whole life. That value in this mode is the criterion of prudential rightness does not and could not conceivably determine what acts it is prudentially right to do. It could only appear to do so by the ambiguity of the word 'what' in the question "What is it (prudentially or otherwise) right to do?" In one sense of 'what' the question may be answered, "Whatever will conduce to the best life possible for you to attain." But in the here pertinent sense, that answer is merely nonrespondent; the question is, "But which act, amongst the alternatives presently open to me, will satisfy that criterion of choice?" And nobody can ever choose a prudent act or refuse an imprudent one without finding the answer to that particular question of empirical fact. The rule of prudential action determines what character of actions it is by reason of which the sanction of prudence attaches to them; namely, their contributing more to satisfaction in one's whole life than any alternative. But what acts have this character, and what fail to have it, has to be determined by looking to the empirical facts of consequences of the act in question. And so in general: any rule of right specifies the criterion, or a partial criterion, of the kind of rightness in question, but the criterion specified must be some quality or character discoverable by inspection in that to which the rule is pertinent. And what activities or acts exhibit this character by reason of which they are right, is determinable only by examination of the activity or act, which may disclose that this act or activity examined has the discoverable character satisfying the criterion or may disclose the absence of this character.

One who asks the question, "What is it right for me to do?" may intend to ask, "What is the criterion of rightness? What is that quality by the having of which any doing of mine, in this present case, will be constituted right?" The answer to that question will be a correct explication of the essential character possession of which will determine any act to be right. And that answer may not be any empirically determined fact at all, and require to have some other than informational ground, if indeed it is valid and has any determinable ground that will be analytic, *a priori*, merely explicative, or else incorrect (a wrong definition or explication of what wants explicating). Or his question may be of a quite different sort. The questioner may be quite clear what character it is the possession of which will constitute any contemplated action right, and what he now asks himself is what alternative, amongst acts now open to him, will have this character. If it is this second question which he asks, then what he seeks to discover is what I here call the objective rightness of any contemplated action. Unless this kind of question is an answerable kind of question, the project of doing right would be completely empty and fatuous.

But some students of ethics, and Kant in particular, confuse this question with the different one of the merit or demerit, innocence or blameworthiness of the action. The first step, leading to this confusion, is recognition that rightness or wrongness of an act is to be assessed by reference to it as a way of acting, and that a way of acting is right if and only if it would be right in all instances. In order that this should not be misunderstood, it is necessary to observe that such being right in all instances requires reference to the circumstances or specificities of an act in question: recognition that stealing candy from children is not the same way of acting as stealing weapons from madmen. Perhaps a good way to make that point secure is to observe that a way of acting is right only if it is always right *in the same premises*. Kant actually leaves that point unclear by indicating what I here refer to as the way of acting involved by referring to the maxim on which one acts. With malice propense one could make a Roman holiday of Kant's conception on this point by observing that it would be a stupid rascal who could not find some innocent maxim covering his rascality. The reason is that any particular action can be subsumed under an indefinitely large number of different maxims, just as any particular object can be subsumed under an indefinitely large number of different class-concepts. Casuistry gets a bad name precisely for this reason. Probity and intelligence in this matter require that the way of acting be taken as specifically as our comprehension of the act we contemplate allows. Any knowable specificity of it can be omitted from account only on the positive understanding that this omitted character of the act is indifferent to its being right or wrong. But we should agree with the Kantian conception that right and wrong is amenable to rule, for the reason that no one can ever comprehend any contemplated act or any which is committed in the infinite specificity of it as concrete event, and the infinitude of its endless consequences.

Kant finds no better way to express the criterion of rightness than this universal rightness of any way of acting which is right, and no better final index to that than one's willingness to see the way of acting in question universally adopted. Let us grant that this is the best of all ready rules of thumb for eliminating wrong ways of acting. It is still not sufficient since, for example, some tribe of men who like to be bossed and annoyed not by necessity of individual decision could will universal regimentation, and those who temperamentally seek the frontier could perhaps will universal anarchy.

But the main point which accounts for Kant's peculiar ethical conceptions is his preoccupation with merit and demerit. No one is blamable for what he does not intend—for unforeseen consequences of his act. The point is debatable, but let us grant it for the present. We shall at least agree that no one is blamable for consequences he *could* not foresee, and in every case of acting there are such consequences unforeseeable to the agent. And admittedly it is only the act as a bringing about of those consequences which are foreseen which can be examined as satisfying or failing to satisfy any rules of action, or, in Kant's terms, any maxim.

Go back to merit or fault. I suggest that in order to be faithful to our own sense of what is blameworthy and what is blameless, we shall have to go further than this in the direction of subjectivity—in regarding what is right as relative to the agent's judgment (which may be mistaken) of what is right. In one respect Kant does go further. He does not allow that an act will be morally praiseworthy merely because it conforms to some maxim which one could will to be universally adopted. To be praiseworthy it must also be done *because* it is thus right. This point in Kant is seldom understood correctly. Kant is quite consistent about it, whether his theory is acceptable or not. Take his own example: honesty is the best policy, but a man who acts honestly because it is the best policy is not, so far, an honest man. When Kant says that the comprehensive principle of right is "So act that you could will the maxim of your conduct to be a universal law," he means by "the maxim of your conduct" the rule which you actually intend to follow: the rule by which you govern your conduct in this and other like instances. The maxim of the man who is honest *because* it is the best policy is "Always act in the most politic manner," and Kant takes it that even the man who acts on that rule could not wish that others adopt it in their dealings with him. His honest action has, therefore, no moral merit. This would be the Kantian answer to one who observes, as I did earlier, that any act may be subsumed under a large number of different maxims. This is the Kantian conception of 'motive'; the motive of an act is that consideration on account of which you choose deliberately to do it, reflected in the rule you deliberately intend to follow in all like cases—in other words, your deliberately adopted active attitude in such cases as the one you now decide.

We shall agree with Kant that the man who acts honestly because that is the best policy is not morally praiseworthy for so doing; at most we give him good marks for being intelligent enough to see that dishonesty does not pay. But this point has, as one consequence, the rigorism or puritanism for which Kant has frequently been reproached. One acquires moral merit only by adhering to the right because it is right, and none by adhering to what right principles dictate because one finds that the act so dictated is what one inclines to do. For example, it happens to be my duty to meet this group at two o'clock on Tuesdays. It also happens that I enjoy doing so. Do I do right in coming? I acquire no moral merit for so doing unless or until I come some day when I am tired or in pain and would rather not. I entirely agree with Kant on this point. But my purpose in coming here is not to acquire moral merit, and if yours is, I could will it to be a universal maxim that you stay away. I could even look indulgently upon your sinfulness if, one day, you neglect a little duty in order to come here because you want to. In other words, I don't agree with the merit-badge theory of morals. Being moral is not the aim of being moral. The end of moral action is finding some good and doing some good, and the good so to be achieved by moral action is not moral goodness itself. Moral goodness is to be determined by relation of the act to a good of some other kind. That is just my point. What constitutes an act right to do is not that property of it by reason of which the doer is morally praiseworthy. Kant is right—up to a point at least—in his delineation of what makes a doer's doing morally praiseworthy. He is wrong in supposing that one can determine what act it is right to do by using the doer's moral merit in doing it as criterion.

But let us return for a further moment to the point that Kant does not go as far as one should in recognizing the subjective nature of the ground of moral merit and demerit. He is right in recognizing that merit and demerit turns upon the reason why the doer deliberately chooses to do it—the maxim expressing the way he intends to act in all such cases. But he passes without mention the fact that people disagree about what such general ways of acting, and what such maxims, are valid, and such that acting in accord with them is right. Even a glance at those cultural disparities which the ethical relativists are fond of emphasizing, or examination of the answers to the sociologist's questionnaire, will reveal that people do what they do, with conviction that this way of acting is right to choose, for the weirdest and most divergent of reasons. And so far as moral merit and demerit goes, shall we not be obliged to recognize that, supposing some of these accepted maxims to be mistakenly identified with those which are valid dictates of right action, the doer who follows his own moral insight, right or wrong, is morally praiseworthy, or at least blameless, in so doing? However stupid one may be in accepting a given maxim as representing a universally right way of acting, we shall be obliged to recognize that the praise-worthy man is he who does what is right, as God gives him to see the right. We may well admit that the Kantian challenge "Suppose every-body were to act that way, just look what the world would then be like; would you choose to live in that kind of world?"—that this challenge might go far to mitigate stupidity in what men accept as right maxims of action. But for a reason already alluded to, it wouldn't go far enough. Totalitarians might be pleased with the picture of a well-regimented world, and sufficiently rugged individualists with a picture of a world in which no man-made law should be enforced. Incidentally, some saintly romantics would be on the same side. Utopians generally are a little stupid in imagining the results of universalizing their proposed pana-ceas. Some people are a little too ready to take the way they see the right as God-given; they get God mixed up with their own romantic sentimentality. But, like little children, they are blameless.

I should like to emphasize that judgment of the rightness and wrong-ness in this mode of subjective rightness, in which any act is right if the doer thinks it right, is both a necessary mode of judgment and the only just way of assessing praiseworthiness and blameworthiness in doing. It is the only just ground on which to mete out rewards and punishments, though we should not omit to note that blameless people and children must sometimes be admonished for their mistaken identi-fications of what it is right to do, both for their own future well-being and the safety of others. Not only justice in some ideal sense, but con-sideration of the social rationale of praising and blaming calls for this mode of assessing the desert of the individual in his actions done. In general those whose intentions are right in this subjective sense will do more good and less harm to others than they would if they acted in subjectively wrong ways—in ways they think wrong. This will remain true even if we be pessimistically convinced that the stupidly well-intentioned can cause more harm than astute rascals are likely to do. The stupid could do even *more* harm if malicious intentions were added to their other shortcomings. Also no socially desirable result is likely to ensue from punishing people for what they do with good intentions but with stupidly mistaken assessment of the consequences. The legal maxim that there is no crime without criminal intent is both just and adjusted to the ends of social security.

It is even just and in the social interest to take the underlying active attitude, which Kant identifies as the motive, rather than the specific action done, as the criterion of desert. It is this underlying attitude, representing the doer's reason for doing, rather than what specifically is done on one occasion, which indicates what the doer will, without correction of his presently dominant attitude, be likely to do on future and similar occasions. The rationale of retributive justice is to be found in the intent of it to correct, by praise or blame, reward or punishment, future behavior. Interest in the act done is, therefore, an interest in it as an index to continuing tendencies to do, hence in motivations or active attitudes, and not in the particular act which may be praised or blamed, rewarded or punished, except as manifestation of such a continuing tendency or motivation. The subjective rightness of the act is that aspect of it in which it functions as such an index to probable future behavior, and judgments of subjective rightness or wrongness are thus the rational basis of retributive justice. The act which is objectively the wrong act to choose, but is chosen by the doer through stupid misjudgment of consequences, is not rationally to be punished, since stupidity is not corrigible in that manner. That is the difference between stupidity and willful negligence. But the supposition that subjective rightness is *the* question of right and wrong would be the supposition that what it is right to do can be as easily and correctly determined by congenital idiots as by men of wisdom.

Let us note in passing that the Kantian motive of an act is not correctly identified with the intention of it. The intention of the act comprises those anticipated consequences which it is willed to bring about in committing it, and this intention is criticizable not merely as reflecting an attitude of good will or ill will but also as a prediction which is a cognitively justified or unjustified foreseeing of consequences and a correct or incorrect evaluation of those consequences. To suppose that the attempt to do right is concerned exclusively with assuring one's own goodness of will in acting, and unconcerned for the correctness of one's foresight and correct evaluation of what one brings about, is ridiculous. But the motive precisely is the intention as adjudged with entire disregard for its validity as cognitive prediction and evaluation. The motive is not the intention of *this act*, but intention in the sense of continuing purpose or attitude and without reference to the specific matter in hand. In short I agree entirely that the subjective goodness or badness of the act—and the underlying motive of it—constitute the absolutely correct criterion of judging people for what they do. But that is quite aside from the question, which any morally and right-minded man may raise: Being fully determined to do what is right and to do it because it is right, *what* in this case ought I to do?

The question what it is right to do is not the question of good will but the question of *what* it is *good to will*; and good will itself offers no criterion whatever for determination of that question. Nothing except some character of the act as a bringing about of what will be brought about by this commitment can afford any ground of decision that this act, and not some other, is that which any good will should choose on this occasion. The ethical problem is to identify this objective character or property of the act, as an alteration of what would otherwise be the case, by reason of which this act is correctly to be chosen instead of omitted by a good will. And a will is good if and only if it is a will to bring about those and only those results which satisfy the criteria of objective rightness. If there were nothing in the nature of acts as the production of certain concrete results to determine which of them are desirable and which are undesirable, there would be no distinction of good will from ill will. Good will is a matter of intended results and of attitudes underlying such intentions, and excludes any question of cognitive validity of the intentions or the validity of assessments of the value made. But if there were nothing independent of the attitude and intention determinative of what a good will should elect to aim at and what to avoid, there would be no ground on which intentions could be determined as good or bad, or right attitudes discriminated from wrong ones.

An act is subjectively right to do if it is that which the doer thinks it *objectively* right for him to do. But if there were no objective ground on which to determine what results ought to be aimed at and what avoided, there would be no ground for thinking one thing right to do and another wrong: no ground on which a good will could choose one act rather than another as rightly to be done.

Kant confuses these two questions of objective right and subjective right by failing to answer a question which is concealed in the dictate, "So act that you could will the maxim of your conduct to be a universal law." That question is, "On what ground could you will your *maxim* to be universally adopted?" Is it that in a community in which this attitude of yours should become universal, would be a community of unqualified good wills and you take that as the supreme social value; or is it that you believe that if all men acted on this maxim, in all cases in which it is pertinent, the results of their so acting would be gratifying to you, or to you and all other right-minded humans, making the world, so far forth, a more desirable one in which to live, but the desirability of it being something other or at least more than the universal moral rectitude of the social order? There must be *some* ground on which a maxim is one to be chosen as fit to be followed universally. The only ground on which one could determine what maxims are to be approved is the kind of acts which those maxims sanction. The goodness of the maxims derives from the goodness of the acts, not the goodness of the acts from the goodness of the maxims. And that any old maxim, just so it may be universally followed, is as good as any other, is plainly ridiculous. The objective rightness of a particular act relates to the desirability of its particular consequences. And the rightness of maxim, which sanctions acts of a certain *kind*, relates to the kind of consequences in general which flow from these kinds of acts which it sanctions. And the subjective rightness of action is the intent to bring about consequences *thought* to be desirable, and avoid consequences *thought* to be undesirable. To meet the question "What ought I to do?" by the answer "You ought to do what you think you ought to do" is nonresponsive, since the questioner seeks light precisely on the point of what one should *think* one ought to do. If there is no responsive answer to this question, then all questions of right are meaningless; and if there is one, then the answer must be found in some criterion applicable to acts as physical bringings about and not as righteous intention, and dividing them into two classes in some manner which is independent of what one thinks about it. If acts do not have or lack some property constituting them right to do, which is independent of our thinking, then there is no such fact as their rightness or wrongness for any thinking to determine. Determination of a criterion or criteria of such objective rightness is the problem of ethics and practical philosophy. Subjective rightness is the subordinate and particular question, what it is right to do to others on account of what they do—particularly, of what they do to the rest of us.

What allows confusion of this subordinate question with the major one of that rightness and wrongness of actions which lies in the value-character of their consequences—their desirability or undesirability—is the predicament in which finite knowers find themselves with respect to every kind of problem of objective fact. What it will be objectively right to do—which act, amongst alternatives open to us, will have consequences exhibiting a certain character not shared by other alternatives, or will have some character in higher degree than others—is a question of empirical fact, a question of objective truth. With respect to this, in any particular case, as with respect to any other question of objective truth, the best that we can do is to determine the answer which is best warranted by consideration of consistency and cogency applied to such relevant evidence as is available to us. Our best answer is simply the cogent answer, insofar as in us lies to achieve cogency. But the cogent answer frequently is not the true one. Whoever believes what is cogent, but as it happens false, commits no fault. And whoever believes and acts on the cogent answer to the question "What is objectively right for me to do?" would be unjustly blamed by others and irrational if he blames himself.

Now shall we say or not say, "There is no criterion of truth beyond the criteria of cogent belief"? I suggest that we shall not say this because, in general, the facts we investigate are always subject to further investigation; and a belief cogently reached on evidence available is always subject to correction by reference to later obtainable evidence. What we believe may be verified or confirmed beforehand or disconfirmed. What we believe, and cogently believe, at any given moment is distinguishable from the truth because there is no time limit on questions of empirical fact. The truth is that conclusion to which the probabilities (cogent beliefs) will eventually converge. But any decision of fact is one taken at some time, on some date, and *rightness* of this decision stops short with its cogency; if cogent, it remains forever the justified decision, regardless of any absolute truth. Let us note, however, that a cogent belief is a belief as to objective fact, not a belief as to its own cogency. And if there were no objective fact, independent of any belief of ours, cogent or incogent, there would be no such thing as cogency in believing, and no distinction between cogent beliefs and incogent ones.

There may be a sense in which there is no time limit on believing, as there is none with respect to investigation. But there is a time limit on decisions of action. And I suggest that the reason there is also a time limit on decisions of belief, and one should not answer all questions of empirical fact by saying, "The matter is not fully determinable," is simply that we have to act, to do or fail to do at that juncture when we may effect something having consequences.

Rightness in action can go no further than to conform itself to the cogent answer to the question, "What in this case is it objectively right to do? What choice of action is best warranted on the available evidence as that whose consequence will be most desirable?" But any answer to any such question, on any date, though cogent, may be false.

The cogent answer to this question is the right one. Action conformable to that right answer is right action. But let us not forget that what the question is about is not its own cogency but the objective fact. If we lose sight of the objective criterion in that to which our cogent decisions seek an answer, we lose sight of that which action is right by aiming at—even when it misses it.

In brief, rightness, in its various modes, is rooted in some corresponding imperative, some nonrepudiatable dictate to conduct ourselves in a certain manner, and/or to conduct ourselves so as to avoid results of a certain kind. I have supposed thinking and believing subject to the dictates of consistency and cogency. I have supposed acting, as physical bringing about, to be subject to two disparate dictates, of prudence and of justice. The nature of prudence, being a simple matter, has been clarified. The nature of justice, being highly complex, has not. It has been suggested—in the case of justice, with no substantiation of it offered—that the principles both of prudence and of justice dictate something to be assessed in terms of value. And, as has been explained, I would consider value, for all modes of evaluation, to be determined by reference to satisfactions to be found. Please accept these assumptions for the moment. The case, then, in the determination of right action is this: there is an imperative (or imperatives) to conduct our action so as to realize certain values, or avoid certain disvalues. That dictate itself, if valid, is *a priori*. What it dictates, in any concrete case, has to be determined by applying correctly the criterion (of value) dictated as the determinant of the corresponding kind of rightness. Such application can be made only by discovering what act will produce consequences having the kind of value which is dictated as criterion of this kind of rightness. Finding the answer to that question of value, and hence of rightness of action, requires judgment of empirical fact. The best we can do, in the case of this or any other empirical fact, is to find the cogent answer, on the available and relevant evidence. The cogent answer, in this or any other question of any character of the empirical, can always fail to be the true answer. But, subject to the time limit on investigation—and decisions of action are so limited—the cogent answer is our best attempt at the true answer. An action is objectively right to do if what is so done—brought about—is cogently judged to satisfy the criterion of rightness, dictated by the imperative which is pertinent to the kind of rightness to be determined. Briefly and inadequately that is right to do which, most probably, will in fullest measure realize the good. That is the perhaps obvious answer to the question of relation between the right and the good.

5. The Individual and the Social Order

The moral you are expected to draw from the discussion of subjective right vs. objective right is that unless there be some discoverable property of particular acts, done or contemplated, which is the criterion by reference to which they are determinably right to do or not right to do, no imperative of doing could ever be applied to any particular act. And in that case, no such imperative could be meaningful, since there would be no act with respect to which one could determine either that this imperative directs the doing of it or permits the doing of it, or directs that it be not done. An imperative directs the doing of acts of a certain kind, or the refraining from acts of a certain kind, or both. Unless it is possible to *pick out* acts which are of that certain kind which the imperative directs us to do or directs us to refrain from doing, choosing to do what is right is a choice we cannot make in practice, and the directive so to choose is empty.

It is entirely possible to take as the criterion of being at fault or being innocent of any fault, in a given choice of action, the criterion of *thinking* the act chosen to have the character of the right to do. I take it that this *is* the criterion we accept in approving or blaming ourselves and others for what is deliberately done—with the qualification that sometimes we regard failure to think, or to think cogently, as itself blameworthy. Further, it is possible, whether it is judicious or not, and whether it accords in fact with the common signification of 'moral' or not, to adopt the convention that 'moral act' is to mean 'innocent act,' 'not blameworthy act.' But even if we take such subjective rightness— as I have chosen to call it—as the significant moral or immoral character of action, we cannot possibly take it to be what the word 'right' means in the statement, "An act is moral (i.e., innocent) just in case the doer thinks it right to do." This must be the case because if we substitute 'moral' for 'right to do' in this definitive statement, we shall have "An act is moral just in case the doer thinks it moral to do"; and that would make any inquiry as to what acts are moral to do an empty inquiry. To inquire whether an act is moral or not, when my thinking it so makes it so, is silly. There is then no character which some acts have and some lack which is the character called 'moral' about which we so inquire. Inquiring is a significant activity only when directed to

---

Written for a proseminar on ethics given at Harvard in 1952.

determination of something which is as it is independently of what one thinks about it; and where 'being X' is synonymous with 'being thought to be X' there is no such character X which inquiry could disclose, or for the disclosure of which inquiry is needed. That X *is* so-and-so just in case it is thought to be so and-so can be the case only where X is immediate to consciousness—an appearance as such or an infallible intuition. That rightness of an act is such an X is, thus, tenable only for the protagonists of the view that rightness of action is determined by an incorrigible and infallible direct insight; and on that view inquiry whether any particular act is right is supererogation: one always knows the answer immediately or else there is none. (Incidentally, what is currently called 'intuitionism' in ethics is not, of course, this conception of an infallible conscience, but the conception that the *criterion* of right action is intuitively apprehended. To know a criterion intuitively, and to know immediately what application of that criterion dictates in a given case, are, of course, two different things.)

If one be convinced that that character of an act by reference to which it is determinably right or wrong is one which it is rational to inquire about, then this character so inquired about is the criterion of what I have called objective rightness. It suggests itself promptly that the objective of any such inquiry is some kind of value which the act, as an empirical bringing about, may have. I have been at no pains to avoid that obvious suggestion; but we do not as yet have a right to it, since we have so far made no investigation of the nature of justice, which is, of course, a highly important kind of rightness which action may have or lack, and according to many ethical conceptions is the only kind of rightness, investigation of which is properly called ethics.

But I take it that our examination of prudential action—which is a much simpler matter—is already sufficient; and certain points to be made are capable of illustration by reference to prudential rightness. The criterion of prudential rightness of an act is its contribution to the doer's own good life of a value exceeding that of any alternative mode of action in the circumstances. That character of the act is a character of its consequences, and the question of it is a question of empirical fact—what consequences to oneself will actually flow from this commitment of action, and what value and/or disvalue will those consequences have as ingredients in one's own life. As we have seen, this question of comparative values is a question of empirical fact.

One who seeks to determine the prudential correctness or rightness of a contemplated choice of action seeks to determine his act by a criterion of empirical fact, future fact which he must, in order to reach the decision, predict. That is the question which determination of objective prudential rightness concerns.

Now the point I want to raise here—and I raise it here with respect to prudence particularly because I think the similar point will arise in connection with justice—is the question whether we shall be speaking judiciously if we say that a decision of prudential action and the act decided on will be objectively right just in case it is true that this action will contribute more of value to the doer's good life than any alternative open to him.

We are here well beyond the point where we can decide such a question by reference to common usage of the term 'right'; if we want to take the above convention for our own, that decision cannot be called wrong. But I take it that there are reasons why we should still be injudicious in adopting that meaning of objective prudential right. What we are seeking to decide in prudential decisions is future facts or events, and the measure of a certain kind of value they will or would have. It is the value so in question which stands as the criterion by reference to which we shall decide. But whether this act *satisfies* that criterion is a question of empirical truth; and with respect to it the best answer we can achieve will be one which cannot be guaranteed to be true but only warranted as more or less probable.

The question is: How *ought* we to decide such prudential matters? What does the imperative to be prudent dictate in such cases? Will it be the case that we shall have decided as we ought if and only if it is true that the act we choose will in fact contribute in maximum degree to our future good life? I take it that this will not be our decision. If, for example, we invest our money in a certain way this year, and next year it turns out that we should have been better off if we had chosen a different investment, I take it that we shall still say that our past decision was rightly taken if we can also say that all the evidence which was available when we made that decision indicated a larger probability that it would turn out well than that this investment which in fact would have resulted better if we had chosen it would turn out advantageously. That is, I take it that we shall say we made the choice to be made in the way in which it is correct to make such choices if we made it according to the *probability*, on the evidence available, that it *would* satisfy the aim of prudent action. We shall say, now that the later facts are before us, that we made a poorer investment than if we had chosen differently. But we shall say—shall we not?—that we chose correctly, if our judgment that, in all probability, the investment we made had the best chance to turn out well was a cogent judgment.

Is this the same as admitting that we did the prudentially right thing to do if and only if we *thought* we were doing the prudentially right thing when we did it? No. If in retrospect, we have to admit that there was evidence then available to us which, if we had considered it, would have indicated that some different investment would probably turn out better, then we shall say that we did not act as prudentially as we might, and our decision was not prudentially justified. We were somewhat imprudent in taking it. We *did* think at the time that our choice was the one most likely to turn out well. But our so thinking was not cogent. To think and decide cogently, and just to think and come to some conclusion, are two different things. The point is that there are criteria of cogency; and what it is cogent to think in any given case is independent of what anybody *does* think, and is determinable from the nature of the specific problem of such thinking.

You may have one further doubt: you *should* have one further question at least. So far as cogency goes beyond consistency and has reference to evidence which is relevant and available, cogency is a discursive character of our thinking, and one may be incogent, not by reason of dealing fallaciously with what comes to his attention, but by failing to attend to what calls for attention in relation to the problem in hand. Perhaps you say also, "Some people have a limited capacity for being cogent, and should not be blamed for an incogency they cannot help." I think we touch here a question of the very nature of logical truth, because one can say of consistency as well as of cogency that the individual capacities for satisfying the imperative to be logical are different and in none of us matches the ideal; yet there is no logical truth independently of the human capacities here in question. Time allows me to say only that relative incapacity to satisfy imperatives which rationality requires us to acknowledge is precisely that fact which obliges the distinction of subjective right from objective right. And the matter of approval and disapproval is the question of subjective right. Objective rightness is an indispensable concept; and it must be delineated in terms of living up to the imperatives we cannot repudiate. I grant that cogency, in any particular problem to be decided, is relative to the conditions of that problem and of deciding it. But if it be conceived of as relative to our personal and subjective limitations in meeting that problem, that will do violence to our very purpose in entertaining this notion of cogency, or any other notion which is normative in its significance.

We here touch upon that sense in which imperatives generally have their root in that character of man we denote by the word 'rationality.' Man is rational by acknowledging imperatives which he is capable of satisfying but, as a descriptive fact, is certain to fail to satisfy on some occasions. And this fallibility is likewise a universal human characteristic. And if it were not for his fallibility, the imperatives he acknowledges would not be imperatives but descriptive generalizations of his behavior.

As you will have noted, I should be willing to define this trait of humanity by saying that to be rational is to acknowledge it as imperative to be consistent, cogent, prudent, and just.

And now we must turn to the question of justice, which is the peculiarly ethical question amongst the questions of the critique of our practice—our deliberate activities—in general.

The three imperatives which we have, so far, sketchily examined are —I suppose—independent of the human social habit, in the sense that if we conceive of a normal man as living, like some Robinson Crusoe, without fellows, we should suppose him to recognize the imperatives of consistency, cogency, and prudence as pertinent to his thinking and doing, but to find no occasion for consideration of any imperative to be just. We should, however, recognize that no normal man—as we should use that term—could grow up to be even consistent, cogent, and prudent without the influence of human society upon his development.

In passing, let us note also that even a Robinson Crusoe with any roots of moral sense would be subject to an other-regarding imperative if he had a dog and a parrot whose lives were affected by his conduct. To note this is to observe a horrible shortcoming of the Western moral self-consciousness, in comparison with the Oriental. The Law of Objectivity calls for compassion toward every other sentient being, though it calls for respect only toward those which are capable of deliberate and self-critical determination of their behavior. If, then, we use 'moral' in the broad sense which I would favor rather than a narrow sense more akin to the literal meaning of 'mores,' we shall recognize that moral problems are not confined to those of justice to one's fellows.

I should like to preface our examination of justice by certain other suggestions (there is not time for anything but suggestions) touching the connections of this topic of justice with facts concerning the social nature of man. I should like to suggest first that not only is our moral sense as including the human sense of the requirement of justice dependent upon the human habit of group living, but it is dependent upon certain peculiarities of human group living as contrasted with other types of group living exhibited by other species. It strikes me that anthropological and sociological studies of human mores, in the literal sense, are prone to interpret these as simply an outgrowth in a species whose survival notably depends upon the habit of group life—the conditioning of man's individual tendencies of response, requisite to food getting and the other modes of adaptation essential to animal life in general, by the superimposed necessities of group life. That accusation is too vague to be tested, and I mean it as nothing more. But what I would suggest is that this overlooks the deep importance, for understanding human mores and human culture, of recognizing precisely what underlies the human moral sense. The most notable and most gratifying peculiarities of the social habit amongst humans are precisely those which turn upon what can only be described as the preservation of individual moral autonomy. No other species is capable of that manner of group life. But men are capable of deviation from this norm; and the menace of statism lies precisely in that fact. If the Russians succeed in their intentions—I don't think they possibly could, even if they were not actively opposed at all, though that is less than no reason for not opposing them—but if they should succeed, they would completely stop the clock so far as human progress is concerned, and probably bring about the extinction of the human race. If humans should survive at all it would be in the manner of adaptation of the anthill and the beehive, in which the individual is no longer individual but a non-autonomous cell in the organism of self-perpetuating hive or colony, apart from which it cannot function.

If I seem to digress in making suggestions of this sort, it is in fact because I think that we cannot arrive at correct conceptions of justice in the human social order if we overlook this indispensability to it of the autonomy of the individual as a self-governing being, determining his individual behavior by reference to his own critical judgment and acknowledging no final authority which can override his own deliberate critique in the light of the immanent imperatives which are authoritative for him because they are thus immanent and cannot be repudiated.

This is, of course, an ancient ideal, and very near the core of Western culture—one of the fundamental tenets of Christianity, and a root-concept in the long tradition of natural law and of government as deriving authority only from consent of the governed. But I think it has implications of a different nature also, some of which may seem opposite in their direction: unorthodox and unchristian even, by the fact that they imply the preservation in human society of individual competition as an instrument for the realization of social purposes. And that, I think, has a definite bearing on the problem which must have been in your minds already as a definite problem of any ethics which would accept prudence, directed to individual ends, and justice, more obviously directed to common purposes, as rationally imperative. The plain divergence, on occasion, of the proximate prudential aim from proximate social aim is what sets this puzzle of social ethics. How are these seemingly antithetic imperatives to be accommodated, compromised, or reconciled in an ethics which accepts both as rationally constraining? But here again, you will recognize a continuing problem of ethics, variously dealt with historically and, as I see it, never satisfactorily. How bring it to appear that the ideally just man, unwilling ever to prejudice the common aim for his personal best good, nevertheless does the best thing for himself; or that an ideally just society, never willing to sacrifice individuals in order to attain group ends, so moves to the realization of the most effective and otherwise ideal realization of the common purpose? That apparently impossible task is intrinsic to ethics, all the way from Plato's *Republic*, which succumbs to the ideal of an insect society with social castes as the paradigm of justice, to the individualism of Kantian Protestant Christianity, which leaves it a miracle which we must trust to the goodness of an unknowable God to bring about as the realization of His kingdom, and to the perfectionist ethics of idealism, which—shorn of its edifying and mysterious talk of Absolute Spirit realizing itself in history—merely exaggerates the importance of the goods of integrity (just as Kant does), recommending the sublimation of our personal sacrifices in the empathic vision of an immanent goal of the wholly rational community. But as Huxley said, long ago, puzzling this same question, it is difficult to see what compensation the eohippus would get for his sorrows in contemplation of the fact that his remote descendant will one day win the Derby. I think it just to shock this beautiful ideal by confronting it with the commonplace practicality that, in this old world as it actually is known, a community of Kantian holy wills, or yearning self-realizationists who forget to be reasonably prudent, will never win any historical prizes or inherit the earth, but merely, like too good children, pass to whatever reward there may be for them in some transcendental and unknowable realm. I do not say there is nothing pertinent in this ethico-religious ideal—men differ from the eohippus on this point. I do say an ethics which leans so heavily upon it is too other-worldly to be practical. And an ethics which is not practical is not valid.

I would touch upon certain considerations which I think pertinent—each worth extended consideration, though they may seem to you remote from ethics. If rationality is to be practical (as Kant thought) its aim of justice must be practicable. And justice without prudence is not.

In the first place, the Absolute of idealistic ethics is a romantic fic-
tionalization of the spiritual but practical fact of the human community
of rational purposes. But these purposes end in values realizable in
individual human lives; Fichte said there is no God save in the mind
of man. I will not go so far, but will suggest that the only valid aims
of ethics are predictable ones—the rest we leave to the unknown God
who may bring about what we cannot predict and so can have no duty
to work for. I translate Fichte into such concrete terms. There are no
good ends to be realized save predictable values capable of realization
in individual lives. There is no transcendent Absolute whose glorious
self-realization we can serve otherwise than by forwarding the aim of
personal and individual good lives as those who live them may find
them. The community has no central consciousness in which to enjoy
or suffer. How horrid transcendental abstractionism may become, we
should now observe when it is given the perverse twist which results
from the unholy marriage of Orientalism and materialism: the individual life counts for nothing against the realization of the ideal community. For that, no individual sacrifice, whether of personal existence
or integrity of personality, is too great. I say there is no value at which
a moral community can rationally and practically aim save those to be
realized in the component real lives of individuals. The community is
a collectivity, and the abstract Society is an idol not even made in the
image of any God which rational man can worship or could serve.

There are also other peculiarities of man as a species, some more and
some less obviously connected with that rationality which is the root
of moral problems and moral aims. There is the trait, seeming remote
from this, that having hands, man is the tool-using animal. The consciousness of self, I suggest, is largely vested in what the individual
will controls. My body is mine because it so generally obeys my will and
realizes my purposes. That is the embodiment of myself which I control; which realizes my will. And that over which I make my will effective is my realized self. The small boy envisages a big self as the loco-
motive engineer, governing this immense instrument of his will as it
thunders down the track, or the aviator who swims up toward outer
space on the perfected mechanical wings which, in his imagination,
never fail him. The tool-using animal can so achieve a bigger self. And
the self-realizationists have a valid and immensely profound point if
they stress the concrete and practical possibilities for enlargement of the
self through the unification of individual purposes with common purposes in a vast and complex and practically well-working society, in
which he may achieve a life which is found good in contributing as an

autonomous individual to a purpose realized in wide-flung organization of common living. The professional man, who makes his social contribution largely with no orders from others but by autonomous decision, is already, in Western society, accorded the great privilege of such a possible self-realization. With the increase of scientific knowledge and its pervasive and growing instrumentation by technology, the proportion of the community whose vocation becomes an exercise of autonomy continually grows. The contrast I would draw is with the biologically and instinctively achieved efficiency of the ant colony. The root of that contrast is in the government of action by imagination, knowledge, intelligence, and the realization of self-hood in the cooperative community of autonomous and self-respecting individuals, mutually respecting each other. The root is in knowledge and the imperatives of rationality. This is the progressive freeing of the human spirit. Hegel missed the essence of it by insufficient recognition of self-fulfillment as doing rather than merely thinking. He so left the way open for the historical antithesis of Feuerbach and the perversion of dialectical materialism.

Another distinctive human trait, so fundamental that it rates as biological, is the possession of language. And the peculiar character of human language, as contrasted with significant animal cries, is that while the latter can direct the attention of others to the immediately observable and directly immanent, human language can convey the past and the envisaged future as well as the present: not merely the presented but that present-as-absent which must be represented. It is so also that it can convey what is removed from presentation by spatial distance, and can communicate the merely possible and the needing to be done. Only by guesswork can we weigh how much this faculty of language has contributed to the fact that humans self-consciously live in a world as far-flung as the distant stars and in a present which finds its place in a march of time in which the here and now discernibly has grown out of its past and moves effectively into the limitless future. Only for man is the past real, beyond the presently felt reverberation and the future a definite locus of the desirable and that which may be planned. The first operation of cognition is translation of the now felt into signification of that which has a place and date in a limitless contemporary world in which all things grow out of their past and move into their future.

This in turn is the deepest miracle of the human social order. Man is the animal—the only animal—conscious of his history as a species, and by this self-consciousness affecting his own evolution and capable of directing it to his human values. Other creatures merely are evolved by natural forces they are incapable of comprehending. But man, by some capacity to penetrate the natural process, in measure controls his destiny. It is so that man alone evolves socially, and in a manner vitally affecting every individual human life, in a manner and with a speed which far transcends the limits of his biological evolution as an animal. If men today are biologically superior to men in—say—ancient Athens, that is hardly by natural selection, but mainly because his young have more to eat and are better spared the laming vicissitudes to which infancy in Athens was subject, by reason of comparative ignorance and the lack of control of conditions of life which that relative ignorance implies.

Each generation of other species begins where its parents began, because there is no social memory: nothing learned from the experience of past generations, no perpetuation in memory beyond the individual memory. For that, human language is essential. Man is the animal that remembers as a species and not merely as an individual. And the great instrument of his evolution, as a self-directed progress, is the social inheritance of ideas—the great traditions of agriculture, of technology, of science, of mores, of music and the arts, of religion and culture generally—by reason of which successive generations, with perhaps no heightening of the average I.Q. or other biological capacities, may still so immensely increase their knowledge and so rapidly extend the possible realization of human value and control of the conditions of good living.

The great instrument of what we call our civilization, which is so produced, is education, in its broadest sense, in which the knowledge and the wisdom man has won, as a result of all past human experience, is passed on to each new generation. And a basic part of that is human mores. These—as the governing institutions of the relation of each individual to his fellows—are the basis of the rest, the condition of individual learning. We are all of us born men and women of the Old Stone Age, with the same equipment of instincts and propensities of action. But the community seizes upon each of us at birth, ministers to our individual needs, girds us with the totality of acquired knowledge, and molds us in the image of its own spiritual attainment.

Oversight of this most impressive of all social facts is ridiculous, the puerile defect of the materialistic theory of history. The vital, the indispensable, factor in human history as human is not material. We live in the same old natural environment as all past generations. Biologically we are little different from our cave-dwelling ancestors. That our lives are so different, society so different, and what we eat and how we come by it so different, and our labor so immensely more productive and all individual activity so much more largely capable of its projected and desirable ends—the secret of all this lies in no material factor, but the spiritual factor of the cognitive and moral nature of man as a social animal. Strip the present generation of all their material trappings and reduce them to naked animals in the old environment, but leave them all their historically acquired knowledge and their acquired mores, it is not then implausible that men might come near to recreating our present human world in a generation or two. But strip the present generation of all faintest recollection of what has been learned since the Stone Age, and all their acquired habits of social living, and it is equally plausible that, in that case, the whole historical process would have, painfully, to repeat itself, and take an equal time. Man is not, as Feuerbach said, what he eats but—if we must pare down human value to the most exigent good of eating—man, at any moment, is what he is by his acquired knowledge and skill in feeding himself abundantly without the Old Stone Age labor of incessantly hunting for berries and digging roots, and chasing prey with a stone club. Economic institutions serve the basic and exigent material needs. And economic progress may largely pace and facilitate all other progress. But the secret of economic evolution is in the spiritual factor of the inherited and evolving idea-system of science and technology, and is no more than limited by any material factor whatever. Materialism is, of course, idiotic on the part of any self-conscious human—the perverse yearning of pseudo-intellectual eggheads to return to wallow in that aboriginal slime from which the human individual is removed by so many million years of progressive differentiation.

And what has all this to do with ethics? Everything. Ethics is man's explication to himself of that spiritual force which is the secret of the distinctive character of the life of the self-conscious animal. The moral imperatives—more largely the rational imperatives of consistency and cogency in his self-directed and self-criticized mental processes, and of prudence and justice in self-directed doing—these are expression of the controlling directives by reason of which human life is what it is and what it may become.

On the one side, every item of what men are aware of as the world around them and the possibilities of their individual doing is something discovered originally to some individual in his individual self-consciousness. The only brains society has to think with and learn with and for perpetuation of itself as a mental and spiritual ongoing force are individual brains. There is no slightest conquest in human history which is due to anything but the thinking of autonomous individual thinkers.

By language, what any individual learns may become a common possession of all. But it is by the sorting and sifting of the social process that although individually acquired ideas are more frequently false than true, the true is elicited and remembered, the mistaken rejected and forgotten. But to impose the social authority of the traditional and accepted upon the spontaneity of individual human thinking would be, obviously, to stop the clock. It is by individual freedom of thought, and the respect for the individual in his own initiative and self-criticism, that human society has become human instead of an ant colony. Only the self-governing and self-criticizing animal is human and could be moral.

On the other hand, the human individual is human only by participation in a human society. The social historical process has made him what he is, and offers the only opportunity he has of what he may achieve and what he may become. Separate him from the social spiritual process, and he must return to the Old Stone Age, or to the level of ape-living even. He is what he is and may realize any value that he individually cherishes only as he meets the conditions of membership in a social order of individuals, cooperating in the pursuit of values cherished in common.

When we come to the ethical questions of justice, and the seeming divergence to the dictate of prudence, on occasion, from the dictate of justice, then let us not forget two things: first, that if one should ask, "What is it that is most indispensable to the individual good of any human?" the readiest and most plausible answer must be, "The privilege of living in a good human society, profiting from its spiritual inheritance of ideas, and sharing in its cooperative institutions, preserved and furthered by its mores" but second, if any community ask itself, "What is it that is most indispensable to our ongoing life, to the distinctive character of the life we share, the source of all we cherish, and the hope of all further social achievement?" there the discerning answer is, "The fact that our social order is composed of autonomous individuals, capable of thinking and learning otherwise than by being told, and subject to their own self-criticism and the ultimate authority of their own self-government in action." If we suppress that self-governing initiative, we destroy that only root from which all that we possess has come to be and from which alone can spring any social advance to be hoped for in the future.

Only for short-term thinking could the contrast of individual prudence and social justice seem fundamental. But only by remembering it can the nature and the valid dictate of real justice be understood.

6. Turning Points of Ethical Theory

There are, I think, three outstanding concepts in ethics: the good, the right, and the just. A particular ethical theory is largely, if not wholly, determined by its analysis of these concepts, and its manner of conceiving their relations to one another.

Justice is, plainly, a derivative concept here. What is just is what is right toward others—what is right in view of our social relationships. Good and right have, each of them, a much wider application than just. Right is what is correct, justified, valid, imperative. The distinction of right and wrong extends over the whole field of man's decisions and his deliberate doing. It applies to all our thinking and inferring, as the distinction between valid and invalid conclusions, and between beliefs which are justified as against those which are mistaken or delusive. It applies to doing as directed to any purpose or kind of purpose, to artistic doing, to any manner of technical doing, and to doing and decisions to do which, like getting one's own breakfast or choosing a comfortable pair of shoes, are as free as possible from any responsibility to other persons. There is, correspondingly, the logically right or wrong, the cognitively valid or invalid, the prudentially justified or unjustified, as well as the artistically right, the politically right, the right answer in arithmetic, the right investment to choose, and the right way to make friends and impress people. In brief, 'right' connotes critique.

Good and bad likewise have wide application, beyond what concerns our relations to others, and are thus just or unjust. Good applies to whatever gratifies or satisfies, or conduces to satisfaction, and hence is desirable and rationally to be wished. The concept of justice occupies so prominent a place in ethics, in spite of being obviously derivative, for two reasons: first, because it seems to require some peculiar principle, not called for in the case of other kinds of right doing, to cover right doing toward others; and second, because so many thinkers in the field of ethics speak and write as if moral rightness and wrongness were exclusively a matter of our obligations to other persons.

Let us grant that this question of justice is the most exigent of moral problems, and what any ethical theory has to say about it is the most important feature of that ethics. But is it in fact the only question of

---

Written in 1951 (according to Schilpp); read before the Harvard Philosophy Club, 1954.

morals? For example, are merely prudential problems questions of ethics, and is it the business of ethics to elicit rules of prudence? If you say "Yes," you outrage any who would follow Kant; and if you say "No," you flout Bentham and the utilitarians. Extraordinary as it may seem at this date, there never has been any clear and common understanding as to what the boundaries of ethics are and what the subject of ethical study is.

I do not think it important how we divide up our problems—though I do think it ought to be recognized as indicating an extraordinary lack if there is to be no attempt at systematic study of right and wrong doing in general and beyond the bound of justice and injustice merely. And I do suggest that the whole business of the conduct of life, and of rightness and wrongness in such conduct at large, is a vitally needed study with which no one can in fact fail to concern himself, and that all questions falling within this broader field are affected with a sense of the moral, because all decisions of the conduct of life must be affected with a sense of right or wrong. If ethics is to be restricted to what concerns justice only, then this broader field of right and wrong doing in general might be called 'practical philosophy,' and ethics will be merely one branch of it.

I would further draw attention to the trouble which ethics has encountered in finding any clear, intelligible, and generally accepted answer to the principal question of justice: the question, namely, "Is it my duty to act with equal regard for the interests of others as for my own; and if so, why?" Could it be that the reason for this difficulty lies in overlooking the fact that right and wrong toward others is only one species of right and wrong; and that we are unlikely to find the root of the imperative of justice if that imperative be thought of as *sui generis* and without parallel? If justice and injustice are one species of right or wrong doing in general, then it might be that the imperative of justice is simply one mode or one application of an imperative which is more general. In that case, it would not be surprising that if we wait to raise the question of the validity of imperatives of action until the specific question of right action toward others comes in view, what we can then find to say about it may prove to be too little and too late.

I wish to suggest that this approach to the question of justice is the auspicious one, from the point of view of theoretical understanding, and that it is best to begin by investigating the broader topic of right and wrong in general, and the imperative in general, and of principles of validity and critique over the whole scope of them. That takes in the normative in general. But it will be obvious that I could not even outline so large a project here. I can only touch upon it here and there, hoping to indicate points which have special importance and are such as can be suggested briefly.

'Right' and its inverse 'wrong' concern some property or character of acts—of whatever is done by decision, and is subject to criticism and such that the doer may be called upon, or call upon himself, to justify it. These terms 'right' and 'wrong' are extended, by that metonymy which characterizes the use of language in general, to whatever connects itself with rightness in action or wrongness in action. But the first and literal meaning, from which the further senses of them derive, is one in which their application is confined to acts, and to acts which are deliberate or corrigible.

I shall wish to use the words 'act' and 'action' here in the above meaning, confining their application to what is done by decision and excluding incorrigible behavior and even unconsidered behavior, except so far as the failure to *consider* it would itself be a matter calling for correction. This is a narrower sense than the common sense usage, but frequent in ethics since it confines act to the sense of 'conduct.' On another point, however, I would use 'act' and 'activity' more widely than is usual by extending these terms to include decisions themselves. Deciding not only is of the essence of any deliberate doing, but deciding is itself an activity, subject to critique and calling for justification. In fact, though a physical doing is not the same fact as the decision to do it, any physical doing is right or is wrong just in case it is something done by decision and that decision is right or is wrong. Rightness and wrongness of decision are, thus, the root of rightness and wrongness in general. All decisions are right or wrong, and nothing else is right or wrong except as it flows from a decision which is right or wrong, or is something the decision to do or to bring about would be right or wrong. And all decisions are right or wrong, justified or unjustified, because all decisions are subject to some imperative. That is right which accords with the imperative and that is wrong which contravenes it.

There will be some, I am sure, who will fail to recognize this fact because, by habit of thought, they associate this word 'imperative' exclusively with felt obligation to others. I can do no more than suggest here very briefly that there are other imperatives than the imperative of justice, and that they are familiar.

There is, for example, the imperative to rightness in inference—the imperative to be consistent in our thinking, by reason of which we are constrained to cry "Touché" when we are found inconsistent or if we refuse a conclusion whose premises we have accepted. At the present moment in history, it is customary to think of principles of logic as formulating a certain kind of fact, and not as normative rules, the adherence to which is an acknowledged dictate for the conduct of our thought. But that there is this normative function of them, determinative of what is justified and is unjustified in conclusions reached, will hardly be denied. At a later point, I shall wish to revert to the kind of facts which logic is supposed to formulate.

Also, believing in general, and disbelieving, have their imperative. And in passing, let us remind ourselves that the greater part of what is called knowing is merely giving credence according to the evidence. The constraint so to conduct our decisions of belief is familiar. There are things we should like to believe but are obliged to consider doubtful. Also we sometimes say regretfully, "That I have to accept as fact." If there are any who could overlook this manner of imperative, it might be persons who conform to it habitually because for them obedience to it represents a bent of mind and professional self-discipline, and any recognized wishful thinking they almost automatically repudiate.

Prudent behavior is also a matter having its imperative. Whether prudential principles are taken to be included in or excluded from ethics, at least it is clear that they concern a problem different from that of social justice. And if prudence lies nearer to inclination, at least we observe in children that prudent decision and action are neither automatic nor dictated by felt inclination; and any of us who has ever postponed a task too long for our own best interests will be able to take the point that prudential dictates operate as imperatives. In fact, the prudential offers a particularly favorable example for distinguishing between inclination and any sense of the imperative, while still observing that the imperative in general cannot be identified with the socially obligatory.

But before probing that matter further, it will be desirable to turn briefly to the concept of the good or valuable, as the third factor in ethical theory. Good and bad, and other value terms, are amongst the most horrendously ambiguous of any—and it makes no difference on this point what language you consider. What makes them so is no perversity or carelessness on our part but the extreme diversity amongst kinds of things we are called on to evaluate. There is, however, one very deep ambiguity, devastating for ethical theory, which lies between what is called good because it represents an aim which is imperative, and what is called good because it gratifies or satisfies. Many, perhaps most, ethical theories try to reduce one of these to the other. Hedonists, for example, try to derive the good as imperative from the good as the gratifying. If, like the social utilitarians, they repudiate egoism and conceive that the good of others lays a duty upon each, they then fail utterly to discover any ground for this imperative of justice. Theories of the opposite sort, like those of Kant and the self-realizationists, make what is good in the sense of imperative aim the first and foremost sense, and try to accommodate the good as gratifying by some preachment extolling the beatitude of the righteous life. I pause to take my hat off to them, but I don't think their arguments prove one cannot be so happy by cutting a few corners. Still other ethical theories, which do not commit either of these reductionist fallacies, do something worse: they dogmatically insist that one or other of these two senses is *the* meaning of good, and content themselves with speaking in edifying ways of their chosen good and speaking disparagingly of good in the other sense. I hope to be neither a reductionist nor a dogmatist here, but I think it absolutely essential for clarity in ethics to distinguish these two meanings. And one of them already has its own distinctive name, just 'imperative.' I wish, therefore, without prejudice to the excellence of righteous living, but simply for purposes of clarity, to separate, brutally and cleanly, these two different concepts, and to speak here only of good or valuable as that which consists in or conduces to satisfaction in living. I have written elsewhere of this; let me here summarize without argument or discussion, for the sake of brevity.

It is patent that the significance of good and ill in human life extends more widely than what we deliberately decide upon and do, or what answers to imperatives, and lies simply in the fact that men, like other animals, enjoy and suffer. The significance of the moral and the right depends on this, though it does not coincide with it. If life were unaffected by any pleasure or pain, joy or grief, no man nor any animal would find one action dictated rather than another. The literally first urge to action is in the fact that the physical performance itself feels good; and the second such urge is found in finding that enjoyment or the relief from pain follows promptly. A prime difference of men from animals (though it is one of degree) is that men learn to identify more remote pains and pleasures as consequences of what they do. Their deliberateness in acting stems genetically from that trait or capacity.

Immediate goodness is the quality of satisfactoriness found directly in experience. Immediate badness is that quality in experience to which we are averse. When the experience in question is immediate, these qualities of good and bad are simply found and need no judgment. When the experience in question is one predicted—perhaps as consequence of action—or one merely viewed as possible, these value-qualities of them must likewise be predicted or judged.

Everything *else* called good or bad is so called in the sense of conducing to such immediate goodness or badness. All other valuable and disvaluable things have value as instrumental, in the broad sense of the word. All values and disvalues in objects and states of affairs are such instrumental goods and bads. The subordinate modes in which these derivative values in objects have to be judged are highly various.

But there is another sense of good and bad, in which the terms apply to experience itself. A life on the whole is a continuum of immediacy, and it may be found good or found bad on the whole. A life on the whole is good insofar as he whose life it is finds it so. Any other and external criterion of it either evaluates it as instrumental of some *other* person's good or to the social welfare, or it represents a grotesque presumption on the part of him who judges. To assess the value on the whole of a possible life which may be his is the unavoidable and impressive necessity under which each of us lies. (And incidentally, one who finds no imperative in that—well, I hope never to argue with him. What I wish to denote by 'imperative' is, I fear, something outside his comprehension.) I would call this value attaching to a life on the whole its quality of *final* goodness. In relation to it, particular passages of immediate experience may call to be reassessed. There are immediate gratifications indulgence in which may detract from it, and immediate privations which may contribute to it. But in any case, the final goodness or badness of a life is no sum of immediate goods minus the sum of transitory bads, nor any product of their duration times their intensity. Such a misplaced passion for arithmetic is too naïve. Life is a temporal gestalt, and has its final value as a composition, not as a bank balance. The good of it is not a summation but a consummation. Its music or its discord is not in any single note, though in nothing apart from all of them.

As each lives his own life, value is relative to persons; that is, what is good *for* is good for somebody or other; and what is good for A may be bad for B—not relative to his wish or inclination. He who supposes that there is nothing good or bad but thinking makes it so may discover his error by trying his recipe. If that doesn't teach him better, let us omit flowers. There is such a thing as social good in the same sense that there are social judgments: that is, individual judgments from the vicarious social viewpoint, or a consensus of individual judgments. The social good is some collation of individual goods and ills; the appropriate method of assuring it is a most serious question of ethics but one I must omit here. Any absolute good of humanity at large is a figure of speech; humanity, as Herbert Spencer observed, has no central consciousness. The analogy of society to an organism is extended and impressive, but it is analogy, not literal truth. The good of humanity is a collective fact, though as collective it *is* a fact. And what contribution to it will or may be made by any act or may result from any objective state of affairs is another fact, though of a kind it is difficult to assess.

In conclusion, let us observe that all goods and bads are empirical facts, and those which are not immediate and must be judged have to be judged on empirical grounds and can be only so judged. Valuation is an empirical science, except that it is too new, in spite of age-old interest, to have developed to the scientific stage. All of us judge values all our lives, and perhaps we come to guess so well as to question what's the use of reckoning.

I have suggested that without values there would be no imperative, but if we seek to derive the imperative straight from value, we are bound to miss its distinctive character. The imperative is imperative whether we like it or not. And it is most clearly discerned where it stands opposed to what we wish. But I have also suggested that we shall not easily see the nature of it by looking to that particular imperative which obliges us to respect the good of others.

Rather our sense of the imperative is simply our sense of fact—but of fact as not immediate. I have used the example of our serious judgment when our own good life is critically in question. It is that same imperative which, as even Hume acknowledged, obliges us practically to act as if our cognitive apprehensions are significant of a real objective world in which we can make valid predictions of the future, in the light of past experience, whether we consider the premises of that practical attitude theoretically sufficient or not. If one makes this investment or takes this job, or studies for this profession or marries at this age, the facts of what will happen and whether they will make for a good life are difficult matters. The consequences of our decision once effected are then out of our hands, and even if we can foretell the future, or estimate it accurately so far as its other features go, we can still blunder devastatingly by mistaking what value-quality will be found in that which we predict and to which we so commit ourselves. To rush in from present inclination and uncriticized emotion is precisely what we would avoid. This is prudential judgment, if you will, though if you say that 'prudence' is a poor word for the responsible attitude, sure, I shall agree and applaud. Our aim is to respect the future fact as that fact will be when it comes: to appreciate it or realize it in that nature it will have experienced, and not as envisaged now in our attempted imaginative presentation of it—colored, it may be, by wishful thinking or romantic daydream. We have two kinds of facts here to respect: the cause-effect facts of natural consequences of our present choice of action, and the value-facts of these consequences as satisfying or dissatisfying ingredients in a life to be lived. From both points of view, our only clues now when we must decide are some manner of immediate presentments. But we would govern our decision not by the immediate quality of this presentment but by the character of what it represents. To heed this imperative will be to decide and to act here and now in view of the objective realities our immediate presentments mediate instead of deciding and doing as present feeling inclines us.

Psychologically, the root of the imperative seems to me quite simple. Herbert Spencer spoke of it as government of the simple presentative feelings by the complex representative feelings. But I suggest that 'representative feelings' is here inapt language. A better name for it is what we know. To subordinate immediate feeling to the objective fact—in this case to what our act affects and what that will in fact be when realized—this is the essence of rationality. But I suggest that our knowing how it will feel to have the tooth pulled tomorrow is not a mental contortion by which we now feel what we predict, and acting with full respect for the nature of that represented factuality is hardly to be governed by the present force of a present representative feeling.

That is—as we commonly conceive it—the difference between a man and an animal. Animals act toward the future and adaptively to future fact. But we suppose that their doing so requires an instinct whose emotive power as now felt exceeds that of any presently opposing inclination. Men are not moved and deterred by the strength of now felt apprehensive feeling but by the sense of an imperative to objectivity in decision. It is so that I would describe the imperative as a felt ingredient in human experience. And the principle of it is simply the principle of objectivity: respect realities apprehended for what they objectively are, and not by reference to your subjective feeling, not according to the quality and intensity of the immediate feeling which mediates them for your apprehension. In other words, be rational, not emotional. Be governed by your intellectual integrity, not by your uncriticized feelings. Taking this as the basic principle of right decision in general, and of moral conduct in the widest sense of 'moral,' is—I hope you note—the exact antithesis of an emotive theory of morals.

And correlatively, this view connects itself with a conception of cognition which, instead of contrasting indicative statements of fact with hortations, persuasions and advice, would point to the essential connection of every statement of fact with corresponding imperatives of action. But these imperatives, unlike commands from one of us to another, or persuasions intended to cozen those addressed into doing what we wish, are such as appeal to the integrity of the one addressed and advise him in the light of it, but do not trespass upon that integrity or upon his freedom of decision and of action.

I have elsewhere developed this pragmatic thought that (analytic statements excepted) every simple indicative statement of objective fact is correlative with and explicated by some set of hypothetical statements of the consequences of possible action. That the stove is hot means, amongst other things, that if you touch the stove you will be burned. Hence the indicative statement which advises of the fact likewise advises, "If you do not want to be burned, don't touch the stove." But this hypothetical imperative, conveyed by the simple statement of fact, "The stove is hot," is not a command originating in the speaker's wish or will and laid upon the one spoken to. If some perverse simpleton should respond, "The stove is hot: if I touch it I shall be burned. So what?", we should naturally reply, "By all means do exactly as you wish, but don't say I didn't warn you." The command of this hypothetical imperative originates in the fact itself, which rules out the possibility of touching the stove without being burned. We merely advise of this. And this advice of action is addressed to the other's rationality. As a categorical command, "Don't touch the stove," it is a prudential imperative of his own intelligence and will, confronting objective fact, or there is no imperative.

If, then, it should be asked, "In what does the imperativeness of the principle of objectivity lie? Why or whence the command to respect objective facts for what they are instead of being governed by immediate feeling?" the answer is, "This imperative lies in your own nature, confronting objective facts, or else there is no imperative in your case. But if you find no imperative in the disclosure of facts, then that must be the end of our concern about you—except as we may feel compassion for dumb brutes we cannot treat as fellows, or be obliged to protect ourselves from the consequences of what they do."

The example here chosen is one in which the implicit imperative of right conduct is, or strikes us as being, merely prudential. The small child who, seeing the glowing stove, feels the urge to touch it and does so, injures only himself. And so likewise in the case of the careless adult, or the occasional pathological mind with the urge to self-inflicted pain. But let us observe that what this trivial example illustrates is the imperative to the good life. The tendency to sacrifice future goods to present urges, especially if the contemplated future be remote, is more frequent, and lapses from the dictate of the principle of objectivity are there more common. The dictate to respect the objective fact of your future satisfactions and griefs for the realities they are, and not to prejudice them by doing as momentarily pleases you—not to sacrifice your birthright for some mess of pottage—is not quite so trivial as our example seems, but the principle is the same. And here too, let us observe, if the validity of this imperative to have regard for a good life on the whole should be challenged by some fool who says, "If I do this I prejudice my interests of ten years from now—so what?" there is nothing to reply. And if his present urges affect our own interests also, there is nothing left but to protect ourselves, as best we may.

It is a common failing of our human nature not to see or feel remote and future interests full size—e.g., to postpone study to the week before exams—and it is by reason of that kind of fact that the principle of objectivity as the dictate of prudence and the good life has the status of an imperative. But it is a dictate which must be self-imposed, and whose validity must be self-acknowledged, or it has none.

The case is the same where the rightness in question is that of right belief. The dictate of objectivity there is obvious: believe what your experience evidences as objective fact, and not according to your simple presentative feelings, your emotions, or what you would like to think. Wishful thinking is, again, a common human failing, and so far as that is the case, the obvious principle of right decision has the status of an imperative: believe what is evidenced as true, or extend your credence as measured by the objectively determinable probabilities.

Incidentally that principle is somewhat more important, theoretically, than it may seem. As some of you will have discovered, it is extremely difficult to express an objective probability on given data as any kind of objective fact. That problem, I suggest, is to be solved by remembering that an objective probability is an advice of right action. "On the given premises, the probability of X is .8" advises "Act as you would if X were to happen in 8 such cases out of 10, and fail to happen in 2 of them." For example, if X is an accident the probability of which is 0.07 and you can insure against it for less than 7 per cent of your loss in case it happens, the right decision is to insure. I suggest that this is the solution of the problem what a probability is: namely, an advice of right decision where there is no certainty. And if we should be convinced that most beliefs are no better than probable, this dictate of right believing is correspondingly important.

I would further suggest that the rightness of logic has no other ground than this self-imposed imperative of the principle of objectivity. There is hardly time to discuss this in detail. Perhaps the main facts, however, are obvious. If it should be asked, "Why be logical?" the question is difficult to take seriously, and perhaps if we try to take it seriously, we might be inclined to look for a prudential sanction: being illogical is a good way to get into various kinds of trouble. But in fact, our sense of rightness in inference as imperative is hardly confined to such cases, but extends as widely as any serious intent in thinking and drawing inferences. Also, though deliberate perversity in inference may be rare, negligence in inference is not. And before such an audience as this, I do not need to emphasize that such correctness is a self-imposed imperative, and that where it is lacking or not responded to, there is nothing left to do but to banish the culprit from our company. And again, logical rightness is an advice of action: be consistent; you cannot eat your cake and have it too.

The advice of rational attitude is the substance of propositions of logic. As rules, logical principles have significance, but as statements of fact they convey no information concerning any object or any state of affairs. They advise our adherence to meanings considered and to premises accepted, but they tell us nothing we do not already know, implicitly at least.

But what of the distinctively ethical imperative: the imperative of justice? I suggest that we do not have to look in any theoretical dark corner for it; the main consideration is right there in plain sight. The other fellow's joys and sorrows are exactly as real and as poignant as your own. Respect them for the objective realities they are, instead of according to any weakly felt and vicarious immediate feeling of sympathy with which they may afflict you. There is more than that, of course, to the question of egoism versus altruism. But time is too short to go into it. If it is the imperative of justice that is wanted, then it is in the principle of objectivity, in application to the question of decisions and actions affecting others. And if one have no sense of this as a valid imperative, then perhaps there is nothing for the rest of us to do but banish him as one we cannot admit to our company and treat as a fellow.

However, if this conception seems to be a weak one, resting simply on a kind of dogmatic dictum when confronted by cynicism in its various current forms, then I think there is a kind of argument by which opponents can be met, though we should first observe the predicament of one who would argue a matter so fundamental. The question here concerns, as I have tried to suggest, imperatives in general, and the basic imperatives—finally, this principle of objectivity itself—must be categorical or else valid in no sense at all. But Kant has confused us about categorical and hypothetical imperatives; the division between the two is not between those which are moral and those requiring a technical sanction or one of antecedent inclination. Instead, this division is between principles which are final and general and apply in all cases, and their application to particular instances. No such general imperative implies a direct and unqualified dictate of rightness in any particular instance. That requires other premises expressing the particularities of the case. There is absolutely no concrete act which is right to do under any and all circumstances. There are even times when you ought to hold your breath instead of breathing. Correspondingly the dictate of right in any particular instance is hypothetical, when fully stated, though let us not overlook the commonplace fact that when the hypothesis of it is satisfied, a hypothetical imperative becomes an unqualified dictate.

Next, let us note the enormity of the demand to validate the basic categorical imperatives. One is being asked to validate the principles of logic as valid directions of inference with no logical premises and no respected rules of inference, to validate the dictate to believe the truth with no prior acknowledgment of antecedent truth believed or any commitment to respect fact when demonstrated. One is asked to show a principle of action right at the same time when the opponent repudiates real and basic rightness of anything at all.

Yet there is a kind of argument which I think can be addressed to any cynic—just by calling attention to the fact that so-called moral imperatives do not stand alone but can be successfully challenged only by repudiating rightness of action altogether.

Time is short, and I must be brief, but let me suggest this argument. It is a *reductio ad absurdum* and also a *petitio principii*—as e.g., any proof in logic must be—but I think it takes a hardy soul to deny its force.

Consider the position of one who says there are no imperatives of right action, and by implication acknowledges that whenever he feels like it or it suits his purposes, he lies or says whatever he pleases. But this admitted pathological liar seeks entry into our serious debate. He wishes us to feel the force of his logic and to believe his conclusion argued for. What he *says*, just like what Epimenides said, may not be self-contradictory. When an admitted Cretan says "All Cretans are liars," the statement he utters may seem plausible to half his audience. But a Cretan's *act of assertion* in saying it vitiates any credibility it could have on the ground of his saying it. Epimenides was in fact intending only to introduce a little comic relief. The contradiction lies in the self-inconsistency of the act of assertion, and may be called pragmatic instead of strictly logical.

The moral is obvious. One who argues that there are no binding imperatives of action intends an assertion, but vitiates any possible serious import of anything he says. He will be properly answered if we tell him we are not amused, or say to one another, "What was that noise; let us go find it and put a stop to it." If for the moment, we should suppose he tells the truth in his own case, then we must find he has no business interrupting our serious and responsible search for truth. And he who repudiates all imperatives cannot, if the repudiation is genuine, be dealt with by arguing. He can but be persuaded with a club, since that may alter his emotions. When the appeal to reason has no effect, force is the only arbiter.

Part III. Epistemology and Metaphysics

1. A Pragmatic Conception of the *A Priori*

The conception of the *a priori* points two problems which are perennial in philosophy : the part played in knowledge by the mind itself, and the possibility of "necessary truth" or of knowledge "independent of experience." But traditional conceptions of the *a priori* have proved untenable. That the mind approaches the flux of immediacy with some godlike foreknowledge of principles which are legislative for experience, that there is any natural light or any innate ideas, it is no longer possible to believe.

Nor shall we find the clues to the *a priori* in any compulsion of the mind to incontrovertible truth or any peculiar kind of demonstration which establishes first principles. All truth lays upon the rational mind the same compulsion to belief; as Mr. Bosanquet has pointed out, this character belongs to all propositions or judgments once their truth is established.

The difficulties of the conception are due, I believe, to two mistakes : whatever is *a priori* is necessary, but we have misconstrued the relation of necessary truth to mind; and the *a priori* is independent of experience, but in so taking it, we have misunderstood its relation to empirical fact. What is *a priori* is necessary truth not because it compels the mind's acceptance, but precisely because it does not. It is given experience, brute fact, the *a posteriori* element in knowledge which the mind must accept willy-nilly. The *a priori* represents an attitude in some sense freely taken, a stipulation of the mind itself, and a stipulation which might be made in some other way if it suited our bent or need. Such truth is necessary as opposed to contingent, not as opposed to voluntary. And the *a priori* is independent of experience not because it prescribes a form which the data of sense must fit, or anticipates some preestablished harmony of experience with the mind, but precisely because it prescribes nothing to experience. That is *a priori* which is true, *no matter what*. What it anticipates is not the given, but our attitude toward it : it concerns the uncompelled initiative of mind or, as Josiah Royce would say, our categorical ways of acting.

The traditional example of the *a priori* par excellence is the laws of

Read at the meeting of the American Philosophical Association, December 27, 1922. Reprinted by permission from *The Journal of Philosophy*, Vol. XX (1923), No. 7, pp. 169–77.

logic. These can not be derived from experience since they must first be taken for granted in order to prove them. They make explicit our general modes of classification. And they impose upon experience no real limitation. Sometimes we are asked to tremble before the spectre of the "alogical," in order that we may thereafter rejoice that we are saved from this by the dependence of reality upon mind. But the "alogical" is pure bogey, a word without a meaning. What kind of experience could defy the principle that everything must either be or not be, that nothing can both be and not be, or that if x is y and y is z, then x is z? If anything imaginable or unimaginable could violate such laws, then the ever-present fact of change would do it every day. The laws of logic are purely formal; they forbid nothing but what concerns the use of terms and the corresponding modes of classification and analysis. The law of contradiction tells us that nothing can be both white and not-white, but it does not and can not tell us whether black is not-white, or soft or square is not-white. To discover *what contradicts what* we must always consult the character of experience. Similarly the law of the excluded middle formulates our decision that whatever is not designated by a certain term shall be designated by its negative. It declares our purpose to make, for every term, a complete dichotomy of experience, instead—as we might choose—of classifying on the basis of a tripartite division into opposites (as black and white) and the middle ground between the two. Our rejection of such tripartite division represents only our penchant for simplicity.

Further laws of logic are of similar significance. They are principles of procedure, the parliamentary rules of intelligent thought and speech. Such laws are independent of experience because they impose no limitations whatever upon it. They are legislative because they are addressed to ourselves—because definition, classification, and inference represent no operations of the objective world, but only our own categorical attitudes of mind.

And further, the ultimate criteria of the laws of logic are pragmatic. Those who suppose that there is, for example, *a* logic which everyone would agree to if he understood it and understood himself are more optimistic than those versed in the history of logical discussion have a right to be. The fact is that there are several logics, markedly different, each self-consistent in its own terms and such that whoever using it, if he avoids false premises, will never reach a false conclusion. Mr. Russell, for example, bases *his* logic on an implication relation such that if twenty sentences be cut from a newspaper and put in a hat, and then two of these be drawn at random, one of them will certainly imply the other, and it is an even bet that the implication will be mutual. Yet upon a foundation so remote from ordinary modes of inference the whole structure of *Principia Mathematica* is built. This logic—and there are others even more strange—is utterly consistent and the results of it entirely valid. Over and above all questions of consistency, there are issues of logic which can not be determined—nay, can not even be argued—except on pragmatic grounds of conformity to human bent and intellectual convenience. That we have been blind to this fact, itself reflects traditional errors in the conception of the *a priori.*

We may note in passing one less important illustration of the *a priori* —the proposition "true by definition." Definitions and their immediate consequences, analytic propositions generally, are necessarily true, true under all possible circumstances. Definition is legislative because it is in some sense arbitrary. Not only is the meaning assigned to words more or less a matter of choice—that consideration is relatively trivial —but the manner in which the precise classifications which definition embodies shall be effected is something not dictated by experience. If experience were other than it is, the definition and its corresponding classification might be inconvenient, fantastic, or useless, but it could not be false. Mind makes classifications and determines meanings; in so doing it creates the *a priori* truth of analytic judgments. But that the manner of this creation responds to pragmatic considerations is so obvious that it hardly needs pointing out.

If the illustrations so far given seem trivial or verbal, that impression may be corrected by turning to the place which the *a priori* has in mathematics and in natural science. Arithmetic, for example, depends *en toto* upon the operation of counting or correlating, a procedure which can be carried out at will in any world containing identifiable things—even identifiable ideas—regardless of the further characters of experience. Mill challenged this *a priori* character of arithmetic. He asked us to suppose a demon sufficiently powerful and maleficent so that every time two things were brought together with two other things, this demon should always introduce a fifth. The implication which he supposed to follow is that under such circumstances $2 + 2 = 5$ would be a universal law of arithmetic. But Mill was quite mistaken. In such a world we should be obliged to become a little clearer than is usual about the distinction between arithmetic and physics; that is all. If two black marbles were put in the same urn with two white ones, the demon could take his choice of colors, but it would be evident that there were more black marbles or more white ones than were put in. The same would be true of all objects in any wise identifiable. We should simply find ourselves in the presence of an extraordinary physical law, which we should recognize as universal in our world, that whenever two things were brought into proximity with two others, an additional and similar thing was always created by the process. Mill's world would be physically most extraordinary. The world's work would be enormously facilitated if hats or locomotives or tons of coal could be thus multiplied by anyone possessed originally of two pairs. But the laws of mathematics would remain unaltered. It is because this is true that arithmetic is *a priori*. Its laws prevent *nothing*; they are compatible with anything which happens or could conceivably happen in nature. They would be true in any possible world. Mathematical addition is not a physical transformation. Physical changes which result in an increase or decrease of the countable things involved are matters of everyday occurrence. Such physical processes present us with phenomena in which the purely mathematical has to be separated out by abstraction. Those laws and those laws only have necessary truth which we are prepared to maintain, no matter what. It is because we shall always separate out that part of the phenomenon not in conformity with arithmetic and designate it by some other category—physical change, chemical reaction, optical illusion—that arithmetic is *a priori*.

The *a priori* element in science and in natural law is greater than might be supposed. In the first place, all science is based upon definitive concepts. The formulation of these concepts is, indeed, a matter determined by the commerce between our intellectual or our pragmatic interests and the nature of experience. Definition is classification. The scientific search is for such classification as will make it possible to correlate appearance and behavior, to discover law, to penetrate to the "essential nature" of things in order that behavior may become predictable. In other words, if definition is unsuccessful, as early scientific definitions mostly have been, it is because the classification thus set up corresponds with no natural cleavage and does not correlate with any important uniformity of behavior. A name itself must represent *some* uniformity in experience or it names nothing. What does not repeat itself or recur in intelligible fashion is not a thing. Where the definitive uniformity is a clue to other uniformities, we have successful scientific definition. Other definitions can not be said to be false; they are merely useless. In scientific classification the search is, thus, for *things worth naming*. But the naming, classifying, defining activity is essentially prior to investigation. We can not interrogate experience in general. Until our meaning is definite and our classification correspondingly exact, experience can not conceivably answer our questions.

In the second place, the fundamental laws of any science—or those treated as fundamental—are *a priori* because they formulate just such definitive concepts or categorical tests by which alone investigation becomes possible. If the lightning strikes the railroad track at two places, *A* and *B*, how shall we tell whether these events are simultaneous? "We ... require a definition of simultancity such that this definition supplies us with the method by means of which ... [we] can decide whether or not both the lightning strokes occurred simultaneously. As long as this requirement is not satisfied, I allow myself to be deceived as a physicist (and of course the same applies if I am not a physicist), when I imagine that I am able to attach a meaning to the statement of simultaneity. ...

"After thinking the matter over for some time you then otter the following suggestions with which to test simultaneity. By measuring along the rails, the connecting line *AB* should be measured up and an observer placed at the mid-point *M* of the distance *AB*. This observer should be supplied with an arrangement (*e.g.*, two mirrors inclined at 90°) which allows him visually to observe both places *A* and *B* at the same time. If the observer perceives the two flashes at the same time, then they are simultaneous.

"I am very pleased with this suggestion, but for all that I can not regard the matter as quite settled, because I feel constrained to raise the following objection: 'Your definition would certainly be right, if I only knew that the light by means of which the observer at *M* perceives the lightning flashes travels along the length *A–M* with the same velocity as along the length *B–M*. But an examination of this supposition would only be possible if we already had at our disposal the means of measuring time. It would thus appear as though we were moving here in a logical circle.'

"After further consideration you cast a somewhat disdainful glance at me—and rightly so—and you declare: 'I maintain my previous definition nevertheless, because in reality it assumes absolutely nothing about light. There is only *one* demand to be made of the definition of simultaneity, namely, that in every real case it must supply us with an empirical decision as to whether or not the conception which has to be defined is fulfilled. ... That light requires the same time to traverse the path *A–M* as for the path *B–M* is in reality *neither a supposition nor a hypothesis* about the physical nature of light, but a *stipulation* which I can make of my own free will in order to arrive at a definition of simultaneity.' ... We are thus led also to a definition of 'time' in physics."[1]

---

[1] Albert Einstein, *Relativity: The Special and General Theory* (New York, trans. R. W. Lawson, 1920), pp. 26–28; italics are the author's.

As this example from the theory of relativity well illustrates, we can not even ask the questions which discovered law would answer until we have first by *a priori* stipulation formulated definitive criteria. Such concepts are not verbal definitions, nor classifications merely; they are themselves laws which prescribe a certain uniformity of behavior to whatever is thus named. Such definitive laws are *a priori*; only so can we enter upon the investigation by which further laws are sought. Yet it should also be pointed out that such *a priori* laws are subject to abandonment if the structure which is built upon them does not succeed in simplifying our interpretation of phenomena. If, in the illustration given, the relation "simultaneous with," as defined, should not prove transitive—if event *A* should prove simultaneous with *B*, and *B* with *C*, but not *A* with *C*—this definition would certainly be rejected.

And thirdly, there is that *a priori* element in science—as in other human affairs—which constitutes the criteria of the real as opposed to the unreal in experience. An object itself is a uniformity. Failure to behave in certain categorical ways marks it as unreal. Uniformities of the type called "natural law" are the clues to reality and unreality. A mouse which disappears where no hole is, is no real mouse; a landscape which recedes as we approach is but illusion. As the queen remarked in the episode of the wishing-carpet: "If this were real, then it would be a miracle. But miracles do not happen. Therefore I shall wake presently." That the uniformities of natural law are the only reliable criteria of the real is inescapable. But such a criterion is ipso facto *a priori*. No conceivable experience could dictate the alteration of a law so long as failure to obey that law marked the content of experience as unreal.

This is one of the puzzles of empiricism. We deal with experience: what any reality may be which underlies experience, we have to learn. What we desire to discover is natural law, the formulation of those uniformities which obtain amongst the real. But experience as it comes to us contains not only the real but all the content of illusion, dream, hallucination, and mistake. The *given* contains both real and unreal, confusingly intermingled. If we ask for uniformities of this unsorted experience, we shall not find them. Laws which characterize all experience, of real and unreal both, are non-existent and would in any case be worthless. What we seek are the uniformities of the *real*; but *until we have such laws, we can not sift experience and segregate the real.*

The obvious solution is that the enrichment of experience, the separation of the real from the illusory or meaningless, and the formulation of natural law all grow up together. If the criteria of the real are *a priori,* that is not to say that no conceivable character of experience would lead to alteration of them. For example, spirits can not be photographed. But if photographs of spiritistic phenomena, taken under properly guarded conditions, should become sufficiently frequent, this *a priori* dictum would be called in question. What we should do would be to redefine our terms. Whether "spook" was spirit or matter, whether the definition of "spirit" or of "matter" should be changed— all this would constitute one interrelated problem. We should reopen together the question of definition or classification, of criteria for this sort of real, and of natural law. And the solution of one of these would mean the solution of all. Nothing could *force* a redefinition of spirit or of matter. A sufficiently fundamental relation to human bent, to human interests, would guarantee continuance unaltered even in the face of unintelligible and baffling experiences. In such problems, the mind finds itself uncompelled save by its own purposes and needs. I *may* categorize experience as I will; but *what* categorical distinctions will best serve my interests and objectify my own intelligence? What the mixed and troubled experience shall be—that is beyond me. But what I shall do with it—that is my own question, when the character of experience is sufficiently before me. I am coerced only by my own need to understand.

It would indeed be inappropriate to characterize as *a priori* a law which we are wholly prepared to alter in the light of further experience, even though in an isolated case we should discard as illusory any experience which failed to conform. But the crux of the situation lies in this: beyond such principles as those of logic, which we seem fully prepared to maintain no matter what, there must be further and more particular criteria of the real prior to any investigation of nature whatever. We can not even interrogate experience without a network of categories and definitive concepts. And we must further be prepared to say what experimental findings will answer what questions, and how. Without tests which represent anterior principle, there is no question which experience could answer at all. Thus the most fundamental laws in any category—or those which we regard as most fundamental—are *a priori,* even though continued failure to render experience intelligible in such terms might result eventually in the abandonment of that category altogether. Matters so comparatively small as the behavior of Mercury and of starlight passing the sun's limb may, if there be persistent failure to bring them within the field of previously accepted modes of explanation, result in the abandonment of the independent categories of space and time. But without the definitions, fundamental principles, and tests of the type which constitute such categories, no experience whatever could prove or disprove anything. And to that mind which should find independent space and time absolutely necessary conceptions, no possible experiment could prove the principles of relativity. "There must be some error in the experimental findings, or some law not yet discovered," represents an attitude which can never be rendered impossible. And the only sense in which it could be proved unreasonable would be the pragmatic one of comparison with another method of categorical analysis which more successfully reduced all such experience to order and law.

At the bottom of all science and all knowledge are categories and definitive concepts which represent fundamental habits of thought and deep-lying attitudes which the human mind has taken in the light of its total experience. But a new and wider experience may bring about some alteration of these attitudes, even though by themselves they dictate nothing as to the content of experience, and no experience can conceivably prove them invalid.

Perhaps some will object to this conception on the ground that only such principles should be designated *a priori* as the human mind *must* maintain, no matter what; that if, for example, it is shown possible to arrive at a consistent doctrine of physics in terms of relativity even by the most arduous reconstruction of our fundamental notions, then the present conceptions are by that fact shown not to be *a priori*. Such objection is especially likely from those who would conceive the *a priori* in terms of an absolute mind or an absolutely universal human nature. We should readily agree that a decision by popular approval or a congress of scientists or anything short of such a test as would bring to bear the full weight of human capacity and interest would be ill-considered as having to do with the *a priori*. But we wish to emphasize two facts: first, that in the field of those conceptions and principles which have altered in human history, there are those which could neither be proved nor disproved by any experience, but represent the uncompelled initiative of human thought—that without this uncompelled initiative no growth of science, nor any science at all, would be conceivable; and second, that the difference between such conceptions as are, for example, concerned in the decision of relativity versus absolute space and time, and those more permanent attitudes such as are vested in the laws of logic, there is only a difference of degree. The dividing line between the *a priori* and the *a posteriori* is that between principles and definitive concepts which *can* be maintained in the face of all experience and those genuinely empirical generalizations which *might* be proven flatly false. The thought which both rationalism and empiricism have missed is that there are principles, representing the initiative of mind, which impose upon experience no limitations whatever, but that such conceptions are still subject to alteration on pragmatic grounds when the expanding boundaries of experience reveal their infelicity as intellectual instruments.

Neither human experience nor the human mind has a character which is universal, fixed, and absolute. "The human mind" does not exist at all save in the sense that all humans are very much alike in fundamental respects, and that the language habit and the enormously important exchange of ideas has greatly increased our likeness in those respects which are here in question. Our categories and definitions are peculiarly social products, reached in the light of experiences which have much in common, and beaten out, like other pathways, by the coincidence of human purposes and the exigencies of human cooperation. Concerning the *a priori* there need be neither universal agreement nor complete historical continuity. Conceptions, such as those of logic, which are least likely to be affected by the opening of new ranges of experience, represent the most stable of our categories; but none of them is beyond the possibility of alteration.

Mind contributes to experience the element of order, of classification, categories, and definition. Without such, experience would be unintelligible. Our knowledge of the validity of these is simply consciousness of our own fundamental ways of acting and our own intellectual intent. Without this element, knowledge is impossible, and it is here that whatever truths are necessary and independent of experience must be found. But the commerce between our categorical ways of acting, our pragmatic interests, and the particular character of experience is closer than we have realized. No explanation of any one of these can be complete without consideration of the other two.

Pragmatism has sometimes been charged with oscillating between two contrary notions: the one, that experience is "through and through malleable to our purpose"; the other, that facts are "hard" and uncreated by the mind. We here offer a mediating conception: through all our knowledge runs the element of the *a priori*, which is indeed malleable to our purpose and responsive to our need. But throughout, there is also that other element of experience which is "hard," "independent," and unalterable to our will.

2. The Pragmatic Element in Knowledge

There are three elements in knowledge: the given or immediate data of sense, the concept, and the act which interprets the one by means of the other. In the matrix of thought these are inseparable; they can only be distinguished by analysis. Not all would agree that even just analysis can separate them. In fact, theories of knowledge might be classified by their insistence upon one or another of these three and the attempt to comprehend the other two within it. Emphasis on the given or immediate characterizes the mystic and Bergson's "pure perception." Subordination of the other two to the conceptual element means idealism or some form of rationalism. Pragmatism is distinguished by the fact that it advances the act of interpretation, with its practical consequences, to first place.

If one ask for a rough and ready expression of the pragmatic creed, I suppose one will be likely to receive the answer, "The truth is made by mind." Qualification, of course, is needed at once. There is equal insistence that the making of truth is directed to some practical situation. And a practical situation implies brute fact, something given, as one element of it: the other element is a human being with his needs and interests. If the pragmatist emphasizes the importance of such needs in determining our human truth, it is equally just to remark that, without the brute fact of the given, the problem of meeting these needs would not arise. Nor would there be anything which could determine that one way of meeting them should succeed and another fail. If the pragmatist maintains, then, that the truth is made, at least he does not believe that it is made out of whole cloth.

Moreover, in conceiving that truth and knowledge represent active interpretation by the mind, pragmatism is not alone. Idealism likewise stresses the creativity of thought. Indeed, the idealist outruns the pragmatist in this respect, conceiving that the object, and so the situation to be met by knowing, has ultimately no existence independent of the mind.

The difference between the two—or *a* difference—lies in this: that for the idealist 'mind' means, in the last analysis, generic mind, the common human mind, or the ideal mind imperfectly manifest in us,

Reprinted by permission from *University of California Publications in Philosophy*, Vol. 6 (1926), No. 3, pp. 205-27.

the Absolute; while for the pragmatist minds are individual, ultimately distinct, and capable of idiosyncrasy. Such personal or racial peculiarities, or differences which time makes in the prevailing temper, may find their expression in the way minds meet the situations which confront them. And so truth may be somewhat personal, and may change with history. It is not rooted in fixed categories which are *a priori.*

These are, then, the bare fundamentals of the pragmatist position concerning knowledge: that knowledge is an interpretation, instigated by need or interest and tested by its consequences in action, which individual minds put upon something confronting them or given to them. On any theory, it is to be expected that minds will largely coincide and that agreement, for various obvious reasons, will be the rule. But the extent and manner of such coincidence is, for pragmatism, something to be noted in particular cases, not simply the result of universal human reason.

As I have suggested, the validity of this general type of conception can be tested by studying the nature and importance in knowledge of the pragmatic element of interpretation, and its relation to the other two, which we may refer to as 'the concept' and 'the given' respectively.

Suppose that we take some outstanding example of knowledge, and, using it as a paradigm, attempt thus to assess the significance of interpretation. Whatever example we choose will be of some particular type, and we must be on our guard against mistaking as general features of knowledge what are only typical of special cases. But if, from lack of time, we thus concentrate on a single illustration, it should represent knowledge at its best. For this reason, I propose the example of geometry. Mathematics comes very close to our ideal of knowledge at least in the important respect of relative certainty. And in the whole field of mathematics, geometry offers the best example because of the concreteness of its applications.

The last quarter-century of mathematical study represents the historical fruition of a great many previous researches and discoveries, so that today we can feel much surer that we understand the nature of mathematical knowledge than it ever has been possible for men to feel before. Three important results emerge from this study. The first is the discovery that all mathematics, and not geometry only, can be developed by the deductive method. A relatively few definitions and initial assumptions suffice to give us all the rest of any branch of mathematics, such as complex algebra or projective geometry.

The second of these results is a necessary consequence of the first: all mathematics is abstract in the sense of being independent of any and every possible application, because if all the theorems follow logically from the definitions and postulates, then we can arbitrarily alter the things which we let the terms, such as 'point' and 'line,' mean, without in the least disturbing any step in the proofs. *Whatever* 'point' and 'line' may mean, given these assumptions about them, these consequences—the rest of the system—must also hold of them, because the theorems follow from the assumptions by pure logic. Thus for any mathematical system, there will be many possible applications, though very likely only one or two of these will have any practical importance. You can let 'points' mean the members of a set of clubs governed by certain rules, or you can let them represent what are usually described as "spheres one inch in diameter." Similarly, the a's and b's and x's of complex algebra may represent numerical magnitudes, or you may let them represent the array of points in space. In this last case, both the applications mentioned are practically important.

The third step was the logical culmination indicated by the two preceding. It was discovered that we can dispense, in mathematics, with all the initial assumptions except the definitions. That is, all the truths of mathematics follow from the definitions of the terms used, without any further assumptions whatever except logic or the principles of proof. This third step could only be proved possible by actually carrying it out. The stupendous labor of thus developing the fundamental principles of mathematics merely from exact definitions of terms, by pure logic, was performed by Mr. Russell and Mr. Whitehead in *Principia Mathematica.*[1]

Our main interest in all this is that it definitely proves something that Plato ventured to assert two thousand years ago: that our knowledge of mathematics is quite independent of that sense-experience which suggests it to us and is the practical motive for our study of it. A club of thorough-paced mathematicians could retire from the world of sense, provided that were somehow possible, and not interrupt their discussions in the least. They would need a means of communication, of course, and some sort of counters, such as words or tally-marks, as the common currency of their discussion. But no application to sense-things is otherwise of the least importance to them. Often they do not assign any meaning at all to their a's and b's; the letters themselves are good enough symbols to serve all their interests.

Thus we discover that the content of pure mathematics is simply

[1] Cambridge, 1910, Vol. I.—Eds.

the deductive or logical order of purely logical entities, a sort of elaborate logical pattern of abstract terms without any denotation at all.

"But," you say, "who wants that kind of mathematics? Who cares whether it is possible or not?" I must not pause to answer that question in detail beyond pointing out the relation which the business of pure mathematics now bears to that of the practical man. The mathematician is a sort of maker of patterns. He keeps a stock of them which is already bigger than anybody has found a need for. He has an infinite number of different geometries, for example, all just as good from his point of view as Euclid, and such curiosities as quaternions and systems containing curves that have no tangents. Mostly he develops these from pure intellectual curiosity. He is exploring the Platonic heavens, and it may seem as important to him as measuring the earth. Sometimes the practical man borrows one of these patterns ready-made and finds for it a previously unsuspected application. Some of the most important advances in physical science have come about in just this way.

But our interest in this lies in the nature which the truth of abstract mathematics is revealed to have. Three points are important:

1. Assuming logic or common modes of valid proof, the truths of mathematics are quite independent of any world of sense, and hence independent of given experience, so far as given experience means perceptible sense-qualities. If there were two mathematical minds, one on the Earth and one on Mars, their experience and their sense-organs might differ in any way you can imagine, and still if only they shared a common logic or modes of valid thinking, all they would need would be some method of communication in order to have all the truths of mathematics in common.

2. In such abstract mathematics, the whole of all truth is open to any logical mind, provided we know precisely what the terms are defined to mean—that is, how they are logically related. To bring out the point, let us contrast mathematical and empirical or sense-knowledge from the point of view of learning. You see this desk. It is a thing of sense. Suppose that we carry away with us whatever knowledge we gain now as we look at it. And then suppose tomorrow someone ask, "Is there a knot on the under surface of the top of this desk?" We do not know. Not only that, but we might be the master minds of all the ages and have thought about it continuously during the interval, and still we could not know. Nothing but a further experience, of us or someone else, could possibly determine the question.

But now suppose that someone write down here the initial principles of some mathematical system—say Euclid's geometry. We may take *that* knowledge away with us, and there is absolutely no mathematical truth of that system which we could not learn merely by thinking about it.

3. An obvious point but for us the most important of all: mathematical truth is a little more certain than almost any other knowledge that we have, precisely for the reason indicated above. We really do not need any further experience to verify it, and no further experience could possibly trip us up and prove us wrong, unless we have been illogical in our thinking. It is the kind of truth called *a priori*, knowable with certainty in advance of any particular sense-experience whatever.

Admittedly not all mathematical knowledge is of this sort. As soon as we raise practical questions about the application of geometry to space or of algebra to stresses and strains, the situation is quite different and more complex. But pure mathematics is, I think, typical of one element which enters into all knowledge. It is because we have here an almost clean separation of this element that I have chosen this example, which in other respects may be a little difficult and uninteresting.

Mathematics is an illustration of the immensely elaborate body of truth which may rise from pure concepts, from the merely logical relations of terms, and terms which need not have any reference to sense-qualities or experienceable things of any sort. Moreover, the initial meanings or relations of these terms are quite arbitrary. The mathematician makes them what he will. Often he chooses them from intellectual curiosity about their consequences, an interest very much like that in the possible moves in a game of chess. When such relations of a few terms are set up, just as when a few rules are imposed as conditions of the game of chess, the logical consequences to which they give rise are almost inexhaustible and absolutely determined.

Now in all our knowledge—particularly in all science—there is an element of just such logical order which rises from our definitions. An initial definition, as we may see, is always arbitrary in the sense that it cannot be false. In itself it does not tell us whether anything is true or not, or what the nature of existing objects is. It simply exhibits to us a concept or meaning in the speaker's mind which he asks us temporarily to share with him and symbolize by a certain word or phrase. Socially, of course, it is important that such meanings should be common, and that words be used in familiar ways. But if a scientist finds a new concept worth developing, he may invent a technical term or use an old word in a new meaning which he takes care to make clear. That the introduction of concepts which are novel and not generally shared may be of the highest importance is something illustrated by almost every major advance in science. Such an initial concept, whether new or old, is a definite logical structure. It sets up precise relations of certain elements of thought. And that structure—or the combination of a few such conceptual structures—may give rise to logical consequences as elaborate as mathematics or the game of chess.

Indeed, before we set out upon any systematic investigation, we must have such initial concepts in our minds. It does not matter how we get them; we can always change them for any reason, or for no reason if it suits our whim. The *real* reasons why we *do* use certain concepts is, of course, practical. That is another story, which I shall come to. But however we come by such initial meanings, it is obvious that we must have them before we address ourselves to any problem. Until we have principles of classification which serve to distinguish what is material from what is immaterial, what is a force from what is not a force, straight from crooked, rigid from non-rigid, the simultaneous from the successive, and so on—that is, until we have certain definite concepts or meanings in mind, we cannot even approach the problem of acquiring knowledge of any sorts of things to which such concepts might apply. We have no handle to take hold of them by.

And whatever our concepts or meanings may be, there is a truth about them just as absolute and just as definite and certain as in the case of mathematics. In other fields we so seldom try to think in the abstract, or by pure logic, that we do not notice this. But obviously it is just as true. Wherever there is any set of interrelated concepts, there, quite apart from all questions of application or the things we use them for, we have generated a whole complex array of orderly relations or patterns of meaning. And there must be a truth about these —a purely logical truth, *in abstracto*, and a truth which is certain apart from experience—even though this is only a part of the truth which we want to discover, and the rest of it is of a quite different sort which depends upon experience.

Ordinarily we do not separate out this *a priori* truth, because ordinarily we do not distinguish the purely logical significance of concepts from the application of words to sensible things. In fact it is only the mathematician who is likely to do this at all. But I should like to indicate that this separation is always possible and that it is important for the understanding of knowledge. To this end, let me use the term 'concept' for this element of purely logical meaning. We can then discriminate the conceptual element in thought as the element which two minds must have in common—not merely may have or do have but absolutely *must* have in common—when they understand each other.

I suppose it is a frequent assumption that we are able to apprehend one another's meanings because our images and sensations are alike. But a little thought will show that this assumption is very dubious.

Suppose we talk of physical things in physical terms, and our discussion involves physical measurement. Presumably we have the same ideas of feet and pounds and seconds. If not, the thing is hopeless. But in psychological terms, my notion of a foot goes back to some immediate image of visual so-long-ness, or the movements which I make when I put my hands so far apart, or to a relation between these two. Distances in general mean quite complex relationships between such visual perceptions, muscle and contact-sensations, the feeling of fatigue, and so on. Weight goes back to the muscle-sensation which we call in New England the "heft" of the thing. And our direct apprehension of time is that feeling of duration which is so familiar but so difficult to describe.

Now in such terms, will your sensory image of a foot or a pound coincide with mine? I am nearsighted; your eyes are good. Or I might have a peculiarity of the eye muscles so that focusing on near objects would be accompanied by a noticeable feeling of effort, while this is not the case with you. When it comes to reaching, there is the difference in the length of our arms. If we lift a weight, there is the difference in strength between us to take into account. So it is with everything. In acuity of perception and power to discriminate, there is almost always some small difference between the senses of two individuals, and frequently these discrepancies are marked. It is only in rough and ready terms that we can reasonably suppose that our direct perceptions are alike.

Even for the large and crude distinctions, what assurance is there that our impressions coincide? No one can look directly into another's mind. The immediate feeling of red or rough can never be transferred from one mind to another. Suppose it should be a fact that I get the sensation you signalize by saying "red" whenever I look at what you call "violet," and vice versa. Suppose that in the matter of the immediately apprehended qualia of sensation my whole spectrum should be exactly the reverse of yours. Suppose even that what are for you sensations of pitch, mediated by the ear, were identical with my feelings of color-quality, mediated by the eye. How should we ever find it out? We could never discover such peculiarities of mine so long as they did not impair my powers to discriminate and relate as others do.

Psychological differences of individuals are indeed impressive. Long before scientific psychology was thought of, the ancient skeptic had based his argument on them. This is what led Gorgias to say that nothing can be known, and if anything could be known, it could not be communicated. There can be no verification of community between minds so far as it is a question of the feeling side of experience, though the assumption that there is no coincidence here seems fantastic.

Yet Gorgias was quite wrong about the communication of ideas. That your sensations are never quite like mine need in no way impede our common knowledge or the conveying of ideas. Why? Because we shall still agree that there are three feet to the yard, that red is the first band in the spectrum, and that middle C means a vibration of 256 per second. At the end of an hour which feels very long to you and short to me, we can meet by agreement, because our common understanding of that hour is not a feeling of tedium or vivacity, but means sixty minutes, one round of the clock, a pattern of relation which we have established between chronometers and distances and rates of movement, and so forth.

When we want to be sure that we share each other's meanings, we define our terms. Now defining terms makes no direct reference to sense-qualities. We set up logical relations of one term to others. The pictures in the dictionary may help, but they are not necessary. We might suppose that such definition chases one meaning back into other meanings, and these into still others, until finally it is brought to bay in some first (or last) identity of meaning which must be identity of sensation or imagery. But all the words used in defining any term in the dictionary are also themselves defined. There is no set of undefined first terms printed at the beginning. The patterns of logical relationships set up by these interconnected definitions of terms themselves constitute the conceptual meanings of the terms defined.

To sum up this matter: the sharing of ideas does not necessarily depend on any identity of sense-feeling. It requires only a certain fundamental agreement in the way our minds work. Given this basis of logic, the process of coming to possess our meanings—and in that sense, our world—in common is secured by the business of living together and the methods of naming, pointing, and learning by imitation, which exhibit the fundamental habits of the social animal. In the end, the practical criterion of common meaning is congruous behavior. Speech is merely that part of behavior which is most significant for securing the cooperation of others.

But while I have been striving to make it plausible that concepts and common meanings are something apart from immediate sensation, you have been preparing an objection, I am sure. "This concept," you will say, "is a mere abstraction. Nobody has one in his mind without connecting it with his experience of objects; and the principal use of concepts is to apply to and name perceivable things."

I must grant this at once. Indeed it is one of the points I should like to make. The purely logical pattern of meaning is always an abstraction. It is exactly like the concepts of pure mathematics in this respect, though other concepts may often lack the simplicity and exactness of the mathematical. Just as in the case of pure mathematics there is a complex and important set of logical consequences which arise merely from the definitions of terms, so also in the case of concepts in general, the pattern of logical relations which is generated simply through our modes of distinguishing and relating is something intrinsically capable of being separated from all application to things of sense, and would then constitute a definite and considerable body of knowledge which could be learned merely by thinking, without any reference to the external world at all. Indeed we know at once that any sort of definition has logical consequences which can be so learned. When we remember that any science, and even common-sense knowledge, can get under way only through our bringing to experience those initial modes of classification and relation which our definitions embody, we are brought to realize that in physics, or chemistry, or any other department of knowledge, we do not study simply the facts of our given experience. We study in part such facts and in part the consequences of our own logical meanings, though usually without any separation of these two.

In our knowledge of the external world, concepts represent what thought itself brings to experience. The other element is 'the given.' It represents that part or aspect which is not affected by thought, the "buzzing, blooming confusion," as James called it, on which the infant first opens his eyes.

It is difficult to make a clean separation of what is given in experience from all admixture of conceptual thinking. The given is something less than perception, since perception already involves analysis and relation in recognition. One cannot express the given in language, because language implies concepts, and because the given is just that element which cannot be conveyed from one mind to another, as the qualia of color can never be conveyed to the man born blind. But one can, so to speak, point to the given. There are some of us who enjoy music passively. We just soak it in, as the infant may confront the world in his first conscious perception. We are transported by it, and all thought is put to sleep. Perhaps others tell us that this is a very uncultivated attitude: that we do not hear the music at all but only a glorious noise. What they mean is that we do not analyze our music and identify its pattern of harmony and melody. Well, for us who listen thus passively, music is pure given, while for those who intellectualize it by analysis it may be something more. But that *more* is not given; the mind brings it to the experience. In every experience there is such a given element, though in very few does it have such immediate esthetic character that we are content to remain confronting it without adding to it by thought.

Perhaps you see already that the mere immediacy of such given experience is never what we mean by knowledge. Or rather, I ought to say, it is not what *most* of us mean by knowledge. There are some, as for instance Bergson and the mystics, who reserve the term 'knowledge' for precisely such a state of luminous immediacy. In the end, it is fruitless to quarrel about the use of terms; we can only note this curious exception to ordinary parlance, and pass on. For the rest of us, knowledge of things does not mean being sunk in such immediacy, but an attitude in which what is given is interpreted and has some significance for action.

If I bite an apple, what is given is an ineffable taste. But if this is the basis of any knowledge, it is because I interpret this taste as significant of what is not just now given, of the quality of the apple or of another bite. At this moment, your immediate apprehension of this thing which I hold in my hand leads you to say that I have here a sheet of paper. But if this should suddenly explode, or if I should proceed to swallow it and smile, you might revise that judgment and realize that it went quite beyond what was absolutely given in perception. Or we might just now hear a chirring, chugging noise which would lead us to think of an automobile outside. But in that case, we are at once aware how very much we have added to the given by way of interpretation.

If time permitted, I should like to make it clear that a state of pure immediacy in which consciousness would just coincide with the given would always be purely passive, and that thought not only is active interpretation but that such interpretation is always significant of our possible action and of the further experience to which such action would lead. But I can omit this, because it is a thought which William James himself made familiar. At least it will be clear that in the knowledge of objects, as much as in the knowledge of propositions or generalizations, this element of active interpretation must always be present. We do not have any knowledge merely by being confronted with the given. Without interpretation we should remain forever in the buzzing, blooming confusion of the infant. This, I suppose, is the biological significance of thinking. It is an activity by which we adjust ourselves to those aspects of the environment which are *not* immediately apprehended in sensation. Knowledge is always something which can be verified. And in verification we always proceed to something which is not just now presented.

It is upon the manner and the nature of this interpretation which we put upon the given that I should like to concentrate our attention. Clearly it is something which we bring to the experience. It is something we are able to make only because we confront what is presented by the senses with certain ready-made distinctions, relations, and ways of classifying. In particular, we impose upon experience certain patterns of temporal relationships, a certain order, which makes one item significant of others. A visually presented quale of the object is a sign of the way it would taste or feel. The taste of it *now* is a sign of the taste of the next bite also. The way yonder door looks to me now is a sign of the distance I must walk to reach it and the position in which I must put my hand to open it. It is by interpretation that the infant's buzzing, blooming confusion gives way to an orderly world of things. Order, or logical pattern, is the essence of understanding. Knowledge arises when some conceptual pattern of relationships is imposed upon the given by interpretation.

Moreover, as we have seen, it is only this conceptual element of order or logical pattern which can be conveyed from one mind to another. All expressible truth about our world is contained in such relations of order, that is, in terms of concepts we find applicable to what is presented in sense.

Now the concepts which we thus impose upon given experience are almost always such as we have formulated only as the need for them arose. Experience itself has instigated our attitudes of interpretation. The secret of them lies in purpose or interest. It is because our concepts have so generally this pragmatic origin that I began with the one illustration where the case is clearly different. Though elementary mathematics is historically rooted in practical need, mathematical concepts have some of them a quite different origin. The mathematician has a whole cupboardful of such conceptual systems for which nobody has found as yet any useful application. *All* concepts have intrinsically the possibility of such separate status; and all truth or knowledge represents an order which is capable of being considered, like mathematical systems, *in abstracto*. The business of learning, and the process by which mind has conquered the world in the name of intelligibility, is not a process in which we have passively absorbed something which experience has presented to us. It is much more truly a process of trial and error in which we have attempted to impose upon experience one interpretation or conceptual pattern after another and, guided by our practical success or failure, have settled down to that mode of construing it which accords best with our purposes and interests of action.

Moreover, this mode of successful interpretation may not be dictated unambiguously by the content of experience itself. The famous illustration of this fact that William James made use of is probably the best. For a thousand years men interpreted the motions of the heavens in terms of Ptolemy's astronomy, based on a motionless earth. Then gradually this was given up in favor of the Copernican system of moving earth and fixed stars. Those who argued this issue supposed they were discussing a question of empirical fact. We now perceive that such is not the case. All motion is relative. The question what moves and what is motionless in the heavens is one which cannot be settled merely by experience. But one choice of axes is highly convenient, resulting in relatively simple generalizations for the celestial motions and enabling celestial and sublunary phenomena to be reduced to the same equations, while almost insurmountable complexity and difficulty attend the other choice. Theoretically if any system of motions is describable with respect to one set of axes, it is also describable in terms of any other set which moves with reference to the first according to any general rule. So that the issue between the Ptolemaic and Copernican choice of a frame of motion cannot be decided on the ground that one describes the facts, the other not. Rather the one describes the facts simply and conveniently, the other complexly and most inconveniently. The only issue is pragmatic.

Similarly with the recent controversy between the physics of relativity and the Euclidean-Newtonian mechanics. Perhaps you and I— certainly I—do not understand the intricacies of Einstein, but so much we have gathered: that since all motion is relative, and since, further, whatever happens at some distant point is known to us only by the passage of an effect through space and time, we cannot measure space without some assumption about time, or time without assumptions about space and the laws of matter which govern clocks, and so on. Therefore at the bottom of our interpretation of events in the physical universe there must be some fundamental assumptions, or definitions and criteria, to which empirical evidence cannot simply say yes or no. One set of assumptions—the relativity ones—means a reduction in the number of independent laws but a reorganization of common sense; the other set obviates this change in current notions about space and time but condemns us to forgo the simplification in fundamental principles. The determinable empirical issues, such as the perturbations of Mercury and the bending of light rays, are—so we may venture to think— by themselves not decisive. If there were no other issue, we should find some way to accommodate these recalcitrant facts to the old categories. The really final issues are pragmatic ones such as the comprehensiveness of laws and economy in unverifiable assumption.

From such striking and important illustrations to the humbler affairs of every day is a far cry. And time does not permit the introduction of further examples which might bridge the gap. But does not history go to prove the point? In any given period, there is some body of generally accepted concepts in terms of which men describe and interpret their experience. Later, these may all be strange. If we go back to the Middle Ages or to the civilization of ancient Greece, and try to view the world as men then saw it, only by an effort can we do so. We might expect that the fundamental things—life, mind, matter and force, cause and effect—would be conceived in the same way. Yet it is exactly here that we find the greatest differences.

These facts are familiar to you, and I need not dwell upon them. But perhaps I may pause for a single illustration. Among the ancients, the distinction between the living and the inanimate was generally drawn between those things which were supposed to have a soul which was the cause of their behavior and development, and those which had no such internal principle which explained their movements. 'Soul' was thus a synonym for 'the vital,' and was a principle of nature, coordinate with the mechanical. Why was this principle of distinction later given up? Has it been disproved that all living things have souls? Or that we must grant, in addition to the mechanical causes of the phenomena of life, an internal vital principle which explains development? We can hardly claim so much. Really to explain this change of categories, we must probably reckon, on the one side, with Christianity and similar influences which, when they came, contrasted 'soul,' as the spiritual principle in man, with the material body. Thus the soul, instead of being conceived as a natural cause of vital phenomena, is now withdrawn from all physical significance. On the other side, the advantage of control which goes with understanding the facts of life, so far as possible, in terms of physics and chemistry has operated to extrude the idea of a soul, as a natural inner principle, from any place in biological conceptions.

With other fundamental concepts, it is much the same. *Words* such such as 'life,' 'matter,' 'cause,' and so on have been used since thought began, but the *meanings* of them have continuously altered. There is hardly a category or principle of explanation which survives from Aristotle or the science of the Middle Ages. Quite literally, men of those days lived in a different world because their instruments of intellectual interpretation were so different. To be sure, the telescope and microscope and the scientific laboratory have played an important part. As time goes on, the body of familiar experience widens. But that hardly accounts for *all* the changed interpretation which history reveals. Not sense observation alone, but accord with human bent and need must be considered. The motive to control external nature and direct our own destiny was always there. Old principles have been abandoned not only when they disagreed with newly discovered fact, but when they proved unnecessarily complex and bungling, or when they failed to emphasize distinctions which men felt to be important.

When things so fundamental as the categories of space and time, the laws of celestial mechanics, and the principles of physics are discovered to depend in part upon pragmatic choice; when history reveals continuous alteration in our basic concepts, and an alteration which keeps step with changing interests; and when we recognize that without interpretation it is not a world at all that is presented to us, but only, so to speak, the raw material of a world; then may it not plausibly be urged that, throughout the realm of fact, what is flatly given in experience does not completely determine truth—does not unambiguously fix the conceptual interpretation which shall portray it?

In short, if human knowledge at its best, in the applications of mathematics and in the well-developed sciences, is typical of knowledge in general, then the picture we must frame of it is this: that there is in it an element of conceptual interpretation, theoretically always separable from any application to experience and capable of being studied in abstraction. When so isolated, concepts are like the Platonic ideas, purely logical entities constituted by the pattern of their systematic relations. There is another element, the sensuous or given, likewise always separable by abstraction, though we should find it pure only in a mind which did not think but only felt. This given element, or stream of sensation, is what sets the problem of interpretation, when we approach it with our interests of action. The function of thought is to mediate between such interests and the given. Knowledge arises when we can frame the data of sense in a set of concepts which serve as guides for action, just as knowledge of space arises when we can fit a geometrical interpretation upon our direct perception of the spatial. The given experience does not produce the concepts in our minds. If it did, knowledge would be pure feeling, and thought would be superfluous. Nor do the concepts evoke the experience which fits them, or limit it to their pattern. Rather the growth of knowledge is a process of trial and error, in which we frame the content of the given now in one set of concepts, now in another, and are governed in our final decision by our relative success—by the degree to which our most vital needs and interests are satisfied.

If this is a true picture, then there are three elements in knowledge, or three phases of the relation of mind to the objects of thought. First, there is the kind of knowledge which we have in abstract mathematics, and the kind of truth which concerns purely logical implications. There is this type of truth for all concepts so far as they are precise and clear. Our knowledge of such truth possesses certainty and finality because it requires only clarity of thought and is entirely independent of experience.

This kind of truth can be, and has been, described in two ways, either of which is accurate when we grasp what they mean. First is the way of Plato, who emphasizes the fact that abstract concepts ("ideas" he calls them) are not created by the mind. What he means is that the mathematician, for example, does not create but discovers the truths that he portrays. Before the non-Euclidean geometries or the possibility of curves without tangents was even thought of, the truth about them was forever fixed.

The second way of describing this realm of abstract entities is to note that such pure concepts have no residence outside the mind. Plato's heaven—so we should say from this second point of view—is merely a fiction to emphasize the absoluteness of conceptual truth. Without our thought concepts would remain forever in the dark limbo of nothingness. Moreover, it is their usefulness, their applicablity to given experience, which moves us to evoke them. We select, or call down from Plato's heaven, those concepts which meet our needs. Plato said we are "reminded" of them by experience; we are more likely to say that we invent or formulate them ourselves. In either case, two points are to be remarked: first, that the logical relations of—and hence the truth about—any determinate concept is fixed and eternal and independent of experience; second, that *what* concepts we shall use or apply we are left to determine ourselves in the light of our needs and interests.

The second phase of the mind's relation to its objects is the element of the purely given in experience. Of this by itself, there is no truth or knowledge in the ordinary sense. Yet the given has significance. There is something which speaks directly to us in just this presentation of the senses, in that immediacy of color or of sound which one who lacked the appropriate sense organ could never imagine nor our description conjure up for him. In particular, the immediate has esthetic significance; perhaps it may also have ethical value and religious meaning. But it is not knowledge in the usual meaning of that term, because it is ineffable; because there is nothing in such direct apprehension which calls for verification; because by itself it has no reference to action.

The third element or phase—the element which distinguishes our knowledge of the external world—is the active interpretation which unites the concept and the given. It is such interpretation alone which needs to be verified, or *can* be verified, and the function of it is essentially practical. Truth here is not fixed, because interpretation is not fixed, but is left for trial and error to determine. The criteria of its success are accommodation to our bent and service of our interests. More adequate or simpler interpretation will mean practically truer. Old truth will pass away when old concepts are abandoned. New truth arises when new interpretations are adopted. Attempted modes of understanding may, of course, completely fail and prove flatly false. But where there is more than one interpretation which can frame the given, 'truer' will mean only 'better.' And after all, even flat falsity can only mean a practical breakdown which has proved complete.

At just this point, however, we may easily fall into misapprehension. In speaking thus of 'new truth' and 'old truth' and of pragmatically 'truer' and 'falser,' I am following a usage which the literature of pragmatism has made familiar. But I think this is a little to be regretted. Most of the paradoxes and many of the difficulties of the pragmatic point of view cluster about this notion that the truth can change. When we see precisely what it is that happens when old modes of interpretation are discarded in favor of new and more successful ones, all these paradoxes will, I think, be found to disappear. What is it that is new in such a case? The given, brute-fact experience which sets the problem of interpretation is not new. And the concepts in terms of which the interpretation, whether old or new, is phrased are—remembering Plato—such that the truth about them is eternal. Obviously what is new is the *application* of the concept, or system of concepts, to experience of just this sort. The concepts are *newly chosen* for interpretation of the given data. That the concepts may also be new in the sense that no one ever thought of them before does not, at bottom, affect the problem at all.

Historically the situation is likely to be slightly more complex; the body of data to be interpreted itself undergoes some alteration. It is possible that old systems of thought should be rejected and replaced by new, simply through reflection and realization of the superior convenience of the novel mode. In fact, this has sometimes happened. But in the more typical case, such change does not take place without the added spur of newly discovered phenomena which complicate the problem of interpretation. The several factors which must be considered are, then: (1) the two sets of concepts, old and new, (2) the expanding bounds of experience in which what is novel has come to light, (3) the conditions of application of the concepts to this new body of total relevant experience.

In the case of the Copernican revolution, it was the invention of the telescope and the increasing accuracy of observation which mainly provided the impetus to reinterpretation. But these new data, though practically decisive, were decisive of simplicity and comprehensiveness only. As we have seen, celestial motions are theoretically as capable of interpretation with respect to axes through the earth as by reference to the fixed stars. Now suppose that mathematicians and astronomers had so much spare time that both these systems had been worked out, for all the data, with some completeness. Which would be the truth about the heavens? Obviously, both. The laws of celestial motion in the two cases would be quite different, and the divergence would extend beyond astronomy to physics. But both would be absolutely and eternally true in their own terms. The one would be better truth, the other worse, from the point of view of workability. But except in the practical sense that we must stick to the one or the other all through and cannot apply them piecemeal, they could not contradict one another.

This situation is not altered by any thought that newly discovered fact may play another than the pragmatic role, and be decisive of truth in a deeper sense. In any case, if old principles were ever true, they must remain true—in terms of the old concepts. To the extent that new evidence can render the old concepts absolutely inapplicable, the "old truth" never was anything but an hypothesis, and is now proved flatly false. It is not, I hope, the point of the pragmatic theory of knowledge to reduce all truths thus to hypothesis. That would be nothing but a cheerful form of skepticism.

Rather the point is—at least the point which I should like to make— that the truths of experience must always be relative to our chosen conceptual systems in terms of which they are expressed; and that amongst such conceptual systems there may be choice in application. Such choice will be determined, consciously or unconsciously, on pragmatic grounds. New facts may cause a shifting of such grounds. When this happens, nothing literally becomes false, and nothing becomes true which was not always true. An old intellectual instrument has been given up. Old concepts lapse and new ones take their place.

It would be a hardy soul who should read the history of science and of common-sense ideas and deny that just this shift of concepts on pragmatic grounds has frequently had important place in the advance of thought. That historically men suppose they are confronted simply with a question of absolute truth when they debate Copernican versus Ptolemaic astronomy, mechanism versus vitalism, relativity versus Newtonian mechanics, and so on, does not remove the possibility that the really decisive issues may often be pragmatic.

Pragmatists have sometimes neglected to draw the distinction between the concept and immediacy, between interpretation and the given, with the result that they may seem to put all truth at once at the mercy of brute-fact experience and within the power of human choice or in a relation of dependence upon human need. But this would be an attempt to have it both ways. The sense in which facts are brute and given cannot be the sense in which the truth about them is alterable to human decision. The separation of the factors is essential. On the one side, we have the abstract concepts themselves, with their logical implications. The truth about these is absolute, and knowledge of them is *a priori*. On the other side, there is the absolute datum of the given. But it is between these two, in the determination of those concepts which the mind brings to experience as the instruments of its interpretation, that a large part of the problem of fixing the truths of science and our common-sense knowledge has its place. Wherever such criteria as comprehensiveness and simplicity, or serviceability for the control of nature, or conformity to human bent and human ways of acting play their part in the determination of such conceptual instruments, there is a pragmatic element in knowledge.

3. Experience and Meaning

Ever since the provisional skepticism of Descartes' First Meditation the attack upon any problem of reality has always been shadowed by the question "How do you know?" The extent to which this perennial challenge has determined the course of modern philosophy requires no exposition. That on the whole the results of it have been salutary will hardly be denied, though it may be said—and has been said—that it leads, on occasion, to the confusion of methodological considerations with positive conclusions. The last thirty-five years have witnessed a growing emphasis upon another such challenge, which bids fair to prove equally potent in its directing influence. This is the question "What do you mean?" asked with intent to require an answer in terms of experience. That is, it is demanded that any concept put forward or any proposition asserted shall have a definite denotation, that it shall be intelligible not only verbally and logically but in the further sense that one can specify those empirical items which would determine the applicability of the concept or constitute the verification of the proposition. Whatever cannot satisfy this demand is to be regarded as meaningless.

For any sufficient consideration of this empirical-meaning requirement it would be essential to sketch those developments which have brought it to the fore: pragmatism and the "pragmatic test"; neo-realism, both of the American school and the similar view of Russell; the new methodology in physics which came in with relativity, especially Einstein's treatment of definition and Bridgman's operational theory of the concept; Whitehead's method of "extensive abstraction," by which certain previously refractory concepts can now be defined in terms of the actually observable and their empirical content thus made evident. Last and most particularly, one would mention the logical positivism of the Vienna Circle, whose program is based throughout upon this consideration of empirical meaning. It would likewise be desirable to consider the divergences between these different movements of thought in their interpretation of the general requirement of empirical meaning.

The presidential address to the Eastern Division of the American Philosophical Association at Amherst College, December 29, 1933. Reprinted by permission from *The Philosophical Review*, Vol. XLIII (1934), No. 2, pp. 125–46.

But before this audience it will be unnecessary to attempt any such survey, either of this development in current theory or of the points of divergence with respect to it. Taking these matters for granted, the purpose of what follows will be to explore a little certain questions concerning the limitations imposed upon significant philosophic discussion by this requirement of empirical meaning—in particular certain issues which are likely to divide those who approach these problems with the thought of James and Peirce and Dewey in mind from the logical positivists. The ultimate objective of such discussion would be to assess the bearing of this limitation to what has empirical meaning upon ethics and the philosophy of values, and upon those metaphysical problems which concern the relation between values and reality. But that objective cannot be reached in the present paper, which will be concerned with prior questions. Even these cannot be set forth with any thoroughness; and I hope it will be understood that the purpose of this discussion is to locate issues rather than to dispose of them, and that criticisms ventured are not put forward in the spirit of debate.

The Vienna positivists repudiate all problems of traditional metaphysics, including the issue about the external world supposed to divide idealists from realists, and any question concerning the metaphysical character of other selves. In the authoritative statement of their position we find the following: "If anyone assert 'There is a God,' 'The ground of the world is the Unconscious,' 'There is an entelechy as the directing principle in the living,' we do not say to him 'What you assert is false' but instead we ask him 'What do you mean by your statement?' And it then appears that there is a sharp line of division between two kinds of propositions. To the one belongs statements such as those made in the empirical sciences: their meaning can be determined by logical analysis; more specifically, it can be determined by reduction to statements of the simplest sort about the empirically given. The other class of propositions, to which those mentioned above belong, betray themselves as completely empty of meaning, if one take them in the fashion which the metaphysician intends. . . . The metaphysician and the theologian, misunderstanding themselves, suppose that their theses assert something, represent matters of fact. Analysis shows, however, that these propositions assert nothing, but only express a sort of feeling of life."[1] According to Carnap all value-theory and nor-

[1] [Hans Hahn, Otto Neurath, Rudolf Carnap.] *Wissenschaftliche Weltauffassung: Der Wiener Kreis* (Wien, 1929), p. 16. (I have translated somewhat freely.)

mative science are likewise without meaning, in the theoretical or empirical sense of that word.[2]

The expression of such feeling of life, and of our evaluative reactions, is, of course, admitted to be a legitimate and worthwhile activity; but, as such expression, metaphysical theses are to be classed with art and poetry. Obviously there is room in such a theory for descriptive ethics, on a psychological or sociological basis, and for the determination of values by reference to a norm which is assumed or hypothetical; but traditional questions of the 'objectivity' of value are repudiated. We may meaningfully ask "When is a character judged good?" or "What is actually approved?" but not "With *what right* is this character said to be 'good'?" or "What is absolutely *worthy* of approbation?"[3]

This repudiation of metaphysics and normative science by the logical positivists cannot, I think, be regarded as an implication of the empirical-meaning requirement alone. At least an important light is thrown upon it by taking into account that "methodological solipsism" in accordance with which their program is developed. Even though they regard this procedure as advantageous rather than prescribed, still the negations or limitations which characterize it seem to underlie their theses, in whatever terms expressed.

On its constructive side this method means no more, at bottom, than a persistent attempt so to define the different classes of objects of our knowledge that the basis of this knowledge in direct experience will be exhibited. It is of the essence of knowledge that it is in the first person. Your mind and your experience can be nothing more, for my cognition, than a construction which I put upon certain data of my own experience. If, then, we are to have a thorough and completed account of knowledge, it is not sufficient that the constitution of objects known should be traced back to experience in the merely generic sense. So far as your observations and reports enter into the construction of that reality which is known to me, they can do so only through the interpretation which I put upon certain modes of your behavior perceived by me. Actually given experience is given in the first person; and reality as it is known in any case of actual knowledge can be nothing, finally, but a first-person construction from data given in the first person.

Consonantly, we have such construction of the objects of science in

---

[2] "Auf dem Gebiet der Metaphysik (einschliesslich aller Wertphilosophie und Normwissenschaft) führt die logische Analyse zu dem negativen Ergebnis, dass die vorgeblichen Sätze dieses Gebietes gänzlich sinnlos sind" ("Uberwindung der Metaphysik durch logische Analyse der Sprache," *Erkenntnis* II [1931], p. 220).

[3] See M. Schlick, *Fragen der Ethik* (Wien, 1930), esp. Chap. I, Sec. 8, pp. 10–12.

general as is outlined in Carnap's *Der Logische Aufbau der Welt*: first, the different kinds of for-me entities (*eigenpsychische Gegenstände*) which are constructed out of elementary experiences (*Elementarerlebnisse*), at bottom, through the relation of remembered similarity (*Ähnlichkeitserinnerung*); second, physical objects, which are constructions out of the simpler for-me things of actually given experience; third, other selves and the mental or cultural in general (*fremdpsychische und geistige Gegenstände*), which are, for actual knowing, constructions out of certain classes and certain relationships of physical things and processes.

In this program we have a consistently maintained effort to be true to the nature of knowledge as we find it. The egocentric predicament is taken seriously; and the "solipsistic" character ascribed to knowing is no more strange or fantastic than Kant's transcendental unity of apperception. The manner in which the *negative* side of logical positivism is related to this same method may, perhaps, be more readily appreciated by reference to cruder but somewhat parallel considerations which are suggested by Berkeley's argument against material substance. (It was Berkeley who first adduced the requirement of empirical meaning in order to prove his opponent's concepts empty and non-significant.)

As has often been noted, the significance and applicability of Berkeley's argument does not leave off at the point where he ceases to use it. By identical logic other selves and the past and future must go the same way as material substance. If you are more than one of my ideas, how can I know it? How can I consistently suppose that I even have an interest in that untouchable you outside my mind which *ipso facto* could make no difference in my experience of you? Also, at this moment, what is that past which I remember, as more than the present recollection, or the future as more than the present experience of anticipation? All must finally dissolve into the eternal now of actually given experience.

There is even one further step for this logic to take. What am I? This self as a recognizable or conceivable particularity can be no more than one of those ideas I call mine. And Wittgenstein gives indication that he accepts the parallel methodological implication: "The subject does not belong to the world but it is a limit of the world. *Where in* the world is a metaphysical subject to be noted? You say that this case is altogether like that of the eye and the field of sight. But you do *not* really see the eye. And from nothing *in the field of sight* can it be concluded that it is seen from an eye. . . . Here we see that solipsism strictly carried out coincides with pure realism. The I in solipsism shrinks to an extensionless point and there remains the reality coordinated with it."[4]

I must not convey the impression that the logical positivists use Berkeleyan arguments, or that they arrive at their conclusions by such a train of thought as the above. Nevertheless this may serve to suggest how methodological solipsism comports with a thoroughgoing empiricism; and it further suggests why this procedure is to be taken as having no metaphysical implications. Subjective idealism, consistently carried through, ends by qualifying every substantive with the prefix "idea of" or "experience of," which by being thus universal becomes meaningless. Whereas Berkeley supposes his argument to establish a subjectivist metaphysics by proving the realistic metaphysics to be empty of empirical meaning, logical positivism points out that the contrary of a meaningless assertion is likewise without meaning, and hence repudiates metaphysical theses of both sorts, and the issue itself, as nonsignificant. Three points, here evident, contain, I think, the gist of the matter. First, when knowledge is envisaged, as it must be, from within the egocentric predicament, all objects known or conceived must reveal themselves as constructions, eventually, from data given in first-person experience. Also, what enters into such construction from past experience can only come in by way of present recollection. (This last is, I take it, the reason for the basic position of the relation of remembered-similarity in the program of Carnap.) Other selves and their experience, or their reports, can enter only as certain items of first-person experience upon which a peculiarly complex construction is put. Second, distinctions such as that between real and imaginary, or between that which is apprehensible to me alone and the object apprehended by us in common, must nevertheless find their genuine place and importance in such construction. The fact that we make these distinctions in practically useful ways evidences that they are not outside the egocentric predicament and metaphysical but inside it and empirical. They are determined by criteria which the subject can and does apply within his own experience. Berkeley, for example, offered the criterion of independence of my will as the basis for the distinction of real from imaginary. And in Carnap one finds such distinctions, and their empirical criteria, meticulously examined. Third, metaphysical issues concerning the external world and other selves do *not* turn upon such empirically applicable distinctions as those just referred to, which can be applied

---

[4] *Tractatus Logico-Philosophicus* (New York, 1922), pp. 151–53. Cf. Carnap, *Der Logische Aufbau der Welt* §65.

within first-person experience. Such metaphysical issues can arise only as it is attempted to give some second meaning to the concepts involved: meanings which do not answer to any empirical criteria which the subject can apply within his own experience. Throughout, a particular and critical point is that only first-person (*eigenpsychische*) data of experience are allowed, in the end, to enter into the construction of objects of knowledge or to function as the empirical content of any meaning.

There is, I think, one further question which is crucial for any theory of knowledge, namely, the question of immediacy and mediation, or transcendence. This has a connection with the preceding considerations; but with respect to this further problem I cannot satisfy myself that I elicit any complete and clear pronouncement from the literature of logical positivism. One can pose the principal issue involved by reference to a statement of Russell's: "Empirical knowledge is confined to what we actually observe."[5] This may seem to be a truism; but I think it is in fact thoroughly false, and demonstrably incompatible with the very existence of empirical knowledge. Let us impose this limitation quite rigorously, in conformity with the considerations set forth above. Knowledge is always in the first person; whatever is known must be known to the subject in question, at the actual moment, within his own experience. The experience of others can enter only as certain items of their subject's own—their reports and behavior perceived by him. And the experience of yesterday or tomorrow can figure in this knowing only as it enters, in the form of memory or imagination, into experience here and now. Hence nothing can be known but what is verifiable in the subject's own experience at the moment when the knowing occurs.

Similarly for meaning. Suppose it maintained that no issue is meaningful unless it can be put to the test of decisive verification. And no verification can take place except in the immediately present experience of the subject. Then nothing can be meant except what is actually present in the experience in which that meaning is entertained. Whatever runs beyond this is unverifiable, and hence meaningless. The result of any such train of thought is obvious; knowledge would collapse into the useless echo of data directly given to the mind at the moment, and meaning would terminate in the immediate envisagement of what is meant.

[5] *Our Knowledge of the External World* (New York, 1929), p. 112. The author makes this statement quite in passing, and perhaps without having in mind the point with which we are concerned.

This is a reduction to absurdity of both knowledge and meaning.[6] If nothing can be known but what is literally within the cognitive experience itself, and what is meant can be only that which is present in the experience which is the bearer of that meaning, then there is no valid knowledge and no genuinely significant meaning, because the *intention* to refer to what transcends immediate experience is of the essence of knowledge and meaning both. Berkeley himself tacitly recognized that, in noting that one idea is "sign of" another which is to be expected; even the skeptic recognizes this intent of knowledge—he is skeptical precisely of the possibility that what is *not* immediate can be known. If that intention of transcendence is invalid, then the further characters of knowledge and of meaning are hardly worth discussing.

Neither the logical positivists nor anyone else (unless a mystic) intends this reduction to absurdity. But if it is something which has to be avoided by any theory which is compatible with the genuine validity of knowledge, that fact becomes important for the just interpretation of the requirement of empirical meaning. In particular, it becomes evident that the experience in terms of which a cognitive meaning requires to be explicated cannot be exclusively the subject's own given data at the moment of the cognition. Thus that manner of reading the implications of methodological solipsism which is suggested above would condemn that procedure to futility. If what the method requires is that objects known should be constructed or defined exclusively in terms of sense-data actually given to the subject at the moment when the knowing takes place, then that method is incompatible with the possibility of knowledge and the reality of empirical meaning.

We are here faced with a problem which runs through the whole history of post-Kantian epistemology—though it is Berkeley rather than Kant who precipitated it in its modern form. How can the knowledge-relation, or the relation of idea to the object it denotes, be valid unless what is known or meant is present to or in the experience which knows or means? But if what is meant or what is known is merely the cognitive experience itself, or something in it, then how can either knowledge or meaning be genuine?

In general there are three types of solution which have been offered. The first of these is representationalism, according to which the object

---

[6] In order to avoid confusion with a quite different problem, the distinction between meaning in the sense of denotation and meaning as connotation should be in mind. It is only the former meaning of "meaning" which is in point in this discussion. In the classification of logical positivism meanings are (1) structural, as in logic and mathematics, or (2) empirical, as in natural science, or (3) emotive, as in art and poetry. It is meaning in sense (2) which is concerned here.

never literally enters into the experience of the subject. This view recognizes, in at least one sense, the transcendence of the object known or meant; and thus avoids the reduction to absurdity which has been mentioned. The difficulty of this view is, of course, to reconcile such transcendence of the object with the possibility of knowing it. Second, there are identity-theories, both idealistic and realistic, according to which the object, or the object so far as it is known, is identical with some content of the subject's experience at the moment when the knowing takes place. The outstanding difficulty of this view is to avoid the reduction to absurdity, because it is incompatible with the supposition that anything can be known which lies beyond the immediate experience of the knower.[7] Such identity-theories are also liable to difficulty with the problem of error.

For the third type of theory—which includes both objective idealism and pragmatism—the object known is definable or specifiable in terms of experience, but the experience in terms of which the object is thus definable is not, exclusively, the experience of the subject at the moment of knowing; it transcends that experience. In rough general terms, objective idealism takes this relation between the experience in terms of which the object is specifiable and the experience which cognizes to be the relation of something *deductively* implied to that in which it is implicit. That is, the present experience in which the knowing occurs—the idea or the given—is taken as determining implicitly the whole object in its reality, and as determining it unambiguously and with certainty, if only we could be explicitly aware of all that is implied. In equally rough terms, pragmatism may be said to take this relation as *inductive*: the given experience of the moment of knowing is the basis of a probability-judgment concerning the experience (or experiences) which would verify, and in terms of which the real nature of the object is expressible.

It would probably be incorrect to take the logical positivists as holding an identity-theory of the cognitive relation.[8] But if they do not, then their conception of the object known, as constructed or 'constituted' in

---

[7] For an identity-theory of the realistic variety, the object known may transcend the knowing experience—because it is known only in part—but the object so far as it is genuinely cognized cannot.

[8] There could be doubt; for example, Carnap says, "Between 'concepts' and 'objects' there is only a difference in the manner of speech" (*Der Logische Aufbau der Welt*, p. 262); and their conception of the relation between physical and mental might be taken to argue an identity-theory. But they have, I think, been principally absorbed in the problem of the *analysis* of the concept (or the object as an intellectual construction), and one should be chary of attempting to elicit from their writings any answer to the present question, which is of a quite different order. At least, I should not wish to presume to do so.

terms of given sense-data, requires to be interpreted so as to avoid an ambiguity which is possible. At this moment I am thinking of the wall behind my back. If I should turn around, I could verify my idea of it. But if at this moment I refer to the wall as a construction from presently given data, then the distinction between 'construction' as present concept and 'construction' as that which this concept means to denote is essential. Both are empirical data, if you like—but they are not the same data. The data which have their place in the concept are memories, visual and tactile images, anticipations; the data which would verify this conception would be perceptions. Not only are memories, ideas of imagination, and perceptions different events, but they are empirically distinguishable kinds of experience-content. Either, then, the wall which my idea denotes is merely the imagination-wall or recollection-wall, which is the immediate datum; or I cannot at this moment know the real wall which I mean; or—the third possibility—it is false that what I now know and mean by 'the wall' coincides with any complex or sense-data now in my mind.

It is on this point that the third type of theory is significant. For the pragmatic form of this third type knowing begins and ends in experience; but it does not end in the experience in which it begins. Hence the emphasis on the temporal nature of the knowing process, the leading character of ideas, and the function of knowledge as a guide to action. Knowing is a matter of two 'moments': the moment of assertion or entertainment and the moment of verification, both of these moments belonging to experience in the generic sense of that word. Knowledge will be true or correct only insofar as the present experience—of the entertainment of the meaning—envisages or anticipates correctly the experience or experiences which would verify it; that is, our knowledge is true if the anticipated experience is genuinely to be met with. But the entertaining experience can be truly cognitive, as against a mere enjoyment of itself, only by the fact that what would be realized in the moment of verification is distinct from the experience which entertains or anticipates it. Otherwise error would be impossible —one cannot be mistaken about the immediate—and hence knowledge, as the opposite of error, would likewise be impossible. I do not mean to say, of course, that at the moment when something is believed or asserted it cannot have a ground in given experience, or be 'partially verified'; but it *is* meant that there must be something more, which is believed in or asserted, than what is verified immediately, if the experience is to have the significance of a knowing as contrasted with an esthetic enjoyment.

The same point can be phrased in another way by reference to the question whether, and in what sense, the datum, by means of which any item of reality is known, is distinct in its being from the cognoscendum.[9]

I should urge that any identity-theory which denies this difference between datum and cognoscendum is incompatible with the cognitive function of the idea or datum. This cognitive function is the guidance of behavior; and in order that the cognizing experience may perform this function there must be at least an element of anticipation or implicit prediction which foreshadows what is *not* here and now present in the datum.

For certain types of realism the problem thus set is taken to be that of the relation between data as items of experience and the reality in its independent existence, which is not any item or complex of items in experience. Pragmatism, in common with idealism and with logical positivism, repudiates the problem in this form as unreal.[10] For all three of these views the relation of datum to cognoscendum is taken to be a relation within experience (in the generic sense), or between one experience and others: not a relation between something in experience and something altogether out of it. The reasons for this attitude would be different in each case; but for all three views the principal ground of this repudiation is the obvious one that a relation of experience to what cannot be brought within experience is a relation which cannot be investigated, and one the very conception of which as cognitive involves a confusion of thought.

All three of these theories would agree that the cognoscendum must be defined, or constructed, or constituted for knowledge, in terms of experience. But if we are not to fall into the opposite error of the reduction to absurdity, which comes from identifying datum and cognoscendum, it must be recognized that the experience of knowing and the experience in terms of which the object is specified cannot be simply identical.

The very simple point which is pertinent to the further issues of this paper is the fact that although knowledge is subject to the here-and-now predicament—the data must be immediate—it is essential to the cognitive function of the present experience that its cognoscendum

---

[9] I borrow this formulation from the recent discussion of [C. A.] Strong and Lovejoy in the pages of *The Journal of Philosophy*, XXIX (1932), 673–87, and XXX (1933), 589–606.

[10] There may be doubt of this. I do not affirm it dogmatically; but this seems to express the intent of Dewey's denial of "antecedent reality," James's insistence that a thing is what is "known as," and Peirce's pronouncement that our concept of the effects of an object, which have practical bearings, exhausts our whole concept of the object.

should *not* be merely here and now. If, for example, there can be knowledge of a future event in one's own life, then the datum which is the vehicle of this anticipation is not the anticipated cognoscendum. And insofar as all empirical knowing has the dimension of anticipation or implicit prediction, the thing known is not to be identified with, or phrased exclusively in terms of, here-and-now experience. What is known now, *now* has the status of being verif*iable*; but in the nature of the case it does not and cannot have the status of being verifiable-now.[11] The only thing which is literally and completely verifiable-now is that which is immediate and now-verified.

This account is, of course, hopelessly inadequate, and raises all sorts of questions which cannot be dealt with here. But the points which are directly pertinent to the further discussion are these. (1) The conception that "empirical knowledge is confined to what we actually observe" is false. To know (empirically) is to be able to anticipate correctly further possible experience. If this is not the whole significance of such knowing, at least it is an essential part of it. (2) What is anticipated, known, or meant must indeed be something envisaged in terms of experience—the requirement of empirical meaning stands. But equally it is essential that what is empirically known or meant should *not* be something which is immediately and exhaustively verified, in what I have called the moment of entertainment.

It will also be of importance to consider a little the sense, or senses, of the word 'verifiable.' Like any word ending in 'able,' this connotes possibility and hence connotes conditions under which this possibility is supposed to obtain. To advance the dictum that what is empirically known, and what is meant, must be verifiable, and omit all examination of the wide range of significance which could attach to 'possible verification,' would be to leave the whole conception rather obscure. But instead of attempting here some pat formulation *a priori*, let us briefly survey different modes of the 'possibility' of the verifying experiences projected by meaningful assertions.

At this moment I have a visual presentation which leads me to assert that my watch lies before me on the table. If what I assert is true, then I could touch the watch, pick it up, and I should then observe certain familiar details which are not discernible at this distance from my eye. This verifying experience is not actual; I do not touch the watch. But nothing is lacking for it except my own initiative. At least I believe

[11] We use the expression "verifiable now" oftentimes in the sense of "verifiable at will." That means literally "verifiable the next moment if I choose to meet certain understood conditions."

that to be the case; and this belief is coordinate with the degree of my felt assurance that the watch is real and is mine. This is, perhaps, the simplest case of verifiability—observability at will. All the conditions of the verifying experience are present except only my intent to make the verification.[12]

Next, let us consider the other side of the moon.[13] This is something believed in but never directly observed. The belief is an inference or interpretation based upon direct observation; the moon behaves like a solid object and must, therefore, have another side. But what is believed in must, in order to be real, possess characters which are left undetermined in our belief about it. For instance, there must be mountains there; or there must be none. To speak more precisely, our belief includes alternatives which are not determined; but, if the thing believed in is what it is believed to be, these alternatives must be *determined in the object*. If there were nothing more, and more specific, to the other side of the moon than what is specifically determined in our construction of it, then it would be a logical abstraction instead of a physical reality. These undetermined characters are what we should see if we could build an X-ray telescope, or what we should find about us if we could construct a space-ship to fly up there and land. What we should observe if these things could be accomplished is what we mean by the other side of the moon as a physically real thing—as something more than a logical construction put upon presently given data.

The projected verification in this case is ideal in a sense which goes quite beyond the preceding example. It is humanly possible, perhaps; men may some day build space-ships or X-ray telescopes. But the conditions of this verification—or any other direct empirical verification of the thing in question—include some which we cannot meet at will. We cannot, by any chain of planned activity, completely bridge the gap between actual conditions and the projected verification. Obviously, then, unless belief in the other side of the moon is meaningless, it is not requisite to such empirical meaning that the verifying experi-

---

[12] Such a single experience would not be a theoretically complete verification of my assertion about the watch. As I have elsewhere indicated, no verification of the kind of knowledge commonly stated in propositions is ever absolutely complete and final. However, an *expected experience* of the watch can be completely verified—or falsified.

[13] It will be obvious that there are modes of verifiability which would fall between the preceding illustration and this one. For example, the verifying experience might be such as could be reached, from actual present conditions, by a more or less complicated chain of circumstances, but a chain every link of which is supposedly related to the preceding one in the manner of the first example.

ence should even be possible at present, in any narrow interpretation of that word 'possible.' To analyse the conception of 'verifiable' which would extend to such cases would be a large order. I shall only suggest what I think might be some of the critical points. (1) As this example serves to illustrate, any reality must, in order to satisfy our empirical concept of it, transcend the concept itself. A construction imposed upon given data cannot be identical with a real object; the thing itself must be more specific, and in comparison with it the construction remains abstract. In making any verification we expect something which we cannot anticipate. This is a paradox in language; but it is, or should be, a commonplace of the distinction between ideas and objects. (2) In making 'verifiability' a criterion of empirical meaningfulness, the primary reference is to a supposed character of what is conceived rather than to any supposed approximation of the conditions of verification to the actual. (3) The requirement of 'verifiability' for *knowledge* is a stricter one, because knowing requires, in addition to meaningfulness, some ground of the assurance of truth. But, as this example makes clear, even the 'possible verification' which is requisite to empirical knowing cannot be confined to the practicalities, or by detailed comprehension of the procedure of such verification. We do not command the means for making any direct verification of our belief in the other side of the moon; but what this signifies is that, with all the means in the world, we do not *know how* to. If it be said that it is required for empirical meaning—or even for knowledge—that we should lay down a rule of operation for the process of verification, it should be observed that sometimes this rule of operation will have to be rather sketchy. This difficulty—if it is a difficulty—will be found to affect not only such extreme cases as the other side of the moon but quite commonplace items of knowledge as well.

I join with you in feeling that such considerations smack of triviality; but certainly a theory which could be overturned by such trivial facts would not be worth holding. Just what we can sensibly mean by 'empirically verifiable' is really a bit obscure. Perhaps the chief requirement ought to be that we should be able to analyse the supposed connection between the projected verifying experience and what is actually given (the 'rule of operation') in such wise that this procedure of verification can be envisaged *in analogy with* operations which can actually be carried out. The degree to which such analogy could be made complete would, I think, justly affect the significance of our supposed knowledge.

As a third example let us take the case of the electron. The existence of electrons is inferred from the behavior of oil-droplets between charged plates, tracks registered on photographs of the discharge from cathodes, and other such actually observed phenomena. But what is it that is inferred; or is anything really inferred? Some physicists, for example Bridgman, would say that our concept of the electron comprehends nothing more than these observable phenomena, systematically connected by mathematical equations in verifiable ways. The layman, however, and probably most physicists, would not be satisfied to think of "electron" as merely a name for such observable phenomena. But what more may they suppose themselves to be believing in? An electron is too small to be seen through any microscope which ever can be made, and it would not stay put if a beam of light were directed upon it. It is equally beyond the reach of the other senses. But is the phrase "too small to be directly perceived" meaningful or is it not? And how direct must a "direct verification" be? Suppose it to be urged that no one can set a limit to scientific inventiveness, or anticipate the surprises which investigation of the subatomic will quite surely present; and that if or when such developments take place, definitely localized phenomena may perhaps be observed within the space to which the mass of the electron is assigned.

Whether this is or is not a question about the real nature of the electron, and what limitations should be imposed on useful conceptions in physics, are matters concerning which I could not have a competent opinion. But there is a general point here which all of us can judge. A hypothetical conception of an empirical reality cannot be definitely ruled out unless we can say categorically that the conditions of its verification could never be realized. Between those conceptions for the verification of which we can definitely specify a rule of operation, and those which we can definitely eliminate as theoretically impossible, there is an enormous gap. And any conception which falls in this middle ground is an hypothesis about empirical reality which possesses at least some degree of meaningfulness. If those who believe in the electron as a sort of ultramicroscopic bullet cannot envisage this object of their belief in such wise that they would be able to recognize certain empirical eventualities as the verification of it, in case the conditions of such verification *could* be met, then they deceive themselves and are talking nonsense. But if they can thus envisage what they believe in, then the fact that such verifying experience is highly improbable, and even that the detail of it must be left somewhat indefinite, is no bar to its meaningfulness. Any other decision would be a doctrinaire attempt to erect our ignorance as a limitation of reality.

The requirement of empirical meaning is at bottom nothing more than the obvious one that the terms we use should possess denotation.

As this requirement is interpreted by pragmatists and positivists and others who share the tendencies of thought which have been mentioned, no concept has any denotation at all unless eventually in terms of sensuous data or imagery. It is only in such terms that a thing meant, or what a proposition asserts, could be recognized if presented to us. But, as the preceding considerations are intended to make clear, the envisagement of what would thus exhibit the denotation or verify the assertion—which is all that meaning requires—has little or nothing to do with the question whether the conditions under which the requisite presentations could be realized can be met or not. Whether such verifying experience is mine or is yours or is nobody's, whether it happens now or in the future or never, whether it is practically possible or humanly problematic or clearly beyond our capacity to bring about—all this is beside the point when the only question is that of theoretical meaningfulness.

One may be tempted, in protest against various forms of transcendentalism and verbalism, to announce the unqualified dictum that only what is verifiable can be known, and only what is knowable can be the subject of a meaningful hypothesis. But such flat statement, while true in general, may nevertheless be misleading on account of an ambiguity in the word 'verifiable.' On the one hand this connotes a certain character of the content of one's assertion or hypothesis. This must be envisaged in sensuous terms; it must be the case that we could recognize certain empirical eventualities as verifying it, supposing that the conditions of such verifying experience could be satisfied. Verifiability in this sense requires an empirical *content* of the hypothesis, but has nothing to do with the practical or even the theoretical difficulties of verification. Whatever further restrictions may be appropriate in physics or any other natural science, the only general requirement of empirical meaning—which alone is pertinent to those hypotheses about reality which philosophy must consider—is this limitation to what can be expressed in terms which genuinely possess denotation.

On the other hand, 'verifiable' connotes the possibility of actually satisfying the conditions of verification. Or, to put it otherwise, verifiability may be taken to require 'possible experience' *as conditioned by the actual*; we must be able to find our way, step by step, from where we actually stand to this verifying experience. Hence practical or theoretical difficulties are limitations of verifiability in this second sense. These limitations may be genuinely pertinent to knowledge, because *knowledge* requires the *assurance of truth*; and whatever would prevent actual verification may prevent such assurance. But verifiability in this second sense has no relevance to meaning, because the assurance of truth is, obviously, not a condition of meaningfulness.

It is of importance to avoid confusing these two senses of 'verifiable' in assessing the significance of those considerations which methodological solipsism makes prominent. If it could be said that actual knowing must rest upon verification which, in the end, must be first-person and must be here and now when the knowing occurs, at least it would be an absurdity to translate this into the negation of meaning to whatever cannot be expressed in terms of first-person experience and of experience here and now. I impute this absurdity to no one; I would merely urge the necessity of avoiding it.

It is likewise important, in the same connection, to bear in mind what have been called the two moments of cognition. It is a fact that past experience is a given datum only in the form of memory; the future, only in the form of imagination. And the reports of others are data for the knower only in that form in which they lie within the egocentric predicament. Hence any idea which can occur with cognitive significance must be a construction by the knower, ultimately in terms of first-person present data. These predicaments, however, are limitations of the moment of entertainment. If one should conclude that because the cognizing experience must take place within the boundaries of the first-person and the immediate, therefore the object of that knowledge, so far as it is genuinely known or meant, must also lie within those limits, one would be overlooking the distinction between the experience which entertains and the projected experience which would verify what is thus entertained. The distinction of these two is of the essence of cognition as contrasted with esthetic enjoyment of the immediate. To identify them would be to reduce knowledge and meaning to absurdity. Again, I do not impute to anyone this identification of the idea, in terms of immediate data, with the object, specifiable in terms of possible experience or experience which is anticipated. I would only urge the desirability of avoiding this fallacy.

In the time which remains it is a bit absurd even to suggest any bearings which the above may be supposed to have upon metaphysical problems. But with your indulgence I shall barely mention three such issues.

One traditional problem of metaphysics is immortality. The hypothesis of immortality is unverifiable in an obvious sense. Yet it is an hypothesis about our own future experience. And our understanding of what would verify it has no lack of clarity. It may well be that, apart from a supposed connection with more exigent and mundane problems such as those of ethics, this hypothesis is not a fruitful topic of philosophic consideration. But if it be maintained that only what is scientifically verifiable has meaning, then this conception is a case in point. It could hardly be verified by science; and there is no observation or experiment which science could make, the negative result of which would disprove it. That consideration, however, has nothing to do with its meaningfulness as an hypothesis about reality. To deny that this conception has an empirical content would be as little justified as to deny empirical content to the belief that these hills will still be here when we are gone.

Next let us consider that question about the external world, supposedly at issue between idealists and realists. One suspects that the real animus of debate between these two parties is, and always has been, a concern with the question of an essential relationship between cosmic processes and human values; and that if, historically, idealists have sought to capture their conclusion on this point by arguments derived from a Berkeleyan or similar analysis of knowledge, at least such attempt has been abandoned in current discussion. So that this question about the external world, in any easily statable form, is probably not pertinent to present controversy. But there is one formulation which, if it is not too naive to be thus pertinent, at least poses an intelligible question about the nature of reality. Let us phrase this as a realistic hypothesis: if all minds should disappear from the universe, the stars would still go on in their courses.

This hypothesis is humanly unverifiable. That, however, is merely a predicament, which prevents assurance of truth but does not affect meaning. We can only express or envisage this hypothesis by means of imagination, and hence in terms of what any mind like ours *would* experience if, contrary to hypothesis, any mind *should* be there. But we do not need to commit the Berkeleyan naiveté of arguing that it is impossible to imagine a tree on a desert island which nobody is thinking of—because we are thinking of it ourselves. It is entirely meaningful, for example, to think of those inventions which nobody has ever thought of, or those numbers which no one will ever count; we can even frame the concept of those concepts which no one will ever frame. Those who would deny this on logical grounds exhibit a sense for paradox of language which is stronger than their sense of fact. Furthermore, *imagination* is sufficient for empirical meaning, though it requires *perception* for verification. I can imagine that future time which I shall never perceive; and humans can meaningfully think of that future when humanity may have run its cosmic course and all consciousness will have disappeared. It may be that the hypothesis of a reality with no sentience to be affected by it is not a particularly significant issue, though the idealist might have an interest in it for the sake of the light which decision about it would throw upon the nature which reality has now. In any case, the fact that it is unverifiable has no bearing upon its meaningfulness. Whether this hypothesis is true is a genuine question about the nature of reality.

Finally, we may turn to the conception of other selves. The importance which this topic has for ethics will be obvious. Descartes conceived that the lower animals are a kind of automata; and the monstrous supposition that other humans are merely robots would have meaning if there should ever be a consistent solipsist to make it. The logical positivist does not deny that other humans have feelings; he circumvents the issue by a behavioristic interpretation of "having feelings." He points out that your toothache is a verifiable object of my knowledge; it is a construction put upon certain empirical items which are data for me—your tooth and your behavior. My own toothache is equally a construction. Until there are such prior constructions as the physical concept "teeth," from given sense-data, neither your toothache nor mine is a possible object of knowledge. And, similarly, until there is a construction involving such prior constructions as human bodies, there is no own-self or yourself as particular objects of knowledge. As knowable things, myself and yourself are equally constructions; and though as constructed objects they are fundamentally different in kind, the constructions are coordinate. That experience which is the original datum of *all* such constructions is, in Carnap's phrase, "without a subject."[14] Nevertheless it has that quality or status, characteristic of all given experience, which is indicated by the adjective "first-person."

With the general manner of this account of our knowledge of ourselves and others I think we should agree. But it does not touch the point at issue. Suppose I fear that I may have a toothache tomorrow. I entertain a conception involving various constructions from present data: my body, teeth, etc. But my present experience, by which I know or anticipate this future toothache, is not an experience of an *ache*. There is here that difference which has been noted between the experience which entertains and the experience which would verify, to which it implicitly refers. A robot could have a toothache, in the sense of having a swollen jaw and exhibiting all the appropriate behavior; but there would be no pain connected with it. The question of metaphysical solipsism is the question whether there is any pain connected with your observed behavior indicating toothache. The logical positivist claims that this issue has no meaning, because there is no empirical content

---

[14] See *Der Logische Aufbau der Welt*, §65.

which could verify the non-solipsistic assertion—that is, no content unless, following his procedure, I identify your pain with observable items such as the behavior which exhibits it, in which case it is verifiable in the first person. To make this identification, however, is to beg precisely the point at issue.

Let us compare the two cases of your toothache now and my toothache tomorrow. I cannot verify your toothache, as distinct from your observable behavior, because of the egocentric predicament. But neither can I verify my own future toothache—because of the now-predicament. My tomorrow's pain, however, may genuinely be an object of knowledge for me now, because a pain may be cognized by an experience in which that pain is not a given ingredient. (The imagination of a pain may be painful; but it is not the pain anticipated. If it were, all future events which we anticipate would be happening already.) *Your* pain I can *never* verify. But when I assert that you are not an automaton, I can envisage what I mean—and what makes the difference between the truth and falsity of my assertion—because I can imagine your pain, as distinct from all I can literally experience of you, just as I can imagine my own future pain, as distinct from the experience in which I now imagine it.

In the nature of the case I cannot verify you as another center of experience distinct from myself. Any verification which I might suppose myself to make would violate the hypothesis by being first-person experience. But there is nothing to which I can give more explicit empirical content than the supposition of a consciousness like mine connected with a body like my own. Whether there is any such would be a terribly important question about reality if anybody entertained a doubt about the answer. Whether you are another mind or only a sleep-walking body is a question of fact. And it cannot be exorcized by definitions—by defining 'meaningful' so as to limit it to the verifiable, and 'verifiable' by reference to the egocentric predicament.

This conception of other selves as metaphysical ultimates exemplifies the philosophic importance which may attach to a supposition which is nevertheless unverifiable on account of the limitations of knowing. Though empirical meaning is requisite to theoretical significance—and that consideration is of first importance in guarding against verbal nonsense in philosophy—still the sense in which a supposition is meaningful often outruns that in which the assurance of truth, by verification, can genuinely be hoped for. In limiting cases like this last question it may even outrun the possibility of verification altogether.

4. Verification and the Types of Truth

In a brief paper, one has the alternatives of taking a small subject and dealing with it in a thorough manner, or choosing a large subject and hoping that its magnitude and importance will serve as excuse for a necessarily inadequate treatment. The former of these alternatives is the more favored, but I shall beg your indulgence in adopting the other. In choosing such a topic as verification and truth, I cannot attempt to deal with more than a narrow phase of it, or to discuss it from any but a strictly limited point of view. It may be well, therefore, to indicate at the outset this angle of approach which is to be adopted.

Philosophical discussion, in this country and in Great Britain, is particularly concerned at the moment with the topic of meaning. With us, this results, in some part, from the pragmatic tradition of Peirce and James and Dewey, with its pragmatic test of meaningfulness and its insistence upon the connection between the significance of any statement and its verifiability. In Great Britain, it reflects the influence of Professor Moore and his analytic school, and their conviction that the hopeful procedure in philosophy is still that which Plato followed in the *Dialogues*—the reflective method, directed to determination of what our fundamental concepts really mean. To this may be added—in both places—the influence exercised by the newly developed methodology of physical science, which has discovered, in the last quarter-century, that philosophical examination of basic conceptions is not mere intellectual fancywork, and which expresses its own critique of scientific concepts in the form of "operationalism." A final and especially important influence is interest in the active school of the logical positivists, or logical empiricists, of the Vienna Circle, and their attempt to apply a method, derived mainly from the new logic which stems principally from *Principia Mathematica*, to a wider field of philosophical problems.

If I attempt to formulate some results of these current developments as a background for the present discussion, you will understand that there is no intent here to be dogmatic. A depiction of anything in philosophy at present is bound to be a snapshot of a moving object. Moreover, there is none of these momentary results which attains the status

Read at Yale and Princeton, 1936–37.

of a philosophic dictum; and there is none which does not reveal further questions with no general agreement about the answers to them.

If there is any precipitate of discussion which might be an exception to this last, it is one which has to do with the nature and criterion of logical truth. There seems to be some general convergence upon the conception that logic consists exclusively of analytic statements or tautologies. Laws of logic, and all propositions whose truth can be ascertained merely by reference to logic, are pronouncements whose truth is independent of any empirical matter of fact. The statement that either A is B or A is not B, for example, does not assert that any examinable state of affairs will possess some particular character rather than some other. The statement exhausts the possibilities, and has no conceivable alternative. The world we live in—or any world we might live in—can, so to speak, be what it likes; but it could not, by any cosmic contortion, evade this logical principle and present a state of affairs requiring revision of it. If we turn this conception—that logic is independent of the empirical—the other way about, it means that logic, and logically certifiable truth in general, contains no information about any matter of fact or any possible content of experience. If the law says anything at all which has an imaginable alternative, what it really expresses is restrictions we impose upon ourselves in the way we identify things by means of names, and the meaning we intend to attach to "either . . . or. . . ." What such a law expresses is our own logical ways of acting, our own logical intentions. The laws of logic, as well as definitions in general and all statements whose truth can be determined merely by application of logical criteria, are such as assert nothing which could conceivably be false; and they contain no information about, nor lay any restriction upon, any matter of empirical fact.

Further, logic and the logically certifiable coincide with the *a priori*. There are no non-analytic—no synthetic—propositions which can be known to be true without proof arising from observation and experiment. The Kantian contention, for example, that mathematical truths represent such synthetic judgments *a priori* is quite generally regarded as being disproved by the development of *Principia Mathematica*, in which the basic laws of mathematics are shown to be logical consequences of appropriate definitions of mathematics alone, without other assumptions than the laws of logic. (There are some exceptions to this, but these are regarded, by those who concern themselves most with such matters, as unresolved puzzles rather than indications of the insufficiency of the procedure.)

If it be said—as it justly may be said—that this mathematical development does not refute Kant's contention, since for Kant "geometry" meant "the truth about our space," while for modern mathematics Euclidean geometry is merely a logical development whose applicability or non-applicability to space is not asserted in mathematics—if this be said, then the answer we are most likely to receive is that the actual character of space is something with respect to which the outcome of observation and experiment—for example, the behavior of a ray of light in passing near the sun—is not irrelevant, and that the truth about our space—the question what geometry is applicable—is an empirical problem, and the answer to it, therefore, is *a posteriori*, not *a priori*.

In ways thus suggested, the conclusion is reached that there are just two classes of propositions: on the one hand, we have logic, definitions, and the logically certifiable in general—including mathematics—which can be known *a priori* because they are purely analytic or tautological. On the other hand, all synthetic propositions, including all pronouncements about any empirical matter of fact, are *a posteriori*, and—as it would commonly be added—are theoretically probable only.

It is an implication of this dichotomy that analytic statements are not, in one possible sense of the word, judgments at all, and apprehension of them is not knowledge. They contain no information concerning matters of fact: they say nothing which has any alternative. But, especially when we remember that mathematics is included in what is thus analytic, such usage of the words "judgment" and "knowledge" would be paradoxical. Possession of such analytic truths is judgment in the sense that mental labor and precision may be required in order clearly to apprehend what our own meanings, represented by definitions we would accept, commit us to. Since we are capable of inconsistency and of erroneously rejecting such merely analytic truths, explicit recognition of what implicitly we have accepted is knowledge as against such possible error. But it is not knowledge which has, or which requires, any empirical verification: not knowledge of what Hume called "matters of fact," or what the Vienna Circle calls "state of affairs," or what a pragmatist might call "the content of any possible experience."

Statements of what are not such merely analytic truths must, all of them, be *a posteriori* and, if true, empirically verifiable. If we know what we mean by any such synthetic proposition, we must be able to specify some empirical eventuality whose occurrence would prove it true or increase its probability, and whose failure to occur, under appropriate circumstances, would prove it false or decrease its probability. Both pragmatists and the adherents of the Vienna Circle are committed to this thesis that empirical or non-analytic propositions, in order to be meaningful, must be such as are intrinsically verifiable. If they are not such that their truth is determinable by reference to criteria which can be stated in eventually empirical terms, then they assert nothing and have no meaning.

There are, of course, major problems about every item of this development which I have so hastily outlined. No one would be willing to commit himself to the theses above set down without qualifying or at least explanatory comment. And nothing here, of course, could be intended as argument designed to render these theses convincing to those who happen not to believe in them. I have attempted only to sketch, in barest outline, a general point of view from which our subject can be approached.

Moreover, agreement amongst those who represent the general tendency of thought which is in question would leave off at about this point. As you know, the Vienna Circle, on the basis of such classification of objectively meaningful propositions as either logical and analytic or empirical and theoretically verifiable, have repudiated all statements which they classify as metaphysical as being meaningless. And Professor Schlick at least, in his *Fragen der Ethik*, has included all normative statements also amongst those which make no assertion and have no factual meaning. Such metaphysical and such normative pronouncements have "emotive" meaning: they may be expressive of the subjective state of one who makes them, and they may have esthetic and possible hortatory significance for those to whom they are addressed. Such pronouncements have their place in life, and their social importance: lyric poetry, for example, is not negligible because it is neither logically nor scientifically verifiable. Also such statements may have psychological or sociological truth: they may express a personal or a social attitude. But since such metaphysical and axiological pronouncements are neither analytic explications of meanings nor verifiable statements of any matter of fact, they make no assertion of any truth for which an objective criterion can be found, and are not, thus, subject to reasonable debate which could be terminated by any disclosure of fact.

Pragmatists generally would not follow these inferences which the Vienna Circle draw from the equation between empirical truth and what is verifiable, as is sufficiently evident from their writings on the topic of ethics. Indeed, pragmatism might almost be defined as the contention that all judgments of truth are judgments of value: that verification is a value-determination, and the criterion of truth is realization of some kind of value. Pragmatism could not consistently admit that value-judgments are incapable of an objective test unless it should be prepared to admit that truth in general is subjective. Its critics have, indeed, urged that precisely that is one implication of pragmatism, but pragmatists themselves have denied the validity of the inference.

Professor Moore also, the central figure in the analytic movement, earlier maintained the objectivity of ethical value-judgments, and gives no indication of having abandoned that position.

So far as metaphysics is concerned, pragmatists and analysts, as well as the logical positivists, have given evidence of regarding at least the traditional content of the subject with suspicion. But they have been more likely to mark a distinction between a profitable and an unprofitable method of metaphysical consideration, or between a more and a less significant type of metaphysical questions, than to follow the Vienna Circle in the complete repudiation of metaphysics.

Since verification is so centrally important for all these current movements which have been mentioned, it suggests itself that their divergences, on topics so fundamental, may find connection with some issue concerning precisely what is involved in verification, and the manner in which verification is connected with meaning and with truth. Even questions so basic as the significance of philosophy itself, the method or methods it can legitimately pursue, and what topics, traditionally subsumed under it, have rightfully this place, may find connection with such an issue.

This problem of the nature and the modes of verification is, in fact, the rock on which these tendencies, which converge up to this point, now split apart. Even the logical positivists are divided amongst themselves upon it; and current discussion has not as yet fallen into any shape presenting clear outlines. In the small suggestion to be made about one such issue concerning verification, in what follows, I cannot claim even the value of information about current developments.

The general nature of verification may appear to be obvious. Whatever is verifiable has the general character of an hypothesis. It is suggested to us because certain consequences of it already appear as empirical fact. But it has other consequences, not yet determined as either true or false. Thus, provisionally accepting our hypothesis as a premise, we make prediction of some empirical eventuality which can be determined by further observation or experiment. Proceeding in the appropriate way, we arrive at the point where what is thus predicted should be found if our hypothesis is true. If the consequence fails to eventuate, then, barring some theoretical defect of our procedure, which prevents the result from being decisive, our hypothesis is proved false. If on the contrary, the predicted consequence is encountered, then our hypothesis is, so far, verified. That is, it is rendered that much more probable—just how much will depend on further considerations which may be omitted here. However, the hypothesis is not completely verified by one such test, because it will have other consequences also, not yet tested. Theoretically, it is doubtful if, even under the most auspicious circumstances, a single observation or experimental result can amount to complete verification. Obviously no hypothesis is completely verified so long as there is any consequence of it for which there is the smallest assignable possibility of its turning out unfavorably. Quite generally, that means that hypotheses possessed of any generality can become no more than highly probable, even though, in the best cases, the difference of this from certainty may be practically negligible.

It is a point of some importance that the so-called "consequences" of an hypothesis, by which we test it, are only occasionally logical consequences, strictly deducible from it. Even in the best cases, as in physical science, they are unlikely to represent anything which follows from the hypothesis without the help of other generalizations, previously accepted. And frequently, the "if...then..." connection between an hypothesis and its consequence is quite innocent of logic. I frame the hypothesis that there is ink in my fountain pen, and I test it by seeing if the pen will write. But the statement, "If there is ink in my pen, it will write," cannot be certified by logic. It is merely something I regard as sufficiently established by previous experience. That is, this assumption that a pen with ink in it will write is itself an hypothesis, but one having a much higher degree of probability than the hypothesis of ink in this pen now, whose truth I am testing.

Perhaps this is a typical case. In testing one hypothesis, we make use of other and better established hypotheses, in order to determine what consequences should follow if the hypothesis to be tested is true. If it is a physical hypothesis which is being tested, we make use of the laws of physics in determining what consequences follow from the hypothesis. But no law of physics is established by logic (unless possibly a few which, like the law of the lever, may be regarded as disguised definitions). These laws of physics are themselves hypotheses, and not completely certain, though their probability is presumably much higher than that of the hypothesis to be tested, in conjunction with which they are used for the prediction of consequences. The important consideration here is that no one hypothesis can be tested in isolation. We test the hypothesis H by reference to its consequence C. C, however, is not a consequence of H alone, but of H together with J and K. If C fails to occur, we attribute this to the falsity of H, because J and K are better established. But if empirical principles in general are of the type called "verifiable"—always having consequences not yet tested, and never more than highly probable—then the J and K of our paradigm will be themselves not theoretically certain; and all that we can be sure of, from the failure of C to occur, is that there is something false in the compound statement, HJK. To revert to our example: I test the hypothesis, "There is ink in my pen," by seeing if the pen will write. But when I suppose that this hypothesis can be tested by that result, I am assuming that pens with ink in them will write. And since this last is itself only a more or less well established hypothesis, I cannot determine with finality whether the failure of my pen to write disproves the hypothesis that there is ink in it, or the more general hypothesis that pens with ink in them will write. All I am certain of is that the compound statement, "There is ink in my pen, and pens with ink in them will write," has at least one false constituent.

If this is, in fact, the typical situation with regard to empirical and verifiable truth, then there are two suggestions which rather naturally arise from consideration of it.

First, it is suggested that the true picture of empirical truth, and of natural science as the best instance of such truth, is somewhat as follows: at any given moment, there is some total body of empirical generalizations which have been accepted because of their explanatory value, because they correctly describe all the facts we know and there is no consequence of them which we know to be false. From time to time, new facts come to light to which such explanation must be extended. Sometimes such new facts are incompatible with this body of previously accepted empirical principles. In that case, the locus of the falsity in our accepted principles is not uniquely determined; a revised explanation, including what is newly discovered, can be achieved in more than one way. We are likely, for obvious reasons, to choose that revision which requires the smallest total alteration, or is most easily accepted for some other reason of the same general type—a kind of reason which is likely to be labeled "pragmatic" (though, as one with leanings to pragmatism, I regret just that use of the term).

This hasty depiction is, of course, lamentably crude, but that the general history of science conforms in measure to the outlines of it will be fairly plausible. Science is a far-flung network of more and less well established hypotheses. From time to time new facts appear which require some alteration of scientific conceptions previously held. But just what alteration in the total body of scientific theory is to be made on this account is seldom unambiguously indicated. The tendency to choose that alteration which accommodates the new fact with least disturbance of the whole body of accepted doctrine, or which accords with some other consideration of intellectual economy, or which gives best hope for some new and advantageous method, etc., is one the working of which seems discernible in the progression of scientific conceptions.

The second suggestion which may be drawn from the above—that is, from the consideration that one hypothesis can seldom, if ever, be tested in isolation from others—is that the actual ultimate test of empirical truth is a kind of coherence in the whole system of acceptable principles. Apart from what are really definitions, there is no single one of our accepted laws which by itself is more than probable: each taken separately is merely hypothesis. These hypotheses are so interrelated that none of them can be decisively tested in isolation. Each depends for its verification not only on the consequences of it but also on the concurrent truth of others. And this dependence of hypotheses is a two-way relation. A given one depends on others, of which it may be, in part or wholly, a consequence; and it depends also upon its own consequences—that is, consequences of it taken together with others. In the light of such considerations, the conclusion may be drawn that the whole body of empirical principles or accepted pronouncements is a vast and interrelated network, every item of which is mutually interdependent with every other, in the end; and the final test of empirical truth is simply that of complete consistency and of such mutual support within the system as a whole.

Both these suggestions begin to appear in current discussion. The conceptions just outlined could not be attributed to any party or individual—for one reason because my depiction is too hasty to be just to anyone's position. But I take it that the general position outlined at the beginning of this paper is forcing us on to something further, though to what exactly is not yet clear.

In spite of their obvious plausibility, I do not think that either of these two suggestions can be accepted without basic qualification, and some addition as well.

The second of them, as we know, is a new form of an older conception: the coherence theory of truth. It is open to the objection that consistency and mutual support of one thesis by another are never a sufficient test of truth—even on the whole. If they were, then we should not need recourse to observation and experiment, but could excogitate our system of empirical truth in a sort of intellectual heaven, under guidance of logical considerations exclusively. Furthermore, to escape from the difficulty that no hypothesis has, all by itself, a finally testable truth, by fleeing to the conception that every acceptable hypothesis is interdependent with every other, would be just an instance of our common human failing of going to extremes. All our accepted empirical principles are, let us say, together in one snarl which we can hardly disentangle. But that does not necessarily mean that each is tied to every other. In some provisionally isolable set of principles—say, the geometrical properties of space—we may find (as we do find by the study of geometry) that our separate theses are pretty well tied together, but that it is by no means the case that each is mutually interdependent with every other. As we know from the example of geometry, we may be able to disentangle whole strings of them, which could be lifted out and replaced by other strings consisting of propositions incompatible with those we have removed but fitting with equal consistency into the system as a whole. There is even better reason for supposing that the system of empirical truth altogether will exhibit the same general character of interwoven but separable strands. Because the world of our scientific discourse is not a loose bundle connected by mere "witness"—to use William James's term—is not a good reason to go to the other extreme and take it to be a "block universe" in which everything depends on everything else. The lines of connection amongst our accepted empirical hypotheses are enormously intricate, but there is no reason to compliment our difficulty in disentangling them with the name of "truth."

The conception that because of the complexity of the total body of accepted principles, and the consequence that we can test no one of them in isolation, there is, therefore, some room for choice in what we shall keep and what we shall throw out when confronted with a new fact which does not fit our system as a whole—that therefore there is a pragmatic factor in the determination of what, at any given moment, we accept as truth, I take to be a just consideration. But if there were no other pragmatic element in truth but this, the label "pragmatist" would be—or ought to be, I think—an uncomfortable one for any of us to wear. Because a choice of hypotheses determined by such consideration of convenience or intellectual economy or simplicity, and so on, if it is a choice which makes any conceivable difference which a future eventuality may affect, is merely a temporary attitude which is at the mercy of such future eventualities. It is doubtless an ever-recurrent predicament that evidence to date leaves some such alternatives still open, and that we must, therefore, choose our working hypotheses from amongst them. In such case, to choose on grounds of convenience, simplicity, etc., is only reasonable, there being no more decisive consideration to which we can, at the moment, appeal. But insofar as future experience can show our choice to be an error, what such "pragmatic" choice determines is not truth but merely the practical attitude where we are unavoidably ignorant, for the time being. That always there remains room for such choice reflects the fact that the best we achieve in the realm of empirical principles remains theoretically no more than probable. But no hypothesis was ever a bit more probable for being simple or otherwise convenient. What such simplicity and convenience determine is not truth or even probability but merely simplicity and convenience, which have their reasonable place in the choice of working hypotheses when no more decisive criterion is presently at hand. (That there is, as I should like to maintain, another and different pragmatic factor in truth—a factor which is not at the mercy of future eventualities, as this one is—is a further consideration which would not be pertinent to the present issue.)

I am sure you feel that even if, in every decision with regard to empirical truth, there is the necessity to consider the consistency and mutual support of all our principles, and even if always there remains some room for choice of hypothesis on grounds such as convenience and simplicity, still the decisive factor in the determination of such empirical truth has so far been omitted. That is the factor of verification itself. On the basis of our hypothesis—or our complicated system of hypotheses—we make a prediction. This prediction is found true or it is found to be false. That is the decisive element in the situation. And in this kind of truth, that what is predicted is or is not so, there is no factor of coherence or any pragmatic factor at all.

I sympathize with this conclusion. But there are difficulties about it which must be considered before we can accept it.

Sometimes a point can be brought out most easily by a trivial example which is so simple as to border on the absurd: let us stick to the one about my fountain pen. I am not sure whether its writing or not writing tests my hypothesis of ink in it, or tests the hypothesis that pens with ink in them will write, or how far it tests one of these and how far the other. In this trivial case, I should, of course, go on to make further tests and decide that point. But in more complex cases like those of physical theory, that might be difficult or not practically possible. If somehow we are balked in going further—that is, to revert to our example, if we cannot make any further and more decisive tests, the question whether to decide that there is no ink in the pen, or to decide that pens with ink in them do not always write, might find no better ground of decision than by reference to the question which of these conclusions would be least upsetting to the whole body of our notions about pens and ink and writing (and all the other things which may enter into such situations). We might choose on the ground of the simplest alteration of this total body of beliefs, or by the criterion of consistency and mutual support. It is quite plausible that this is what we usually do, in fact, and that the result of such choices by reference to pragmatic convenience or considerations of coherence is what we are likely, at any given moment, to accept as our body of "truth."

But the non-pragmatic element which illustrates our present point is that the pen won't write. That, we say, is an absolute fact, and the one which precipitates the problem. And it is absolute facts of just that order which stand at the center of every such problem, and constitute the final tests of any verifiable truth or hypothesis. We may have a complex and difficult problem about what any verification tests; but if we have any verification at all, there is an absolute truth about that.

Unfortunately for us, the matter is not quite so simple. We should be right if there were some propositions which we absolutely find true or false by looking directly and simply to the given experience in the moment of verification. But it can be doubted that there are any such. Again, let us take our example. We are inclined to say that the absolute and certain truth in that case is that when we try it the pen won't write. But suppose someone to observe: "Your test depends on your supposition, based on previous experience, that your pen writes when there is ink in it. Now suppose that to be true—leave aside any doubts about that: still, are you sure that this present experience of not writing, is a test of it? Would you wager your life that this is your pen, the experience of which is the basis of the supposition that it tests your hypothesis? Would you be willing to stake the future welfare of all humanity on the proposition that you have a real pen in your hand, even, and that it is not writing?"

If I could have the smallest doubt on any such point, if I should even look twice before betting my life on this thing in my hand, I give my case away. Because by that I confess that the supposition that my present experience proves what I say—"My pen won't write"—is only very probable. It is just another hypothesis to add to the complicated set I already have on hand.

Or, to leave our illustration and speak in general terms: the predictions which we make, for the purpose of testing hypotheses, are propositions. Therefore, to test the hypothesis, even partially, we must find that proposition which states the predicted consequence of the hypothesis either true or false. But can any experience give an absolute test of any proposition? Is there any proposition we can frame which we can, in a directly given experience, absolutely and finally and beyond all theoretically possible doubt, find true or false? If not, then we are back with those who tell us that we can never get beyond some total body of interrelated probabilities; and our so-called "truth" must in the end be determined either pragmatically or by reference to the consistency and mutual support of such hypotheses.

Now we shall have to admit, I think, that propositions that we take to express some present fact, which would verify something, are, in the typical case, not really what we take them to be—are not something absolutely and finally determined to be true by what we see or hear or otherwise experience when we, as we say, make the verification. That my pen won't write—or doesn't write—is not absolutely proved in the so-called verifying experience, because there is theoretical doubt that this thing in my hand is my pen, or a pen, or even that it isn't writing—that there is not something terribly strange about my perceptive apparatus just now, or that I am not dreaming. At least, the propositions that this is a real pen, and that it is not writing, are statements which have some further implications, and could be themselves tested in further experience. Their truth implies something more than what I now experience: and if this more should fail to come to pass in the predicted way, we should have to call them in question. We shall have to admit that they are, theoretically, no more than hypotheses, although their probability is so large that the difference from certainty is practically negligible.

The supposition that there are any statements of objective fact whose truth can be fully determined in any given experience is, in fact, difficult or impossible to defend. Whenever we assert that an objective property belongs to an objective thing—that this desk is yellow, that the blackboard is rectangular, that this is a piece of paper in my hand—what we assert outruns what our momentary perception can completely assure. If I were a magician intent on mystifying you, you might well reserve judgment on any one of these matters. You would then know how to test these statements: you would demand a better light on the desk or blackboard, or a light you had yourself examined, or a view from some other angle, or you would demand to take this thing I am holding in your own hands. Such further experience would have a bearing on the truth in question, would be essential to the verification of it; and the statement of such supposed truth is thus proved to have the present status of partially verified hypothesis and not of complete certainty. When we remember—for one thing—the omnipresent possibility of illusion and mistakes of perception, we shall have to grant, shall we not, that assertions of objective states of affairs, matters of fact, never get theoretically beyond the point of being probabilities of the order, let us say, of 99.9 (and as many more 9's as you choose to add on) but never 100 per cent certainty.

Nevertheless, you object to the conclusion that, with regard to empirical truth, we are forced back upon an exclusively pragmatic test of it or solely to considerations of coherence. You say, perhaps, that if empirical truth did not somehow come down to experience in the end, then not only is the phrase "empirical truth" a terrible misnomer, but the whole body of it becomes a fantastic fabrication, a mere play of the logical faculty operating in a vacuum. If—you say—what is supposed to establish science and commonly accepted principles, as probable hypotheses at least, were itself nothing more than probable, then what we call "probable" would really be only probably probable, or probably probably probable . . . ; and there would be no test of anything and not even a genuine probability. At least, I hope you would say these things, because they seem to me to be inescapable facts.

However, if our convictions on these points are justified, we shall have to look a little further for the absolute *pou sto* of certainty in the realm of matters of empirical fact. We shall not find it in the region of objective assertions about objective things. Such objective propositions, one and all, turn out to involve predictions, to be further testable, and hence theoretically no more than probabilities. If I say this pen will not write, it is subject to examination whether it is a pen ; if I say the blackboard is rectangular, we can get a carpenter's square and proceed to verification of it. Any such statement of the objective character of anything would have such further implications, and no such statement can be brought down simply to what a directly given experience can confirm.

However, our mistake here is only that, in our natural impatience of the distinction between practical certainties (the very highly probable) and genuine theoretical certainties, we have stated ourselves too hastily, and in terms which turn out to be indefensible. We cannot claim, with hope of justification, that a verification consists in finding something true or false which could be stated as an objective character of an objective thing. What I am genuinely certain of, in my direct experience, is not that this thing in my hand is my pen, but that it appears just like my pen as I remember it. What I am completely sure of is not that the blackboard *is* rectangular, but that it *looks* rectangular to me now. I may justly add that, as my previous experience assures me, what appears to me just like my pen very probably *is* my pen, and that things the size of the blackboard which look rectangular to me probably are rectangular or not much different from the rectangular. But what we absolutely find true, in the verifying experience, is not such assertions of objective properties, but is just that something looks or sounds or feels in such and such a determinate fashion. When we phrase ourselves with complete accuracy, what we shall state, as our absolute truths, will be just such formulations of the content of our given experience. And it is on such formulations of the given that the whole pyramid of our more and less probable hypotheses will rest, with simple but objective assertions like "The blackboard is rectangular" and "This is my pen" very near the base but not really coinciding with this foundation of it.

I fear that you will think that I have traveled far to disclose a small and very obvious point. But if we examine this small point closely, it turns out to have rather surprising importance. Not only does it resolve the problem in question—that there is an eventual criterion of empirical truth quite other than the pragmatic one of convenience or the logical one of coherence; but also it has further implications for the just conception of meaning, and for the relations of other kinds of truth to the truth of science. Let us remind ourselves that the general point of view which we assumed for the purposes of our discussion characterizes all empirical truth as verifiable. It holds that the nature of empirical truth consists in such verifiability, and that only those empirical statements which are verifiable possess factual meaning. The small point which we have noted upsets all these conceptions. If it is compatible with the intention of them, still it shows this intention to be poorly realized in these expressions of it, and that the necessary qualifications will result in a quite different picture of empirical truth and empirical meaning.

Let us examine the nature of those formulations of directly given experience which we have found to represent the absolute certainties on which all other empirical truth is eventually based.

First, they are not, in any proper sense of the word, verifiable statements. The reason that they are certain is that they are not subject to anything which could happen in future. If I say, "This blackboard *is* rectangular," that is verifiable; and by the same token future eventualities may oblige the reconsideration of it. But if I confine myself to the certainty "This blackboard looks rectangular to me now," nothing that can happen in future will have any bearing on the truth of that. In the only sense in which such formulations of the given can be said to be verifiable, they are already verified when they are made. There is no question for the maker of such a statement, of its truth or falsity: as intended, it either expresses what he knows to be true, or it is a false statement, and he knows that. The test of the truth of such statements does not consist in the outcome of any process of verification but merely in an observed relation of accord between the intended denotation of the language used and the determinate content of an experience which meets or satisfies that intent.

Thus truth which is tested by verification—and that includes the truth of all empirical generalizations and of all assertions of objective matters of fact—depends eventually upon truth of another kind, which is not tested by verification and does not need to be verified.

If we could follow out all the implications of such considerations, we should find, I think, that they have a bearing on further problems—for instance upon value-theory in general and upon ethics. You will remember that the Vienna Circle has drawn a line between empirical and verifiable statements, on the one hand, which have the character of objective truth or falsity and have literal meaning, and merely expressive pronouncements, on the other hand, the truth of which cannot be tested by any verification. To these latter they deny any factual or cognitive meaning and grant only an "emotive" meaning. Concordant with this distinction, they regard science, taken as consisting of assertions which can be tested by some process of verification and which have objective meaning, as the all-inclusive truth; and they repudiate other classes of statements, including those of metaphysics and normative ethics, as neither true nor false, and not literally meaningful, because they are merely expressive of what is subjective.

Now as we have seen, there *is* a real line of division between any verifiable assertion about the objective quality of an objective thing (the rectangularity of the blackboard, for example) and the formulation of the immediate content of given experience (the seen character of the blackboard as I look at it). If I say that the blackboard is rectangular, I imply something about the further possible experience of it: implicitly I predict that its now-given visual character is a more or less permanent possibility of experience; also that this appearance would alter, with change of my angle of vision, in certain ways and not in others; that a carpenter's square placed at the corners would coincide with the edges of it, and so on. "Rectangularity" as an objective property of the blackboard represents a whole complexus or series of given visual and other sense characters in experience: no single immediate datum is sufficient to determine the actuality in the blackboard of this

objective quality. It is for this reason—that is, because of the complexity or temporal spread of what the objective predicate "rectangular"
as applied to the blackboard means, or requires for its truth—that the
assertion "The blackboard is rectangular" is something verifiable, and
requiring verification for establishment of it as fact.

However, we also see that the truth of such an objective assertion
about an objective property rests eventually upon the truth of statements of a different sort: the kind which formulate the verification
itself and are merely reports of the immediately given in some experience. Such reports are ordinarily not formulated at all; and every-day
language is ill-adapted for the making of them. When we wish to convey just that immediate visual quality with which the blackboard now
impresses us, we find no other words available than just the names of
objective properties, such as "rectangular," and we have to achieve our
precise meaning by some locution such as "looks like" or "appears to
be." But if we observe what it is that we thus intend to formulate, and
just what meaning our words—perhaps "rectangular looking"—are
here intended to have, we find, do we not, that such formulations of
the given in experience should properly be classed with the sort which
the Vienna Circle would condemn as philosophically and scientifically
negligible, because they do not have the character of verifiable assertions, but are merely expressive statements of the subjective. Their
proper classification is with those of the kind to which the logical positivists would deny factual or cognitive meaning and ascribe only "emotive" meaning.

Whoever uses language to report given experience is, in fact, giving
it a meaning which is merely expressive, which connotes nothing to be
verified in later experience, and which makes it significant of the subjective (that is, immediate) rather than the objective. He is using language in just the fashion in which it is used in lyric poetry for example.
The blackboard would make a poor subject for a poem. But the expression of just that directly given quality with which it strikes us now
would be precisely the expression of the sort of thing which Professor
Prall calls an "esthetic surface," which poetry and art attempt to convey. It is this kind of meaning, apparently, which the Vienna Circle
would label "emotive."

However, if such meanings as these are to be called "subjective,"
still, so far from being philosophically and scientifically negligible, they
are such as must constitute the ultimate test and the ultimate significance of science and of every kind of empirical truth; because the truth
of whatever is verifiable comes down eventually to the truth of just

such statements of the experience in which it must be verified, if it is verified at all. If such expressive and subjective statements, which are not subject to any further verifying tests, do not have genuine meaning, and genuine truth or falsity, then empirical generalizations and science itself must likewise be without literal meaning, as a result.

Thus the consequences of the little point we have observed may eventually extend so far as to break down the supposed line of division between objective scientific pronouncements and those so-called subjective meanings which are merely expressive and which figure in the formulation of immediately apprehended quality. That this might have a bearing on the kind of truth we can expect in ethics and in esthetics, and the relation of this to scientific truth, will be fairly obvious.

It would not be possible to follow out these issues here, and determine whether such suggested consequences for other philosophical problems could genuinely be elicited or not. But at least we see that the upshot of the general point of view, outlined at the beginning of this paper, is no foregone conclusion. If there is, to a degree, this convergence of certain current tendencies which has been suggested, still the further development of it is something which could go on in more than one way. What the ultimate consequences of it are to be, is, I suppose, a matter which will not be concluded by the present generation. Perhaps some of you who are now before me will have a hand in determining it.

5. Some Logical Considerations Concerning the Mental

It is a conception as old as Socrates and as modern as our current logical analyses that the central task in philosophic discussion of any topic is to arrive at and elucidate a definition. That, I take it, is what is properly meant by a philosophic "theory"; a theory of X is a more or less elaborate definitive statement having "X" as subject, together with such exposition as will remove difficulties of understanding and serve to show that this definition covers the phenomena to be taken into account.

I fear that what this occasion calls for is such a theory of mind. But if so, then I am unprepared for it. I am unable to present any statement of the form "Mind is . . ." (where "is" would express the relation of equivalence of meaning) which would satisfy me or which I should expect would satisfy you. I can only put forward certain statements intended to formulate attributes which are essential to mind: to point to phenomena of which we can say, "Whatever else is or is not comprehended under 'mind,' at least it is intended to include *these.*" In particular, I shall wish to emphasize that whatever is called "content of consciousness" is so included, and to consider certain consequences of that simple fact.

In so doing, however, I am aware of one danger. Confronted with problems of analysis which there is trouble to resolve, one may sometimes circumvent them by changing the subject. We find ourselves unprepared to formulate any sufficient criterion of X which precisely accords with what is comprehended under "X" and what excluded. But we are—it may be—prepared to elaborate systematically and ingeniously some *other* definitive statement using the same term in a somewhat different signification: some definition of the *word* "X" devised with a view to skirting what is dark to our insight and ruling out whatever we find unmanageable in current usage of the term. Theories are sometimes achieved in this way. But this fallacy of changing the subject, I would above all else avoid. I can not express precisely and clearly what you and I mean by "mind"; but if anything I have to say should be found incompatible with that common meaning, then I should not wish to persist in maintaining it.

Read, with omissions, at the meeting of the Eastern Division of the American Philosophical Association, Philadelphia, December 26, 1940. Reprinted by permission from *The Journal of Philosophy*, Vol. XXXVIII (1941), No. 9, pp. 225–33.

It is one such essential feature of what the word "mind" means that minds are private: that one's own mind is something with which one is directly acquainted—nothing more so—but that the mind of another is something which one is unable directly to inspect.

If that is, in fact, a required feature of what we should call "a mind," then indeed it must be admitted to be a question whether minds—anything having this character—exist. It must also be admitted that the statement itself, asserting the existence of mind in this sense, might contain some irremovable unclarity or some implicit inconsistency, rendering it a non-significant affirmation. However, any such possible doubts can, I think, be removed.

But first, let us observe that if the above statement is correct, when measured against the intended signification of "mind," that of itself is sufficient to preclude certain prevalent theories. Whatever else such theories may be true of or false of, as statements about what is meant by "mind" they are literally not pertinent. Behavioristic interpretations of mind are thus not pertinent, nor is any identification of mind with brain states or brain functionings.

The point has been raised often enough and will not need to be elaborated here. All men are directly acquainted with their own minds, but no one is directly acquainted with the present state of his brain. We know nothing about our brain states except by complicated and more or less uncertain inferences. And if technical difficulties of observing our own brains should be overcome, still the man who should be suffering pain and at the same time observing his own brain, would be aware of two things, not one; and only by an inductive inference would he be led to suppose that the one of them had anything to do with the other.

Sometimes when such arguments as this are put forward, however, it is not realized that they depend fundamentally upon what kind of thing is *meant* by "mind." That is the case: otherwise this type of objection to a behavioristic or brain-state interpretation of mind could be easily met. It could be observed, for example, that one may see a thing held in the hand and at the same time feel it with the fingers. And one who thus saw and felt the same object might not know that what he visually observed was the same thing that he tactually observed. An infant or a man who suddenly receives the sense of sight must learn to make such identification of the visually with the tactually perceived; it requires to be inductively inferred. Nevertheless, identification in this case is valid. And it might be argued that identification of the mental with the behavioral or with brain-states is similarly valid, in spite of the objection. However, in such a case as this, in which an identification which is valid requires to be established by inductive inference, there are also two things—or more than two—whose *non*-identity is witnessed by the necessity of such learning. In our example, there is the tactually felt as such—the tactual datum—and there is the visually apprehended as such—the visual datum. There is also the object held in the hand, which is a different kind of entity from the other two. Thus in one signification of the phrases "what is seen" and "what is felt," they may denote the same thing, though this identity requires to be inferred from some course of experience. In another signification, what is seen is *not* identical with what is felt; and this non-identity is proved merely by the possibility of observing both without being able to identify them.

If, then, this kind of objection to behavioristic and brain-state interpretations of mind is sound, it is so because of the meaning of terms referring to the mental: because these are so intended that if A is a present phenomenon of my mind, then anything I can not directly inspect is not identical with A, and anything I could observe without being able to identify it with A would be in fact not identical with A.

This characteristic of the intended meaning of terms applied to the mental is not peculiar to them; nor is the kind of controversy which can arise on account of the type of ambiguity here illustrated. The question whether the sound of music is or is not correctly identified with certain harmonic motions is a closely similar issue, which depends on the meaning of the language which is used, and upon appeal to criteria which are different according as it is one or another of two possible meanings which is intended.

Apparently there are two classifications of namable things: one of them such that "A" and "B" can denote the same entity only if a person who directly observes what "A" names and what "B" names will also be able to observe that they name the same thing, and the other classification such that what "A" names can be identical with what "B" names even though one may observe what "A" names and what "B" names without being able to make the identification. If I knew how to draw a sharp and clear line between these two classifications of namable things, I suspect that this distinction might be important for our present topic. But I do not know how to draw it in a manner at once comprehensive and faithful to our actual intentions in the use of language.

There is, however, one consideration which seems pertinent and clear. Some terms—or some terms in some uses—name what presents itself, or could present itself, as such: name appearances or data. The intent of this use of terms we may, for convenience, label "phenomenal meaning"; and the language thus used may be called "phenomenal language." Other terms—or the same terms in a different and more frequent usage—name things which may appear but are in any case distinct from their appearances, that is, name something to which a given appearance may be attributable but something to which also more is attributable than could present itself to any single observer on one occasion. Physical objects are all of them included in this latter classification. And it is entities of this classification for which it may be true that A and B are identical, though one who observes what "A" names and observes also what "B" names may still be unable to make the identification. Phenomena of consciousness—it suggests itself—all of them belong in the former classification. They have universally the character here labeled "datum"; and language used to name or apply to any conscious content as such has phenomenal meaning. It denotes an appearance or appearances. Such data, when given, are entities whose identity and character it is impossible to mistake—though admittedly any language used to name them may be inappropriate or inadequate and fail to express just what is intended. An appearance or datum is just what it seems to be, and is nothing more than or other than what it appears to be.

If this is correct, then it may serve to explain the pertinence of the argument that mental facts can not be identified with brain facts or facts of physical behavior because we directly inspect and are fully acquainted with the mental factuality but may be ignorant of the brain-state or the behavior; or if we should be also aware of these latter, may still be ignorant of any connection between them and what is mental. Admitting this phenomenal meaning of language used to denote the mental, such argument is entirely sound, and proves its point.

These considerations may also serve to locate more precisely one issue between those who interpret the mental in terms of behavior or of brain-states and those who would repudiate such interpretation. We who criticize these conceptions are talking about phenomenal entities as such when we use terms referring to the mental; they, by contrast, are in search of something belonging to the other classification: some entity to which these mental phenomena may be attributed, but a thing which by its nature transcends any possible phenomenal appearance which could be given at any one time. This thing is, on their account, a state of the physical brain or of the behaving organism.

If this does in fact correctly locate the issue—or *an* issue—then I think there is something further to be said about it which is obvious. It may well be that there are two kinds of namable entities to be talked about when the mental is under discussion : the directly given phenomena of consciousness, and a something—a substance, if you please—to which these are attributable. That there is such a thing or substance of which mental phenomena are attributes, and that this thing is the brain or the behaving organism, is one view, to be considered alongside others, including the dualistic conception of a non-physical substance as that to which mental states are attributable. But at least there are two things to be talked about : the substance of which the mental phenomena are attributes, and the directly given phenomena themselves which are to be attributed. There is a truth about these latter, and a kind of truth peculiarly patent, concerning which we can be mistaken only by some inadvertence. It is, moreover, this truth of the phenomenal which sets the problem in any search for that substance to which contents of consciousness are attributable. It is these phenomena which are to be accounted for, and the phenomenal facts about them which must be looked to in order to determine the correctness or incorrectness, or the plausibility, of any solution which may be offered for this problem which I have ventured to call the problem of substance.

In their preoccupation with this substance-problem, the proponents of behavioristic and brain-state theories of mind sometimes speak as if there *were* no such entities as the directly inspected contents of consciousness, or appear to deny that there is any truth which can be told about them except in terms of those things—on their view, physical things—of which the mental are manifestations. By implication, they seem to accuse us, who would try first of all to state facts about these directly presented phenomena themselves, of talking nonsense or speaking of what does not exist. Such implication, intended or not, is certainly without justification. Whoever would deny that there are directly inspectable facts of the content of consciousness would deny that which alone makes a theory of mind desirable and significant, and that which supplies the only final test of such a theory.

There is a second point which is pertinent to these issues, and can also be approached from grounds of analysis or logic. A definition, or a philosophic theory, should explicate the subject of it by specifying that criterion by which the thing in question could be selected from amongst all possible things which could be presented to us or imagined. It is not sufficient in a definition—and it should not be thought satisfactory in a theory—to characterize A by reference to XYZ, where XYZ are characters which, under conceivable circumstances, might be determined as present but leave us still in doubt whether what is presented is *A*. If we know what we mean by "*A*" and if what we mean by "*A*" is expressed by "*XYZ*," then it could not conceivably happen that *XYZ* should be determined as present but there could be rational doubt whether what is presented is *A*.

Behavioristic and brain-state interpretations of mind do not satisfy this prime requisite of definition and adequate theory. They do not satisfy it for the same reasons that the relation between mental phenomena and behavior or brain-states is something which can only be inferred inductively.

Let it be granted that there is some more or less complex character of behavior such that whenever behavior of just this character occurs there is consciousness, and whenever there is not behavior of this sort there is no consciousness. Let it be further granted that for every qualitative specificity of consciousness there is some equally specific and correlated character of behavior. Still the definitive explication of the mental in terms of the behavioral can not meet our requirement. First, because it would still be possible, for example, to be in doubt whether the angle-worm on the fish-hook suffers pain; and we should be unable to dispel this doubt by observing its behavior. The criterion of consciousness in terms of behavior breaks down in such borderline cases, simply because nobody can specify this criterion except in some arbitrary fashion whose truth to what we mean by "consciousness" he merely guesses at. Second, the various modes of one's own consciousness—suffering pain, hearing music, seeing green—are directly distinguishable by inspection. But no one could recognize these specificities of his own mentality in terms of behavior, because neither he nor anyone else can state precisely what character of behavior is unexceptionably present when there is pain or heard music or the seeing of green, and unexceptionably absent when there is not this specific mode of consciousness.

It is sufficiently evident that identification of the mental with the behavioral, or with brain-states, represents a locution comparable to the physicist's statement that a specific pitch *is* a particular frequency of harmonic motion, and that sound *is* harmonic motion within a certain range of frequencies. Such locution represents first an empirically discovered correlation of two independently recognizable phenomena, a pitch and a rate of vibration. If "middle C" did not *first* mean something identifiable without reference to vibration, and if "vibration of 256 per second" did not *first* mean something identifiable without reference to sound, this correlation of the two could never have been empirically established and statement of it would be unintelligible verbiage. Eventually we may come to have a degree of inductive assurance of this correlation which exceeds our confidence in identifications of pitch by other means than physical determination of this frequency. That being the case, our most trusted criterion of pitch, and of the objectivity of sound, comes to be this criterion in terms of harmonic motion. To that extent and in that sense, it becomes understandable and even justifiable if the phenomena of sound are *defined* in terms of harmonic motion.

Such definition, which represents a type quite common in science, is of a peculiar sort which may be called "definition by description" (definition by reference to some non-essential character but one uniformly found present in all actual cases of the thing in question and found absent in all other cases which are actual). A traditional example would be "Man is the animal that laughs." It is a distinguishing feature of such definition by description that the relation of definiens to definiendum which it states is one requiring to be established by induction and incapable of being established by logical analysis alone. Correlatively, the criterion of the definiendum which such a definition specifies is one (supposedly) sufficient for selecting what the definiendum denotes in all actual circumstances, but *not* sufficient to select what is defined under all thinkable circumstances or from amongst all imaginable things.

The behavioristic or the brain-state theory of mind involves such definition of the mental by description. The principal difference of it from the example just discussed is that, whereas the correlation between sound and harmonic motion is well substantiated in all details, the correlation of mental phenomena with equally specific brain-states or modes of behavior is less well substantiated as a general thesis, and is quite undetermined in many of those specific details which the general truth of it requires. That being so, the definition of the utterly familiar specificities of the mental in terms of supposedly correlated brain functions or behavior is definition of the known in terms of the unknown.

There is also the consideration that whereas in natural science, which concerns itself exclusively with the existent, such definition by description has its pragmatic justification, such justification is lacking in philosophy, whose concern is not that of establishing synthetic *a posteriori* truths. From this point of view, the behavioristic or the brain-state theory of mind substitutes an hypothesis which only the future development of natural science can corroborate or disprove for our more appropriate business of the analysis of meanings.

It has been regarded as a strong point in favor of interpreting the mental in terms of behavior or of brain functions, and a strong point against any theory of the sort indicated by what has here been said, that minds other than our own, as anything distinguishable from certain physical phenomena, are unverifiable entities. And affirmations of what is unverifiable have sometimes been said to be meaningless. You will not expect me to attempt, in the space that remains, any adequate discussion of the questions here involved. But one or two considerations which are pertinent may be briefly indicated.

All of us who earlier were inclined to say that unverifiable statements are meaningless—and I include myself—have since learned to be more careful. This dictum is unclear, and in the most readily suggested interpretations of it is too sweeping to be plausible. Also, the main point here does not have to do with verification at all. With empiricists in general and pragmatists in particular, such reference to verifiability as essential to meaning is only a roundabout way of pointing out that unless you are somehow prepared to recognize the factuality you assert, in case that factuality should be, or could be, presented to you, your verbal expression is not a matter-of-fact statement because it affirms nothing intelligible. Any conditions of verification over and above this one requirement that a matter-of-fact assertion must have empirical sense—whether these further conditions be "practical" or "theoretical"—are irrelevant to the question of meaningfulness. And clearly the belief in other consciousness than one's own satisfies this one requirement of the meaningful: that there must be some criterion for recognition, some sense content indicative of what is meant. We can envisage the conscious experience of another, by empathy, in terms of our own. And we do. Any denial of that would be too egregious for consideration.

We significantly believe in other minds than our own, but we can not *know* that such exist. This belief is a postulate. At least I should have said this earlier—and did say it. But I now think this statement was a concession to an over-rigorous conception of what deserves the name of "knowledge." For empirical knowledge, in distinction from merely meaningful belief, verification is required. But there is what we call "indirect verification" as well as "direct"; and there is "complete" or "decisive verification" and also "incomplete verification" or "confirmation" as more or less probable. There are reasons to think that these two distinctions—direct or indirect and complete or incomplete—reduce to one: that in any distinctive sense of "directly verifiable," that and that only is directly verifiable which is also completely and decisively verifiable. (The plausibility of this may be suggested by the thought that whatever is incompletely verified does not present itself in its full nature but is observed only in certain manifestations.) Most of what we call "knowledge" is not only incompletely verified at any time but—when the matter is considered carefully—must remain so forever. (It may be completely verifiable, or completely confirmable, in the sense that there is nothing which the truth of it requires which could not, given the conditions of verification, be found true or found false; but it is not completely verifiable in the sense that verification of it can be completed—somewhat as there is no whole number which can not be counted, but counting of the whole numbers can not be completed.)

In view of these facts (if these suggestions indicate fact), it may be that there is no fundamental difference, by reference to its verifiability, between the belief in other minds and the belief, for example, in ultra-violet rays or in electrons. It might even be that the belief in other minds, though always incompletely verified and incapable of becoming otherwise, is supported by inductive evidence so extensive as to be better confirmed than some of the accepted theses of physical science.

6. The Modes of Meaning

The discussion will mainly be confined to meanings as conveyed by words, by series of ink-marks or of sounds. But it will be well to acknowledge at the outset that verbal meanings are not primitive: presumably the meanings to be expressed must come before the linguistic expression of them, however much language may operate retroactively to modify the meanings entertained. Also, other things than verbal expressions have meaning; in fact, one may well think that words are only surrogates for presentational items of other sorts which are the originals in exercise of the meaning-function. As Charles Peirce pointed out, the essentials of the meaning-situation are found wherever there is anything which, for some mind, stands as sign of something else. To identify meaning exclusively with the characters of verbal symbolization would be to put the cart before the horse, and run the risk of trivializing the subject. The generic significance of meaning is that in which *A* means *B* if *A* operates as representing or signifying *B*: if it stands for *B*, or calls it to mind. Still, it is doubtful that there are, or could be, any meanings which it is intrinsically impossible for words to express: it may well be that in discussing verbal meanings exclusively, we do not necessarily omit any kind of meanings, but merely limit our consideration to meanings as conveyed by a particular type of vehicle.

Even with this limitation to meaning as verbally expressed, it is impossible, within reasonable limits of space here, to present our topic otherwise than in outline only. Nor will it be possible to make desirable comparisons between the outline to be offered and other discussions of the same subject. But because such outline-presentation may easily have the air of dogmatism, I should like to express my conviction that if there be any one analysis of meaning in general which is correct, then any number of other analyses will be possible which are equally correct: for much the same reasons that if any set of primitive ideas and primitive propositions are sufficient for a mathematical system, then there will be any number of alternative sets of primitive ideas and propositions which likewise are sufficient. Amongst alternative analyses of meaning which should be so fortunate as to be correct in all details, choice would presumably be determined by such considerations as convenience, simplicity, and conformability to some purpose in hand.

Reprinted by permission from *Philosophy and Phenomenological Research*, Vol. IV (1943–44), No. 2, pp. 236–49.

In general, the connection between a linguistic sign and its meaning is determined by convention: linguistic signs are verbal symbols. A *verbal symbol* is a recognizable pattern of marks or of sounds used for purposes of expression. (What is recognized as the same pattern, in different instances, is partly a matter of physical similarity and partly a matter of conventional understanding.) Two marks, or two sounds, having the same recognizable pattern, are two *instances* of the same symbol, not two different symbols.

A *linguistic expression* is constituted by the association of a verbal symbol and a fixed meaning; but the linguistic expression cannot be identified with the symbol alone nor with the meaning alone. If in two cases, the meaning expressed is the same but the symbols are different, there are two expressions, not one. If in two cases, the symbol is the same but the meanings are different, there are two expressions, not one. But if in two cases—as in different places or at different times— the meaning is the same and the symbol is the same, then there are two *instances* of the expression but only one expression.

An instance of a symbol is often called a symbol, and an instance of an expression is often called an expression; but these modes of speech are unprecise. An ink-spot or a noise is a concrete entity; but a symbol is an abstract entity; and an expression is a correlative abstraction.

A linguistic expression may be a term or a proposition or a propositional function. As it will turn out, propositions and propositional functions are terms; but some terms only are propositions, and some only are propositional functions; and these two latter classifications are mutually exclusive.

A *term* is an expression which names or applies to a thing or things, of some kind, actual or thought of.

It is sometimes said that what is not actual cannot be named. But such assertion is either an arbitrary and question-begging restriction upon use of the verb "to name"—since plainly whatever is thought of can be spoken of—or it is merely silly. One does not easily imagine what those who make this assertion would say to persons who have named a hoped-for child or inventors who have named a never-completed machine. However, there are difficulties connected with this point which are genuine; and it will be the intention so to write here as to minimize dependence upon it. In line with that intention, the above definition of a term may be rephrased: a term is an expression *capable* of naming or applying to a thing or things, of some kind.

In common speech, a term is said to denote the existent or existents to which it is applied on any given occasion of its use. For example, in the statement "Those three objects are books," "book" is said to denote the three objects indicated, or any one of them. This usage has the awkward consequence that what a term is said to denote is not, in most instances, the denotation of it. We shall, however, continue to use both "denote" and "denotation" with their commonplace significances.[1]

All terms have meaning in the sense or mode of denotation or extension; and all have meaning in the mode of connotation or intension.

The *denotation* of a term is the class of all actual or existent things to which that term correctly applies. The qualification "actual or existent" here is limiting and not merely explicative: things which are, or would be, namable by a term but which do not in fact exist are not included in its denotation.

A term which names nothing actual has *zero-denotation*. But it would be a mistake to say that such a term as "unicorn" or "Apollo" has no denotation, especially since this would suggest that it has no meaning in the correlative sense of meaning. A term has meaning in the mode of denotation if it is intended to function as a name; and any locution not so intended is not a term.

When it is desirable to refer to whatever a term would correctly name or apply to, whether existent or not, we shall speak of a *classification* instead of a class, and of the comprehension of the term. The *comprehension* of a term is, thus, the classification of all consistently thinkable things to which the term would correctly apply—where anything is consistently thinkable if the assertion of its existence would not, explicitly or implicitly, involve a contradiction. For example, the comprehension of "square" includes all imaginable as well as all actual squares, but does not include round squares.

Much confusion in analysis may be avoided by the clear distinction of denotation from comprehension.

The *connotation* or *intension* of a term is delimited by any correct definition of it. If nothing would be correctly namable by "T" unless it should also be namable by "A_1," by "A_2," and ... and by "A_n," and if anything namable by the compound term "A_1 and A_2 and ... and A_n" would also be namable by "T," then this compound term, or any which is synonymous with it, specifies the connotation of "T" and may be said to have the same connotation as "T." This leaves "connotation" subject to one ambiguity, which will be discussed later. But for the present, the characterization given will be sufficiently clear.

---

[1] Some avoid the awkward consequence mentioned by saying that a term *designates* a thing that it names. This terminology is apt, but is not adopted here.

Traditionally the term "essence" is used to indicate that characteristic of the object or objects named which is correlative with the connotation of the term. It is, of course, meaningless to speak of the essence of a thing except relative to its being named by some particular term. But for purposes of analysis, it is desirable or even necessary to have some manner of marking this distinction between characters of an object which are essential to its being named by a term in question, and other characters of the object which are not thus essential. We shall say that a term *signifies* the comprehensive character such that everything having this character is correctly namable by the term, and whatever lacks this character, or anything included in it, is not so namable. And we shall call this comprehensive essential character the *signification* of the term.[2]

Abstract terms are those which name what they signify. Thus for abstract terms, signification and denotation coincide. Things which incorporate the signification of an abstract term, "*A*," but possess other characters not included in what "*A*" names, are instances of *A* but are not named by "*A*."

Non-abstract terms, whose denotation is distinct from their signification, are *concrete*.

By the idiom of language, there are certain words and phrases—e.g., predicate-adjectives like "red"—which when they occur as grammatical subject are abstract terms, but which may occur as concrete terms in the predicate. Such words and phrases are sometimes called *attributive*. But this classification is primarily linguistic; the words and phrases in question are not strictly terms but only ambiguous symbolizations having now one, now another, meaning. The classification "attributive" is worth remarking only in order that certain confusions about abstract and concrete terms may be avoided.

A *singular* term is one whose connotation precludes application of it to more than one actual thing. A non-singular term is *general*. (The dichotomy, singular or general, is not significant in the case of abstract terms; if it be applied to them, all abstract terms must be classed as singular.)

It should be observed that singularity or generality is a question of connotation, not of denotation. "The red object on my desk" is a sin-

---

[2] Some may be minded to insist that it is the *sign* which *signifies*, and not the term or linguistic expression, constituted by association of the sign with a meaning. Our usage here of the words "signify" and "signification" is, of course, arbitrary: other and possibly more appropriate words might have been chosen instead. But what we use these words to refer to is a function of the term or expression, and is *not* a property which (like its shape) can be attributed to the sign regardless of the meaning associated with it.

gular term, and "red object on my desk" is a general term, regardless of the facts about red objects on my desk. If there is no red object on my desk, or if there is more than one, then "the red object on my desk" has zero-denotation, but its being a singular term is not affected.

The question what should be regarded as comprehended by a singular term involves the consideration that, although singularity is connoted, still the connotation of a singular term is never sufficient—without recourse to other and logically adventitious facts—to determine *what* individual is named, i.e., to select this individual from amongst all thinkable things satisfying the connotation of the term. Thus the denotation of a singular term is a class which is either a class of one or is empty. But its comprehension is the classification of *all* the things consistently thinkable as being the one and only member of that class.

It will be noted that, for any term, its connotation determines its comprehension; and conversely, any determination of its comprehension would determine its connotation, by determining what characters alone are common to all the things comprehended. In point of fact, however, there is no way in which the comprehension can be precisely specified except by reference to the connotation, since exhaustive enumeration of all the thinkable things comprehended is never possible.

The connotation of a term and its denotation do not, however, mutually determine one another. The connotation being given, the denotation is thereby limited but not fixed. Things which lack any essential attribute, specified or implied in the connotation, are *excluded from* the denotation; but what is *included in* the denotation, and what not, depends also on what happens to exist, since the class of things denoted —as distinguished from what the term comprehends—is confined to existents.

Also, the denotation of a term being determined, the connotation is thereby limited but not fixed. The connotation cannot include any attribute absent from one or more of the things named; but it may or may not include an attribute which is common to all existents named by the term, since such an attribute may or may not be essential to their being so named. "Featherless biped," for example, does not connote rationality, even if the class denoted contains only rational beings.

We should also remark that a term may have zero-comprehension. For example, "round square" has zero-comprehension; the classification of consistently thinkable things so named is empty. But many terms —e.g., "unicorn" and "non-rational animal that laughs"—have zero-denotation without having zero-comprehension; things which would be correctly so named are consistently thinkable.

The classic dictum that denotation varies inversely as connotation is false; e.g., "rational featherless biped" has the same denotation as "featherless biped." But this relation does hold between connotation and comprehension. Any qualification added to a connotation (and not already implied) further restricts the comprehension; and with any omission of a qualification from a connotation, the classification comprehended is enlarged to include thinkable things which retention of that qualification would exclude.

This relation of connotation and comprehension is worth remarking for the sake of one consequence of it: a term of zero-comprehension has *universal* connotation. This may at first strike the reader as a paradox. But the correctness of it may be observed from two considerations. Only terms naming nothing which is consistently thinkable have zero-comprehension. And "*A* is both round and square," for example, entails "*A* is *y*," for any value of *y*. That is, the attribution of "both round and square" entails *every* attribute; and the connotation of "round square," since it includes every mentionable attribute, is universal.[3]

This fact clarifies one matter which might otherwise be puzzling. Plainly, it is incorrect to say that terms like "round square" have no connotation, or that they are meaningless. This term is distinguished from a nonsense-locution like "zuke" by definitely implying the properties of roundness and squareness. And it is only by reason of this meaning—this connotation—which it has, that one determines its inapplicability to anything consistently thinkable.

Thus what is (presumably) intended by the inaccurate statement that such terms are meaningless can be stated precisely by saying that they have zero-comprehension, or that their connotation is universal.

The diametrically opposite kind of term—those having universal comprehension and zero-connotation—are also often said to be meaningless. "Being" and "entity"—supposing everything one could mention is a being or entity—are such terms. And again, the accurate manner of indicating the lack of significance which characterizes these terms

---

[3] "*A* is both *x* and not-*x*" entails "*A* is *x*."

And "*A* is *x*" entails "Either *A* is both *x* and *y* or *A* is *x* but not *y*."

Hence "*A* is both *x* and not-*x*" entails "Either *A* is both *x* and *y* or *A* is *x* but not *y*."

But also "*A* is both *x* and not-*x*" entails "*A* is not *x*."

And "*A* is not *x*" entails "It is false that *A* is *x* but not *y*."

Hence "*A* is both *x* and not-*x*" entails "It is false that *A* is *x* but not *y*."

But "Either *A* is both *x* and *y* or *A* is *x* but not *y*" and "It is false that *A* is *x* but not *y*" together entail "*A* is both *x* and *y*."

And "*A* is both *x* and *y*" entails "*A* is *y*."

Hence "*A* is both *x* and not-*x*" entails "*A* is *y*."

is to observe that attribution of them implies no attribute that could be absent from anything: that their connotation is zero and their comprehension unlimited. But if they genuinely lacked any meaning—any connotation—this character of them could not be determined.

The modes of meaning mentioned above for terms—denotation or extension, connotation or intension, comprehension, and signification—are likewise the modes of meaning of propositions and of propositional functions. This is the case because propositions are a kind of term; and propositional functions are another kind of term.

A proposition is a term capable of signifying a state of affairs. To define a proposition as an expression which is either true or false is correct enough but inauspicious, because it may lead to confusion of a proposition with the *statement* or *assertion* of it, whereas the element of assertion in a statement is extraneous to the proposition asserted. The proposition is the assertable content; and this same content, signifying the same state of affairs, can also be questioned, denied, or merely supposed, and can be entertained in other moods as well.[4]

"Fred is buying groceries" asserts the state of affairs participially signifiable by "Fred buying groceries (now)." "Is Fred buying groceries?" questions it; "Let Fred buy groceries" presents it in the hortatory mood; "Oh that Fred may be buying groceries" in the optative mood; and "Suppose Fred is buying groceries" puts it forward as an hypothesis. Omitting, then, this adventitious element of assertion—or any other mode of entertainment—we find the assertable content, here identified with the proposition itself, as some participial term, signifying a state of affairs, actual or thinkable.

It will be noted that the state of affairs is the *signification* of the proposition, not its denotation. When any term denotes a thing, it names that thing as a whole, not merely the character or attribute signified. And what a term denotes or applies to is, by the law of the Excluded Middle, also denoted by one or the other of every pair of mutually negative terms which could meaningfully be applied to it. Thus there would be a failure of analogy, on a most important point, between propositional terms and the more familiar kind of terms, if we should regard propositions as denoting the state of affairs they refer to. And the denotation or extension of propositions would not be subject to the law of the Excluded Middle. The denotation or extension of a proposition, as application of that law leads us to see, is something

---

[4] I am indebted to conversations with Professor C. W. Morris for this way of putting the matter—though he may not approve the conception that a proposition is a term.

which is likewise denoted by one or other of every pair of mutually negative propositional terms, i.e., one or other of every pair of mutually contradictory propositions. And this thing denoted is not that limited state of affairs which the proposition refers to, but the kind of *total* state of affairs we call a world. The limited state of affairs signified is merely the *essential attribute* which any world must possess in order that the proposition in question should denote or apply to it. A statement asserting a proposition *attributes* the state of affairs signified to the actual world. And the denotation or extension of a proposition— since denotation is in all cases confined to what exists—is either the actual world or it is empty. Thus all *true* propositions have the same extension, namely, this actual world; and all *false* propositions have the same extension, namely, zero-extension. The distinctive extensional property of a proposition is, thus, its truth or falsity.

A proposition *comprehends* any consistently thinkable world which would incorporate the state of affairs it signifies: a classification of Leibnitzian possible worlds. This conception of possible worlds is not jejune: the actual world, as far as anyone knows it, is merely one of many such which are possible. For example, I do not know at the moment how much money I have in my pocket, but let us say it is thirty cents. The world which is just like this one except that I should have thirty-five cents in my pocket now is a consistently thinkable world— consistent even with all the facts I know. When I reflect upon the number of facts of which I am uncertain, the plethora of possible worlds which, for all I know, might be this one, becomes a little appalling.

The *intension* of a proposition includes whatever the proposition entails; it comprises whatever must be true of any possible world in order that the proposition should apply to or be true of it—a sense of the meaning of propositions which is familiar and fundamental.

An *analytic* proposition is one which would apply to or be true of every possible world: one, therefore, whose comprehension is universal, and correlatively, one which has zero-intension. At this point, the distinction previously remarked between terms of zero-intension and locutions which have no meaning becomes important. An analytic proposition does not fail to have implications—though all entailments of it are likewise analytic or necessary propositions which would hold true of any world which is consistently thinkable. That an analytic proposition has zero-intension is correlative with the fact that in being true of reality it imposes no restriction or limitation on the actual which could conceivably be absent.

A *self-contradictory* or self-inconsistent proposition has zero-comprehension, and could apply to or be true of no world which is consistently thinkable. Correlatively, such a proposition has universal intension: it entails all propositions, both true and false.

All *synthetic* propositions, excepting the self-contradictory, have an intension which is neither zero nor universal, and a comprehension which is neither universal nor zero. They entail some things and not other things. Consonantly, their truth is compatible with some consistently thinkable states of affairs and incompatible with other consistently thinkable states of affairs.

The discussion of propositional functions must be even more compressed—suggested rather than outlined.

A propositional function is essentially a kind of predicate or predication: a characterization meaningfully applicable to the kind of entities names of which are values of the variables. For a propositional function of the general form "x is A" (where "A" is some non-variable expression), it is "being A" which is this predicate or characterization; for one of the general form "x R y" (where "R" is some constant), it is "(the first mentioned) being in the relation R (to the second mentioned)," or "(the ordered couple mentioned) being in the relation R."

Speaking most judiciously, there is only one variable in any propositional function. In what are called functions of two variables, x and y, this one variable is the ordered couple (x, y); in what are called functions of three variables, it is the ordered triad (x, y, z), etc. In the verbal form of the propositional function, so construed, the characterization which essentially is the function itself is predicated of this one variable. What are called variables are, in fact, merely syntactic devices for preserving the essential structure of the predication itself. Otherwise put: variables are constituents of discourse which have no meaning except one conferred by their context, including the syntax of that context.

Propositional functions are participial terms, as propositions are. But whereas the propositional characterization (if we may so call it for the moment) "John being now angry" could only characterize reality or some thinkable world, the propositional-function characterization "being angry" or any of the form "being A" or of the form "being in the relation R" could not be a characterization of a world, but only of a thing, or a pair of things, etc. And a function-characterization which is predicable of one thing would be meaningfully predicable of many.[5]

---

[5] This does not mean that the kind of term which is a function is necessarily a general term. "Being now the President" is meaningfully predicable of many things; but by its intension it must be *falsely* predicable of any existent but one: hence it is a singular term.

The denotation or *extension* of a propositional function is the class of existent things (individuals or ordered couples or triads, etc.) for which this predication holds true. It may be a class of many or a class of one or an empty class.

The *comprehension* of a function is the classification of things consistently thinkable as being characterized by this predication. This comprehension may be universal or zero or may include some consistently thinkable things and exclude others.

The *connotation* or intension of a function comprises all that the attribution of this predicate to anything entails as also attributable to that thing. This intension may be universal or zero or neither.

Propositional functions of the sort sometimes called *assertable*—the kind that logicians write down in expounding their subject (when they do not make mistakes)—are functions having universal comprehension: falsely predicable of nothing which is consistently thinkable. And they have zero-intension, imposing no limitation on anything thinkable in being held true of it. It is by this fact alone that their status as assertable functions can be certified.

At almost every point of this outline, questions requiring to be met have been omitted. But even with this condensation, insufficient space remains for indicating applications of it to moot questions of theory. We shall mention briefly two such only: application to the question of meaningfulness in general, and the ambiguity of "intension" which was mentioned earlier.

If one should wish to speak of *the* meaning of a term or proposition or propositional function, it will be evident that meaning in the mode of intension would be the best candidate for this preferred status. Expressions having the same connotation or intension must also have the same denotation or extension, the same signification, and the same comprehension. One might suppose, in consequence, that two expressions having the same intension would have the same meaning in every called-for sense of the word "meaning." Nevertheless, that would be an error.

That two locutions expressing the same intensional meaning may still be *distinct expressions*—and not two instances of one expression— is a point which has already been covered; they may be distinct by the fact that the *symbols* are different, though the meaning is the same. However, not every pair of expressions having the same intension would be called synonymous; and there is good reason for this fact.

Two expressions are commonly said to be synonymous (or in the case of propositions, equipollent) if they have the same intension, and *that intension is neither zero nor universal.*[6] But to say that two expressions with the same intension have the same meaning, without qualification, would have the anomalous consequence that any two analytic propositions would then be equipollent, and any two self-contradictory propositions would be equipollent. Also, any two terms like "round square" and "honorable poltroon" would then be synonymous.

The desirable restriction requires us to add a further specification to intensional meaning in the case of complex expressions.

An expression in question is *elementary* in case it has no symbolized constituent, the intension of which is a constituent of the intension of the expression in question itself. Otherwise the expression in question is *complex*.

The intension of any complex expression has, in addition to the intensions of its symbolized elementary constituents, an element of syntax. But we can avoid discussion of syntax here if we recognize that the syntax of a complex expression, so far as it is not already implicit in the intension of constituents taken separately (e.g., by their being substantives or verbs, etc.), is conveyed by the *order* of these constituents.

When we think of the ways in which complex expressions can be analyzed into constituents and a syntactic order of them, we may refer to *analytic meaning*. This expression will not be defined: instead, we shall characterize the relation "equivalent in analytic meaning." Two expressions are *equivalent in analytic meaning* (1) if at least one is elementary and they have the same intension, or (2) if, both being complex, they can be so analyzed into constituents that (a) for every constituent distinguished in either, there is a corresponding constituent in the other which has the same intension, (b) no constituent distinguished in either has zero-intension or universal intension, and (c) the order of corresponding constituents is the same in both, or can be made the same without alteration of the intension of either whole expression.

Thus "round excision" and "circular hole" are equivalent in analytic meaning. Likewise "square" and "rectangle with equal sides," since these terms have the same intension and one is elementary. But "equilateral triangle" and "equiangular triangle," though they have the same intension, when taken as whole expressions, are not equivalent in analytic meaning, since there is no constituent of the former which has the

---

[6] "Equipollent" is doubtfully appropriate here; there is no term which unambiguously names that relation of propositions which is parallel to the relation of synonymity between terms.

intension of "equiangular" and no constituent of the latter which has the same intension as "equilateral."

We shall be in conformity with good usage if we say that two expressions are synonymous or equipollent (1) if they have the same intension and that intension is neither zero nor universal, or (2) if, their intension being either zero or universal, they are equivalent in analytic meaning. And we shall be in conformity with good usage if we take the statement that two expressions have the *same meaning*, when the intended mode of meaning is unspecified, as indicating that these expressions are synonymous or equipollent.

We turn now to the ambiguity of "intension" which has been referred to.

Intension or connotation may be thought of in either of two ways, which we shall call respectively linguistic meaning and sense meaning.

Linguistic meaning is intension as constituted by the pattern of definitive and other analytic relationships of the expression in question to other *expressions*.[7] One who, for example, tried to learn the meaning of a French word with only a French dictionary at hand, might—if he be poorly acquainted with French—be obliged to look up also words used in defining the one whose meaning he sought, and the words defining them, and so on. He might thus eventually determine a quite extended pattern of linguistic relations of the word in question to other words in French. If the process of this example could, by some miracle, be carried to its logical limit, a person might thus come to grasp completely and with complete accuracy the linguistic pattern relating a large body of foreign words but—in an obvious sense—without learning what any one of them meant. What he would grasp would be their linguistic meaning. And what he would still fail to grasp would be their sense meaning.

Sense meaning is intension in the mode of a criterion in mind by which one is able to apply or refuse to apply the expression in question in the case of presented things or situations. One who should be able thus to apply or refuse to apply an expression correctly under all imaginable circumstances would grasp its sense meaning perfectly. But if, through faulty language sense or poor analytic powers, he could still not offer any correct definition, then he would fail to grasp (at least to grasp explicitly) its linguistic meaning.

Because many logicians have of late been somewhat preoccupied with language, intension as linguistic (or "syntactic") meaning has

[7] Some would say "syntactic" here, instead of "analytic." A relationship is analytic if the statement of it is an analytic statement.

been overemphasized, and sense meaning has been relatively neglected. These two modes of intensional meaning are supplementary, not alternative. But for many purposes of theory of knowledge it is sense meaning the investigation of which is more important. For example, those who would demand theoretical verifiability or confirmability for significance in a statement have in mind sense meaning as the prime requisite for meaningfulness in general. Likewise those who would set up the criterion of making some (practical) difference, and those who emphasize the operational significance of concepts are emphasizing sense meaning.

For sense meaning, imagery is obviously requisite. Only through the capacity called imagination could one have in mind, in advance of presentation, a workable criterion for applying or refusing to apply an expression to what should be presented. But for reasons made familiar by the long controversy between nominalists, conceptualists, and realists, sense meaning cannot be vested directly and simply in imagery. The nominalist denies the possibility of sense meaning on such grounds as the impossibility of imagining dog in general or triangle in general, or of having in mind an image of a chiliagon which is sufficiently specific to distinguish between a polygon of 1000 sides and one having 999. It is the persistence of such nominalism which, in large measure, is responsible for the current tendency to identify meaning with linguistic meaning exclusively.

The answer was given by Kant. A sense meaning, when precise, is a schema: a rule or prescribed routine and an imagined result of it which will determine applicability of the expression in question. We cannot imagine a chiliagon, but we easily imagine counting the sides of a polygon and getting 1000 as the result. We cannot imagine triangle in general, but we easily imagine following the periphery of a figure with the eye or a finger and discovering it to be a closed figure with three angles. (Many protagonists of operational significance forget to mention the imaged result, and would—according to what they *say*—identify the concept or meaning exclusively with the routine. Presumably this is merely an oversight: no procedure of laying meter sticks on things would determine length without some anticipatory imagery of a perceivable result which would, e.g., corroborate the statement that the thing is three meters long.)

Many epistemological problems may be clarified by reference to sense meaning—for example, the question as to the meaningfulness of asserting that there are mountains on the other side of the moon. Practical difficulties of confirmation have no relevance: the routine and result which would corroborate the statement are in mind with a clarity sufficient for determination—perhaps with a clarity equal to that with which we grasp what it would mean to verify that there are elephants in Africa. The two assertions equally have sense meaning.

If it be said that analytic statements have no sense meaning, then it is in point that all analytic statements have zero-intension, and impose no limitation upon any consistently thinkable total state of affairs or world in being true of it. Analytic statements are, so to say, verifiable by the fact that no total state of affairs in which they should fail of truth can be imagined. But if *constituents* in analytic statements did not have sense meaning, in the more limited fashion of having criteria of their application which are sometimes satisfied and sometimes not, then this universal applicability of the analytic statement could not be certified by reference to imagination and without recourse to particular perceptions, and hence would not be knowable *a priori*.

Likewise, if it be said that the self-contradictory has no sense meaning, it is in point that the self-contradictory expression has universal intension and zero-comprehension. The situation in which it should apply is precluded in ways which imagination alone is sufficient to discover. But again, this fact would not be certifiable *a priori* if constituents in the self-contradictory expression did not have sense meanings which are self-consistent. We can certify the impossibility of what is expressed by the experiment of trying to relate these sense meanings of constituents in the manner which the expression as a whole prescribes.

By their ultimate reference to concrete sense meaning, even the analytic and the self-contradictory have a kind of empirical reference. And without that, they would be genuinely non-significant for any experience in the world of fact. They are independent of any *particular* state of affairs or of what the world that exists is like in its details, because their applicability or inapplicability in general, or their truth or falsity in general, is certifiable from experiments in imagination.

7. Professor Chisholm and Empiricism

Professor [Roderick] Chisholm questions the adequacy of the account of perceptual knowledge which I have put forward, on the ground that this account is incompatible with "the familiar facts sometimes referred to as 'the relativity of sense perception.' "[1]

I have held that what the statement of a perceptually learned objective fact, such as "This (seen object) is red" or "This is square," means—in one specific, and specified, sense of the word 'meaning'—is explicable by some set of statements representing predictions of possible experience and having the form "If S be given and act A initiated, then in all probability E will follow," where 'S', 'A', and 'E' each refers to some recognizable item of direct experience, and the colloquial phrase "in all probability" is intended to suggest a probability approximating to certainty.

Professor Chisholm's criticism is restricted to a single point. (And I wish to express my admiration for the succinctness he achieves, in discussing a complex matter, without injustice to the conception discussed.) He believes that no such prediction in terms of direct experience follows from the statement of an objective and perceptually evidenced fact without an *additional* premise or premises concerning objective conditions of the predicted experience—such as the lighting conditions in the case of "This is red," or the condition of the angle of perspective in the case of "This is square." And he believes that, because such additional premises are required, the objective statement ("This is red" or "This is square") can not be said to entail anything whatever in terms of direct experience.

Professor Chisholm's discussion convinces me that, in my summary,[2] I was injudicious in saying that the objective statement "entails" such predictions in terms of direct experience, and calling these consequences "analytic" without making certain explanatory comments.[3] I shall attempt to make good that deficiency in concluding this note.

Reprinted by permission from *The Journal of Philosophy*, Vol. XLV (1948), No. 19, pp. 517–24.

[1] Roderick M. Chisholm, "The Problem of Empiricism," *The Journal of Philosophy*, Vol. XLV, No. 19 (1948), p. 512.

[2] *An Analysis of Knowledge and Valuation* (La Salle, Ill., 1947), Chap. VII, Sec. 16.

[3] The points in question are explained later in the book [*ibid.*], Chap. X.

The more important point, however, concerns his allegation that no statement of objective fact has any consequence in terms of direct experience without further premises specifying objective conditions of the experience in question. If that objection can be sustained, then I agree with him in thinking that the type of empiricism of which my account is one variant—verification-theories and confirmation-theories of the meaning of empirical statements of objective fact—will be altogether indefensible. And the suggestion will be that some kind of coherence-theory of empirical truth should be considered instead (though Professor Chisholm does not commit himself to this suggestion).

This will be the case because if the perceptually learned fact, "This seen object is red," has no consequences in terms of direct experience without additional premises such as "The illumination is sufficient," "The light is white and not red," "My eyes are normal," and so on for all conditions which could affect the red appearance of the thing, then obviously such further required premises will be very numerous in any given instance. Also, since these conditions will be matters of objective fact which are as difficult to assure with certainty as the statement "This object is red" itself, that statement will not be verifiable or even confirmable by anything presented or presentable in immediate experience. Only the immensely complex kind of statement, "This seen object is red, and is sufficiently illuminated with white light, and my eyes are normal, and . . . ," can be subjected to any experiential test of truth: hence the suggestion that only a coherence-theory will be tenable and that no verification-theory or confirmation-theory can be maintained.

My own belief is that if Professor Chisholm's point can be made good, then there will be nothing left for us but skepticism, because I am convinced that any coherence-theory will have defects which are fatal.

It is important to remember here that although various relativities of the content of presentation to conditions of observation—both conditions affecting the object and conditions affecting the subject's observation of it—are commonplaces of experience, we nevertheless do obtain empirical knowledge from experiences so affected, and that what we are here discussing is no debater's point or preciosity of semantics but one of the obvious and cognitively important facts of life. When we view a square object from an angle, for example, we may see a nonrectangular appearance and not something which looks like this—

□

but we may nevertheless learn from this experience that the object viewed is square. For this conclusion, we do *not* require antecedent information about our angle of vision, for the simple reason that the appearance itself evidences the angle of perspective as well as the objective shape of the thing seen. A square object seen from an angle and an object of the indicated non-rectangular shape seen from straight in front do not appear exactly the same; we discern a directly apparent difference of the two. Otherwise, visual experience would be a wholly untrustworthy index of the objective shape of things.

The relativities of perceptual content to the conditions of observation do indeed often defeat our attempts to learn objective facts from direct experience, and are a frequent source of illusions and mistaken judgments of perception. But, in general terms, there are only three possibilities of the relation between a given appearance affected by such relativity and the objective character this appearance may lead us to ascribe to the thing observed: (1) the objective condition to which the appearance is relative will be evidenced in the character of the appearance itself, so that just this appearance is still a trustworthy index of the objective property ascribed—as in the example just discussed; or (2) the given appearance may not be discernibly different from that of some other kind of object, under conditions other than those which actually affect this observation—so that the appearance could "deceive" us under conditions which, for all we know, may presently obtain—but because the condition which would lead to this "deception" is one which is exceptional, there is a high correlation between just this given character of the appearance and the objective property it leads us to ascribe to the thing observed, in which case it remains the fact that the given appearance is a valid *probability*-index of the objective property; or (3) on account of relativities of this kind of perception to conditions which are frequent and are not reliably reflected in any discernible difference of the given appearance, this manner of appearance is not even a probability-index of the property we ascribe to the object observed.

In case (1), such relativity is no bar to veridical judgment of the objective property ascribed on the basis of the given appearance, though superficial or careless observation might lead to error on account of this relativity. That kind of fact is a commonplace of perceptual cognition. In case (2), although the relativity in question may lead to erroneous belief in a particular instance, and this through no fault of our own, the belief induced will still be justified as *probable*, on account of the high correlation mentioned. That even the best kind of direct evidence may occasionally be affected by some unguessable condition which leads to mistaken perceptual judgment is again a commonplace of empirical cognition. In case (3), the judgment of objective fact from the appearance given is not justified and is not knowledge, whether the guess one makes happens to be lucky or to be unlucky.

These facts I have intended to incorporate in my account. That almost any perception will be found to be an instance of case (1) in some respect hardly affects the matter, since when one refers to what is given, this reference should be to the appearance in all its specificity and include all characteristics of the immediate experience which are pertinent to the judgment made. What is more important to observe is that perceptual knowledge of objects and states of affairs is always, in some respect or manner, an instance falling under case (2). There are all degrees of reliability of the connection between given qualia of the content of perception and objective characters of things observed which we are thus led to believe. In no case—I have supposed—is this reliability 100 per cent and sufficient for theoretical certainty. But it is often sufficient for practical certainty: sufficient to justify our acting on the belief without hesitation. In the remaining cases—that is, where we hold the judgment as practically certain but in fact the correlation between given appearance and objective fact believed does not justify this assurance—our belief is not knowledge but an invalid perceptual judgment.

Professor Chisholm's criticism, as phrased, does not refer directly to this relation between given appearance and objective fact—though that is involved—but to the connection between statement of the objective fact and predictions of further experiences which might confirm it. Let us turn to that point, in terms of our previous example. If what I am looking at has the appearance of a square object seen from an angle, and I believe that this thing is in fact square, then innumerable possible corroborations of that belief may be suggested—e.g., that if I take three steps to the right, the appearance of a square object seen from directly in front will then be presented. If I make this test, with the anticipated result, my belief will be confirmed in some measure; and if I make it with a result divergent from what I expect, it will be disconfirmed. The statement of what I believe—"This object is square" —has the consequence "If S (the now apprehended presentation) be given, and act A (three steps to the right) initiated, then in all probability E (the appearance of a square seen from directly in front) will follow."

The qualification "in all probability" is interjected here because it could happen that, although the object viewed is really square and my attempted confirmation of that fact is well judged, the test of it in this instance might give a negative result—because this particular experience is affected by some condition which I do not control and of which there is no evidence in the given presentation S. But if this kind of untoward result should be the rule and not the exception, then my belief on the basis of this presentation or this attempted confirmation of it—one or both—would be ill-judged and not an instance of knowledge; and it would be false that the statement of objective fact, "This object is square," has this particular consequence of the form "If S and A, then in all probability E."

What I think Professor Chisholm overlooks, in his criticism, are two facts to which attention has now been drawn: first, the specificity of given appearances by which a presentation which is 'relative to' some condition of observation frequently contains a sufficient clue to this objective circumstance which affects it. Perhaps he makes use of examples in which the 'S' of my paradigm is allowed to be ambiguous or unduly circumscribed in its reference to given presentation and does not include all aspects of the experience-content which are pertinent to the prediction—or examples which are instances of observation so superficial and inattentive that judgment based on them could not properly be taken as justified. Second, he appears to overlook the importance of the probability-qualification in predictions of confirming experience. That qualification covers the point that, in cases where the given presentation is an actually justifying ground for the objective belief (and hence for prediction that further tests of it will give a positive result), it still remains true that "mistake is possible," on account of some exceptional and unguessable condition affecting a particular observation. Correlatively, one who supposes that justified perceptual judgments are instances of theoretical certainty misreads the actual nature of empirical knowledge. Taken together, these two considerations seem to me to indicate his error in alleging that an objective statement of the kind of facts we think to learn from perception does not have as consequence any prediction of the form "If S be given and act A initiated, then in all probability experience E will follow," without additional hypotheses concerning conditions affecting the particular observation or test.

However, Professor Chisholm does well to observe that if it be supposed that a statement of objective fact 'P' ("The object viewed is square") entails or has as analytic consequence a certain prediction of this form—"If S be given and act A initiated, then in all probability experience E will follow"—then we shall encounter the seeming difficulty that some further premise, 'Q', may be such that the conjoint statement 'P and Q' will have as consequence a prediction which is incompatible with this consequence of '*P*' alone. In our example, for instance, the additional premise "The object seen is really behind me and I am viewing it in a mirror" would lead to the prediction that if I take three steps to the right what I shall see is my own reflection instead of any square-looking appearance. That the premise of objective fact, '*P*', may have the consequence '*T*' but the hypothesis '*P* and *Q*' may have a consequence incompatible with '*T*' is paradoxical, because it is a familiar rule of logic that when '*P*' entails '*T*', '*P* and *Q*' (for any additional premise '*Q*') must likewise entail '*T*', and can not entail anything incompatible with '*T*' if '*Q*' is consistent with '*P*'.

What needs to be observed here—and what I omitted to mention in my summary statement of the matter—is that this familiar rule, "If '*P*' entails '*T*', then for any '*Q*', '*P* and *Q*' entails '*T*' ", can not be applied, in the manner one is likely to attempt, where '*T*' is any kind of probability-statement. Probabilities are relative to the premises (factual or hypothetical) from which they are determined. And in consequence of this fact it can be—and frequently is—true that on the premise '*P*' alone something, '*R*', is highly probable, but on the premise '*P* and *Q*', '*R*' is highly *im*probable and something else, '*S*', which is incompatible with '*R*', is highly probable. In such a case, what must be noted is that, although '*R*' and '*S*' are incompatible as unqualified statements of fact, the two statements, "On the premise '*P*' alone, '*R*' is highly probable" and "On the premise '*P* and *Q*', '*S*' is highly probable," *can not be incompatible since both are true* and no true statement can ever be incompatible with any other which is also true. (It must also be noted that the probability-consequences themselves, " '*R*' is highly probable" and " '*S*' is highly probable", are not incompatible because, in this form, they are incompletely stated and require the preface "Relative to '*P*' " or "Relative to '*P* and *Q*' " in order to be accurate statements of fact.)

Let us take an example. "These two dice are marked in the usual manner" gives a high probability for the prediction "In one hundred throws of these dice double-six will occur less than twenty times." But the premise "These two dice are marked in the usual manner and are loaded to show double-six" does not justify the prediction of less than twenty double-sixes in a hundred throws, but an opposite prediction instead. And for the sake of comparison with Professor Chisholm's argument, let us also remark here that when one predicts less than twenty double-sixes in one hundred throws as a (highly probable) consequence of the premise "These two dice are marked in the usual manner," one does *not* require the additional information, or assumption even, that the dice are honest. This prediction is justified if we *know nothing about* their being honest or loaded but only that, for properly marked dice in general, twenty double-sixes in a hundred throws is highly exceptional.

In my account of perceptual knowledge, it is *probability*-consequences of objective statements which are in question. These consequences are themselves hypothetical in form—"If S and A then E"—but that affects nothing here in question: in our example of the dice, for instance, we might have considered a consequence of the form "If I throw these dice, then with a probability of 35 to 1, double-six will not appear," without otherwise affecting that illustration.

It seems to me that the plausibility of Professor Chisholm's argument depends upon overlooking the importance of the probability-qualification in the predictions of direct experience which figure in my account and the facts about probability-consequences in general which are pointed out above. When these are remembered, I think it may be evident that he adduces no consideration which is sufficient to support his critical conclusion.

In my account, objective statements of fact are said to *entail* such probability-consequences because it is consequences of this sort which are *contained in what it means*—in one sense of meaning—to assert the objective statements from which they are derivative. It is such probable eventuations of experience, as results of possible ways of acting when certain appearances present themselves, which represent what we learn when we learn objective facts; and there is no directly testable content of any belief in any objective state of affairs beyond what could be specified in such predictions.

8. The Given Element in Empirical Knowledge

Since I have already said in print how I would propose to deal with our present topic, let me here omit any attempted summary and try instead to emphasize those basic considerations which, as I see it, dictate this conception of an incorrigible datum-element underlying empirical beliefs which are justified.

Empirical knowledge—if there be any such thing—is distinguished by having as an essential factor or essential premise something disclosed in experience. That is a tautology. To express this tautological fact circumstantially and circumspectly can be a matter of some difficulty; but, if anyone should deny what we so attempt to state, he must impress us as philosophizing by the Russian method of the big lie, and argument with him might well be useless. It is this essential factor in knowledge which comes from experience which I would speak of as 'the given.'

But since experience and the functioning of it as the basis of empirical knowledge is something open to the inspection of all of us, each in his own case, how comes it that we tell such different tales about it? The account which I have offered has frequently met with dissent; and this dissent with respect to something which, if correctly stated, should be obvious gives me pause. If those who so find fault held a rationalistic theory, I might offer myself the excuse that they philosophize in the interest of an unsound major premise. But the greater number of my critics have been as firmly empiricistic in their professed convictions as myself. That is just what puzzles me most, because I seem to find only two alternatives for a plausible account of knowledge: either there must be some ground in experience, some factuality it directly affords, which plays an indispensable part in the validation of empirical beliefs, or what determines empirical truth is merely some logical relationship of a candidate-belief with other beliefs which have been accepted. And in the latter case any reason, apart from factualities afforded by experience, why these *antecedent* beliefs have been accepted remains obscure. Even passing that difficulty, this second alternative would seem to be merely a revival of the coherence theory of truth, whose defects have long been patent.

Read in a symposium on "The Experiential Element in Knowledge," at a meeting of the Eastern Division of the American Philosophical Association, Bryn Mawr College, Bryn Mawr, Pennsylvania, Dec. 29, 1951. Reprinted by permission from *The Philosophical Review*, Vol. LXI (1952), No. 2, pp. 168–75.

There undoubtedly is some logical relation of facts—or more than one—to which the name 'coherence' might aptly be given. And there is equally little doubt that such logical and systemic relationships are important for assuring credibility—once a sufficient number of antecedent and relevant facts have been otherwise determined. But no logical relationship, by itself, can ever be sufficient to establish the truth, or the credibility even, of any synthetic judgment. That is one point which logical studies of the last half century have made abundantly clear. Unless the beliefs so related, or some of them, have a warrant which no logical principle can assure, no logical relation of them to one another constitutes a scintilla of evidence that they are even probable.

Let us assume that the whole of the truth has even that strongest type of coherence illustrated by a system of geometry. The statements of the system (postulates and theorems together) are so related that, if we should be doubtful of any one of them, the other statements of the system would be sufficient to assure it with deductive certainty. But that relationship, as we know, is insufficient to determine any truth about the geometric properties of actual things. If Euclid is thus coherent, then so too are Riemann and Lobachevsky; though given any denotation of the geometric vocabulary, these three geometries are mutually incompatible systems. If the truth about our space is ever to be ascertained, something disclosed in experience must be the final arbiter. Since this is the case for geometric truths, which cohere by the strong relations of deductive logic, *a fortiori* it must be the case for empirical truth at large, for the determination of which we must so often rely upon induction, which affords a probability only, on the supposition that our premises are certain or that they have some antecedent probability on other grounds.

In brief, we have nothing but experience and logic to determine truth or credibility of any synthetic judgment. Rule out datum-facts afforded by experience, and you have nothing left but the logically certifiable. And logic will not do it.

Such argument by elimination is admittedly not final, and I would not rest upon that but would appeal additionally to the facts of life. However, I would ask my critics where they stand on this point. Have they repudiated a fundamental requirement of any empiristic theory? Are they rationalists who think to extract from logical considerations alone some sufficient ground for empirical beliefs? Or are they really skeptics who dislike to acknowledge that fact in so many words? Or do they find some third alternative which I have overlooked?

One class of those who disagree have made their point of objection clear; it concerns my supposition that what is given in experience is incorrigible and indubitable. Empiricists generally are agreed that non-perceptual synthetic knowledge rests finally on knowledge which is perceptual, and so find the root problem in the nature of perception. Practically all empiricists recognize that some items of perceptual cognition are less than indubitable; perception is subject to illusion and mistake. They differ among themselves as to whether all perceptions, or some only, are subject to doubt. Mr. Moore, for example, regards such convictions as "This is my hand" (under appropriate circumstances) as subject to no doubt. But many, perhaps most of us, can find differences of degree only in the valid assurance of perceptual judgments: we recognize that most of them have what may be called 'practical certainty' but think that none of them is theoretically and validly certain. Those of us who come to this conclusion are then confronted with the following question: Is there, either antecedent to and supporting the perceptual belief in objective fact, or in the perceptual experience itself, an element or factor which is the basis of the perceptual judgment but is not, like this judgment of objective fact, subject to theoretical doubt?

My own answer to this question is affirmative. When I perceive a door, I may be deceived by a cleverly painted pattern on the wall, but the presentation which greets my eye is an indubitable fact of my experience. My perceptual belief in a real door, having another side, is not an explicit inference but a belief suggested by association; nevertheless the *validity* of this interpretation is that and that only which could attach to it as an inductive inference from the given visual presentation. The given element is this incorrigible presentational element; the criticizable and dubitable element is the element of interpretation.

The arguments which have been offered in criticism of this view are literally too numerous to be mentioned here. Some of them have been of the casual variety which may be advanced without reference to any attempted full account of empirical knowledge. The objections of Goodman and Reichenbach, however, are not of that sort but are made in the interest of alternative views which are complex and worked out. Neither of them has had time to do more than suggest his alternative conceptions; and I shall have time only to suggest where, as it seems to me, some of the critical issues lie.

I hope I shall not give offense if I say that Reichenbach's view impresses me as being an unabridged probabilism: a modernized coherence theory with two immense advantages over the older one so named. First, he makes provision for observation-statements, though he insists that these should be in objective ('physical') language, and that they are both dubitable and corrigible. And second, he substitutes for the vague relation, historically called 'coherence,' meticulously described relations of probability-inference.

First, as to observation-statements: let us suppose that I look over yonder and report that I see a horse. You (being epistemologists) may reply that you find my report ambiguous: that statements of the form "I see an X" are assertions of objective fact if and only if the constants substitutable for 'X' are understood to be confined to expressions denoting physical entities, but that statements of this form are in the protocol or expressive idiom if and only if the expressions substitutable for 'X' are understood to be designations of *appearances*. In the one case—you observe—I have made a dubitable assertion of an existent horse; in the other case, I have merely reported a specific given presentation which, whether dubitable or not, at least asserts no real horse as being present. This protocol statement, in its intended meaning—so I would claim—will be true just in case I am not lying or making some verbal mistake in the words I use. I am unable to see that Reichenbach's denial of this second and expressive idiom is other than a dogmatism. (Even his 'phenomenal language' seems not to coincide with what I deem essential for any formulation of the given in experience.) I would, moreover, emphasize that the near absence of any restricted vocabulary or syntax for expressive statements is an unimportant matter for empirical knowledge itself: no one needs verbal formulation of his own present experience in order to be aware of it; and obviously, nobody else's protocols are indubitable to us. Protocol expression is as inessential to what it expresses as a cry of fear is to the fearful apparition which may cause it. It is for purposes of epistemological discussion that the notion of protocol statements is principally needed, though there are, of course, statements so intended, and the requisite idiom is one which finds exemplification in natural language.

Let us pass these points, however, and take it that the observer of the horse has formulated his observation in objective ('physical') language, and that what he reports is dubitable and only probable. Reichenbach himself refers to the difficulty which then arises (attributing the objection to Russell): a statement justified as probable must have a ground; if the ground is only probable, then there must be a ground of it; and so on. And to assess the probability of the original statement, its probability relative to its ground must be multiplied by the probability of this ground, which in turn must be multiplied by the probability of its own ground, and so on. Reichenbach denies that the regressive series of probability-values so arising must approach zero, and the probability of the original statement be thus finally whittled down to nothing. That matter could be discussed for an afternoon or longer;

it makes a difference whether one is talking about determined probabilities on known grounds, or merely what are called 'a priori probabilities.' However, even if we accept the correction which Reichenbach
urges here, I disbelieve that it will save his point. For that, I think he
must prove that, where any such regress of probability-values is involved, the progressively qualified fraction measuring the probability
of the quaesitum will converge to some determinable value other than
zero; and I question whether such proof can be given. Nor do I think
that the difficulty can be removed by his 'argument from concatenation.' It is true that, by the rule of inverse probabilities, we may proceed in either direction, determining the probability of a 'consequence'
from the probability of a 'ground,' or of a 'ground' from a 'consequence.' But what I would emphasize is that, as Reichenbach mentions,
you cannot take even the first step in either direction until you are
prepared to assign numerical values to the 'antecedent probabilities'
called for by the rule. These must literally be determined *before* use of
the rule will determine the probability of anything. And, if the answer
be given that these can be determined by another use of the rule, the
rebuttal is obvious: in that case you must make that *other* use of it
before you can make *this* one. An interminable progressus or regressus
need not defeat theoretical purposes provided you are on the right end
of it—the end from which its members are successively determinable.
But in the kind of case here in point, one is always on the wrong end
of any segment of the series, always required to determine something
else first before one can determine what one wants to determine. The
supposition that the probability of anything whatever always depends
on something else which is only probable itself is flatly incompatible
with the justifiable assignment of any probability at all. Reichenbach
suggests that the craving for some certainty here is a retained trace of
rationalism; my countersuggestion would be that it is the attempt to
retain a trace of empiricism.

Even more crudely put: the probabilistic conception strikes me as
supposing that if enough probabilities can be got to lean against one
another they can all be made to stand up. I suggest that, on the contrary, unless some of them can stand alone, they will all fall flat. If no
nonanalytic statement is categorically assertable, without probability
qualification, then I think the whole system of such could provide no
better assurance of anything in it than that which attaches to the contents of a well-written novel. I see no hope for such a coherence theory
which repudiates data of experience which are simply given—or no
hope unless a postulate be added to the effect that *some* synthetic statements are probable *a priori*: the postulate, for example, that every per-

ceptual belief has *some* probability just on account of being a perceptual belief.[1]

There is time only for very brief comment on one other point. Both Goodman and Reichenbach would impose a requirement of consistency —or 'inductive consistency'—on protocols. This goes along with their supposition that what protocols report is dubitable and corrigible. Briefly and inadequately, there is no requirement of consistency which is relevant to protocols. A protocol is a report of given appearances, of experience as such. Looking out over an audience, I see in one place two heads on one neck. When I lift my own head a bit, I see only one head there. But that is no reason to alter my first protocol and deny this apparition of two heads. I do not, of course, believe the two apparent heads to be actual. It is at *that* point that the requirement of inductive consistency comes in. But the critique by which I avoid that conclusion as to objective fact is criticism of a suggested interpretation— of a perceptual *belief*—and not a criticism of what the protocol reports. What it further indicates is only the desirability of some objective explanation of this apparition. The careless observer's protocols, the insane man's direct experience, and the content of the dreamer's dream must not be corrected or eliminated in the interest of consistency; to do that would be simple falsification of facts of experience. The problem of empirical knowledge at large is the problem of an account of objective facts which will accord with the occurrence of the experiences reported in all truthful and verbally accurate protocols. That is one test of adequate empirical knowledge. And the capacity of the objective account to explain any puzzling and apparent incongruities of experience is a further such test. To call a given experience an illusion, or a dream, or a careless observation is to indicate the kind of objective fact which will explain it—just as the laws of optics and the fact of my looking through the edge of my glasses explains my apparition of two heads. We must not forget that experience is all that is given to us for the purposes of empirical knowing, and that such knowledge of objective facts as we achieve is simply that body of beliefs which represents our overall interpretation of experience. If we could not be sure of our experience when we have it, we should be in poor position to determine any objective fact, or confirm the supposition of one, or assign any probability to one.

I regret not to make the further and detailed comments which Goodman's paper merits. Disbelieving that my conception of an indubitable

---

[1] This was suggested to me by Professor Paul Henle—though not as a supposition which he would adopt.

given element in experience can be maintained, he suppresses further criticisms he might have, in the interest of a possible pragmatic reformulation of statements describing experience.

Putting it oversimply one may say that what he proposes is the interpretation of observation-statements in terms of the forward looking import of what they lead us to expect. But that proposal is, I fear, a little more pragmatic than I dare to be. However plausibly such reformulation could be carried out, it would fail to satisfy me because of a conviction I have concerning the task of epistemological study—the conviction, namely, that a principal business of epistemology is with the *validity* of knowledge. And validity concerns the character of cognition as warranted or justified.

In order to be knowledge, empirical judgment must not only have predictive import of what will verify or confirm it; it must also be distinguished from a merely lucky or unlucky guess or hazard of belief by having some justifying ground. And in the nature of the case, what so justifies an empirical judgment cannot be something future to it and presently uninspectable but must lie in something antecedent to or compresent with it. Where it is perceptual cognition which is in question, the point is that the interpretation of experience—the perceptual belief —*is* significant of the future and verifiable, but, in order that this belief have *validity*, that which functions as the ground of it must be present and given.

That is precisely the point with which I am here principally concerned. It is on account of that point that I have felt it necessary to depart from or to supplement other pragmatic theories. And it is on account of that point that I could not accept Goodman's pragmatic proposal: by interpreting empirical findings in terms of what is future to them, it would invite confusion of the ground of knowledge which is there and given with what is not there but anticipated. It is also on that same account that I must disagree with various other current theories, put forward as empirical, which fail to recognize the datum-element of experience. In terms of such conceptions—so I think—no explanation of the validity of knowledge is forthcoming or even possible, and the holders of them can escape the skeptical conclusion only by failing to look where they are going.

I consider skepticism something worse than unsatisfactory; I consider it nonsense to hold or to imply that just any empirical judgment is as good as any other—because none is warranted. A theory which implies or allows that consequence is not an explanation of anything but merely an intellectual disaster.

9. A Paradox of Nominalism

I offer the following as a paradox implicit in nominalism. I would not assert the theses set down, or maintain dogmatically that the train of reasoning is valid. But I should know something which I do not presently know about current nominalism if I should find out what that is here set down the nominalist takes exception to, and how he would argue for his exception or exceptions taken:

(1) That which is or can be the same in two instances is abstract.
(2) Nothing which is not the same in two instances can be recognized.
(3) That which is not recognizable is not identifiable.
(4) Hence if any non-abstract entities are real they cannot be identified.
(5) What cannot be identified cannot be known.
(6) According to nominalism, only non-abstract entities are real.
(7) Hence, admitting nominalism, if anything is real it cannot be known.
(8) Hence the only consistent nominalist is one who is also a skeptic.

Skeptics should not make statements about the character and limits of the real, since they admit that all such statements are unprovable.

Perhaps thesis (4) is a critical member of the set. If so, the point would not be that non-nominalists admit (4) but that they have a way of obviating it; and the question may be whether any consistent theory of knowledge, obviating (4), is open to the nominalist.

Written on June 6, 1953.

10. A Comment on "The Verification Theory of Meaning"

In his article on "The Verification Theory of Meaning," Professor [Everett] Nelson adopts "as a procedural device" reference to "Professor C. I. Lewis' theory of objective beliefs as a paradigm." I fear, however, that this is a compliment which I do not deserve—that my conception involves too many peculiarities to be recognized as typical by others who hold some form of the verification, or confirmation, theory of meaning. On the other hand, it grieves me that I seem thus to acquire a certain amount of guilt by association and become responsible for sins I do not remember committing.

That, however, would be a complicated matter to untangle and of no great importance. Suffice it to say that I do not altogether recognize myself in Nelson's pages. What it will be important to consider is the searching criticisms he makes of this type of theory and his interests in making them. These interests—if I judge correctly—are reflected in his reference to "the principle underlying verification theories, namely, the restriction of meaning to empirical meaning," and in his sentences as follows:

I embrace certain of the positive epistemological commitments of the proponents of the [verification type of] theory but believe that these lead to the impossibility not only of knowledge but of meaning itself unless they are supplemented by a nonphenomenalist metaphysics. . . .

Now I want to show that, even if every empirically decidable proposition implied by an objective belief is a sense-datum proposition, this theory rests on ontological assumptions of a nonempirical kind. . . .

The meaningfulness of an objective belief presupposes that it involves a nonempirical organizing concept which provides the unity and connectedness which we have found necessary, or which performs the functions traditionally attributed to substance and causality.

In the first place, it must be pointed out that if I am any kind of representative of the verification theory, then the theory does not require "the restriction of meaning to empirical meaning." I have devoted a hundred dullish pages to the thesis that there are two dimensions of meaning, the extensional and the intensional, both of them essential for logic and epistemology, and that empirical meaning—namely, meaning as a criterion in mind by reference to which the applicability of a term

Reprinted by permission from *The Philosophical Review*, Vol. LXIII (1954), No. 2, pp. 193–96. This article was originally titled "A Comment."

or the believability of an empirical statement is to be attested in experience—is simply one mode of intensional meaning.

Also I must protest against any suggestion that a verification theory of meaning implies phenomenalism. That supposition appears to have originated with people who understood meaning only in the sense of applicative, denotative, or extensional meaning and who did not grasp the sense of meaning as implicative and intensional. They therefore supposed that if one say, e.g., that "Today is Monday" is equivalent in meaning to "Tomorrow is Tuesday" (equivalent with respect to all that either statement implies, since they imply each other), he must somehow be identifying Monday with Tuesday and the present with the future. They similarly supposed that in identifying the conceptual and implicative significance of "This object is an apple" with the empirical eventuations which would attest its believability, one must somehow be reducing the substantial apple to the sum of its various appearances in experience. Hence the epithet "phenomenalism." It is discouraging that people who know better should speak as if they were subject to this confusion. "Phenomenalism" is the name for a metaphysical theory like Kant's; the verification theory of meaning has nothing to do with that. (Incidentally, Kant was able, within the limits of his phenomenalism, to find considerable organizing significance in the concepts of substance and causality.)

There are, in my opinion, metaphysical presuppositions which are essential to epistemology: for example, the nature of knowledge itself presupposes a reality to be known which transcends the content of any experience in which it may be known. And my own metaphysical convictions are, as it happens, realistic. But I have thought it both possible and desirable to investigate the nature and validity of knowledge in some independence of the question whether Cartesian dualism or Berkeleian idealism or Kantian phenomenalism or current neopositivism is the correct metaphysical doctrine.

I agree, however, that the main question which Nelson urges— whether a verification theory must be supplemented by admission of some nonempirical organizing concept or concepts in order to avoid the consequences mislabeled phenomenalistic and other difficulties— is a pertinent and important issue, whether it is a metaphysical issue or not.

With respect to that question I must observe that, on one point which is critical, Nelson either misunderstands my conception (and language I have used could be responsible for that) or he makes an assertion about it which I cannot accept. The various "terminating judgments" implied by an objective belief are *not* independent. Insofar as finding one such consequence to be true confirms (increases the antecedent probability of) the objective belief itself, it must likewise increase the probability of any other such consequence which this belief implies. This manner of relation between terminating judgments implicit in the same objective belief is of course precisely that of *"dependent* statements" (or "events") in probability theory. The terminating judgments implied by any single objective statement thus form what I have called a "congruent set," the members of which are mutually relevant and mutually supporting in their corroborative significance.[1] Thus I would suggest that perhaps the "organizing concept" which Professor Nelson seeks is already at hand; it is just the concept expressed by statement of the objective belief itself, implying as it does the mutual relevance and mutually corroborative relationship of all the various eventualities which would be evidence favorable to it.

In this same connection, I further agree that not only a verification theory of meaning but any theory of the meaningfulness of empirical statements and the validity of empirical knowledge requires the assumption of a relationship of items of experience which is not sense-observable—though given that there *is* such a relationship, particular instances of it become sense-confirmable. This required relationship is the one which Berkeley observed when he remarked that, owing to divine beneficence, "one idea is sign of another which is to come." For any validity of induction in general, it must be the case that one eventuation of experience can validly function as probability-index of another. Lacking that, not only could there be no validity for empirical predictions, but there could be no apprehension of any object, knowable through its diverse appearances. I have made this required assumption, without metaphysical trimmings, simply on the ground that, without what is so assumed, there could be for us no apprehension of a world of objective facts and things.[2] This is merely the acknowledgment that we address ourselves to a reality to be known. But if what is so acknowledged can be further illuminated by metaphysical discussion or any other kind, I should welcome that as an important contribution.

[1] *An Analysis of Knowledge and Valuation* (La Salle, Ill., 1947), pp. 249, 343ff.
[2] *Ibid.*, pp. 272f., 362.

11. Realism or Phenomenalism?

Philosophy begins in wonder, and the content of that original wonderment is metaphysical. The history of the subject shows this true of the race, and one may surmise that it is likewise characteristically true of the individual who philosophizes. But whatever answers are first hazarded to the metaphysical questions, doubts arise as to our assurance of them. This doubt attaches first, perhaps, to the particular conjectures advanced as solutions of the metaphysical problems. But in any case it soon extends to any possible such conjecture. So the philosopher begins over again, but this time with the epistemological question: Whatever the ultimate nature of things may be, can we find it out, and if so, how? The thought is, perhaps, that once we have settled this second kind of question, we can then return to the metaphysical ones and settle them too. Descartes made such a new beginning in philosophy and squared accounts with all the fundamentals in his six *Meditations*.

However, we are born too late for that. In spite of the fact that the cognitive processes lie more fully open to our inspection than the world at large and what goes on in it, the epistemological questions fail to show progress toward any clearer and better assured determination of them than do the metaphysical ones. And this difficulty we find in arriving at any general consensus on matters which are as familiar and easily observable to any one of us as to any other may arouse suspicion that the questions themselves are not well put: that there is some lack of clarity as to what, if it could be determined, would constitute an acceptable answer to them, or even whether there is any answer which could be given and would prove final. Such examination of the questions themselves sends us back to a third kind of problem: "What does this issue mean? Is it perhaps meaningless?" Even this, as we are all aware, is not the end. Meanings are something entertained by individuals in the privacy of their own minds; but any conveying of them depends on language. Also, we largely think in words; and language, being mainly developed for practical rather than theoretical purposes, can betray a philosophic question or subvert an intended answer. Some

Read at the annual meeting of the Pacific Division of the American Philosophical Association, September 9, 1954. Reprinted by permission from *The Philosophical Review*, Vol. LXIV (1955), No. 2, pp. 233–47.

penetration of the ambiguities and obscurities of language is called for, and perhaps some devisement of linguistic instruments having a higher order of precision. So we retreat once more, this time into syntax and semantics. And here, finally, we discover one further question still: "What is it that is meant by 'meaning'?" We encounter the complication that there is more than one sense of that which language can express and more than one dimension of the import of thought itself.

We might be moved to suspect that what so shows itself is mainly significant of the philosophic temper: that there is something about this reflective bent of mind, or in the kind of questions which it raises, or the kind of assurance without which it will accept no answer, by reason of which it is destined to discover that, whatever topic it pursues, there will always be some other kind of question to be answered first; and it is fated to retreat from every problem faced into some other and supposedly anterior one, in search of a *pou sto* which is not there. On second thought, however, it must be admitted that this widening and deepening of the philosophic problems is inevitable; their involvement with one another lies in the nature of the case. Such light as may be thrown upon any one of them may serve to illuminate those first and last questions which represent the perennial interests of philosophy. It is only to be hoped that these centrally important topics will not be permanently lost sight of in a thicket of subordinate questions and side-issues.

It is to one of those perennial questions that I would revert on this occasion: the issues which lie between idealism, phenomenalism, and realism. No full discussion will be expected in so short a paper. I shall wish nevertheless to suggest, in broad terms, the kind of answer which I think holds most of promise. But I am sensible also of the predicament indicated above, by reason of which any suggested answer must raise more and other kinds of questions than the one addressed, and proceed upon assumptions which themselves are questionable. For that, I see no help. I must hope that if you find my premises debatable—as of course they will be—there may still be something of interest in the interconnection of questions so involved. And I shall be myself as much concerned with such interrelationships and with some measure of the possible separation of problems as with any other consideration which affects these issues.

The problem of realism, idealism, or phenomenalism is at one and the same time epistemological and metaphysical, because it concerns the subject-object relation, instead of any relation both ends of which lie in cognitive experience itself. In that it differs from another kind of problem, more exclusively epistemological: that of the critique of cognition as valid or invalid, justified or unwarranted, correct or mistaken. The problem of such criticism is already implicit in the fact that cognition is called knowledge only on the presumption of its correctness. These questions of critique concern what is determinable by application of those criteria satisfaction of which is required by, and will be sufficient for, warranted validity of empirical belief and by reference to which any disclosure of experience is to be taken as confirming or as disconfirming a belief in point. Questions of that kind call for answers which can be formulated in terms of experience itself and criteria applicable to experience, for the simple reason that there is nothing beyond experience which can be adduced for our inspection and to which such criteria can be applied, nor anything other than disclosed or disclosable characters of experience upon which the decision they may afford can turn.

That is not to say that knowledge—empirical knowledge—can be divested of its objective reference. Just as we do not call cognition knowledge except on presumption of its validity, so too we do not call empirical cognition knowledge except on the presumption of objective actuality in some sense corresponding to it. But that actuality can be mediated to us only by experiential apprehension; and our only possible assurance that what is so mediated is actual is our assurance that the apprehension of it is valid. The correctness of empirical apprehension can, in some measure at least, be determined by reference to characters and relations within cognitive experience itself. And the actuality of that which empirical cognition signifies to us cannot otherwise be assured at all. The content of cognition is belief. What is so believed is some objective state of affairs: that some thing or things, or some kind of things, exist or do not exist. As implication of that, it is also believed that certain experiences will be realizable under specifiable conditions requisite for attesting this belief as to the objectively actual. But any critical judgment as to the correctness of this belief can be made only by reference to some content disclosed or to be disclosed in experiences which will test it. Any principles of the cognitive critique require to be phrased in terms which reflect this nature of the problem. They cannot, without confusion of it, be formulated in terms of anything beyond what experience presents or may present.

Let us also remark, in passing, that the principles and criteria themselves, by reference to which cognitive apprehensions and empirical conclusions are to be judged as justified or not so justified, must be capable of being elicited by critical reflection, addressed to empirical knowledge in general or to the particular kind of case in point. They are in a sense self-imposed or simply acknowledged and are antecedent to any cognitive project. No other than a reflective corroboration of them is possible: the tests of validity cannot themselves be attested valid by anything further and not implicit in them; and any supposed demonstration of their acceptability must be circular. Any principles of epistemological criticism must be in this respect like those of logic. Indeed one could question whether the critique of empirical knowledge is not a part of logic or logic a part of it. Certainly this critique and what is called inductive logic are essentially involved with one another.

The attempt at this manner of formulation of the critique of empirical knowledge, confining it to what is statable in terms of experience exclusively, became inevitable, I think, when Berkeley emphasized the fact that an idea cannot be compared with an objective entity beyond experience but only with another idea or content of experience. One idea is sign of another which is to come. In attributing to the present experience this import of a sign, we can have no other assurance than inspectable characters of it—which Berkeley himself specified as clearness or vividness, independence of the will, and its hanging together with other content according to natural law. And the cognitive significance attached is to be verified or falsified by the signified empirical eventuality when it comes, and not by any ideation which jumps out of its experiential skin and superposes conscious content on an independently existent object to see whether the two are congruent. The whole transaction of signifying as predictable and of verifying the prediction must be carried out within experience itself.

I hope that there is nothing essentially wrong with the type of epistemological procedure so suggested—so long as it confines itself to what pertains to the distinction between cognitive validity and cognitive mistake or error. Segregation of that kind of question from those which concern the subject-object relation is in the interest of problems of both types. The critical assessment of cognition turns, and can turn, only upon what is immanent to cognitive experience itself. And by recognizing that limitation of it we may gain a measure of independence from metaphysical suppositions as to the relation between knowledge and the independently existent actualities of which knowledge takes itself to be significant. But by the same token, any metaphysical conclusion supposedly implied by so epistemologizing must show itself, upon examination, to be so inferred only by some fallacy. The notion seems to have gained currency that this manner of separating off the problems of the critical assessment of empirical beliefs, and stating them in the only terms in which any determination of them could be reached, becomes phenomenalistic merely by this manner of its formulation. That is a confusion of thought or else an unfortunate misuse of the term "phenomenalism."

It is, perhaps, an inevitable suggestion to go on from the Berkeleian thought above mentioned in the Berkeleian way, to a metaphysics which is likewise confined to terms of conscious experience and its content. But unless one follow through consistently to solipsism, reference to independent factuality will be sure to break in upon this soliloquy of self-entertaining experience and do violence to its methodological inhibitions. The thought that thinks itself thinks nothing. Without that other than its own content to which it refers, there is no distinction of fact from fancy, and the thought could not be either true or false. There is no *critique* of objective truth other than the critique of credibility and of the confirmation of empirical belief. But neither the credibility of a belief nor its status as confirmed is the truth of it. Truth concerns the subject-object relation: "snow is white" is true just in case snow is white. The epistemological problem is how we know that snow is white: how well it is evidenced by experience and how in experience it may be further corroborated or disconfirmed. And the remaining problem is the metaphysical one, what snow being white is.

Independent reality is not something to be proved but an original acknowledgement which all men make confronting the facts of life. We find ourselves in the presence of that which is as it is and not otherwise and must be accepted as we find it, antecedently to any effort to mold it nearer to desire. It shows itself obdurate to our wish and will, though in some measure alterable if first we submit ourselves to learn in what respects and in what manner it is amenable to our manipulation. Even wishing and willing would be of no import if it were not that what we face is fixed antecedently to the desiring and with characteristics which we fain would alter. It is that which is so fixed independently of our apprehension which we must learn. To think—that is, to think seriously and to know, as against the idle self-entertainment of the day-dreaming consciousness—is to posit that which is and is other than the apprehension of it, and does not arise with or from the apprehension of it but bespeaks another ground. If independent factuality did not force itself upon us, we should have to invent it in order to exist as beings who think and wish to do. Even Fichtean idealism rests upon that: in the beginning was the act, and the first act is self-assertion. But in positing itself, the ego posits the non-ego, which stands over against the ego and resists the will.

No idealism, of course, whether of the Berkeleian or the absolutist variety, denies independent reality. Berkeley's ultimate is the mind of God, responsible for the content and sequence of those presentations to human consciousness which constitute the proximate reality recognized by common sense. And the difference of this common-sense reality from the unreality of dream and illusion is as important on his view as on any other. Absolute idealism likewise does not fail to recognize that the external world of common-sense objects is as independent of our finite and fallible knowing as any philosophic conception has ever represented it to be. Though any generalization so large is also loose, one may suggest that the primary interest of idealism has never been in any distinctive thesis concerning common knowledge, but rather in the validity of values: in supporting the conviction that human ideals of the good and the right find some sanction in a reality more ultimate than the everyday world of our common thinking and doing. Like phenomenalism, idealism interprets the objects of our common knowledge as independent *factualities* but as manifestations of a reality more ultimate, rather than as being realities in their own right and such that their ultimate nature is simply that which is apprehended in the sensuous encounter with them. Idealism reduces this familiar and universally credited reality to the status of appearance; and the basic difference of this conception from the phenomenalism of Kant is that it conceives the ultimate reality behind this phenomenal world to be also knowable, and knowably spiritual—though such knowledge of the ultimate, even on this idealistic interpretation, can be reflective only and not perceptual. The point I would emphasize here is that for idealism, as for phenomenalism, the external world of our ordinary perceptual encounter, though apparent rather than ultimately real, is still a world of independent factuality. For idealism as for phenomenalism and also for realism, there is an antecedently fixed fact wherever there is anything to be cognitively discovered through experience, and it is this independent factuality which determines truth and falsity in the world as it presents itself. The external world, whether a reality which appears to us in its own nature or an appearance determined by reality more ultimate, and whether that more ultimate reality is also knowable or not, is in any case a world which is as it is and not otherwise and to be apprehended as it is by empirical knowledge.

Taking the objects of empirical knowledge as they are so known to us, whether appearances as they must appear to humans, or constituent in reality with just those characters we apprehend when empirical knowing is correct, we have the question what is implied by this status of recognized empirical actuality, in contrast to empirical nonactuality. Traditionally, our problem here would concern the category of substance. I take it that discussion of substance has been largely abandoned as unhelpful. The residue of it is found in the question whether an object is merely a bundle of attributes—that and the surd of existential fact: the fact that some things we think of are actual and some are not.

On this point, as on others, I must summon hastily and present briefly such thoughts as seem to me pertinent to the final suggestion I would offer. I would set over against this traditional conception of substance a thought drawn from Whitehead—even though I do some violence to his way of thinking in so extracting it. An object is an event: some continuous volume in space-time comprising a history of enduring. Characteristically, the process of change in this kind of event is never too abrupt or too pervasive; and what we recognize as an object is so recognizable only by some persistence of character. On that point, we may make connection with something to be found in traditional discussions of substance: one must either find in the object something which persists unaltered, or one must penetrate to some lawlike or predictable mode of such alteration, characteristic of the kind of thing the object in question is recognized to be. If the question should be asked, "Could any arbitrarily designated continuous volume in space-time be regarded as an object?" I think the plausible answer must be that in fact we do recognize as objects only such events as show, in the process of them, some recognizable manner of their hanging together—some lawlike phases of the life-history, characteristic of the kind of thing whose endurance this event is. And let us admit at once that, in so understanding the process internal to an object, we must often advert to causal connections between constituent events within the object's life-history and events which are external to it and comprised in the life-histories of other objects, related to this one. That is, some processes within the object are understood, and reveal their lawlike character, by being interpreted as lawful interactions between the object in question and other things, or characteristic behavior of this kind of object as affecting and affected by others. Both in such interactions with other objects, and in its internal processes, we must find in any object recognized, some "nature" of it, exhibited in the way it spatio-temporally behaves. And some properties or propensities of behavior, simple or complex, must be discernible as persisting as long as this object endures and is recognizable.

Some modes of such persistence, or continuities of a distinctive type, are very precious—our own continuity of memory, for example, or other aspects of our self-recognition. But if some exquisite and super-precious "being-in-itself" is to be attributed, then I think that at least it is inexpressible.

The trouble, then, with the bundle-of-attributes notion of existent things would seem to be its omission of the relations of properties; but if it be said that this relationship is itself just another property, I would observe only that it is a different order of property from those related—an organization of properties.

There are two further points about anything recognizable as an object which are pertinent to the phenomenalist-realist issue. First, whatever is an object is an individual. And second, the properties ascribable to an object are never simply identifiable with characters we sense in observation of it, but are "ways of behaving" or propensities exhibited.

If an individual is a bundle of attributes, at least it is an infinite bundle. It is a mark of an individual as existent, as against a supposititious one, that the whole truth about it, whether within or beyond our knowing, is fixed in the actuality of it. It answers to the Law of the Excluded Middle, and the answer to any question which could meaningfully be asked about it is determined in the fact of its existence. The number of such questions is endless: however many have been asked and answered, there is always another the answer to which is not yet implied. Leave out the answer to that, and just this actual individual, as against some other which is thinkable as having existed instead, is not yet specified. In the tree of Porphyry (as usually printed in the text-books) "Being" is at the top, and "Socrates, Plato, etc." at the bottom; but between these proper names and what stands next above, there is an unbridgeable gap. All that we know of Socrates is some bundle of ascribable attributes, but leave out an actual eyelash, and it could be some other who might have been ordained to be born instead of Socrates. The idealists' doctrine of internal relations is impeccable and even *a priori*—except that consequences which they drew from it do not follow. All that we can ever know of an individual, which will be some limited complex of properties, will never imply all that still remains undetermined in what we know but fixed in the actuality of it as it exists. We *posit* individuals, though we shall never verify the individuality of any object by full acquaintance; and we make this posit in recognition of the fact of life that there is always another unanswered question about anything that exists. All we shall ever know of a referred-to individual, however, is some bundle of its attributes.

Properties of objects are, of course, universals. But universals are of several distinct types, differently related to our knowledge, and different in the manner of their being. If that ancient wheeze "Do universals exist?" is ever to be answered, we shall have to distinguish these different orders of universals as well as the different senses of the verb "to be." For our present purposes, however, we need only distinguish properties of objects in general from qualia of sense-presentation. Any property of an object has that manner of being which is obvious: just that of being a property of an individual. Some such universals are actual—actually instanced—and some which we can think of, like hundred-footed mammalia, have no actual instance. Any quale of sense-presentation, if correctly specified, has the distinction from any other type of universal that two instances of it are discriminable to sense only by reference to their context. (What I want to say here is a little difficult. But I think this is correct if we understand that two *disparate* qualia coincidentally instanced—an apparent shape and an apparent color, for example—are to be interpreted as mutually contextual.) Any quale is abstract in the sense of being literally abstracted from its given context by attention, and in the sense of having more than one instance, but not abstract in the sense of triangularity, whose instances may be immediately discriminable, as different shapes, without respect to context. It is universals of this last-mentioned type which precipitate the nominalistic objection to acknowledgment of their factuality. They cannot be at once precisely and adequately imaged. Anything we can imagine precisely is a quale or some complexus of such. And if qualia imagined or represented were not also comparable with those of sense, no knowledge could ever be gathered from our sense-experience, because nothing presented could be recognized.

We persistently confuse sense-qualia and objective properties of things, though no possible instance of one of these can ever be an instance of the other. It is by such confusion that an early form of the phenomenalist-realist issue arises. Locke inquired whether the blueness of the sea was in the sea as in our perception of it (though the example we here select is an adverse one) or whether the visual appearance of blueness was simply in our perception or consciousness, as apprehended pain is. The property of blueness which is in the sea, or in the blue cloth or blue chalk, is in no case identifiable with an immediately apprehended visual quale. And this fact is not due to our using "blue" for a whole range of the color-properties of objects, as well as for a whole gamut of visual qualia. It is still true if we identify the objective property in question by reference to a particular and smallest-observable area of the color-pyramid, or as a single wave length of the spectrum, and likewise specify the appearance-quale so as to satisfy the requirement that two instances of it are indiscriminable except by context. Make "blue" as precise a word as the artist's "crimson lake" when he buys a tube of paint, and it is still true that this specific property of any object presents itself to the eye by some whole range of visual qualia—dependent upon variations of illumination, as well as upon variations in the visual purple and other conditions of the eye which sees. Even the artist cannot tell crimson lake paint from magenta paint by looking at it under sufficiently adverse conditions. The immediate presentational quale, with due reference to apprehended circumstances, is simply one manifestation of the objective color-property attributable to the objective existent, and one means of confirming that objective property, more frequently used than the many other ways in which that property also manifests itself in presentation, some of which, like those which figure in spectroscopic examination, are both more precise and more decisive. The visual quale and the objective color of an object could not be identical because they belong to different categories of being. We use the same color-words because the visual manifestation of a color-property is the most frequently useful clue to it, though only one of the ways in which it manifests itself and by reference to which it may be confirmed as objectively factual. The objective color of a thing is a potentiality or dispositional trait inherent in the nature of this object, and evidenced in various observable ways, including a variety of effects upon human eyes under specifiable circumstances. It is a propensity of behavior, resident in the nature of the object, which it has and will retain unless or until it undergoes some objective alteration of that nature. And the sense in which it is independent of eyes, or even minds, and would have been the same if eyes had never evolved, as well as the sense in which it would have been a *different* potentiality if there had never been eyes, is a question for those who enjoy resolving verbal puzzles. We may know that an object has a certain color-property, and we may be well enough assured of it for all practical purposes, merely by looking at it under propitious conditions; but what is so known is the reliable predictability of certain visual and other manifestations, the potentiality for production of which resides in the nature of this object. However, so far as empirical knowledge can be guaranteed, what we so know is a character which the object really has in itself—the objective property which will variously manifest itself in these predictable ways.

The point is not confined to the traditional secondary qualities. Similar things are to be said of the shapes of objects, for example. Berkeley said some of them, in psychologically crude terms but acutely. A specifiable objective shape manifests itself by a whole gamut of presentational patterns in the visual field, as well as by a lesser gamut of tactual impressions, totally different in presentational quality from the visual clues to objective shape but reliably correlated with them. When we know the objective shape which a thing has, what we know is such reliability, attributable to the nature of it, of the various ways in which it will manifest itself, either by direct effect upon experience or by observable effects on other objects when, for example, it is introduced into the same confined space with them.

What we may know, when we say that we know an object, is some property or properties of it. We never know all the properties of any individual thing, and never can have such exhaustive knowledge of any. And there is nothing other than attributes of it (including its relations to and interactions with other things) which we can ever learn about it. Concerning some things we can, with sufficient trouble and a measure of good luck, find out properties sufficient for its identification as an individual—though only because not all the things which might consistently be thought of are to be found in this actual world. But even the individual objects we identify with a minimum of risk are never wholly known to us. Sometimes there is something further which is implied by what we presently know of them and which could be elicited simply by cogent reflection; but in all cases, it is also the fact that there is something true of the object—some properties truly resident in the nature of it—which are neither explicitly known to us nor implicated in what we already know.

It is precisely on this last point that realism differs from idealism. (That matter calls for development; but there is no time for it.) Already, I am sure, you anticipate my little suggestion—I will not call it a conclusion since the discussion has, perforce, been too limited and sketchy for cogent concluding.

The suggestion is that we know objects only as we know certain objective properties of them, which are potentialities or reliable dispositional traits resident in the nature of them as they objectively exist, and whose manifestations are variously observable: directly in the presentational content of human experience to which they give rise, and indirectly through the observable interactions of objects with one another. We never know or can know all the properties of any individual thing, but what we do or may know is metaphysically veridical; these properties are in the things themselves as in our knowledge of them—provided we do not fall into confusions about the nature of our knowledge.

All empirical knowledge must be, eventually, mediated to us by presentational qualia and the patterns of them in experience, including temporal pattern and interrelation with the temporal pattern of our own activities as likewise directly observable to us. Coincidence of these qualia with properties resident in objects is precluded in the metaphysical nature of the case, and by facts of life which should be obvious. What may become known to us of the nature of objects is reliable dispositional traits of them so manifested. We could have no practical interest in any other conceivable manner of knowing them—just this manner of knowing suffices for all that we conceivably might be able to accomplish in any world of things existing independently of being known by us. (I will not say, however, that such knowledge is sufficient to *every* human interest—especially in view of the unlimited character of human curiosity.)

Plainly the manner in which properties resident in objects are manifested in our presentational experience confronting them is dependent on our own nature as well as on the nature of the objects in themselves. How widely it may be true that objective existents possess properties which, by reason of human limitations, are forever beyond our finding out, we can only guess. Conjecture on that point can run to any length. It is not even precluded to ask if objects, as we distinguish them, are not abstracted by relation to something distinctive of the human. There are stars in the heavens, but constellations only for our seeing. Perhaps likewise there are molar masses only for our senses, directed upon the quanta or wavicles which inhabit the ocean of energy. But at least the potentiality of so appearing to us, instead of otherwise, and of being discriminable as just these molar masses, in just these relations to one another, is in the ocean itself, as constituted independently of us. Whatever consolatory consideration phenomenalism could support by this thought of a human ignorance we cannot transcend is wide open; though as Kant observed, there could be no justified belief on such a point without some rationally impelling consideration other than the cognitive. Let us remark, however, the many and previously unguessed ranges of reality which science has progressively brought within the scope of human observation by methods that are indirect. Even the knowable is sufficiently wider than the known to afford a considerable field for presently unprovable but not hopelessly implausible conjectures, of the sort which are often bracketed with the metaphysical.

Such knowledge as we have, or ever can expect to have, of what exists must be mediated to us by appearances of things, but it is not *of* appearances. Whatever directly appears is never, by itself, knowledge of any existent. What we do or may know—objective properties of things—is certain reliable traits constituent in the apprehensible natures of objects. And there is nothing in this character of knowledge or in any consideration pertinent to it which justly should suggest that our knowledge, though partial, is not, so far as it extends, a knowledge of existents as they are in themselves.

I do not know whether so conceiving the matter is appropriately to be classed as phenomenalism or as realism. My preference would be for "realism." I remind myself that a conception remotely similar was put forward years ago by my colleague, Professor [Jacob] Loewenberg.[1] He labeled his view "Problematic Realism." But my divergences are too considerable to allow my borrowing his title; and this presentation is too undeveloped to justify my involving anyone else in these suggestions.

[1] In G. P. Adams and W. P. Montague, II, eds., *Contemporary American Philosophy* (New York, 1930), pp. 55–81.

Part IV. Logic and the Philosophy of Logic

1. Implication and the Algebra of Logic

The development of the algebra of logic brings to light two somewhat startling theorems: (1) a false proposition implies any proposition, and (2) a true proposition is implied by any proposition. These are not the only theorems of the algebra which seem suspicious to common sense, but their sweeping generality has attracted particular attention. In themselves, they are neither mysterious sayings, nor great discoveries, nor gross absurdities. They exhibit only, in sharp outline, the meaning of "implies" which has been incorporated into the algebra. What this meaning is, what are its characteristics and limitations, and its relation to the "implies" of ordinary valid inference, it is the object of this paper briefly to indicate.

Such an attempt might be superfluous were it not that certain confusions of interpretation are involved, and that the expositors of the algebra of logic have not always taken pains to indicate that there is a difference between the algebraic and the ordinary meanings of implication. One may suspect that some of them would deny the divergence, or at least would maintain that the technical use is preferable and ought generally to be adopted. As a result, symbolic logic appears to the uninitiated somewhat as an *enfant terrible,* which intimidates one with its array of exact demonstrations, and demands the acceptance of incomprehensible results.

In the algebra of logic, 'p implies q' is defined to mean 'either p is false or q is true' $[(p \supset q) = (\backsim p \vee q)$ Df.].[1] But this last expression

---

Reprinted by permission from *Mind,* Vol. XXI (1912), No. 84, pp. 522–31.

[1] I choose this form of the definition partly because it is the one used in the most economical development of the calculus of propositions—in the *Principia Mathematica* of Russell and Whitehead—and partly because of its convenience for the discussion in hand. Other defined equivalents of '$p \supset q$' are:

(1) $p = pq$ (the assertion of p is equivalent to the assertion of p and q both);

(2) $\backsim (p \backsim q)$, or $p \backsim q = o$ (that 'p is true and q is false' is a false assertion; or, the proposition which asserts p and denies q is false); and

(3) $(p \vee q) = q$ ('either p is true or q is true' is equivalent to 'q is true').

It comes to the same thing in the end, whichever one of the four mentioned definitions of implication be chosen. Any one of them may be deduced as a theorem in a properly constructed system which adopts any other at the start. The choice depends solely upon the method of developing the particular system (see Whitehead, *Universal Algebra* [Cambridge, 1898, Vol. I], p. 40).

The symbolism which will be used in the paper is that of the *Principia Mathematica* with slight modifications. The letters, p, q, stand for propositions or 'propois equivocal. Implication is defined in terms of disjunction, but 'either-or' propositions may have at least three different meanings. One of these is ruled out when we understand that 'p or q'—either p is true or q is true—must not be taken to exclude the possibility that both p and q may be true. Disjunctions in the algebra do not signify mutual exclusion. If p be true, it is not implied that q is false. A convenient statement of this takes the form, "*At least one* of the propositions p and q is true." Two meanings of disjunction still remain. The implication of the algebra of logic bears the same relation to the one of these that the Aristotelian "implies" bears to the other. Hence the need of distinguishing carefully between these two sorts of disjunction.

Compare, if you will, the disjunctions: (1) Either Caesar died or the moon is made of green cheese, and (2) Either Matilda does not love me or I am beloved. In both cases, at least one of the disjoined propositions *is* true. The difference between the two may be expressed in a variety of ways. The second disjunction is such that at least one of the disjoined propositions is "necessarily" true. Reject either of the possibilities and you thereby embrace the other. Suppose one of its propositions false and you are in consistency bound to suppose the other true. If either lemma *were* false, the other would, by the same token, be true. None of these statements will hold for the first disjunction. At least one of its propositions is, as a fact, true. But to suppose it false that Caesar died, would not bind one to suppose the moon made of green cheese. If 'Caesar died' *were* false, the moon would not necessarily be made of green cheese—if conditions contrary to fact have any meaning at all. It is this last which the algebra is, according to its meaning of disjunction and implication, bound to deny.

The most significant distinction, however, remains to be noted. The second disjunction is such that its truth is independent of the truth of either member considered separately. Or, more accurately, its truth can be known, while it is still problematic *which* of its lemmas is the true one. It has a truth which is prior to the determination of the facts in question. The truth of 'either Caesar died or the moon is made of green cheese' has not this purely logical or formal character. It lacks this independence of facts. Its contradiction would not surprise a logical mind unacquainted with history.

It requires careful analysis to separate these two meanings of 'either-or' propositions, though their main features may seem sufficiently dis-

---

sitional functions.' $\supset$ signifies 'implies.' $\vee$ is the sign of disjunction. $\frown p$ may be read 'not-p' or 'the negation of p' or 'p is false.' Similarly p may be read as written or as 'p is true.'

tinct. We may call disjunctions like (1), whose truth cannot be known apart from the facts, extensional disjunctions; those of the type of (2), whose truth can be known while it is still problematic which member is true—or whether both are true—we may call intensional. These two may be further distinguished by considering their negatives. If one take 'either Caesar died or the moon is made of green cheese' to be a false statement, one may mean thereby that a certain relation is falsely asserted of the two propositions 'Caesar died' and 'the moon is made of green cheese.' If Smith asserts, "Either my name is not Smith or this is my hat," one might reply: "No, you are wrong; there may be other Smiths in the hall with names in their hats." One does not deny that Smith knows his own name, or that this is his hat. One denies only that his statement exhausts the possibilities. The negative of intensional disjunction is, thus, the negation of the disjunctive relation itself and not the negation of either member. To take another example: (3) either London is in England or Paris is in France; one may deny that any "necessary" disjunction is here involved, though either half of the statement by itself is true. If either member of the disjunction *were* false, the truth or falsity of the other would not thereby be affected. Perhaps we cannot ever be certain of the possibility of such a contrary-to-fact condition. Still we *know what we mean* when we suppose it. The negation of intensional disjunction is, then, the negation of a logical relation of propositions, and is entirely consistent with the truth of one or both of the disjoined assertions. One denies only that the disjunction has any truth apart from the facts in question.

The negative of extensional disjunction is the denial of *both* its members. Taking 'either-or' in their reference to extension, neither (1) nor (3) can be denied. The truth of extensional disjunction is secured by the truth of either member, regardless of "logical connections," and the negation of extensional disjunction accordingly negates both the disjoined propositions.

That the meaning of disjunction in the algebra of logic must consistently be confined to the extensional follows from the fact that, in the algebra, the negative of a disjunction is the negation of both its members $[\backsim (p \lor q) = \backsim p \backsim q]$,[2] and the negative of a "product"— e.g. 'both p and q are true'—is the disjunction of the negatives of its factors $[\backsim (pq) = (\backsim p \lor \backsim q)]$.[3] Every intensional disjunction is also extensional, or, more accurately, the intensional disjunction of p and q implies their extensional disjunction also. But the reverse does

[2] De Morgan's theorem.
[3] De Morgan's theorem.

not hold. Of every intensional disjunction, at least one member *is* true; but not every 'either-or' proposition with at least one true member is an intensional disjunction. If, however, any one suppose that the algebra can treat of intensional disjunctions "because they are a special class of extensional disjunctions," let him consider the fact that, in negating *any* disjunction, the algebra negates both its members. If p and q are disjoined both extensionally and intensionally, still the algebra treats only of their extensional disjunction. That this is not mere "logic-chopping" will appear when we come to convert disjunctions into implications.

Before leaving the subject of disjunctions, we should note two further characters of the intensional variety. A genuine intensional disjunction does not, of course, suffer any alteration of its logical nature if one of its members is known to be false, or one known to be true, or when both things are known. 'Either Matilda does not love me or I am beloved' loses none of its intensional character if it is discovered that Matilda does not, in fact, love me, or that I am actually beloved. In argument, one produces a dilemma[4] for the purpose of introducing later the falsity of one member and thus proving the truth of the other. The dilemma has the same meaning to the speaker who knows its solution and to the hearer who does not. Its character as intensional disjunction is attested by the fact that the hearer can know its truth before knowing its solution—and by the further fact that both speaker and hearer, after reaching the solution, are still bound by the condition which turns out to be contrary to fact. If the true member *were* false, the other would necessarily be true.

Again, intensional disjunction is not restricted to the purely formal or *a priori* type of (2). Suppose a wholly reliable weather forecast for the 16th of the month to be "warm." This implies that (4) either today is not the 16th or the weather is warm. On the supposition made, this is an intensional disjunction. One might know its truth even if one could not find a calendar and were suffering from chills and fever. But strike out the initial assumption and the disjunction becomes, if still true, extensional. Knowledge of its truth now depends upon verifica-

---

[4] A dilemma *may be* an intensional disjunction with the restriction that its members cannot be true together. Extensional disjunctions admit of the same limitation while still remaining extensional. This last type, however, do not appear in discourse except as mere truisms or as figures of speech. Example (1)—either Caesar died or the moon is made of green cheese—belongs to this class. It is a truism, or—if meant to be taken as *intensional* disjunction—hyperbole. Thus we might have distinguished four types of disjunction instead of three. But the important division is that of intensional in general from extensional in general.

tion of one or both of its members. We may say that extensional disjunction concerns actualities; intensional disjunction, possibilities. But one or more facts being given, the possibilities are thereby narrowed, and an intensional disjunction which is not *a priori* may be *implied*.

As has been said, intensional disjunction bears the same relation to inferential or "strict" implication[5] that extensional disjunction bears to the algebraic or "material" implication. Intensional disjunctions when converted into implications, according to the equivalence which the algebra states, become strict implications. Extensional disjunctions, by the same rule, produce material implications. In either case '*p* implies *q*' is equivalent to 'either *p* is false or *q* is true'—to 'either not-*p* or *q*' $[(p \supset q) = (\backsim p \lor q) \text{ Df.}]$. Taking the intensional disjunctions: if we let *p* represent 'Matilda loves me' and *q* 'I am beloved,' example (2) states exactly 'either not-*p* or *q*.' 'Either Matilda does not love me or I am beloved' is equivalent to 'Matilda loves me implies that I am beloved.' Since 'either-or' states a reversible relation, we may equally well let *p* represent 'I am beloved,' and *q* 'Matilda does not love me.' 'Not-*p* implies *q*' will then read: 'I am not beloved' implies that 'Matilda does not love me.' By the same process, (4)—'Either today is not the 16th or the weather is warm'—may be transformed into 'Today is the 16th implies that the weather is warm' and 'The weather is not warm implies that today is not the 16th.' Remembering that (4) is an intensional disjunction only in the light of a certain presupposition, we may observe that, in this case also, intensional disjunction produces strict implication.

If *p* and *q* are intensionally disjoined, then—whether *p*, or *q*, or both are, in fact, true—if *p* were false, *q* would be true. The negation of *p* implies *q* in the ordinary meaning of "implies." Also if *q* were false, *p* would be true; *p* can *validly be inferred* from the proposition which negates *q*.

Examples (1) and (3) are extensional disjunctions. If we let *p* represent 'Caesar died' and *q* represent 'the moon is made of green cheese,' 'not-*p* implies *q*' will read, 'Caesar did not die' implies that 'the moon is made of green cheese.' Interchanging *p* and *q* above—since 'either-or' is reversible—we have 'the moon is not made of green cheese' implies that 'Caesar died.' Thus we get the implications of the algebra. The former of these is a good example of the sense in which a false proposition implies anything; the latter well illustrates how a true proposition may be implied by any proposition. By the same method (3)

[5] We may call this kind of implication "strict" at least in the sense that its meaning is narrower than that of the algebraic implication.

'either London is in England or Paris is in France' gives us 'London is not in England' implies that 'Paris is in France,' and 'Paris is not in France' implies that 'London is in England.' Each of these last may be regarded as a case of a false proposition implying any proposition and, at the same time, of a true proposition being implied by any. *Any two true propositions* whatever might have been substituted for 'London is in England' and 'Paris is in France'; the implications would have resulted in the same way. The denial of the one would imply the other; the denial of the other, the one.

In order that it may be clearer that implication has, in the algebra, *no other significance* than that exemplified by the transformations of (1) and (3), let us consider what is involved in *denying* the algebraic implication relation. Take any false proposition p—e.g. 'Rome is still burning'—and any true one q—e.g. 'Christmas is coming.' At once the extensional disjunction 'either p is false or q is true' is satisfied—by the falsity of p alone, or by the truth of q alone—and it follows that p implies q $[(p \supset q) = (\frown p \vee q)$ Df.]. To deny that p implies q is to deny the equivalent disjunction 'Either p is false or q is true' $[\frown (p \supset q) = \frown (\frown p \vee q)]$. To deny this disjunction is, according to the algebra, to deny the truth of both its members, i.e. to assert p and deny q $[\frown (\frown p \vee q) = (p \frown q)]$. Thus, if one would deny that 'Rome is still burning' implies 'Christmas is coming,' one must assert that Rome still burns and deny the advent of Christmas.

Or we may take any two problematic propositions, as (p) 'Swift married Stella,' and (q) 'There are other universes beyond ours.' At once we can assert, according to the algebra, that if p does not imply q, q implies p. If p is false, that alone satisfies the extensional 'Either p is false or q is true' and proves that p implies q. Similarly if q is true. If p is true and q is false—the only situation for which p does not imply q—then it is at once doubly certain that q implies p. Of any two false propositions, each implies the other; and similarly, of any two true propositions, each is implied by the other. If one of two propositions is false and the other true, the former implies the latter. Either 'Swift married Stella' implies that 'there are other universes beyond ours,' or 'there are other universes beyond ours' implies that 'Swift married Stella.' And there is an even chance that the implication is mutual. Indeed the algebra of logic allows us to make these assertions prior to all knowledge of the content of p and q and apart from any consideration of what would ordinarily be called their logical import.

Most theorems in the algebra admit of being exemplified within the field of strict implications and intensional disjunctions. Aside from those which involve the negative of a disjunction, there are only a few which do not. All of these are the results of a single assumption of the calculus of propositions, the so-called principle of addition. This principle states that p implies 'either p or q'—if p is true, then either p is true or any other proposition q is true $[p \supset (p \vee q)]$. We have already noted it in observing that an extensional disjunction is satisfied simply by the fact that one of its members is true. That this principle is formally false for intensional disjunctions is apparent when we note that—in the strict sense of implies—p does not imply that if p *were* false, any other proposition q would necessarily be true. From the fact that today is Monday, we cannot infer that if today were not Monday, the corn crop would be destroyed.

Assuming 'p implies (either p or q),' the proof that a false proposition implies any proposition is short and easy. Substituting not-p (p is false) for p, we have 'not-p implies (either not -p or q).' Replacing 'either not-p or q' by its defined equivalent 'p implies q,' not-p implies that 'p implies q'—'p is false' implies that 'p implies any other proposition, q.' If or when p *is* false, the consequence 'p implies q' follows. A false proposition implies anything. Resuming the proof in symbols: Addition—$p \supset (p \vee q)$. Substituting $\smallsmile p$ for p throughout, $\smallsmile p \supset (\smallsmile p \vee q)$. $(\smallsmile p \vee q) = (p \supset q)$, by definition. $\therefore \smallsmile p \supset (p \supset q)$. The proof that a true proposition implies any proposition requires one additional principle—that disjunctions are reversible $[(p \vee q) = (q \vee p)]$. Assuming that '$p$ implies (either p or q),' we may reverse the disjunction and get 'p implies (either q or p).' Substituting not-q for q, 'p implies (either not-q or p).' Replacing this disjunction by its equivalent 'q implies p,' the result is 'p implies that q implies p.' If p is true, it is also true that any other proposition q implies p. A true proposition is implied by any proposition. Addition—$p \supset (p \vee q)$. $(p \vee q) = (q \vee p)$. Substituting $\smallsmile q$ for q, $p \supset (\smallsmile q \vee p)$. $(\smallsmile q \vee p) = (q \supset p)$, by defininition. $\therefore p \supset (q \supset p)$.

The existence of these two theorems in the algebra brings to light the most severe limitation of the algebraic or material implication. One of the important practical uses of implication is the testing of hypotheses whose truth or falsity is problematic. The algebraic implication has no application here. If the hypothesis happens to be false, it implies anything you please. If one find facts, x, y, z, otherwise unexpected but suggested by the hypothesis, the truth of these facts is implied by one's hypothesis, whether that hypothesis be true or not—since any true proposition is implied by all others. In other words, no proposition could be verified by its logical consequences. If the proposition be false, it has these "consequences" anyway. Similarly, no contrary-to-fact condition could have any logical significance, whether one happen to know that it *is* contrary to fact or not. For if the fact *is* otherwise, the proposition which states the supposition implies anything and everything. In the ordinary and "proper" use of "implies" certain conclusions can validly be inferred from contrary-to-fact suppositions, while certain others cannot. Hypotheses whose truth is problematic have logical consequences *which are independent of its truth or falsity.* These are the vital distinctions of the ordinary meaning of 'implies'— for which '*p* implies *q*' is equivalent to '*q* can validly be inferred from *p*'—from that implication which figures in the algebra.

That the definition of implication in terms of extensional disjunction is in accord with any ordinary or useful meaning of the term can hardly be maintained with success. There can be, however, with regard to such a definition, no question of truth or falsity in the ordinary sense. As one of the assumptions or conventions of the calculus of propositions, the definition represents only the exact statement of the way in which expressions are to be equated or substituted for one another. Provided it is possible so to equate them without contradiction, it is meaningless to call the equations untrue. We may, however, object to the definition on the ground that a more useful one is possible; and especially will this be the case when the system in question is one, like logic, which we wish to apply in some field of practical human endeavor. The present calculus of propositions is untrue in the sense in which non-Euclidean geometry is untrue; and we may reproach the logician who disregards our needs as the ancients might have reproached Euclid had he busied himself too exclusively with the consequences of a different parallel postulate.

Nothing that has preceded should be taken to imply that the algebra of logic is necessarily unequal to the task of symbolizing such logical processes as those of inference and proof, or the more general processes which the algebra itself has the value of bringing to light. Our conclusions militate not against symbolic logic in general, but against the calculus of propositions in its present form. As a matter of fact, a few simple changes would remove all the "absurdities" from the present calculus and bring it into agreement with the strict meaning of implication. The principle of addition—*p* implies 'either *p* is true or *q* is true'—is the only one of an economical set of postulates of the present calculus[6] which is false for the intensional meaning of disjunction and,

---

[6] See those of the *Principia Mathematica* (Cambridge, 1910), Vol. I, pp. 98-101.

consequently, for strict implication. If this were removed, and disjunction confined—as a matter of interpretation—to the intensional variety, we should be well on our way to a new calculus. One other change would be necessary. The equivalence of "products" with the negatives of disjunctions and of the negatives of products with disjunctions $[pq = \frown (\frown p \vee \frown q)$ and $\frown (pq) = (\frown p \vee \frown q)]$ is inconsistent with the exclusion of purely extensional disjunctions.[7] The product pq—'p and q are both true'—would, accordingly, appear as a new indefinable, though capable of clear interpretation. In place of the principle of addition, the principle of simplification—'p and q are both true' implies 'p is true' $[pq \supset p]$—would be assumed. "Addition" could no longer be deduced from it, as at present, when the negatives of disjunctions and products had no symbolic equivalents.[8] A careful analysis of what these changes involve leads one to discover certain ambiguities and confusions which exist even in what ordinarily passes for sound reasoning.

An alternative and more fruitful method of developing the calculus of strict implication would be to retain both extensional and intensional disjunction, symbolize them differently, and define implication in terms of intensional disjunction only. The extensional disjunction would now have its negative in a product, as at present, and the principle of addition could be retained, but only for extensional disjunction. As a consequence, such theorems as 'a false proposition implies any proposition' would still not appear, but the principle of simplification $[pq \supset p]$ could be deduced instead of being assumed. This second mode of development would produce a calculus which retained all the theorems of the present one which hold for the ordinary meaning of implication, and would reject automatically those which appear to the uninitiated as "absurd." It would also be much wealthier in theorems than the present calculus, because of the fact that the intensional disjunction of p and q implies their extensional disjunction also, though not vice versa. And, owing to the distinction of these two meanings of 'either-or' propositions, this calculus would prove a valuable instrument of logical analysis. Its primary advantage over any present system lies in the fact that its meaning of implication is precisely that of ordinary inference and proof.

[7] De Morgan's theorem holds only for extensional disjunction.
[8] Both would still have important *implications*.

2. Types of Order and the System Σ

It is a commonplace of current theory that mathematics and exact science in general is capable of being viewed quite apart from any concrete subject matter or any system of physical facts to which it may usefully be applied. Geometry need not appeal to any intuition of spacial complexes or to a supposititious space form; it has no need to rely upon diagrams or make use of 'constructions.' Arithmetic makes no necessary reference to the sensible character of collections of marbles or of areas. Dynamics does not require the dubious assumption that the 'moving particles' of which it treats are possible of experience or verifiable physical entities. The 'points' of geometry and kinematics, the 'numbers' of arithmetic, and so on, are simply terms—x's, y's, z's, entities, anything—and the question what concrete things may be successfully regarded as such x's and y's is a question of application of the science, not one which need be considered while the system itself is in process of development.

If considerations of usefulness and of application are important in determining what assumptions shall be made or what systems developed, still such pragmatic considerations are principles of selection amongst actual and possible systems, and not internal to the systems themselves.

An arithmetic, a geometry, a kinematics, is thus capable of being viewed simply as a complex of relations and operations (relations of relations) which obtain amongst entities the nature of which, apart from those properties which follow from the relations assumed, is wholly indifferent. Such a system may, in fact, admit of various interpretations and applications, more or less useful, all of which satisfy the requirement that these relations and operations be valid. As Professor Royce is accustomed to put it: a system of science is a type of order, the distinguishing characteristics of which are the kind of relations—symmetrical or unsymmetrical, transitive or intransitive, etc.—which obtain among its terms, and the relations of these relations, by means of which the terms are 'ordered' and the relations 'transformed.'[1]

Reprinted by permission from *The Philosophical Review*, Vol. XXV (1916), No. 3, pp. 407–19.

[1] I do not know that Professor Royce has anywhere printed just this statement, and my way of putting it may not be satisfactory to him, but Harvard students in "Philosophy 15" will remember some such formulation.

The growing recognition of the advantages of so viewing systems of pure science is one of the prime motives for the present interest in symbolic logic, or logistic. For logistic is the science which treats of types of order. One may reach the particular type of order which it is desired to portray—the arithmetic or geometry—by further specification of that minimum order which must obtain among entities if they are to 'belong together' in a set or system—the order of logic. This can be done in a variety of ways, which may be roughly divided into two groups. These two methods are distinguished by the fact that in the one case the 'numbers' of arithmetic or 'points' of geometry are treated as (conceptual) complexes having a definite internal structure, while in the other the 'numbers' or 'points' are the simple and indifferent terms, the x's and y's of the system. The former mode of procedure is best illustrated by the investigations of Russell's *Principles of Mathematics* and *Principia Mathematica* of Russell and Whitehead. The other method is exemplified by Dedekind's *Was sind und was sollen die Zahlen,* by the *Ausdehnungslehre* of Grassmann, and by the paper of Mr. A. B. Kempe, "On the Relation between the Logical Theory of Classes and the Geometrical Theory of Points."[2] But this second method appears in its best and clearest form in the paper of Professor Royce on "The Relation of the Principles of Logic to the Foundations of Geometry."[3] Each of these procedures has its advantages and its difficulties. Of late, the first method has received a disproportionate share of attention. For this reason, if for no other, I deem it important to call attention to the second method in general and to Professor Royce's paper—its notable exemplification—in particular.

Professor Royce generalizes upon certain relations previously pointed out by Kempe, in the paper mentioned above—certain relations which are fundamental both for logic and for geometry. If $ac \cdot b$ represents a triadic relation in which a and c are the 'even' members and b is the 'odd' member, $ac \cdot b$ is capable of various significant interpretations. If a, b, and c represent areas, $ac \cdot b$ may be taken to symbolize the fact that b includes whatever area is common to a and c and is itself included in that area which comprises what is either a or c (or both). The same relation may be expressed in symbolic logic as

$$ac \prec b \prec (a+c) \; ; \; \text{or} \; \bar{a}b\bar{c}+a\bar{b}c = 0.$$

---

[2] *Proc. London Math. Soc.,* Series I, Vol. 21, pp. 147–82. See also his earlier "A Memoir on the Theory of Mathematical Form," *Phil. Trans.,* Vol. CLXXVII, pp. 1–70, and the Note thereon, *Proc. Royal Soc.,* Vol. XLII, pp. 193–96.

[3] *Trans. Am. Math. Soc.,* Vol. 6, pp. 353–415.

This relation may be so assumed that it has the essential properties of serial order. Taking it in the form just given and presuming the familiar laws of the algebra of logic, if $ac \cdot b$ and $ad \cdot c$, then also $ad \cdot b$ and $bd \cdot c$. Hereupon we may translate $ac \cdot b$ by 'b is between a and c,' and the relation will then have the properties of the points a, b, c, d, in that order. Further, if a be regarded as an origin with reference to which precedence is determined, $ac \cdot b$ may represent 'b precedes c,' and $ad \cdot c$ that 'c precedes d.' Since $ac \cdot b$ and $ad \cdot c$ together give $ad \cdot b$, if 'b precedes c' and 'c precedes d,' then 'b precedes d.' Hence this relation has the essential transitivity of serial order, with the added precision that it retains reference to the origin from which 'precedes' is determined.

Professor Royce points out to his students that the last-mentioned property of this relation makes possible an interpretation of it for logical classes in which it becomes more general than the inclusion relation of ordinary syllogistic reasoning. If there should be inhabitants of Mars whose logical sense coincided with our own—so that any conclusion which we regarded as valid would seem valid to them, and vice versa—but whose psychology was somewhat different from ours, these Martians might prefer to remark that "b is 'between' a and c," rather than to note that "all a is b and all b is c." These Martians might then carry on successfully all their reasoning in terms of this triadic 'between' relation. For $ac \cdot b$ meaning $\bar{a}b\bar{c} + a\bar{b}c = 0$ is a general relation which, in the special case where a is the 'null' class contained in every class, becomes the familiar "b is included in c" or "all b is c." By virtue of the transitivity pointed out above, $oc \cdot b$ and $od \cdot c$ together give $od \cdot b$, which is the syllogism in *Barbara*, 'If all b is c and all c is d, then all b is d.' Hence these Martians would possess a mode of reasoning more comprehensive than our own and including our own as a special case.

The triadic relation of Kempe is, then, a very powerful one, and capable of representing the most fundamental relations not only in logic but in all those departments of our systematic thinking where unsymmetrical transitive (serial) relations are important.[4] In terms of these triads, Kempe states the properties of his 'base system,' from whose order the relations of logic and geometry both are to be derived. The 'base system' consists of an infinite number of homogeneous elements,

---

[4] It should be pointed out that the triadic relation is not necessarily unsymmetrical: $ac \cdot b$ and $ab \cdot c$ may both be true. But in that case $b = c$, as may be verified by adding the equations for these two triads. Further, $ab \cdot b$ is always true, for any a and b. Thus the triadic relation represents serial order with the qualification that any term may be regarded as "preceding" itself or as "between" itself and any other.

each having an infinite number of equivalents. It is assumed that triads are disposed in this system according to the following laws :[5]

1. If we have $ab \cdot p$ and $cb \cdot q$, r exists such that we have $aq \cdot r$ and $cp \cdot r$.

2. If we have $ab \cdot p$ and $cp \cdot r$, q exists such that we have $aq \cdot r$ and $cb \cdot r$.[6]

3. If we have $ab \cdot c$, and $a = b$, then $c = a = b$.

4. If $a = b$, then we have $ac \cdot b$ and $bc \cdot a$, whatever entity of the system c may be.

To these, Kempe adds a fifth postulate which he calls the 'law of continuity' : "No entity is absent from the system which can consistently be present." From these assumptions and various definitions in terms of the triadic relation, Kempe is able to derive the laws of the symbolic logic of classes and the most fundamental properties of geometrical sets of points.

But there are certain dubious features of Kempe's procedure. As Professor Royce notes, the 'law of continuity' makes postulates 1 and 2 superfluous. And it renders entirely obscure what properties the system may have, beyond those derivable from the other postulates without this. For the negative form of the 'law of continuity' makes it impossible to assume the existence of an entity without first investigating *all* the properties of *all the other* entities and collections in the system, where some of these other entities and collections exist only at the instance of the 'law of continuity' itself. Consequently the existence of any entity or set not explicitly demanded by the other postulates can be assumed only at the risk of later inconsistency. Also, in spite of the fact that Kempe has assumed an infinity of elements in the base set, there are certain ambiguities and difficulties about the application of his principles to infinite collections.

In Professor Royce's paper, we have no such 'blanket assumption' as the 'law of continuity,' and the relations defined may be extended without difficulty to any finite or infinite set. We have here, in place of a 'base system' and triadic relations, the 'system Σ' and 'O-collections.'

The system Σ consists of simple and homogeneous elements. Collections of these may contain any finite or infinite number of elements; and any element may be repeated any number of times, so that x and

---

[5] See Kempe's paper, "On the Relation . . . ," pp. 148–49.

[6] If the reader will draw the triangle *abc* and put in the "betweens" as indicated, the geometrical significance of these postulates will be evident. I have changed a little the order of Kempe's terms so that both 1 and 2 will be illustrated by the same triangle.

x-repeated may be considered a collection, x, x-repeated, and y a collection, and so on. Greek letters will signify determinate collections in Σ. Collections in Σ are either O-collections or E-collections. $O(\text{———})$ signifies that (———) is an O-collection; $E(\text{———})$ that (———) is an E-collection, i.e., that it is not an O-collection. Assuming for the moment the principles of the algebra of logic, $O(pqrs\cdots)$ signifies that $pqrs\cdots + \overline{pqrs}\cdots = 0$. [Both the laws of the algebra of logic and the properties of O-collections which render them thus expressible are, of course, derived from the postulates and not assumed in the beginning.] It will be clear that the order of terms in any O-collection may be varied at will.

'x is equivalent to y' means that in every collection in which x or y occurs the other may be substituted for it and the collection in question still remains an O-collection.

If two elements in Σ, say p and q, are such that $O(pq)$ is true, then p and q are said to be *obverses*, each of the other. Since it will follow from the postulates of the system that all the obverses of a given element are mutually equivalent, and that every element has at least one obverse, a 'unique representative' of the obverses of x may be chosen and symbolized by $\bar{x}$. Pairs of obverses will turn out to have the properties of negatives in logic.

Any q such that $O(\beta q)$ is true is called a *complement* of β.

Any r such that $O(\beta p)$ and $O(qr)$ are both true is called a *resultant* of β.

The postulates of the system Σ are as follows:[7]

I. If $O(\alpha)$, then $O(\alpha\gamma)$, whatever collection γ may be.

II. If, whatever element b_n of β be considered, $O(\delta b_n)$, and if $O(\beta)$ is also true, then $O(\delta)$.

III. There exists at least one element in Σ.

IV. If an element x of Σ exists, then y exists such that $x \neq y$.

V. Whatever pair (p, q) exists such that $p \neq q$, r exists such that while both $O(rp)$ and $O(rq)$ are false, $O(pqr)$ is true.

VI. If w exists such that $O(\theta w)$, then v also exists such that $O(\theta v)$ and such, too, that whatever element t_n of θ be considered, $O(vwt_n)$.

From these assumptions the whole algebra of logic can be derived in such wise that the system Σ has the order of the totality of logical classes. To see this, we must first define the F-relation. If $O(pqrs\cdots)$ to any number of terms, we may represent the same fact by $F(\bar{p}/qsr\cdots)$, $F(\overline{pr}/qs\cdots)$, $F(r/\overline{pqs}\cdots)$, etc., where the rule for transforming

[7] See p. 367 of the Royce paper.

the O-collection into the corresponding F-collections is that we introduce a bar, separating any one or more elements of the O-collection from the remainder, and then replace each of the elements on one (either) side of the bar by its obverse.[8] Since the order of terms in O-collections is indifferent, terms on the same side of the bar in any F-relation are independent of the particular order in which they are written. Also, it follows immediately from the definition of the relation that $F(pq/\overline{rs})$ and $F(\overline{pq}/rs)$ are equivalent. Where the F-relation holds for three terms, it turns out to be identical with the triadic relation of Kempe, and the Kempean $ac \cdot b$ is thus a special case of the F-relation, namely $F(b/ac)$, or $F(ac/b)$, or $F(a/b\overline{c})$, or $F(\overline{a}/\overline{b}c)$, or $F(b/ca)$, etc., all of which are equivalent. We may, then, define the 'illative' relation—'b is included in c' where b and c are classes, 'b implies c' where b and c are propositions, 'b precedes c,' where b and c are points or terms in one-dimensional array—as the special case of any of the above F-relations in which a is the 'zero element,' or 'null class,' or 'origin.' But these F-relations are equivalent, by definition, to $O(a\overline{b}c)$ and $O(ab\overline{c})$. Hence $b \prec_a c$ may be defined to mean $O(a\overline{b}c)$ and $b \prec c$ to mean $O(o\overline{b}c)$. Thus in terms of the totally symmetrical O-relation, the unsymmetrical, transitive dyadic relation which characterizes both serial order and syllogistic reasoning can be defined.

As is well known, the entire algebra of logic may be derived from a class K, the idea of negation, and the illative relation, hence also in terms of the system Σ and O-collections. The 'zero element' or 'null class' is any arbitrarily chosen member with reference to which all illative relations are supposed to be specified. Such an element o itself bears the illative relation to any other x, since $F(ox/o)$, or $O(o\overline{o}x)$, holds for any element x. The element 1, the 'universe' of the algebra of logic, may then be defined as the negative or obverse of the o chosen. In the system Σ, o and 1 do not differ from any other pair of obverses, apart from the arbitrary choice of a reference element for illative relations. The logical product of two terms, x and y, is then definable as any P such that $F(ox/P)$, $F(oy/P)$, and $F(xy/P)$. The logical sum of x and y is definable as any S such that $F(1x/S)$, $F(1y/S)$, and $F(xy/S)$. P, so defined, will be such that $P \prec x$ and $P \prec y$, while any w such that $w \prec x$ and $w \prec y$ will be also such that $w \prec P$. For S it will be true that $x \prec S$ and $y \prec S$, and any v such that $x \prec v$ and $y \prec v$ is also such that $S \prec v$. S and P are, in fact, the

---

[8] This definition presupposes the proof of the principle that if $O(pqr..)$ then also $O(\overline{pqr}..)$, as well as the proofs which make possible the notation $\overline{pqr}$, explained above. See pp. 367-71 of the Royce paper.

'lower limit' and 'upper limit,' with reference to the chosen zero element, of all the F-resultants of x and y, an F-resultant being any z such that $F(xy/z)$. These definitions for the product and sum of two elements may be extended immediately to any number of elements, or any collection β, if we replace x and y by 'any element of β, however chosen.' The usual laws of the algebra of logic, connecting sums and products, terms and their negatives, and the elements o and 1 may then be verified for the system Σ. This order of logical entities is contained in Σ in an infinite variety of ways, since any pair of obverses may be arbitrarily chosen for 1 and o. F-relations and O-relations, not confined to dyads and triads, *are capable of representing this order in a generalized form.*

There is, moreover, a wealth of order in the system which the algebra of logic, even in terms of any polyadic relation, does not require. It is this difference which renders the system Σ capable of being viewed as a generalized space form.

It follows from postulate V that if $p \neq q$, then there is an element 'between' p and q. The postulate states: Whatever pair (p, q) exists such that $p \neq q$, r also exists such that while both $O(rp)$ and $O(rq)$ are false, $O(pqr)$ is true. $O(pqr)$ or $F(pq/\bar{r})$ gives, by definition of the illative relation, $r \prec_q p$ and $\bar{r} \prec_p q$, or r is 'between' p and q. And $\bar{r}$ must be distinct from p and q both, for otherwise, it follows from the definition of obverses, one of the two $O(\bar{r}p)$ and $O(\bar{r}q)$ will be true. Hence postulate V may be restated in the form: For every pair of distinct elements, there exists an element, distinct from both, between them. It is at once obvious that if the elements be 'points' and $p \prec_o q$ mean that p is between o and q, postulate V requires that the order of points in Σ should be dense in every direction (with reference to every pair of points). It is further clear that if we take any pair of distinct points, o and z, and postulate t between them, we shall be required to postulate also r between o and t, v between t and z, and so on. Owing to the transitivity of the illative relation, we are thus required to postulate for every pair (o, z) an infinite number of elements in the order $o \prec_o r \prec_o t \prec_o v \prec_o z$. Such an ordered collection is continuous. We have already seen that it is dense. It remains to see that it satisfies the requirement that every fundamental segment has a limit. Consider two selections from the collection, $\varkappa$ and λ, such that if k is any element of $\varkappa$, every element j such that $j \prec_o k$ belongs to $\varkappa$, and every element l such that for every element k of $\varkappa$ $l \prec_o k$ is false, belongs to λ. There is, then, an element, call it S, such that for every element k in $\varkappa$ $k \prec_o S$, and if l is any element such that for every element k of $\varkappa$ $k \prec_o l$, then $S \prec_o l$. Such an element S is the 'sum' or 'upper limit' of x, defined above. Hence every fundamental segment has a limit. Any collection thus characterized by a transitive unsymmetrical relation and continuous order deserves to be called a 'line.' Every pair of distinct elements in Σ determines such a line.

For every pair of distinct points, o and q, there exists p such that F (oq/p) and hence $O(oq\bar{p})$. By the definition of the F-relation, if $O(oq\bar{p})$ then $F(\overline{oq}/p)$. Hence if o and q determine a line $o \cdots p \cdots q$, there exists also a line $\bar{o} \cdots \bar{p} \cdots \bar{q}$, or $\bar{q} \cdots \bar{p} \cdots \bar{o}$, in which appear the obverses of all the elements in $o \cdots p \cdots q$. But it also follows from $O(oq\bar{p})$ that $F(o\bar{p}/\bar{q})$, or $q \prec_o \bar{p}$. Thus if $o \cdots l \cdots z$ be any line determined with reference to an 'origin' o, the line containing the obverses of the elements of $o \cdots l \cdots z$ may be determined by reference to the same origin. And if two elements of $o \cdots l \cdots z$, say m and n, are such that $m \prec_o n$, then $\bar{n} \prec_o \bar{m}$. If we further consider the order of elements in both lines $o \cdots l \cdots z$ and $\bar{z} \cdots \bar{l} \cdots \bar{o}$, with reference to the origin o and its obverse $\bar{o}$, the two lines appear as a single line which passes from o to $\bar{o}$ through l, and from $\bar{o}$ back to o through $\bar{l}$. Let m and n be any two elements of $o \cdots l \cdots z$ such that $F(on/m)$. We have $m \prec_o n$. Hence $\bar{n} \prec_o \bar{m}$. But if we have $F(on/m)$, then also $O(on\bar{m})$ and so $F(\bar{o}m/n)$. Hence $n \prec_m \bar{o}$. Thus any two elements, m and n, such that m is between o and n, are also such that n is between m and $\bar{o}$. From the transitivity of the illative relation, $m \prec_o \bar{o}$. But if $m \prec_o \bar{o}$, then from the above $m \prec_o o$. Thus we have the continuous line $o \cdots m \cdots n \cdots \bar{o} \cdots \bar{n}$ $\cdots \bar{m} \cdots o$, or $\bar{o} \cdots \bar{n} \cdots \bar{m} \cdots o \cdots m \cdots n \cdots \bar{o}$, which has so far the character of the projective line with o as origin and $\bar{o}$ the point at infinity. And if m, n, r occur in that order in one 'direction' from the origin, then $\bar{m}, \bar{n}, \bar{r}$ occur in that order in the 'opposite direction' from the origin.

Certain further characteristics of order in the system may be mentioned briefly. In general, lines such as those considered above may 'intersect' any number of times. From the definition of obverses, $O(a\bar{a})$ and $O(c\bar{c})$ always hold. But by postulate I, if $O(a\bar{a})$, then $O(a\bar{a}\bar{p})$, and hence $F(a\bar{a}/p)$, for any element p. Similarly, if $O(c\bar{c})$, then $F(c\bar{c}/p)$. Thus collections consisting of the F-resultants of different pairs may have any number of elements in common. But in terms of such operations as were in question in the definitions of 'sums' and 'products,' sets of resultants may be determined such that they have one and only one element in common. Thus certain selected lines in the system intersect once and once only. There are any number of such sets.

In general, if any pair of elements in a set are obverses of one another, all the other elements of the set will be resultants of this pair, and their entire array will be 'one-dimensional' so far as dimensionality may be attributed to such a collection. The problem of selecting sets suitable for any space form—any n-dimensional array—is the problem of selecting so that O-collections will be excluded. Such sets, containing no obverses, are the 'flat collections' of Kempe. As he pointed out, the excluded obverses will form an exactly similar set, so that 'spaces' come in pairs somewhat suggesting companion hemispheres. In terms of 'flat collections,' one-dimensional, two-dimensional, n-dimensional arrays may be specified in any number of ways.

Once the order of the system Σ is generated in terms of O-relations and F-relations, the determination of such more specialized types of order is a problem of selection only. In the words of Professor Royce, "Wherever a linear series is in question, wherever an origin of coordinates is employed, wherever 'cause and effect,' 'ground and consequence,' orientation in space or direction of tendency in time are in question, the dyadic asymmetrical relations involved are essentially the same as the relation here symbolized by $p \prec_y q$. This expression, then, is due to certain of our best established practical instincts and to some of our best fixed intellectual habits. Yet it is not the only expression for the relations involved. It is in several respects inferior to the more direct expression in terms of O-relations. . . . When, in fact, we attempt to describe the relations of the system Σ merely in terms of the antecedent-consequent relation, we not only limit ourselves to an arbitrary choice of origin, but miss the power to survey at a glance relations of more than a dyadic or triadic character."[9]

With this hasty and fragmentary survey of the system Σ, we may turn to considerations of method. It was suggested in the introduction that the procedure here exemplified differs in notable ways from the method of such studies as those of *Principia Mathematica*. In that work, we are presented at the outset with a simple, though general, order— the order of elementary propositions so related to one another that one is the negative of another, two may be such that at least one of them is true, and so on. In terms of these fundamental relations, more special types of order—various branches of mathematics—are built up by progressive complication. In some respects this is the necessary character of deductive procedures in general; in other respects it is not. In particular, this method differs from that employed by Mr. Kempe and Professor Royce in that *terms*, as well as relations, of later sections are themselves complexes of the relations at first assumed. The complica-

---

[9] Pp. 381–82 of the Royce paper.

tion thus made necessary can hardly be appreciated by those who would regard a number, for instance, as a simple entity. To illustrate: In *Principia Mathematica*, the 'cardinal number' of x is the class of referents of the relation 'similar to' where x is the relatum.[10] The 'class of referents' of any relation R is defined as α such that α is identical with x such that, for some y, x has the relation R to y. 'Relatum' is similarly defined. 'm is identical with n' means that, for any predicative function φ, ψm implies φn. I do not pause upon 'predicative function.' α is 'similar to' β means that, for some one-to-one relation R, α is identical with the class of referents of R and β is identical with the class of relata of R. A 'one-to-one' relation is a relation S such that the class of referents of S is contained in 1 and the class of relata of S is contained in 1.[11] '1' is defined as α such that, for some x, α is identical with *the x*. '*The x*' is my attempt to translate the untranslatable. The attempt to analyze 'is contained in' would require much more space than we can afford. But supposing the analysis complete, we discover that the 'cardinal number of x' is ———, where ——— is the definition first given, with all the terms in it replaced by *their* definition, the terms in these replaced by *their* definition, and so on. All this complexity is internal to the *terms* of arithmetic. *And only when this process is complete* can any properties or relations of 'the cardinal number of x' be demonstrated. An advantage of this method is that the step from one order to another 'based upon it' is always such as to make clear the connection between the two. It preserves automatically the hierarchic arrangement of various departments of exact thinking. The process of developing this hierarchy is tedious and taxes our analytic powers, but there is always the prospect of assured success if we can perform the initial analysis involved in the definitions. But the disadvantages of this complexity can hardly be overemphasized. It is forbidding to those whose interests are simply 'mathematical' or 'scientific' in the ordinary sense. Such a work as *Principia Mathematica* runs great risk of being much referred to, little read, and less understood.

In contrast with such complexity, we have, by the method of Mr. Kempe and Professor Royce, an order completely generated at the start, and such that the various special orders contained in it may be arrived at *simply by selection*. Little or no complication within the

[10] I shall, perhaps, be pardoned for translating the symbolism—provided I do not make mistakes.

[11] More accurately, "every member of the class of referents of S is contained in 1, and every member of the class of relata of S is contained in 1," because all relations are, in *Principia Mathematica*, taken in the abstract.

terms is required. Involved as the structure of the system Σ may seem, it is, by comparison, a marvel of simplicity and compact neatness. With this method, there seems to be no assurance in advance that any hierarchic relations of different orders will be disclosed, but we shall certainly discover, and without difficulty, whatever analogies exist between various orders. Again, this method relies much more upon devices which may be not at all obvious. It may not tax severely the analytic powers, but it is certain to tax the ingenuity.

In another important respect, advantage seems to lie with this method. One would hardly care to invent a new geometry by the hierarchic procedure or expect to discover one by its use. We have to know where we are going or we shall not get there by this road. By contrast, Professor Royce's is the method of the pathfinder. The prospect of the novel is here much greater. The system Σ may—probably does—contain new continents of order whose existence we do not even suspect. And some chance transformation may put us, suddenly and unexpectedly, in possession of such previously unexplored fields.

Which of the two methods will prove, in the end, more powerful, no one can say at present. The whole subject is too new and undeveloped. Certainly it is to be desired that the direct and exploratory method be increasingly made use of, and that the advantages of studying very general types of order, such as the system Σ, be better understood.

3. The Structure of Logic and Its Relation to Other Systems

There are, in general, three types of logical theory: (1) The view which treats logic as formal and at the same time as concerned with the actual modes of right thinking. Traditional logic is of this type. (2) The view which regards logic as concerned with the actual processes of right thinking, and *for that reason* repudiates the formalistic conception of logic as inadequate. The so-called "modern logic" illustrates this type. (3) The view which treats logic as formal and renounces all attempts to portray the actual psychological processes which lead to the discovery of truth. Recent mathematical logic—what Mr. E. G. Spaulding has called the "new logic"—belongs to this type.

The critical comparison of these three theories is an important and interesting topic, but it cannot be accomplished in a short paper. Instead, we shall here take the third type of view as our point of departure, and proceed to certain consequences of it which concern the application of logic to more general problems.

From the present point of view, then, logic does not have to do with the modes of reasoning, either actual or ideal, but only with *criteria* of validity in inference—or, viewed in another way, with the fundamental types of order. It is related to our thought processes somewhat as the tests of an artistic masterpiece might be related to the psychology of genius. We throw our ideas into the deductive forms for the sake of testing their consistency; we seldom do or can make use of them in the actual constructive process of thinking.

No criticism is here implied of any investigation of those thought-processes which normally lead to correct results. When the coincidence of forms of thought with modes of logic is given up, the portrayal of the normal or typical successful thought-process is no less important for being separated from logic. The "new" logicians can recognize the significance of this problem, set by the "modern" logicians, even if the "modern" logicians refuse to return the compliment. The insistence is only upon the separation of questions of psychology from questions of validity.

Again, the new logic regards the deductive system not as a method of proving truth so much as a method of presenting results and estab-

Read, with omissions, at the twentieth meeting of the American Philosophical Association, at Columbia University, December 29, 1920. Reprinted by permission from *The Journal of Philosophy*, Vol. XVIII (1921), No. 19, pp. 505–16.

lishing relations. The most successful logical structures which thought has produced are the systems of deductive mathematics. The illusion that such systems are demonstrations of complex facts from simple and self-evident axioms was dispelled by non-Euclidean geometry and investigations of the infinite. In modern developments, the selection of primitive propositions is governed solely by their deductive power and simplicity and by the system which is to be developed. Such postulates are no more evident or certain than theorems. Frequently they are less so. *Principia Mathematica* triumphantly demonstrates on page 83 of volume II that $m + n = n + m$, but some of its postulates are fairly dubious (the "axiom of reducibility" for example). It is as much the assumptions which are verified by the theorems as the reverse. Or, more accurately, it is the internal order of the system and its *general* conformity to fact which helps to verify any particular proposition which might otherwise be in doubt. Such verification—as it is important to note—is always partial and inductive, since it is possible that another deductive system, with slightly different and equally acceptable assumptions, may contain all the propositions observed to conform to fact and exclude those which are in doubt. The more or less deductive developments of "Newtonian" and relativity physical theory may serve as an illustration.

It is an important consequence of this view that the attempt to establish incontrovertible truth by deductive procedures is nugatory. The traditional rationalistic conception that metaphysical first principles can be shown to be logically necessary, or that what is logically prior is more certain or self-evident, is a conception to which the actual structure of logical systems lends no support. In genuinely rigorous deductive systems, "logically prior" means only "deductively more powerful" or "simpler." The supposed necessity of presuppositions most frequently turns out to be nothing more significant than lack of imagination and ingenuity. And in the remaining cases, that which is presupposed is not, by that fact, proved true. The plurality of possible beginnings for the same system, and the plurality of equally cogent systems which may contain the *same* body of already verified propositions but differ in *what else* they include, dispel the notion of indispensability or peculiar importance in that which is logically prior.

An exception to these strictures will probably be urged for the fundamental principles of logic itself. The laws of logic—it will be said—are not only presupposed by science and rational investigation in general, but their necessary truth is further attested by the fact that they are implied by the very attempt to negate them. To deny them is to reaffirm them. Here is a veritable foundation stone for the rationalistic procedure. Here is the indubitable basis upon which we can build anew the entire structure of exact science, and perhaps eventually of philosophy, assuming only that which no rational mind can deny. Is not this what the most notable examples of the new logic themselves make evident?

But the laws of logic are, in fact, no exception. That the denial of a proposition leads to its reaffirmation by no means establishes its truth. This foundation stone will not bear its own weight, to say nothing of the proposed superstructure. To see that this is so, we must first examine the nature of "reaffirmation through denial." Whoever asserts a self-contradictory proposition does not in one and the same breath affirm and deny the content of his assertion. He affirms it in fact; he denies it by implication only. Or to put it otherwise: he affirms it, and the question whether he also denies it is the question of what his assertion implies. Now the question of what an assertion implies is precisely a question of logic. The content of logic is the principles of inference. Whoever, then, denies a principle of logic may either draw his own inferences according to the principle he denies, or he may consistently avoid that principle in deriving his conclusions. If one deny a principle of inference, but inadvertently reintroduce it in drawing conclusions from his statement, he will indeed find that he has contradicted himself and admitted what originally he denied. But if he denies a principle of inference and consistently reasons in accordance with his own statement, he need incur no self-contradiction whatever.

It is a fact that for one who stands *within* a given system of logic, the denial of one of its principles will imply the principle itself. But this signifies nothing more profound than the fact that deductions *in* logic are inevitably circular.[1] In deducing our theorems of logic, we must make use of the very principles which the deduction is supposed to demonstrate. If, then, I use "bad" logical premises but "good" logical reasoning, I shall contradict myself, quite as surely as if I use two premises which are mutually inconsistent. Perhaps an example here will be of assistance. Take the law of contradiction in the form "That x is A and x is not A, is false." Its contradictory will be, "x is A and x is not A." Let us take this last statement as a preimse and draw the inferences from it.

(1) "x is A and x is not A" implies its latter half, "x is not A."

(2) "x is not A" implies "It is false that x is A."

(3) "It is false that x is A" implies "That x is A and x is not A, is

---

[1] Omitting from consideration the development of logic, as a purely abstract system, by the "operational" instead of the "postulatory" method. These omitted considerations serve to strengthen, not to weaken, what we here set forth.

false." (Just as " 'Today is Monday' is false" implies "That today is Monday and it is raining, is false.") Thus from the denial of the law of contradiction, we have deduced the law of contradiction itself. But we have done so only because, though denying it in the premise, we have reintroduced it in step (2) of the reasoning. If we had, consistently with the premise, refused to take step (2), we should never have got any such conclusion.

Every good or correct logic, then, will be such that its principles are undeniable without contradiction; the denial of any one of them leads to formal inconsistency. But this is true only because so long as we remain *within* our system of logic, we shall use the very principle in question in drawing inferences from the denial of it, and thus beg the question of its truth.

A *good* logic *must* be circular. But what should lead anyone to suppose that this character belongs exclusively to systems of *good* logic? Apparently those who set store by the "reaffirmation through denial" have committed the fallacy of illicit conversion; they have reasoned: "A logic whose principles are true will give their reaffirmation through denial. Therefore, whatever principles meet this test must be true."

All logic and pseudo-logic is similarly circular. A little ingenuity suffices to construct a bad logic in which, reasoning badly according to our bad principles, we always get consistently bad results. And if we deny one of these principles, still by sticking to our bad method of reasoning, we can reaffirm the bad principle in conclusion.[2] Since a bad

---

[2] One family of such systems—consistent in their own terms, and such that the denial of any principle leads to its reaffirmation as a consequence—is determined by the presence in the system of the proposition

$$q < [p < (p < q)]$$

where p, q, etc. are propositions, and $p < q$ represents "p implies q," or "if p is asserted, q may be asserted." This proposition allows of two distinct meanings of $p < q$, neither of which coincides with the usual one; and the properties of this relation may be further specified in a variety of ways. *Some* of the systems in this family might be regarded as "good" logic, but most of them are "bad." Such a "bad" logic may be developed logistically from the following formal postulates:

A. $-(-p) = p$ (Def. of $-p$, the denial of p)
B. $-(p < -p)$
C. $(p < q) < (-q < -p)$
D. $[p < (q < r)] < [q < (p < r)]$
E. $(q < r) < [(p < q) < (p < r)]$
F. $(p < q) < (-p < -q)$

Postulate F is obviously false as a general law of implication. It is interesting that postulate B seems to exclude the possibility that any proposition should lead to its own denial as a consequence, yet if P be any principle of the system, we can prove that $-P < (-P < P)$. Hence the assertion of $-P$ leads to the assertion $(-P < P)$.

logic, whose principles are false, may still be such that the denial of any one of these principles will lead to its reaffirmation, it follows that the test of "reaffirmation through denial" does not, in logic, prove the truth of the principle thus reaffirmed.

It should be added, to avoid misunderstanding, that, in spite of what has just been said, the test of self-criticism or circularity is a valuable test of any deductive development of logic. That the principles proved are precisely the principles used in the demonstration of them is here a matter for congratulation. That the method of our proof coincides with the result of it is a test of both method and result. It is not a test of truth, however; it is a test of formal or methodological consistency. The error of taking self-criticism to be a test of logical *truth* lies in overlooking the fact that a thoroughly false logic may still possess this merely methodological consistency.

One further bit of explanation seems required also. We do not mean to say that there are no necessary propositions. Whoever takes a given logic to be true will find its principles undeniable without contradiction (i.e., in his logic) and therefore necessary. Some logic is true, and hence some logical principles are necessary. The point is simply that the truths of logic are not *proved* by any such procedure—since, as proof, it always begs the question. The basic necessities cannot be proved but only recognized or assumed—and they are assumed at the risk of error.

This disposes of "reaffirmation through denial" as a test of logical truth sufficient to establish first premises. But it may still be questioned whether the test has not valuable applications outside logic altogether. One may admit its insufficiency to establish the truth of a logical principle, should that logical principle really be in doubt; but one may still urge that, once the principles of logic have been recognized and accepted, this test of reaffirmation through denial becomes applicable outside the field of logic, and that, furthermore, the use of the test outside logic does not involve any circularity.

The answer is that there are, in fact, necessary and self-contradictory propositions which are not of logical import, and that the test in question would be entirely legitimate and final here if it were not for the unfortunate circumstance that whatever is taken to be thus established will be found in each instance either to have been already assumed or not to be really demonstrated. Any case in which this test is supposedly used to establish truth should be subject to close scrutiny; there is always a colored gentleman in the woodpile. Indeed, the fallacies involved in current examples of the reaffirmed-through-denial and the self-contradictory are so simple as hardly to need pointing out.

For example, the fallacy of arguing from the undeniable existence of thinking to the self which does the thinking vitiates Descartes' use of the "I think." But quite apart from that, the man who should assert "I am not thinking," so far from contradicting himself, would give the best possible evidence of the truth of his statement. The proposition "I am not thinking" does not imply "I am thinking." It may be that the attitude of will which we suppose to underlie the making of *any* assertion is such as to be incompatible with the admission "I am not thinking," so that we may be sure that whoever could make such a statement would find himself at cross purposes. But the reason for this is contained neither in the proposition nor in any implication of it. There is here no logical inconsistency whatever.

Again, it is said that the statement "There are no propositions" is self-contradictory—because it is itself a proposition. So far from being self-contradictory, it is quite plausible. There are important considerations which point to the conclusion that the idea of a proposition is one which can never be exemplified in human speech or thought—that "proposition" is a sort of ideal like the absolute good. Also, we may note in passing that Mr. Russell, who admits the existence of propositions, would deny that "There are no propositions" is itself a proposition. But suppose we forget all this, and agree that it is a proposition. Still it is not self-contradictory. It *is* a proposition—we agree—but it neither states nor implies that it is a proposition. A proposition does not assert its own existence any more than a bar of pig-iron asserts its own existence. What a proposition asserts is its *content*. Moreover, even if it *did* imply its own existence, it would not serve as an example of "reaffirmation through denial" proving new truth. For whoever assumes that "There are no propositions" is itself a proposition has assumed already that there are propositions and that this one is false. But if one does *not* assume that "There are no propositions" is itself a proposition, then its implication of its own existence would not be the implication that *a proposition* exists, and no contradiction would develop.

These two examples are typical. There *are* necessary propositions, and some of them can be proved—from other necessary propositions as premises—but they cannot be proved by being implied by their own denial. Without qualification, nothing can be shown to be so implied unless it is already assumed. The use of reaffirmation through denial is never legitimate as demonstration of new truth, though it *is* legitimate, and frequently valuable, as a means of pointing out inconsistency of assumption.

Questions of logical priority are often confused by use of the term "presuppose." This word has no single meaning, but it is commonly used to designate what is logically prior with the added thought that it is also necessary. Correctly speaking, what is logically prior to X will imply X, but it will not, in general, be implied by X. In the language of mathematics, if A is logically prior to B, then A must be a sufficient condition of B or at least one of a sufficient set of conditions; but "sufficient condition" must not be confused with "necessary condition."

Frequently, there is a concealed argument from the particular to the general in the appeal to "presupposition." Physics presupposes mathematics in the sense that physics cannot be developed without mathematics, while mathematics contains no necessary reference to physics. And in the same sense all the special sciences presuppose logic. But if what is presupposed in this sense be regarded as thereby established or proved necessary, the fallacy involved is easily detected. If I assert that two feet and two feet are four feet, I do not thereby commit myself to the proposition that $2 + 2 = 4$. It is required only that this should be true of linear measure. Gases under pressure or living organisms might—for all that is here in question—be governed by very different mathematical laws. The particular fact does not even require that there should be *any* general laws of mathematics. There can be little doubt that this fallacy has played its part in the traditional *a priori*. Presuppositions, so called, are always general in their import. The facts that presuppose them are particulars. Now A is not a necessary condition of B unless "A is false" implies "B is false," i.e., unless B implies A. *No general principle is a necessary condition of any particular fact or assertion unless the particular fact or assertion implies the general principle.*[3] And even if this should be the case, it would be the particular and not the general which was, so far, logically prior and the original premise.

If we avoid this fallacy and take "A presupposes B" to mean "A is a necessary condition of B," i.e., "B implies A," then we should be so

---

[3] If I am not mistaken, there is such a class of general principles which are genuinely implied by all subsumed particulars—the laws of logic. This depends, however, upon a meaning of "implies" which cannot here be taken for granted. Further, the discussion of this class of "necessary presuppositions" would alter nothing which precedes, since these presuppositions cannot be *proved* from the fact that they are thus universally implied. The reason is obvious: they would have to be first assumed in order to provide the demonstration itself. They are "presupposed" in exactly the same sense that they are "necessary"—that is, only in the system in which they are *first assumed*.

cluttered up with presuppositions that the fine glamour of the word would be wholly lost. Presuppositions would be truly necessary conditions—that is, relatively necessary—but instead of being first facts they would be last facts, or later facts, and would ordinarily rest upon all sorts of assumptions. Their necessity would ordinarily be whatever necessity had already been established for the fact which presupposed them—that and nothing more.

There are two further meanings of "presupposition"[4]—two which differ from the previous ones by affording some ground for the metaphysical respect in which presuppositions have been held. "Presupposition" may be taken in the literal meaning of "earlier assumption." Mathematics truly stands to the laws of physics in this relation, and logic to all the special sciences. So understood, a presupposition is logically prior. But the idea of necessity is given up. Where the body of facts which such a presupposition implies is considerable and well established, and there are no implications of it which are known to be false, the presupposition gains that kind of verification which particulars can give to general principles—that is, the partial and inductive verification of it as an original hypothesis.

The one remaining meaning which has been referred to attaches to "presupposition" a significance which is psychological rather than logical. It may be maintained that certain general laws are required, not in the sense of being logically inescapable, but in the sense that they are *necessarily assumed* by every rational mind. It seems likely that historical rationalism has regarded the fundamental necessities as psychological in precisely this sense. If there are universal presuppositions in this sense, their necessity is simply the necessity which a rational being recognizes in the criteria of his own rationality. So viewed, the crux of the question concerns the existence or non-existence of such universality of rational intent.

The discussion of this question is not strictly required for our point, because what is necessarily assumed is confessedly such that its necessity is incapable of demonstration. But it may be of value to indicate briefly a point of view which is compatible with what precedes, and to suggest some of the reasons for it.

If there are any such universal principles of rational activity, we should certainly expect to find them exemplified in logic, since inference is the very archetype and exemplar of rational action in general.

---

[4] I omit from consideration a meaning which Mr. Spaulding has given—"*p* presupposes *q* when '*p* implies *q*' implies '*q* implies *p*' "—because I have never been able to exemplify it. One comment may be made: if '*p* implies *q*' implies '*q* implies *p*,' then *p* and *q* are equivalent propositions, and hence *equally* necessary.

If there is any universality of rational intent, it will most clearly exhibit itself in a common logical sense.

Now whoever enters a discussion, pragmatically assumes that the logical sense of those engaged is the same with his. The pursuit of common enterprises, regarded as rational, rests at bottom upon a similar assumption. But in making this assumption—as we are frequently aware—we take a certain risk. In the interest of our rational enterprise we must take this risk. The principles of rationality—in logic as well as in ethics, jurisprudence, and politics—are not empirical facts but social demands. They are ideals; and ideals are things which do not exist as empirical facts. They do not exist even as universality of intent. The only common ideal is the ideal of unanimity—the demand of each that all shall agree with him. And this is as true in logic as in other matters. The facts of social life evidence a fairly general unanimity about the criteria of valid inference. But precisely where we should hope to find this unanimity complete—that is, amongst students of logic—it is, in fact, most notably and lamentably absent. The ideal of a universal logical sense is one strongly demanded by its importance to all social enterprises, and is more closely approximated in fact than most of our ideals. But sticking to facts, in the spirit of facts, we are obliged to admit that it does not completely exist and probably never will. It is easy to beg the question by defining "rationality" in one's own terms. But that can lead only to the familiar conclusion, "All the world is strange save thee and me—and thee's a little strange." With respect to ideals, we all of us stand in the egocentric predicament; we can only assert our own and hope for agreement.

The whole development of the last quarter-century goes to enforce the fact that no deductive system, logic itself included, can justly claim to be demonstration of certain truth from indispensable first principles. That is not what a deductive system is. Instead, as has been said, it is simply the orderly exhibition of certain important relations *amongst* facts or propositions. Whatever verification it affords extends quite as much and quite as simply to premises or assumptions as to conclusions. Such verification can never be complete or final except for those who are already determined to accept what the system sets forth as absolute truth.

It may seem to some that what the preceding discussion has chiefly demonstrated is the unimportance of deduction in general and the new logic in particular. Such a conclusion would be hasty. What the new logic is, in fact, capable of revealing is the existence of a new method for philosophy—or a new significance for the old deductive procedure—which has not yet been sufficiently recognized and exploited. It offers the deductive procedure *not as a method of proof but a method of analysis*. Instead of taking the field of arithmetic, or of logic, etc., as one in which indispensable premises are to lead to previously uncertain or undiscovered conclusions by a process of demonstration, it takes the generally accepted facts of arithmetic, or of logic, as a problem for analysis and orderly arrangement. In the process of making such an analysis and reconstructing our facts upon the basis of its results, we may—and most frequently do—come upon previously unsuspected facts or principles which are required by those more commonly recognized. And we may also discover reasons for discarding some conceptions previously accepted. But in general we accept the results of previous experience; the need is not so much to substantiate as to understand those results. For example, long before Dedekind and Cantor, it was sufficiently clear that the *use* of irrationals by mathematicians was a valid one. And the propositions stating their properties in use and their merely functional relations to other numbers were fairly well established. What was *not* clear was the *nature* of the irrationals. The problem was, as Dedekind's title puts it, *"Was sind und was sollen die Zahlen?"*

Similarly, the point of *Principia Mathematica* is not to prove that $m + n = n + m$ and $2 \times 2 = 4$, but to discover the nature of the various types of numbers, to indicate by its orderly development their relation to the more general categories of logic, to investigate the structure of the field of the various mathematical relations, to segregate those propositions which require more than purely logical assumptions, and to state those assumptions most simply and precisely.

Mr. Whitehead's recent book, *Principles of Natural Knowledge*, extends this procedure to the field of fundamental physical concepts. Although this development does not have the character of formal deduction, yet whoever reads it with care and compares it with the earlier study, *Mathematical Concepts of the Physical World*, will discover in it another exemplification of this method of deductive analysis. Here too, we have no *demonstration* of the facts of nature, but an analysis of the real meanings of such familiar terms as "moment," "duration," "point," "motion," "location," "coexistent," and "sequent." The point is not in the corroboration of proximate physical facts. So viewed, the book might amount to the proof that one and one make two in the physical world, that there are events and things, that the horse can run and the cat can really see. Its significance lies rather in that combination of insight and ingenuity with which proximate facts are analyzed, and the fundamental categories of physical science and our common-sense dealings with the external world are cleared of confusion and connected in an orderly way. By such analysis, Mr. Whitehead provides a reasonable basis for accepted fact, but a basis which still is to be regarded as verified by its logical consequences rather than as verifying such consequences.

Whenever our knowledge of a body of facts approaches that completeness which makes it possible, the deductive development of those facts both serves to present them in the most economical way and provides the best possible understanding of their nature. It is by their orderly connection and their common derivation from a few simple ideas that *explanation* of them is afforded. The claim of uniqueness or exclusive truth for such explanation is commonly unwarranted. The same facts may admit of various explanations, from different points of view, i.e., based upon different fundamental categories.

The use of this method has been coupled, most frequently, with a realistic philosophy. But it does not require the more general realistic position. It dictates no metaphysics, and comports also with idealism or pragmatism. The prominence which it gives to such criteria as simplicity and sufficiency, and the emphasis upon plurality of possible developments, are suggestive of pragmatism. The part played by internal consistency, and the verification of particulars through their relation to a systematic whole, emphasize conceptions which are prominent in idealism. It can even be claimed, of course, that the significance here given to the deductive system is essentially the same with that of historic idealism—that the acceptance of the facts of science and common experience and the discovery of more fundamental truths by making of these a problem in explanation is exactly what Kant and his successors accomplished. The question how far such a claim is warranted need not here concern us. It is complicated by the fact that the so-called deductions of the post-Kantians are formally defective, that idealism has usually insisted upon a psychological conception of logic, and by the occurrence in some idealistic arguments of the fallacies of presupposition which have been mentioned. Our only concern will be to point out that the claim of indispensability for a single set of first principles, or of exclusive truth for one method of analysis—the idea of the traditional *a priori*—is a claim which finds no place in the newer method and no justification in the logic which it applies.

To be sure, it is reasonable to suppose that as deductive analysis conquers successively larger and more varied fields of fact and brings these special fields into consonance by explanations of a higher order, the number of possible modes of development will be restricted. Perhaps finally, when human wisdom shall be summed up in an all-embracing and systematic deduction of everything, only one such analysis will be found possible and adequate. But an eventuality so remote does not warrant serious consideration.

It is just in the notion that the most general questions are presently capable of unique solution by a deductive procedure that traditional rationalism commits its glaring error. The fact is, of course, that the method is more applicable to subordinate questions than to such general problems. It is only when our knowledge of proximate facts becomes fairly comprehensive, detailed, and exact, that deductive analysis is capable of rendering valuable service. But it is also just to remark that it is precisely where no such procedure is applicable that the results of philosophic investigation are least subject to logical criteria and, consequently, most liable to error. The most general problems of philosophy are a field for speculation rather than proof. Yet even here, the mental habit which this method enforces—the search for explanation through analysis and open-minded consideration of alternative possibilities—has a value which should not be disregarded.

4. Facts, Systems, and the Unity of the World

The purely logical approach to metaphysical problems is somewhat out of fashion. High *a priori* grounds and necessary being are threatened with banishment. Yet metaphysics is relatively little concerned with the particular, and there is a considerable portion of it which has to do only with what would be true of any world which is logically conceivable. The issues of pluralism or monism, internal and external relations, the character of the individual, the relation of datum and object, and the nature of truth—all turn upon such considerations. Moreover, the advances of logic in recent years, especially with reference to the structure of systems, is capable of shedding new light on these problems: and there is one logical method of attacking them which has never been properly exploited. It is the purpose of this paper to illustrate that method by applying it to one of the central problems of metaphysics, the problem of the unity of the world. As we shall see, a perfectly definite answer can thus be given to the question whether and in what sense reality is one or many, and the considerations which afford this answer are unusually free from doubt.

Most metaphysical studies have begun by taking the world as constituted of objects or individual things. Undoubtedly the world is such an array of objects, of some sort or other. But this approach to the problem is inauspicious for two reasons: first, because no object is or can be exhaustively known, and second, because this procedure immediately involves us in questions about the relations of objects, which are highly complex and divert the discussion promptly to subordinate issues.

It is equally true that the world is a system of facts, taking "fact" to indicate that which a proposition (some actual or possible proposition) denotes or asserts. That the world can be exhaustively construed as an array of such facts follows from this: if there were any phase, part, or aspect of the real not comprised in some fact, then the real would contain what could not be stated or asserted, and hence could neither be known nor imagined, guessed at nor inquired about. So far at least as the real is intelligible, it is constituted of facts and their relations. In the array of all facts, objects and their relations will be comprehended, just as all facts would be determined in the array of objects. Hence

Reprinted by permission from *The Journal of Philosophy*, Vol. XX (1923), No. 6, pp. 141–51.

either of these methods must lead to the same results in the end. But the approach through facts may succeed where the other fails because of the simpler relation of fact to knowledge. The *object* always transcends our particular knowledge or judgment—as the whole transcends the part, or the real transcends the apparent, or as the complex structure transcends its simpler and more superficial elements. But the *fact* is, by its very nature, the unit of knowledge. It represents exactly that which thought can surely grasp in judgment and express in a proposition, that which our knowledge can completely possess or surround. Moreover, the relations of facts are simpler to deal with because they are at once the relations treated by the logic of propositions : facts may imply one another, as propositions imply one another, and facts are compatible or incompatible, as are the propositions which express them. Such relations are comparatively simple in type, and we possess the technique adequate to deal with them.

But the logic of facts is hampered at the outset by a difficulty of terminology. Ordinarily the word "fact" is restricted to that which a *true* proposition denotes. But in addition to the form of words which asserts or means, there is that which is asserted or meant, as much when the statement is false as when it is true. And lacking some word to indicate this objective or designatum of a proposition, without respect to its truth or falsity, there are certain problems which it is difficult to discuss at all. Let us, then, stretch the word "fact" to this meaning, by omitting its usual connotation of truth, and intend by it simply what a proposition—some proposition—asserts. When it is desirable to distinguish what is denoted by true propositions exclusively, we may speak of "actual facts." This is not to assign to "unreal facts" any dubious metaphysical status ; it is merely a convenience of language. Just as it is immaterial whether we say that "Kilkenny cat" denotes no object or that what it denotes is unreal, so it is merely a question of propriety or convention whether we shall say that "All the world is apple pie" asserts what is not a fact or that the fact which it asserts is non-actual. The second choice of language is the more convenient because the logical relations of facts are unaltered by their actuality or non-actuality, just as the logical relations of propositions are unaffected by their truth or falsity.[1]

---

[1] If space and continuity permitted, it would be in place here to discuss the various types of fact, particularly positive and negative (which does not coincide with the distinction of affirmative and negative propositions), as well as the relations of facts to "things" and to "events." But there is no horrid mystery in these matters if we do not go about it to make one.

The properties of facts which are metaphysically important are all due to their interrelation in systems, or complexes which possess some definite structure. The notion of system, especially in its connection with knowledge and truth and with the nature of the real, has played a most important role in philosophy. "Systematic unity," "organization," "deductive system," "coherence"—the significance of such conceptions requires no comment. But the notion of "system" ("deductive system" excepted) has usually been very vague, and when definite, highly special or complicated. For the most important metaphysical consequences, we find that the simplest and most comprehensive meaning of "system" is the only one which is required. In the meaning which we shall assign, any set of facts constitutes a system if it meets the following requirements:

(1) If A is a fact of a given system—call it Σ—and A is inconsistent or incompatible with B, then B is not in Σ.

(2) If C is in Σ, and C requires or implies D, then D also is in Σ.[2]

(3) If E and F are facts in Σ, then Σ contains also the joint-fact EF. This third condition is relatively unimportant; it is the correlate of the obvious truth that whenever two propositions are asserted separately, the proposition which states both together can be asserted.[3]

Systems are, then, sets of mutually consistent facts such that whatever system contains a given fact will contain also all the consequences of that fact. No idea of order or arrangement is here intended, and it is not essential that such systems be constructed or constituted by any mental operation. The logical relations of facts exist whether anyone notes those relations or not; that A is consistent with B, or follows from B, is something which we do not create, but discover.

To each system of facts will correspond the system of the propositions which assert those facts. Deductive systems will be amongst those thus defined; indeed, systems in general will correspond exactly with all the different sets of propositions which could be generated by deduction (in each case from a set of consistent assumptions) if the assumptions of a system were allowed to be as numerous as you please. But there are other systems than those which would ordinarily be thought of as deductive. It is a significant consideration that any part of our

[2] "Implies" is here used in its ordinary meaning, which the writer has elsewhere discussed as "strict implication." A is "inconsistent" or "incompatible" with B if A implies the falsity of B or B the falsity of A.

[3] The insertion of this condition is necessary only because A and B together may imply C when neither alone implies C. A system will contain not only the logical consequences of each of its facts separately, but also the consequences of any combination of them.

knowledge, as well as our knowledge as a whole, must determine such a system. The *logical* conditions of truth are here summed up. What we truly know of physics, of space, of biological forms, or of the world altogether will determine a system. But we must be careful here to say "determine" and not "constitute." We are never aware of all the logical consequences of what we know · our knowledge fixates a whole system of facts but can not possibly exhaust it.

We know a great deal about the properties of systems in general, largely because deductive systems are special cases which are included. Some of these characteristics can be pointed out without lengthy discussion. First, there is more than one such system. Second, one system may contain another; all the propositions or facts of one may belong also to the other. (As the term is here used, however, two systems consisting throughout of identical facts will be identical systems, regardless of any notion of deductive order.) Third, two systems may be such that they have some facts in common, although the further facts in each are incompatible or inconsistent with those of the other. For example, Euclidean and a non-Euclidean geometry will have all those propositions in common which follow from their postulates without the parallel-postulate, or postulate concerning coplanars.[4] But in two such geometries the postulate concerning coplanars, and most of the propositions which follow from it, are different in the two systems, and those of the one are incompatible with those of the other. From these commonplaces, which need no demonstration, follow consequences of the first importance, in particular that the same fact A may be consistent both with another, B, and with the contradictory of B. Some facts are independent even though they should be jointly true. This is often overlooked or even denied in metaphysics.

However, the existence of facts which are independent of given systems does not immediately settle the question of the structure of reality, because it may be claimed—and often is claimed—that this independence is due to the limited character of the system: that the plurality of systems and independence of facts disappears when we consider reality as a whole, and that as the organization of actual facts becomes more and more adequate we approach a single unitary system all of whose parts stand in relations of rigid necessity and such that no actual fact can be independent of it. It is precisely this notion that every fact of our world is somehow determined by every other—that reality has no independent parts—which we find to be false. But admittedly, any con-

---

[4] I.e., when geometry is taken in the concrete, as the truth about space, and identical terms have the same definitive meaning.

ceivable world will be more complex than most systems, and it will be infinitely more complex than those systems, such as geometries, which have hitherto been adequately investigated. Hence, to elucidate the issues of our problem, we must consider the structure of "possible worlds."

Any conceivable world is a system, since all its facts must be mutually consistent, and any consequence of facts in it will also be a fact in it. But not every system is a world. If we speak of facts which are asserted by propositions which contradict one another as "contradictory facts," the difference between a world and a system which is not a world lies in this, that a system may omit both a fact and its contradictory—as a geometry omits both the existence of the color blue and anything contrary to it—while a world must contain one or other of every contradictory pair. The law of contradiction holds of a system, but the law of the excluded middle does not. A world, however, must satisfy both these laws; it must be such that every proposition is either definitely true or definitely false of it. In other words, a system which is not a world (a mathematical system, for example) will be indeterminate in ways which no possible world could be.

We may, then, call any set of facts a "possible world" if it meets the following requirements:

(I) If A is a fact of a given world—call it Ω—and A is incompatible with B, then B is not in Ω.

(II) If C is not in Ω, then the contradictory of C is in Ω.

(III) If E and F are in Ω, then Ω contains also the joint-fact EF. Conditions (I) and (III) for worlds are identical with (1) and (3) for systems, but condition (II) is more comprehensive than (2), which follows from (I) and (II), as the reader will readily see.

It is obvious that a given system may be contained in more than one possible world. This relation of a system to any world which includes it is the more important because it is the relation of knowledge to reality. The problem of knowledge (the practical, not the epistemological problem) turns largely upon this, that the facts which are accepted as belonging to the actual world, and thus constitute our knowledge at any given moment, determine a system (if we are fortunate enough to avoid inconsistency), but we can hardly suppose that they determine a world. The advance of empirical knowledge enlarges our system by the addition of new facts which may be independent of previous knowledge, and we approach the world of reality by means of such an ever-growing system. But we never reach the point of discovering *which* of various equally possible completions of our system of known facts the actual world is. So far as we can determine, *the real world is always merely one of many which must be viewed as equally possible.*

It is precisely this situation which is reflected in the use of inference. When we infer from our previous experience, instead of turning to new data, we make a psychological addition to our knowledge which is trustworthy simply because the conclusion will be true of *any possible* world which contains the facts stated in the premises. "If *A*, then *B*," may be translated, "Any world in which *A* should be true and *B* false, is impossible," or, "Any possible world which contains *A* must also contain *B*." Where inference is impotent and we wait upon further evidence, the addition to our knowledge which is sought must consist of independent facts, not contained in the system which our knowledge determines.

No one will ever discover all the consequences of what he knows, so that we cannot say offhand whether the system determined by anyone's knowledge is adequate to a world or not. But the supposition that all truth (including details about prehistoric individuals, facts about the invisible stars, etc.) could be determined without further experience or anything beyond the implications of what we already know is a conception so fantastic as hardly to deserve consideration. Certain arguments for metaphysical monism seem to make precisely this claim, but in a form which suggests a confusion of facts with objects. If one say, "The logical consequences of what I now know include all fact and all reality," we must observe the evident ambiguity of the word "what." *What* I know is a real object in all its complexity; what I *know* is merely a limited and superficial set of facts pertaining to this object. If we could know our object completely, it may be that our knowledge would determine all reality—that is another question. The "flower in the crannied wall" or "the bit of chalk I hold in my hand" may be a microcosm of reality; but our facts do not thereby extend to all reality, since they comprise only a few characters of this microcosm. I may be assured that "when I drop this chalk I shake the farthest star," but that does not enable me to calculate the perturbations of Mercury. Our meager knowledge of the individual thing does *not* imply all actual fact; and as for the object, it implies nothing. Only facts and assertions can have implications.

Such arguments, turning upon the relations of objects, have frequently been adduced to prove for the world that kind of unity which makes every part depend upon every other part or upon the whole. And this in turn has been construed to mean that everything in the world is necessarily as it is, and every fact of it a necessary fact. The question of the relations of objects, whether external or internal, we here omit from consideration. But we shall now proceed to demonstrate that, regarded as a complex of facts, the world cannot have this kind of unity. Since the argument is a bit involved, let us outline it in advance: I. If any world is logically conceivable, then more than one is logically conceivable, because (*a*) every self-consistent system must be contained in or "true of" at least one possible world, and (*b*) there are systems, equally self-consistent, which cannot be true of the *same* world. II. Every possible world will contain some facts in common with any other. Hence, III, the actual world contains some facts in common with worlds which are conceivable but not actual. Therefore, IV, reality cannot be such that all its facts are necessary and necessarily related. It is characteristic of the real world to contain facts which are mutually independent or "external."

Consider any system—call it $\Sigma(o)$—and any proposition, p. Either the propositions in $\Sigma(o)$ imply p, or they imply its contradictory, not-p, or they imply neither. In the last case, p is completely independent of $\Sigma(o)$; both p and not-p are compatible with the system as a whole. Hence if $\Sigma(o)$ is self-consistent, then it already contains p, or it contains the denial of p, or either of these may be adjoined to it and the resulting enlarged system will also be self-consistent. Any other proposition, q, will be related to the system $\Sigma(o, p)$ or the system $\Sigma(o, \text{not-}p)$ in precisely similar fashion: if neither q nor not-q is contained in $\Sigma(o, p)$, then the systems $\Sigma(o, p, q)$ and $\Sigma(o, p, \text{not-}q)$ are both self-consistent.

We should like to go on and say: Therefore one or other of every contradictory pair of propositions, neither of which is contained in $\Sigma(o)$, can be adjoined to it, and *the result will describe a possible world of which $\Sigma(o)$ is "true."* That we cannot say this is due to two considerations: first, if p and q are both independent of $\Sigma(o)$ and independent of each other, still q may not be independent of $\Sigma(o, p)$ or $\Sigma(o, \text{not-}p)$. Hence in expanding our system in the direction of a possible world, of which it shall be "true," we can deal with independent propositions only one at a time. And second, the multitude of facts or propositions is such that no one-at-a-time process can ever exhaust them. The collection of all facts has a magnitude at least as great as that of any set of entities whatever—so great that, to put it in paradox, there can be no such number. One of *every* contradictory pair can consistently be adjoined to $\Sigma(o)$, but in such a case this does not mean that one or other of *all* pairs can be so adjoined. However, it does mean that of all the facts that ever will be known, guessed or merely hazarded, doubted or denied or put in question, one or other of all the contradictory pairs belongs together with $\Sigma(o)$ in a self-consistent system. The limitation of our proof is simply the limitation of possible knowledge in general. No conceivable knowledge can ever be adequate to a world: the notion of Reality or The Universe is simply a regulative ideal of reason in the Kantian sense. And our argument *is* sufficient to prove that if there be any self-consistent system which is *not* true of some possible world, then that fact itself is forever beyond all knowledge. In the only sense in which we can speak of a world at all, whether actual or possible, there is a possible world for every self-consistent system.

For greater clarity, we repeat the gist of this in illustration. Let the original system be Riemann's geometry. Either Riemann's geometry contains, when all its implications are developed, the law of gravitation, or it contains the proposition which states the falsity of that law, or this law is completely independent of the system. In the third case, the system is compatible both with the law and with its being false. Supposing that it is thus independent, we may adjoin either the law or its denial to the geometry to form a new system which will also be self-consistent. In precisely the same fashion any other proposition—say the law of Mendelian inheritance—is either contained in this enlarged system, or its denial is contained, or the proposition and the system are mutually independent and either Mendel's law or its denial may consistently be adjoined. Every mentionable proposition can be similarly dealt with. Thus, so far as any conceivable knowledge or guesswork can ever go, Riemann's geometry is true of a logically conceivable world.

If this were not the case, then there must be some proposition, X, such that the statement "Either X is true or X is false" will of itself imply the falsity of the system as a whole, and the system is not self-consistent. A similar remark applies to all the other geometries, interpreted in whatever terms, and to every system whatsoever. So long as we accept the self-consistency of mutually incompatible systems, such as rival geometries, we are bound to maintain that more than one world is logically conceivable. Whoever would deny this may rightfully be challenged to produce the proposition X and prove the inconsistency— the purely logical inconsistency—of all the geometries but one. But as is well known, the correspondences between Riemann's or Lobachevsky's and a modernized Euclid are such that if one fails of self-consistency the other must also.

Second, every world which is logically conceivable will have something in common with every other. For if this were not the case, there could be at most only two such worlds, the world of all the propositions actually true, and the world consisting of the denials of each of these propositions. But the contradictories of true propositions are not all consistent *with each other* and could not describe a possible world. Therefore, either there is only one such world—which has been disproved—or every such world has something in common with every other.

Third, since every world which is logically conceivable has something in common with every other, every world, including the actual one, contains mutually independent parts.[5]

Let the system of propositions common to two possible worlds, Ω_1 and Ω_2, be designated by $\Sigma(\omega_1 \omega_2)$, and let the propositions which are true of Ω_1, but false of Ω_2, be designated by $\Sigma(\omega_1 - \omega_2)$. These two systems are both contained in Ω_1. And no proposition of $\Sigma(\omega_1 - \omega_2)$ follows from the propositions in $\Sigma(\omega_1 \omega_2)$, because in Ω_2 all the propositions of $\Sigma(\omega_1 \omega_2)$ are true, but those of $\Sigma(\omega_1 - \omega_2)$ are false. If we compare Ω_1 and another possible world, Ω_3, we must find similarly that Ω_1 contains an independent part $\Sigma(\omega_1 - \omega_3)$, which is not the same as $\Sigma(\omega_1 - \omega_2)$, for in that case Ω_2 and Ω_3 would be identical.

Thus any possible world—in our illustration Ω_1—must contain independent parts or systems of facts, which will be more or less numerous according to the number of other possible worlds with which it has something in common. Since the number of possible worlds is at least as great as the number of self-consistent and mutually incompatible systems, the structure of any possible world, and hence of ours, can be determined from the number of mutually incompatible systems. If there should be n such systems, then every possible world must be such that it can be divided into independent parts in at least n different ways. And if the number of such systems should exceed 2^n, then every possible world will contain at least $n + 1$ systems each of which is completely independent of all the others. The reasons for these particular mathematical relations may be omitted, since it is sufficient for our present purpose to note that in general the number of independent parts in any possible world must increase as the number of mutually incompatible systems increases.

But we know that there are an *infinite* number of such mutually incompatible systems. To choose the simplest confirmation, Riemann demonstrated that there are an infinite number of geometries, each

---

[5] There is one system which is contained in *every* possible world and hence is not an independent part of any—a consideration which it is not necessary to go into here.

inconsistent, as a complete system, with every other, and every one of them consistent in itself and logically as sound as Euclid. In various other ways also, it might be demonstrated that the number of mutually incompatible systems is infinite. The only question is whether it is simply infinite, like the natural numbers, or an infinity of a higher order. Hence it follows necessarily that reality contains an infinite number of independent parts, or logically independent sets of facts. Such formal demonstration does not make us see *how* this is so (and we hope that no one will attach any esoteric meaning to our procedure), but *that* it is so admits of no rational doubt.

It would be easy, however, to misapprehend the nature of this necessary pluralism. The world is *not* such that, given any one of its facts, all the others are thereby determined. But no matter how numerous the possible worlds may be, any one of them, including the actual, may be a closed system in the sense of having no single fact in it which is not determined by other facts of it. Indeed it is difficult to see how this could fail to be the case. Even relatively simple systems have this character. Identically the same system may be generated by two sets of postulates having no members in common. The postulates of the one set will all follow as theorems from those of the other. Hence in such a system there is no proposition which is not a consequence of other propositions in the system. Yet some of the propositions in it may be independent of others; in particular, each postulate may be independent of the other postulates; and hence some of its propositions may belong also to another system, even though the two systems as a whole are mutually incompatible and each has this "closed" character. Thus nothing in the preceding forbids the notion that the actual world is a very tight system of interlaced facts. On the other hand, that every actual fact depends upon other such facts (as is highly probable) is very far from meaning that all actual facts are "necessary" or their contraries inconceivable. The issues of monism or pluralism have frequently been taken in a somewhat rough and ready fashion. As they are usually stated, the truth lies somewhere between them.

These considerations have an important bearing upon the connection between coherence and truth. "Coherence" is a very vague term. If it be taken to mean the relation between the various parts or members of a system, still that does not cure its vagueness, since this relation may be that of logical consequence or simply the relation of consistency without dependence. Such relations of consistency with, or dependence upon, other accepted facts constitute the only criteria of truth which are available, so long as we do not find or call upon further empirical evidence. And when the various limitations of sense-knowledge are remarked, the importance of these relations is apparent. But compatibility with other facts is only a negative, never a sufficient and determining condition. Even that every fact is implied by others in the system does not determine truth. Each of the facts of Euclidean geometry is coherent with the other facts of it; it follows from these others. Yet that does not serve to verify a single proposition. It does not even mean that Euclidean geometry must be accepted or rejected as a whole. Some portion of Euclid may be true of our space and the rest entirely false. The selection of a set of propositions acceptance of which would commit us to the system as a whole is a very nice matter. And when it is accomplished, we have made a beginning toward splitting up the whole system, in various ways, into sets which can be accepted or rejected independently. Since any of these independent sets or subsystems may belong to or be true of a different possible world, it is obvious to how limited an extent coherence is a sufficient test of truth.

A pluralism of "incoherence" is false, if coherence means consistency. Mutually incompatible propositions *ipso facto* cannot be true of the same world unless that world be alogical—whatever that may mean. But a monism which identifies the necessary with the actual, the actual and the all-possible, is incompatible with conceptions which are logically fundamental.

5. Review of *Principia Mathematica*

In the years since the first edition was published (Vol. I, 1910; II, 1912; III, 1913), the nature of the project undertaken in *Principia Mathematica* has become sufficiently understood. It is the demonstration that pure mathematics is rigorously deducible from correct definitions of its fundamental concepts alone, without other assumptions except such as are sufficient for a logic which provides an adequate canon of proof in general. For the completion of this project, it was necessary not only to dispense with the usual postulates of the various branches of mathematics but also to analyze the basic concepts, usually taken as undefined ideas, in such manner that these could all be defined solely in terms of the initial concepts of logic. That is, all such notions as ordinal and cardinal number (in general), the ordinal and cardinal numbers, $1, 2, 3, \ldots, \omega, \aleph$, etc., the relations $+, \times$, etc., the ideas involved in serial order and in the various types of series, in linear, vector, and angular measure, and so on, must all be defined in terms, eventually, of such concepts as "either-or," "elementary proposition," "negative of," and "propositional function."

This seemingly impossible task was carried out for the fundamental branches, excepting geometry, in the three volumes of the first edition. The fourth volume, on geometry, has not appeared, and probably is no longer to be expected. Although Part VI, in Volume III, covers concepts of quantity and measurement applicable in geometrical branches, it remains a matter of conjecture how far and by what procedures geometrical postulates could have been dispensed with in this fourth volume.

In the new edition, the text of the first edition is reprinted without change, except for the correction of misprints and similar errors. Any other procedure would be most difficult, since it would disturb the whole system of backward references in proofs. Accordingly, the desirable alterations are indicated and discussed in an "Introduction to the Second Edition" and in three appendices to Volume I.

These alterations fall under two heads: economies of procedure which have been proved possible by work in logic done since the first edition, and discussion of a new and less comprehensive assumption in place of the "axiom of reducibility."

Reprinted by permission from *The American Mathematical Monthly*, Vol. XXXV (1928), No. 4, pp. 200–205.

The alterations of the first sort are two: substitution of the Sheffer-Nicod "stroke-function" for other undefined ideas of logic, and elimination of "asserted propositional functions."

In the first edition, the undefined ideas are eight: (1) elementary propositions (those involving no variable or unspecified term) symbolized by $p, q, r, \ldots$, (2) propositional functions (statements involving an undetermined or variable constituent) symbolized by ϕx, $\psi(x, y)$, etc., (3) assertion of a proposition, (4) assertion of a propositional function, (5) negation of a proposition p, symbolized by $\sim p$, (6) disjunction $p \vee q$, meaning exactly "At least one of the two, p and q, is true," (7) the idea "ϕx is true for all values of x," symbolized by (x). ϕx, (8) "ϕx is true for some values of x," symbolized by $(\exists x)$. ϕx. All the logical principles necessary for mathematical proof are derived from seven symbolic postulates in terms of the above, together with certain postulates (which are really principles of logical operation) which cannot be symbolized.

Professor H. M. Sheffer showed[1] that the two undefined ideas, negation and disjunction, can be replaced by one, p/q, meaning "p and q are, one or both, false." (Sheffer, Nicod, and Russell all read this "p and q are incompatible," which is misleading, since obviously two propositions which are both false, or one true and one false, may be compatible or consistent in the ordinary sense. This relation is to "material implication," on which the logic of *Principia Mathematica* is based, as the ordinary meaning of inconsistency is to the "implies" of ordinary inference. If we represent "p materially implies q" by $p \supset q$ and the ordinary meaning of "p implies q" by $p < q$, then

$$(p \supset q) = (p/\sim q) \quad \text{and} \quad (p < q) = \sim (p_0 \sim q),$$

where $p_0\, q$ represents the usual meaning of "p is consistent with q.")

In terms of this stroke-function, the negation of p is definable as p/p, and the disjunction of p and q as $(p/p)/(q/q)$. Following this paper of Sheffer's, Jean Nicod[2] reduced five of the symbolic postulates of *Principia Mathematica* to one:

$$[p/(q/r)]/\{[t/(t/t)]/[(s/q)/((p/s)/(p/s))]\} \, .$$

The rather startling result is the proof that all the propositions of mathematics (unless we must except geometry) can be derived from three symbolic postulates in terms of the idea p/q.

The second economy of procedure results from the recognition that

[1] *Transactions of the American Mathematical Society*, Vol. 14, pp. 481–88.
[2] *Proceedings of the Cambridge Philosophical Society*, Vol. 19, pp. 32–41.

the idea of "asserted propositional function" is unnecessary. In the first edition, a theorem such as $p \supset \sim q . \supset . q \supset \sim p$, "If p implies that q is false, then q implies that p is false," is regarded as a propositional function, since p and q are undetermined or variable. Now propositional functions cannot in general be asserted, being neither true nor false (e.g., "x is a rational fraction" is neither true nor false until the variable x is replaced by some one of its "values"). But certain propositional functions, such as this theorem, *can* be asserted: they are true *formulas*. However, in all such cases the function is assertable only because it holds for all values of its variables. Hence any statement of the form

$$p \supset \sim q . \supset . q \supset \sim p$$

is equivalent to another, of the form

$$(p) : . (q) : p \supset \sim q . \supset . q \supset \sim p ,$$

"for all values of p and all values of q, if p implies that q is false, then q implies that p is false." This last statement is not a propositional function but a proposition, of the general type $(x) \cdot \phi x$. Thus all "asserted propositional functions" are in reality propositions, and any theorem of the first edition, having the form of a function, should be regarded as a proposition asserting this function to hold for all values of its variables.

The recognition of this fact works another improvement, which the book does not note. Since the idea "negation of p" is symbolized by $\sim p$, we ought to be able to express the fact that a deduction-formula (let us say, $p . \supset . p \supset q$) is false by its symbolic negation, $\sim (p . \supset . p \supset q)$. But this is not possible, because $p . \supset . p \supset q$ covers the special case $p . \supset . p \supset p$, which is true. Hence we can assert neither $p . \supset . p \supset q$ nor its symbolic contradictory, which seems incompatible with the principle that one of every pair of contradictory assertions must be true. When $p . \supset . p \supset q$ becomes $(p) : . (q) : p . \supset . p \supset q$, this difficulty disappears, because its contradictory then is

$$(\exists p) : . (\exists q) : \sim (p . \supset . p \supset q) ,$$

"for some values of p and some values of q, $p . \supset . p \supset q$ is false." This last is, of course, true.

The emendation in the above fashion of the logic of elementary propositions, contained in Sections *1 to *5 of the first edition, is very simple. It is merely sketched in the new Introduction. The logic of propositional functions, in terms of the stroke-function, is more involved and also more fundamental. The principles of it, sufficient for all later proofs, are developed in a new Section *8, to replace Section *9 of the first edition. This new section is printed as Appendix A.

The second main novelty of the new edition—limitation of the use of the "axiom of reducibility"—touches one of the most recondite features of *Principia Mathematica*. In ordinary developments of mathematics no need is felt for the axiom of reducibility or any substitute for it, because the existence of classes in general is taken for granted if defining properties of the class can be specified. (Existence of a class does not here mean existence of members of the class: null-classes may "exist".) But the authors desired to avoid such assumption, both because it seemed theoretically doubtful and because it contributed to "vicious-circle fallacies," which are encountered in the theory of assemblages. These are such as Burali-Forti's paradox about the ordinal number of all ordinals, and the paradox of the "least indefinable (transfinite) ordinal." Accordingly, propositions which would ordinarily be interpreted as being about some class are, in *Principia Mathematica*, treated as statements about some propositional function which holds for every member of the class. Thus if ϕx be "x is an ordinal number," any proposition about the class of ordinals is rendered by some statement $f(\phi x)$ about the propositional function ϕx. Moreover, the "theory of types," adopted to avoid the vicious-circle fallacies, restricts the significance of any propositional function to some one type—to individuals, or classes of individuals, or classes of such classes, and so on. The result of these two limitations—the absence of the assumption that classes exist, and the theory of types—is to render it difficult to prove anything about certain legitimate totalities such as all the classes to which a given term belongs, or all the properties of a term. For instance, "All those properties which belong to 1 and are such that if they belong to n then they belong to $n + 1$, are properties of every finite number." The axiom of reducibility was assumed to obviate such difficulties. It has two cases (ed. 1, Vol. I, p. 174):

$$*12 \cdot 1 \vdash : (\exists f) : \phi x . \equiv_x . f!x \quad \text{and}$$
$$*12 \cdot 11 \vdash : (\exists f) : \phi(x,y) . \equiv_{x,y} . f!(x,y) .$$

These differ only in that $*12 \cdot 1$ is for functions of one variable, $*12 \cdot 11$ for functions of two. The first may be read "For any propositional function ϕx, there is some predicative function $f!x$, which is always true when ϕx is true, and false when ϕx is false." A "predicative function," as nearly as can be briefly put, is a single predicate, while the predicate ϕ in the axiom may be complex. Thus what the axiom assumes is that for any compound or complex statement about a term *x*, there is some single predicate which holds when the complex statement is true and fails when it is false. This allows such statements as would ordinarily be made by reference to some totality of classes to which a term belongs (or the totality of properties of the term) without allowing the notion of any totality of propositional functions which the term satisfies. This last kind of totality is what leads to the vicious-circle fallacies and is forbidden by the theory of types.

However, this axiom of reducibility is dubious. Hence the new edition proposes for consideration the substitute assumption that "A [propositional] function can only enter into a proposition through its values" (ed. 2, Appendix C, p. 659). This substitution requires the rewriting of many proofs, particularly those concerning Frege's "ancestral relation" by which the procedure of mathematical induction is shown to be completely deductive. But all the theorems essential to mathematical induction can still be demonstrated; the revision of these proofs is carried out in Appendix B. However, a similar revision for theorems concerning the real numbers and well-ordered series in general is not found possible. "There is, . . . so far as we can discover, no way by which our present primitive propositions can be made adequate to Dedekindian and well-ordered relations. . . . It is upon this that the theory of real numbers rests, real numbers being defined as segments of the series of rationals. . . . If we were to regard as doubtful the proposition that the series of real numbers is Dedekindian, analysis would collapse" (ed. 2, Vol. I, p. xliv).

The real purpose both of the axiom of reducibility and of the proposed substitute is to be able to treat all the propositional functions which figure in mathematics in a manner which would be valid without further assumption if it were established that all such functions can be analyzed into purely logical relations of their ultimate constituents. The difficulty of establishing this, in *Principia Mathematica*, is due, I believe, in part at least, to the preconception that all logical functions are truth-functions—that is, such that their truth or falsity depends solely on the truth or falsity of their terms. (See Appendix C, *passim*.) All the functions of logic are, by the method of *Principia Mathematica*, treated as such truth-functions. For example, the material implication, $p \supset q$, can be defined by the accompanying table, where $+$ represents "true" and $-$

p	q	$p \supset q$
$+$	$+$	$+$
$-$	$+$	$+$
$+$	$-$	$-$
$-$	$-$	$+$

"false." That is, "p materially implies q" fails when p is true and q false, and otherwise holds.

The conception that all mathematics is concerned only with such truth-functions leads to difficulty, because a truth which depends, in any part, upon the *form* of propositions *cannot* be determined in this fashion merely from the truth or falsity of its constituents; while if differences of form are not significant in mathematics, all equivalent propositions will be identical. If, further, logical equivalence means only equivalence of truth-value, this view leads inevitably to the conclusion that there are really only two propositions, one true and one false; and all mathematics will thus collapse into an immense tautology. Essentially this conclusion was accepted by Frege and has been renewed by Wittgenstein; Mr. Russell[3] seems to draw back from it without being willing to abandon the premises which lead to it.

As a fact, I take it, form is of the essence of both logic and mathematics. Logical truth, such as what is ordinarily meant by "q is deducible from p," depends in part upon the form of p and q and cannot be determined from their truth or falsity alone. If I should be correct in this, it is not a matter for surprise if a procedure which depends upon treating all mathematical assertions as logical functions of their constituents, while at the same time holding logical functions to be exclusively truth-functions, should stop short of complete success. Actually, in spite of the fact that the relations assumed as primitive are all truth-functions, the method of this work is largely dependent upon considerations of form and is, I believe, inconsistent with the theoretical conceptions of the nature of mathematics which are expressed in it.

In Volume II, the prefatory statement of symbolic conventions is considerably expanded. In the remainder of the volume, and in Volume III, I do not find any material alterations.

---

[3] I refer to Mr. Russell because he is alone responsible for the revisions of this edition, and because I do not think Mr. Whitehead would subscribe to the content of this Appendix C.

6. Alternative Systems of Logic

From Aristotle down, the laws of logic have been regarded as fixed and archetypal; and as such that they admit of no conceivable alternatives. Often they have been attributed to the structure of the universe or to the nature of human reason; and in general they have been regarded as providing an Archimedean fixed point in the realm of thought. Opinion to this effect still prevails generally, although modern studies in exact logic reveal certain facts in the light of which any such belief becomes highly problematic. For example, in *Principia Mathematica*, the fundamental laws of mathematics are derived from a logic which is distinctly not in accord with traditional Aristotelian conceptions; yet this deduction is notably successful, and certainly could not be called fallacious. There are, moreover, an indefinitely large number of other such non-Aristotelian systems. These differ from one another, and from traditional logic, not in any superficial fashion—as, for example, syllogistic modes differ from those of hypothetical reasoning—but in such wise as to represent different determinations of the fundamental categories of deduction. For instance, the implication-relation of *Principia Mathematica*, Section A, which is made the basis of the deduction, does not permit that any two propositions should be mutually independent (such that neither implies the other); and it permits that two propositions should be consistent (such that neither implies that the other is false) only if both are true. More precisely, it does not allow the ideas of consistency and independence to be significantly applied to propositions. Nor does it allow the modal conceptions, "possible," "impossible," and "necessary," to apply to propositions.

This logic of *Principia* is based upon the fundamental dichotomy of true and false. Recently, Professors Lukasiewicz and Tarski have developed an analogous system, based upon a tripartite division of propositions in general, and resulting in a logic for which the law of the Excluded Middle becomes similarly *non-significant*. They have also indicated a simple rule by which divergent systems of the same general type may be constructed in unlimited variety.[1] Other systems than

Reprinted by permission from *The Monist*, Vol. XLII (1932), No. 4, pp. 481–507.

[1] *"Philosophische Bemerkungen zu mehrwertigen Systemen des Aussagenkalküls," Comptes Rendus des Séances de la Société des Sciences et des Lettres de*

those belonging to the class indicated by these authors can also be developed. And—strangest of all—every one of these systems is capable of being interpreted in such a way that all its laws are true, and represent logical principles in an easily definable and quite proper sense. It is not the case that if one such system is true, then all the others must be false: nevertheless they are alternatives, in the sense that if one such system be taken as the canon of deduction—as it can be—then principles belonging to other systems must be abandoned as inapplicable, inexpressible, or non-significant. The non-significance of the "consistency," "independence," "necessity," etc., of propositions, in the logic of *Principia*, is a case in point.

Such logistic systems are not mere playthings for an idle hour. The plurality and variety of them, the facts of their general structure, and their relation to one another must inevitably result in problems of the first magnitude concerning the nature of logical truth and the character of inference. For example, it can be demonstrated beyond all reasonable doubt that the number of different implication-relations, in terms of which our inferences might be drawn (with complete validity in every case), is unlimited. It follows, of necessity, that the reasons why we use the particular implication-relation (or relations) which actually figure in our deductions are not exclusively considerations of logical truth and falsity: some further criterion, independent of truth and falsity, is required.

A just conception of the scope and meaning of these results cannot be conveyed without a more extended survey of such systems than could be given in brief space. But a few examples may be presented, in outline, to illustrate their general character. The consequences which appear to follow may be indicated summarily:

(1) There are no "laws of logic" which can be attributed to the universe or to human reason in the traditional fashion. What are ordinarily called "laws of logic" are nothing but explicative or analytic statements of the meaning of certain concepts, such as truth and falsity, negation, "either-or," implication, consistency, etc., which are taken as basic.

A "system of logic" is nothing more than a convenient collection of such concepts, together with the principles to which they give rise by analysis of their meaning.

(2) There are an unlimited number of possible systems of logic,

---

Varsovie, XXIII (Warsaw, 1930), Classe III, pp. 51–77. [The article in question was written by Professor Lukasiewicz alone, not by Lukasiewicz and Tarski.]

each such that every one of its laws is true and is applicable to deduction. These systems are alternatives in the sense that concepts and principles belonging to one cannot generally be introduced into another—because of fundamental differences of category.

Also, the unlimited multiplicity and variety of such systems and principles transcends the limits of human apprehension: practically it is necessary to make a choice amongst them, if there is to be any canon of inference at all.

(3) Sufficiency for the guidance and testing of our usual deductions, systematic simplicity and convenience, accord with our psychological limitations and our mental habits, and so on, operate as criteria in our conscious or unconscious choice of "good logic." Any current or accepted canon of inference must be pragmatically determined. That one such system should be thus accepted does not imply that alternative systems are false: it does imply that they are—or would be thought to be—relatively poorer instruments for the conduct and testing of our ordinary inferences.

II

Two primary difficulties beset the problem of presenting any system of non-Aristotelian logic. First, we lack any criterion for judging its correctness in its own terms: our "intuitions" may not apply. Second, the development of any system involves inference: how shall we avoid reverting to the Aristotelian manner of drawing such inferences, when we are supposed to be thinking in non-Aristotelian terms? The procedure which obviates both these difficulties is the "matrix method," by which certain rules, to be carried out mechanically, are sufficient to determine what laws belong to the system and what do not. After a little practice—strange as it may seem—the reader will have no more difficulty in thinking in non-Aristotelian terms than he would, for example, in performing his arithmetical calculations in a number system based on the radix 12 instead of the familiar system on radix 10. Aristotelian logic is no more prescribed by reason than the fact that we have ten fingers is prescribed by reason.

As has been indicated, the calculus of propositions in *Principia Mathematica* is non-Aristotelian; but it is relatively familiar, and many students have got to the point where they suppose it to be "correct," and Aristotle incorrect insofar as the two fail to coincide. Since this is the simplest of all systems which can be developed by the matrix method, we may use it to exemplify the general procedure.

Suppose we represent the fact that any proposition p is true by writing $p = 1$, and the fact that p is false by writing $p = 0$. These two properties, truth and falsity, represented by 1 and 0, constitute the basic categories of this system and are called its "truth-values." Every proposition is either true or false; it has either the value 1 or the value 0; and the fact that the system is concerned exclusively with what is definable in terms of truth and falsity may be expressed by saying that it is "two-valued." All the logical "functions" which figure in the system are definable in terms of these two values. For example, the negation of p, "not-p" or "p is false," may be defined by the fact that when p has the value 1 (truth), not-p has the value 0 (falsity), and when p has the value 0, not-p has the value 1. This relation of the truth or falsity of not-p to the truth or falsity of p sufficiently determines the exact meaning of "not-p." Again the logical function "either p or q" can be defined by the fact that it always has the value 1 except when p and q both have the value 0. If a person found himself unclear as to just what was meant by "not-p" or "either p or q," these meanings could be unambiguously determined by the following scheme: 1 represents "true," 0 represents "false," $\sim p$ represents "not-p," and $p \lor q$ represents "either p or q." In the following matrix, or table, the values of p are in the left-hand column, the values of q at the top. The corresponding values of $p \lor q$ are found where column and line intersect. The values of $\sim p$, corresponding to those of p, are in the right-hand column under the symbol $\sim$:

$\lor$	1	0	$\sim$
1	1	1	0
0	1	0	1

Thus the square in the middle of the table summarizes the following facts:

(1) If $p = 1$ and $q = 1$, then $p \lor q = 1$,
(2) If $p = 1$ and $q = 0$, then $p \lor q = 1$,
(3) If $p = 0$ and $q = 1$, then $p \lor q = 1$,
(4) If $p = 0$ and $q = 0$, then $p \lor q = 0$.

Since we know that $p = 1$ represents "p is true," and $p = 0$, "p is false," these four facts together tell us exactly what $p \lor q$ represents. The column under the symbol $\sim$, when compared with the first column, which contains the values of p, summarizes the facts:

(5) If $p = 1$, then $\sim p = 0$,
(6) If $p = 0$, then $\sim p = 1$.

These two together tell us exactly what $\sim p$ symbolizes.

All the other expressions which occur in the two-valued logic can be defined in terms of these two functions, $\vee$ and $\sim$. Three other relations of propositions are usually represented in the system:

$$p \supset q = \sim p \vee q \quad \text{Def.}$$

That is, $p \supset q$ (read "p implies q") is defined to mean "Either p is false or q is true."

$$p\,q = \sim(\sim p \vee \sim q) \quad \text{Def.}$$

That is, $p\,q$ (read "Both p and q," or "p is true and q is true") is defined to mean "It is false that either p is false or q is false."

$$p \equiv q = (p \supset q)(q \supset p) \quad \text{Def.}$$

That is, $p \equiv q$ (read "p is equivalent to q") is defined to mean "p implies q, and q implies p."

The truth-values of any one of these defined expressions can be determined from those for the functions $\vee$ and $\sim$, given in the original matrix. We give the determination of the values of $p \supset q$, to illustrate the method:

p	q	$\sim p$	$\sim p \vee q\ (= p \supset q)$
I	I	O	I
I	O	O	O
O	I	I	I
O	O	I	I

Here, the first two columns, under p and q, represent the four possible combinations, (1) p true and q true, (2) p true and q false, (3) p false and q true, (4) p false and q false. The values under $\sim p$ correspond to those under p, according to the rule given by the original matrix: when the value of p is 1, the value of $\sim p$ is 0, and when the value of p is 0, the value of $\sim p$ is 1. The values of $p \supset q$ (or of its defining equivalent, $\sim p \vee q$) are then determined from those of $\sim p$ and q, according to the rule of the original matrix. As we see, $p \supset q$ is true except when p is true and q false. If anyone object that the relation "p implies q" does *not* always hold when p and q are both true propositions, or both false propositions, or when p is false and q true, the answer is that the relation $p \supset q$, in this logic, *does* hold under these conditions—that is what it *means*. One may call it by some other name than "implies" if one choose, and certainly it is a very special meaning of "implies," but it is a perfectly good relation for inferring q from p, as we shall see.

The other defined relations may be similarly fixed in meaning by finding their "truth-table" values. Following the rules of the original matrix, the results will be as given below:

p	q	pq	$p \equiv q$
I	I	I	I
I	O	O	O
O	I	O	O
O	O	O	I

Thus pq is that relation which holds when p is true and q is true and and fails to hold under any other conditions. And $p \equiv q$ is that relation which holds when p and q are both true or both false and fails to hold when one is true and the other false. Thus $p \equiv q$ means "p and q are equivalent in point of their truth or falsity."

The non-Aristotelian character of this logic follows from the non-Aristotelian *meanings* of the logical functions $p \supset q$ and $p \equiv q$ (and from the slightly special meaning of $p \lor q$, which is one of *two* meanings of "either-or," *both* of which occur in traditional logic). Given these meanings, there is nothing "queer" about the processes of reasoning involved.

We may now determine the laws of the system by this same truth-table method. The process is somewhat tedious but utterly reliable.

What is a law of logic? It is a true *formula*. Just as a law of algebra is a formula which holds true whatever numbers *a*, *b*, *c*, etc., represent, so a law of the logical relations of propositions is a formula which is true whatever propositions *p*, *q*, *r*, etc., represent. Thus, in terms of our truth-tables, any expression represents a law if it always has the value I, no matter what the values of *p*, *q*, *r*, etc., may be. Expressions which do not always have the value I are not laws.

As an example, let us determine whether the expression $p \supset q . \supset . \sim q \supset \sim p$ represents a law. (The dots in the expression are merely marks of punctuation, used instead of parentheses.) To save space, the expression itself is represented in the table by "*Law*."

p	q	$p \supset q$	$\sim q$	$\sim p$	$\sim q \supset \sim p$	*Law*
I	I	I	O	O	I	I
I	O	O	I	O	O	I
O	I	I	O	I	I	I
O	O	I	I	I	I	I

The values in the column under $p \supset q$ here may be taken from the first truth-table given. We may also use this column as the rule for determining the values of $\sim q \supset \sim p$ from those of $\sim q$ and $\sim p$. The same rule determines the values of the whole expression, in the last column, from those of its members, $p \supset q$ and $\sim q \supset \sim p$. The expression in question is a law of the system: whether p and q have the value 1 or the value 0, $p \supset q . \supset . \sim q \supset \sim p$ always has the value 1. This law may be read "If p implies q, then not-q implies not-p."

Let us similarly test the expression $p \supset q . \supset . q \supset p$:

p	q	$p \supset q$	$q \supset p$	$p \supset q . \supset . q \supset p$
I	I	I	I	I
I	O	O	I	I
O	I	I	O	O
O	O	I	I	I

This is not always true; it has the value 0 when $p = 0$ and $q = 1$: "If p implies q, then q implies p" is not a law of the system.

Considerations of space forbid further examples. But the process is always the same (except that if three propositions, p, q, and r, appear in the expression, we need eight lines instead of four to represent all the combinations of their truth-values; for four propositions, sixteen lines, etc.). The class of expressions which always have the value 1, as determined by the rules of the original matrix and the definitions, coincides exactly with the laws which are deducible from the postulates given in Section A of *Principia Mathematica*.

The reader would find that a certain amount of practice is necessary in order to use this matrix method with facility.[2] But for present purposes, such facility is unnecessary, if only the method itself be understood. Two points are of cardinal importance:

(1) The legitimate, correct, or valid meaning of any function in the system (such as $\sim p$, $p \vee q$, $p \supset q$, etc., above) is to be determined from the meaning of the truth-values (0 and 1) by the matrix or truth-table for the function in question. Whatever English expression exactly summarizes the relation of this function to the truth or falsity of its constituent p's and q's is the correct rendering of its meaning in the system. Sometime such precise interpretation in language would be too long or involved to serve as the ordinary "reading," and a loose phrase may be substituted—as "p implies q" for $p \supset q$. But always any function

---

[2] Those who have some acquaintance with mathematical methods of demonstration will observe that it is nothing more than a convenient device for applying the method of "perfect induction" (exhaustion of the possible cases).

has such an exact meaning; and this is determined by the original matrix and the definitions, from the meaning assigned to the truth-values.

(2) If the interpretation assigned to the truth-values is such that what has the value I is true, or is validly assertable, then for that interpretation of the functions which is valid, all the laws of the system will be *universal truths*. The manner in which a law is established, by the matrix method, absolutely assures that.

III

On the basis of what has now been explained, it would be possible to prove directly that there are any number of different systems of logic, every one of them such that all its laws are true. But without something further in the way of concrete examples, it would be difficult to appreciate just what this fact means. Let us, then, exhibit very briefly and in outline two other systems, neither of which is completely Aristotelian.

The first of these is the three-valued system of Lukasiewicz and Tarski which has been mentioned. It is generated by the following matrix:

C	I	½	o	N
I	I	½	o	o
½	I	I	½	½
o	I	I	I	I

Here Np represents "not-p" or "p is false": it has exactly the same meaning as $\sim p$ in the two-valued system. The other function, pCq, is the implication-relation of the system; but its meaning is *not* identical with that of $p \supset q$. Definitions of the system are:

$pOq. = :pCq.C.q$ Def.   ("p or q")
$pAq. = :N(Np.O.Nq)$ Def.   ("p and q")
$pEq. = :pCq.qCp$ Def.   ("p is equivalent to q")

(The dots, as before, are merely for punctuation: two dots (:) is a stronger mark of punctuation than one dot.) It must be understood that the readings of the functions here suggested are only loose phrases: their exact meanings remain to be determined.

The fundamental matrix, and the definitions, give the following truth-table for the functions of the system. (For convenience of printing, we replace the sign of the intermediate truth-value, ½, by the symbol ?.)

p	q	pCq	pOq	pAq	pEq
I	I	I	I	I	I
I	?	?	I	?	?
I	O	O	I	O	O
?	I	I	I	?	?
?	?	I	?	?	I
?	O	?	?	O	?
O	I	I	I	O	O
O	?	I	?	O	?
O	O	I	O	O	I

There is an obvious analogy here between this and the previous system: pCq is the analogue of $p \supset q$; pOq, of $p \lor q$; pAq, of $p\,q$; and pEq, of $p \equiv q$.

On account of its having three truth-values, instead of two, certain functions are definable here which have no analogues in the two-valued system.

$$Mp.=:Np.C.p \quad \text{Def.} \quad \text{("p is possible")}$$

If Mp is "p is possible," NMp will be "p is impossible," MNp will be "p is possibly-false," and $NMNp$ will be "It is impossible that p be false" or "p is necessarily true." We can also define "p is doubtful" (Dp) as equivalent to "p is both possible and possibly-false":

$$Dp.=:Mp.A.MNp \quad \text{Def.}$$

The truth-values of these functions, as determined by the fundamental matrix and the definitions, are as follows:

p	Np	Mp	NMp	MNp	$NMNp$	Dp	NDp
I	O	I	O	O	I	O	I
?	?	I	O	I	O	I	O
O	I	O	I	I	O	O	I

A brief comparison of important laws of the two-valued and the three-valued systems is as follows:

2-1 $p \supset p$ 3-1 pCp
 p implies p; every proposition implies itself.

2-2 $p\,q.\equiv.q\,p$ 3-2 $pAq.E.qAp$
 "p and q both" is equivalent to "q and p both."

2-3 $p \equiv \sim(\sim p)$ 3-3 $p.E.NNp$
 p is equivalent to not-not-p.

2-4 $p.\supset.p\lor q$ 3-4 $p.C.pOq$
   p implies "p or q."

2-5 $pq.\supset.p$ 3-5 $pAq.C.p$
   "p and q both" implies p.

2-6 $p\supset q.\equiv.\sim q\supset\sim p$ 3-6 $pCq.E:Nq.C.Np$
   "p implies q" is equivalent to "not-q implies not-p."

2-7 $p\supset q.\supset:q\supset r.\supset.p\supset r$ 3-7 $pCq.C:qCr.C.pCr$
   If p implies q, then "q implies r" implies "p implies r."

2-8 $p.\supset.q\supset p$ 3-8 $p.C.qCp$
   If p is true, then q implies p: a true proposition is implied by any proposition.

2-9 $\sim p.\supset.p\supset q$ 3-9 $Np.C.pCq$
   If p is false, then p implies q: a false proposition implies any proposition.

2-10 $p.\supset.\sim p\supset p$ 3-10 $p.C:Np.C.p$

If p is true, then not-p implies p: every true proposition is implied by its own negation.

So far, the two systems are completely analogous. It is to be observed that laws 1 to 7 hold also in Aristotelian logic. But laws 8, 9, and 10 illustrate the fact that, in both these systems, the meaning of "implies" is non-Aristotelian. The following principles, which hold in the two-valued system but not in the three-valued, exhibit certain fundamental differences between the two:

2-11 $\sim p\supset p.\supset.p$ 3-11′ $Np.C.p:C.p$ does not hold.

2-12 $p.\supset.\sim(p\supset\sim p)$ 3-12′ $p.C:N(p.C.Np)$ does not hold.

2-13 $p\supset\sim p.\supset.\sim p$ 3-13′ $p.C.Np:C.Np$ does not hold.

2-14 $p\lor\sim p$ 3-14′ $p.O.Np$ does not hold.[8]

The last four laws of the two-valued system may be read: (11) If not-p implies p, then p is true; (12) If p is true, then it is false that p implies

---

[8] If a given law holds in the three-valued system, the analogous law will always hold in the two-valued; but the converse statement is not true, as 11–14 illustrate. In any truth-table for the three-valued system, if we strike out every line in which the truth-value ? occurs, the result is the corresponding truth-table for the two-valued system. The comparison just mentioned follows from that fact: a law will hold in the three-valued system only if (1) it holds for the values 0 and 1, and (2) it also holds for the value ?, and for combinations of ? with 0 and 1.

not-p; (13) If p implies not-p, then p is false; (14) Either p is true or p is false. It is to be observed that all these principles are Aristotelian.

The fact that 3-14′, $p.O.Np$, does not hold, is particularly important, because $p \lor {\sim}p$ expresses the law of the Excluded Middle. The reason why this principle is not, and cannot be, contained in the three-valued system depends upon the meaning of the function pOq, and is a very good illustration of the principles which govern the interpretation of such systems. If we refer to the truth-table for pOq, we find that this expression has the value ? when p and q both have that value. Also, as the table for Np tells us, if $p = ?$, then $Np = ?$. Hence when $p = ?$ (and therefore $Np = ?$) $p.O.Np$ must have the value ?. Thus it cannot be a law of the system, since a law must always have the value 1. If we interpret O as being the "either-or" relation, and $p = ?$ as "p is doubtful," then in this system "Either p or not-p" is doubtful when p is doubtful.

But the trouble here is one of interpretation. We have said that the valid interpretation of any function must depend on the meanings assigned to the truth-values. What can $p = 1$, $p = 0$, and $p = ?$ validly mean in this system? At once it is evident that if $p = 1$ means "p is true," and $p = 0$, "p is false," there is nothing left for the intermediate value, ?, to represent—that is, nothing left *unless* we suppose that a proposition may be neither true nor false. *That* depends on what is meant by "proposition": if we accept the usual meaning, "a statement which is either true or false," then that question is settled: the truth-values of this system cannot be interpreted in this fashion.

Suppose, however, that $p = 1$ have the same meaning here as in the calculus of probabilities, "p is *certainly* true," and $p = 0$ mean similarly, "p is *certainly* false." Then $p = ?$ can mean, "p is neither certainly true nor certainly false," i.e., "p is doubtful." Thus this is a valid interpretation which can be imposed on the truth-values. Now let us return to the relation represented by pOq. This function has the value ? when both p and q have that value. But is it a fact that when p is doubtful and q is doubtful, "Either p or q" is doubtful? In general, yes; but this fails to be the case when the two propositions p and q happen to be so related that if one is false the other must be true. When that is the case, p and q may both be in doubt, but "Either p or q" admits of no doubt. Thus the fact that $p.O.Np$ is not always true in this system does not mean that for this logic the law of the Excluded Middle is *false*: it reflects the fact that, when validly interpreted, pOq does not mean precisely "At least one of the two, p and q, is true." That meaning of "either-or" is *inexpressible* in terms of the categories "certain," "certainly-false," and "doubtful"—is not significant when propositions are thus classified. One whose logic was based upon this trichotomy would have no use for the law of the Excluded Middle: he would ignore it as irrelevant to deduction.

What the function pOq truly represents is a little difficult to express in a manner which is at once precise and obvious; it is: "At least a designatable one of the two, p and q, is true." That is: suppose that we are called upon to bet on one or the other of the two, p and q, as we choose. Suppose both are doubtful. The one we choose to bet on will then be doubtful. This will be the case even when q is the negative of p, so that "Either p or q" is a certainly true statement. Thus $p.O.Np$ is doubtful when p and Np are both doubtful, though "Either p or not-p" is certainly true.

The valid interpretation of the other functions, if 1 represents "certain," o "certainly-false," and ? "doubtful," is as follows:

pAq, "It is not the case that a designatable one of the two, p and q, is false."

pEq, "p and q both have the same truth-value."

pCq, "Disregarding degrees of uncertainty, if you exchange a bet on p for a bet on q, you will not be disadvantaged."

This last may seem to be a very funny implication-relation; but it satisfies the requirement that when it holds, and p is known to be true, q must be true. It is an absolutely safe basis for inference.

Interpretation of the functions of one variable is a simpler matter:

Np, "p is false."

Mp, "p is not certainly-false."

NMp (is equivalent to $p = 0$), "p is certainly-false."

MNp, "p is not certainly-true."

$NMNp$ (is equivalent to $p = 1$), "p is certainly-true."

Dp (is equivalent to $p = ?$), "p is doubtful."

NDp, "p is certainly-true or certainly-false—is not doubtful."

With these interpretations, all the laws of the system are universally true principles.

The system selected as an example of the four-valued type is closer to our usual logical conceptions—so close, in fact, that most of its laws coincide with them. The matrix for this system is as follows:[4]

---

[4] This system, as here outlined, is due to Dr. W. T. Parry; see his doctoral dissertation, on file in the Harvard University Library. It satisfies the postulates for "Strict Implication" (1.1–1.7 and 2.2 in Lewis, *Survey of Symbolic Logic* [New

V	1	2	3	4	~	◊
1	1	1	1	1	4	1
2	1	2	1	2	3	1
3	1	1	3	3	2	1
4	1	2	3	4	1	4

Here 4 corresponds to the 0 of previous systems, and 2 and 3 are intermediate values. The relation $p \lor q$, defined by the square portion of the matrix, is capable of the same interpretation, "Either p or q," as in the two-valued system. Of the two functions, defined in the columns at the right, $\sim p$ is "not-p," as previously; and ◊p may be read "p is possible." This last is *not* identical with Mp in the three-valued system.

Additional definitions of the system are:

$$p\,q \;=\; \sim(\sim p \lor \sim q) \quad \text{Def. (``p and q are both true'')}$$
$$p < q \;=\; \sim\!◊\,(p\!\sim\! q) \quad \text{Def. (``p implies q'')}$$
$$p\,O\,q \;=\; ◊\,(p\,q) \quad \text{Def. (``p and q are consistent'')}$$
$$(p = q) \;=\; (p{<}q)(q{<}p) \quad \text{Def. (``p is equivalent to q'')}$$

Laws of the system include the following; analogues of those cited for the previous systems have the same number:

4-1 $\;p<p$

4-2 $\;p\,q.=.q\,p$

4-3 $\;p.=.\sim(\sim p)$

4-4 $\;p.<.p\lor q$

4-5 $\;p\,q.<.p$

4-6 $\;p<q.=.\sim q<\sim p$

4-7 $\;p<q.<:q<r.<.p<r$

4-8′ $\;p.<.q<p$ does not hold.

4-9′ $\;\sim p.<.p<q$ does not hold.

4-10′ $\;p.<.\sim p<p$ does not hold.

4-11 $\;\sim p<p.<.p$

4-12 $\;p<\sim(p<\sim p)$

4-13 $\;p<\sim p.<.\sim p$

4-14 $\;p\lor\sim p$

If the reading of these laws gives any trouble, it may be determined by reference to that given for the corresponding principles of the previous systems. It will be noted that 8, 9, and 10, which do not hold

York, 1932], Ch. V) together with the additional postulate 1.9 suggested by O. Becker, "*Zur Logik der Modalitäten,*" *Jahrbuch für Philosophie und Phänomenologische Forschung* [Halle], 1930, Bd. XI; see p. 511.

here, are non-Aristotelian, and that this system differs from the two-valued by not including them. It differs from the three-valued by including 11–14: and these laws are Aristotelian. Respects in which the Aristotelian character of this system is subject to doubt will be referred to later. The interpretation of the truth-values for which it approximates to traditional logic is as follows: $p = 1$, "p is necessary (such that its denial involves a contradiction)"; $p = 2$, "p is true but not necessary"; $p = 3$, "p is false but not impossible"; $p = 4$, "p is impossible."

Brief as it must be, the above should be sufficient to indicate that all such systems developed by the matrix method are exact, and that two such may have laws in common but will differ with respect to others. It is definitely provable that an unlimited number of such matrix systems exist, and that every one of them can validly be interpreted as a calculus of logic.[5] If we should insist upon giving their symbolic ex-

---

[5] Lukasiewicz and Tarski *(op. cit.*, p. 72) give the following rules for constructing a system on any finite number, *n*, of truth-values:

Let p and q designate certain numbers of the interval $(0 - 1)$, e.g., 0, 1/2, 1, or 0, 1/3, 2/3, 1, etc. Let the values of pCp ("p implies q") be determined as follows: If $p \leqq q$, then $pCq = 1$; and if $p > q$, then $pCq = 1 - p + q$. Let Np ("p is false") be determined by the rule: $Np = 1 - p$. If from the interval $(0 - 1)$ only the limiting values 0 and 1 are chosen, the resulting matrix is that of the two-valued system above. If in addition the number 1/2 be taken, then we have the matrix of the three-valued system. In similar fashion, 4, 5, ... *n*-valued systems can be constructed.

For every system constructed by this rule, there is an interpretation such that all its laws are true. Moreover this rule by no means exhausts the possibilities: for example, the four-valued system above is no one of these. *Any* such matrix system can be generated mathematically, and interpreted, by the following principles. Only one assumption (1. below) is necessary; further principles are either conventions (C) or demonstrable propositions (T):

The Abstract System

1. A class K_n, consisting of a specified finite number of elements, is assumed.

(C) 2. The "variables" of the system, $p, q, r, \ldots$ denote, ambiguously, members of K_n. If $p = m$, where m is an element of K_n, m is said to be the "value" of p.

(C) 3. Any function in the system $f(p, q, \ldots)$ is determined by assigning a value of $f(p, q, \ldots)$ for each combination of the values of its variables, or by being defined in terms of such functions, previously determined.

(T) 4. The variables $p, q, \ldots$ are themselves functions in the system.

(C) 5. An element i in K_n is arbitrarily chosen as the "designated element." (A system may have more than one designated element. If there is but one, the element 1 is usually chosen.)

(C) 6. Any function $L(p, q, \ldots)$ such that, for every value of the variables, $L(p, q, \ldots) = i$ is a "law of the system."

(C) 7. If every function which can be determined by a matrix on the *n* values

pressions arbitrarily predetermined meanings, then any or all of them might be false, in part or altogether. But if the principles of interpretation explained above are adhered to, then every law of every one of these systems must be a universally true formula.

IV

Examination of these systems, and their interpretations, will serve to bring out a number of important points.

The truth-values, as interpreted, become the basic categories of the system. That two systems, based on numerically different classes of truth-values, do not admit of coincidence in these categories should be at once evident. One cannot exhaust the possibilities in a two-, a three-, a four-fold way by the same principle of division, or in such wise that the resultant divisions coincide. For example, since the two-fold distinction, true or false, is exhaustive, these two cannot represent categories of any system based on more than two values: there would be nothing left for the intermediate values to designate. Where the num-

---

of the system can also be expressed in the symbols of the system, the system is said to be "symbolically complete."

(T) 8. For a specified number n of elements, any two systems based on K_n are mathematically equivalent if they have only one designated element and are symbolically complete.

(T) 9. Two systems on the same number of elements may be nonequivalent by being symbolically incomplete in different ways.

(T) 10. There are at least as many such systems as there are finite numbers.

Principles of Interpretation

11. The variables p, q, r,... are interpreted as propositions (entities capable of being asserted or denied).

12. The elements in K_n are interpreted as some set of properties of propositions such that (a) every proposition must have at least one of this set of properties, and (b) the property represented by any designated element i is such that whatever proposition has this property is validly assertable.

Condition a is satisfied by any exhaustive classification of propositions, in accordance with a particular principle of division.

"Assertability," as required by condition b, is a character common to a variety of more specific properties—e.g., truth, universal truth, logical necessity, probability-value $= 1$.

13. The valid interpretation of any function in the system is to be determined by the relation of its values to the values of its variables; i.e., the meaning of the values having been assigned in accordance with 11, the meaning of any function is determined by the array of its values for all combinations of the values of its variables.

(T) 14. For every such abstract system, there is at least one interpretation satisfying conditions 10 and 11.

(T) 15. Any interpretation such that it satisfies conditions 10, 11, and 12 is also such that every law of the system represents a universally true principle of the relations of propositions.

ber of values exceeds two, it may be the case that two systems coincide in their limiting values—as "certain" and "certainly false" allow the intermediate ground between them to be variously divided. But they cannot coincide throughout, for obvious reasons.

As a consequence, the logical truths which are expressed by the laws of one system will not, in general, be expressible in terms of others. For example, the properties of the relations of consistency, inconsistency, and independence of propositions, as defined in the four-valued system above, cannot be expressed in any two- or three-valued system.[6] For this reason, acceptance of one such system as the canon of deduction would mean the repudiation of others. We cannot base the systematic principles of our logic, at one and the same time, on fundamentally different modes of classifying propositions.

Something of the logical significance of such basic categories (which appear as the truth-values in systems like the foregoing) may be crudely suggested if we imagine a mind which should be as much at home in non-Aristotelian distinctions as we are in those of Aristotle. For example, a mind bent upon adhering to the certainty, uncertainty, and certain-falsity of the three-valued logic might greet the idea of "truth unadorned" with the comment: "If you mean that what you affirm is certain, in what is 'truth' different from certainty? And if you do not mean that, why affirm it? Apparently you are trying to invent a logic for sophists, in which what nobody knows can be asserted. When you can give me a clear example of uncertain 'truth,' or show me how uncertain 'truth' would be different from uncertain '*un*truth,' I shall be prepared to listen: until then, I think you are talking nonsense." Obviously such a mind would be unlikely to "speak our language," but equally obviously, such mental blindness would not mean irrationality.

The propositional calculus of *Principia Mathematica*—to use an opposite illustration—similarly ignores all distinctions not expressible in terms of simple truth and falsity. Its two-valued logic cannot incorporate the idea of consistency between propositions, for example. But a person who thought exclusively in its terms might contend: "A proposition is either true or false, and cannot be both. If two propositions being 'consistent' means being both true, the idea is superfluous; and if it means being both false, or one true and one false, I don't see the point of it." Before such obtuseness, a differently minded person could only throw up his hands.

---

[6] A system on a larger number of values may contain one on a smaller number as a subsystem, but this is not generally the case. Also two systems on the same number of values may be distinct.

To some degree and in some respects, such obtuseness is inevitable to all of us. For example, if a proposition is necessary, does it follow that it is also necessarily-necessary? If a proposition is self-consistent, does it follow that the denial of its self-consistency is self-contradictory? Perhaps the reader cannot answer these questions—and finds himself disinclined even to consider them. But whether the four-valued system, above, coincides with Aristotelian categories or not, turns precisely upon the answer to these questions. If we are inclined to disregard the technicalities of matrix systems, on the pragmatic ground of their "triviality," at least we ought to be alive to our own logic and its difference from them. Here is an opportunity to make a contribution to logic, because nobody has ever answered these questions.

It may be well to point out, however, that the answers to these questions will not settle *the truth* of logic. What would be determined is not such truth but, instead, the exact meaning of the ideas of "necessity" and "possibility" which conform to our logical practice. There are *two* ideas of "necessity" and "possibility," for one of which the questions must be answered affirmatively, and for the other, negatively. There is an exact logic which incorporates the affirmative answers, and another for the negative answers. These two systems are no more alike than a geometry of curved space is like Euclid.

There are two points which—we hope—this illustration may serve to enforce. First, that the determination of our canon of deduction, on such a point, is not the determination of an absolute truth—the discovery that the equation, "necessary = necessarily-necessary," is true or is false—but is only the determination which, of two equally exact and equally possible ideas of necessity, we intend to incorporate in our thinking. And second, that such determination is, nevertheless, no mere trivial question for logicians to play with, any more than the question whether the surveyor's geometry is Euclidean or Riemannian is a trivial question for geometers to play with.

Possibly one could press this analogy a little. It may be that the scope of actual logical practice is too limited to provide an answer to the questions. In that case, we might be pragmatic about our choice of an exact canon of logic, for reasons similar to those which led Poincaré to be pragmatic about our choice of a geometry. However, if the conclusions of this paper are correct, logic is *not* pragmatic in this sense that the absolute truth about it is not practically determinable. Rather, any canon of deduction must be pragmatically determined for the reason that the absolute truth includes *alternatives*—different systems, with different basic concepts—and wherever or whenever we are confronted with the necessity of choosing, we may do so deliberately, and without any possibility of being wrong—if we are clear in our own minds—in either case.

That any other logic than that exemplified in our actual deductions would be practically defensible, we are not in the least concerned to argue. But the genuinely pragmatic basis of this logic may become clearer if we examine considerations which would favor the practicability of some other.

Of the systems examined, the three-valued is at the farthest remove from common sense. Yet there are quite important and highly plausible points of view from which it might be urged that a just logic should be three-valued. There is a class of statements, called "propositional functions," which are sometimes true and sometimes false—in contrast to propositions, strictly so called, which are definitely true or false and if once true are always true. Examples of propositional functions are "Today is Monday," "The sum of the angles exceeds two right angles," "A is less than B." If p, q, r, etc., represent such statements and if $p = 1$ represent "p is always true," and $p = 0$, "p is always false," then obviously there will be a middle ground between these. Not only will a three-valued logic be applicable, but it would satisfy certain fairly obvious interests of deduction. Furthermore, it may be urged that all ordinary statements are such propositional functions, and that the only genuine "propositions," containing no variable element, would be quite negligible assertions such as "Napoleon is Bonaparte." The reasons for this contention are too lengthy to be included here, but some of them, at least, will probably occur to the reader.

Again, a similar conclusion is indicated by the actual character of what are ordinarily called "negative propositions." "X is white" and "X is not white," in ordinary use, are not genuinely contradictory, because "white" and "not-white" are not genuinely negative terms; they exhaust the possibilities only within some limited "universe of discourse"—that of color, in this instance. The precise contradictory of "X is white" is "It is false that X is white"; and this last is not a negative but an "infinite" proposition, of a sort which rarely, if ever, reflects the content of an actual judgment. Mutually negative judgments, such as "X is white" and "X is not white" leave an undetermined middle ground, or an area outside both: an election, a bargain, an argument, beauty, the parallel postulate are neither white nor not-white, but fall into this indeterminate third. That the dichotomy of genuine contradictories is more conformable to actual thinking or inference than the trichotomy "A, not-A, and neither A nor not-A," is a thesis extremely difficult to establish.

Again, the mathematical logician Brouwer has maintained that the law of the Excluded Middle is not a valid principle at all. The issues of so difficult a question could not be discussed here; but let us suggest a point of view at least something like his. If we should be interested exclusively in concepts and the relations of concepts, instead of individual concrete objects, we should have to admit that there are various assertions which are neither true nor false, because concepts are indeterminate with respect to what falls outside their "essence." For example, "Infinity is odd" and "Infinity is even," "The Cheshire cat has a tail" and "The Cheshire cat has no tail," are neither true nor false. (We could also go further, and say: "We can know objects only through concepts; hence our knowledge, and therefore our logic, must terminate in concepts.") Thus there is a *certain way of construing* propositions for which the law of the Excluded Middle becomes inapplicable or non-significant, and the dichotomy, true or false, would have to be replaced by the trichotomy, true, false, or indeterminate. Any resultant logic would be three-valued.

The law of the Excluded Middle is not writ in the heavens: it but reflects our rather stubborn adherence to the simplest of all possible modes of division, and our predominant interest in concrete objects as opposed to abstract concepts. The reasons for the choice of our logical categories are not themselves reasons of logic any more than the reasons for choosing Cartesian, as against polar or Gaussian coordinates, are themselves principles of mathematics, or the reason for the radix 10 is of the essence of number.

But one says: "The canon of deduction cannot possibly be subject to arbitrary choice. When one infers, one does so validly or invalidly; and you can no more change or avoid the laws which determine such validity than you can alter the law of gravitation." First let us use a trivial illustration here: I go to X's office at ten o'clock and find he has left word, "If anyone calls before eleven, I shall be in the Library." I reason that I am somebody, and have called before eleven; therefore if the word he left is trustworthy, X will be in the Library. Is my reasoning invalid? No. But is there any "necessary connection" between my calling and X's being in the Library? No: this is not the usual "if-then" relation of our more frequent speech. It is, nevertheless, perfectly safe for the purposes of inference. Granted the truth of this "if-then" statement, and the truth of the antecedent in the relation, the consequent also will be true.

There are an indefinitely large number of such "implication-relations," each and every one of which is perfectly safe for inference. The one above exemplifies the $p \supset q$ of the two-valued system: it is broader than the usual meaning of "if-then" and includes that meaning. The pCq of the three-valued system is different but equally reliable for inference; and the $p<q$ of the four-valued system is likewise utterly safe but not at all the same relation. Indeed, we are grossly understating the case. If we define the class of "implication-relations," pIq, as such that when pIq holds and p can be asserted, q also will be true, then there are four such implication-relations in the two-valued system; 2916 which are definable in terms of the categories of a three-valued system, and over a million in a four-valued system. Each of these is different from every other, in some respect, and answers to different laws; but each and every one of them is absolutley safe for the purpose of drawing inferences from true premises. This strains one's credulity, no doubt; but not to the breaking point, let us hope, since the matter is demonstrable. Let us hasten to add that we have no least intent to urge this multiplicity of implications as being, in general, any contribution to the practical business of deduction. But when, from such a plethora of possible bases of valid inference, we make use, at most, of two or three—and feel, perhaps, that only a single one should be incorporated in a "good" logic—can there be any explanation, other than pragmatic, for this situation?

This leads to a final point, which is almost certain to be raised: Is not the identification of *any* such system as the foregoing with the canon of inference a falsification of the nature of logic? Should not logic include *all* true principles of *all* such systems—if they really are true, as has been claimed? The answer is that one may quite reasonably use the word "logic" in this comprehensive manner if one wish: any argument on that point would be verbal. But "logic" in this sense could not be synonymous with the—or a—canon of deduction, for reasons which should now be clear. The attempt to include all modes of classification, and all resultant principles, would produce, not a canon, but a chaos. Some choice is necessary: and in the nature of the case, the grounds of choice can only be pragmatic.

7. Notes on the Logic of Intension

The expression "extensional logic" will here be used in the sense which has become familiar and is illustrated by the early sections of *Principia Mathematica*. What will be meant by "intensional logic" is illustrated by Strict Implication (the system S2, as in C. I. Lewis and C. H. Langford, *Symbolic Logic*, Chapter VI and Appendix II) and by the extension of that system to propositional functions in the paper of Dr. Ruth Barcan Marcus.[1]

Confining attention to the logic of propositions, we can distinguish an extensional calculus by the fact that all asserted expressions are truth-functions of the proposition-variables. Any useful calculus of propositions having the character called "intensional" will be more complex. Every asserted expression in it will be either (1) of the form $\sim \lozenge \sim A$, where '$\sim \lozenge \sim A$' is that expression which is true when and only when 'A' is analytic; or (2) equivalent to some expression of the form $\sim \lozenge \sim A$, by the laws of equivalence of the system itself; or (3) of the form A, where $\sim \lozenge \sim A$ is also provable in the system. Among asserted functions of class (3), there may be truth-functions which are analytic, as is illustrated by the fact that all assertions of the *Principia* calculus of propositions are provable theorems of S2.

As this calls to our attention, the difference between an extensional and an intensional system is not one with respect to the analytic character of asserted functions; no valid calculus of logic includes any non-analytic assertion. The difference is that, in an extensional system, the analytic character of postulates and theorems is not asserted and not distinguished from the character of nonanalytic truth, because "A is analytic" cannot be symbolized or defined in terms of the logical constants of the system without addition. In an intensional system, the modalities of functions—"analytic," "nonanalytic"; "consistent," "inconsistent"; "deducible," "nondeducible"; and so on—are symbolized and distinguished from nonmodal truth. As a consequence, in any application of an extensional calculus, the peculiarly logical questions of analyticity, consistency, and deducibility have to be discussed in terms

Reprinted by permission of the Bobbs-Merrill Company from Paul Henle, Horace M. Kallen, and Susanne K. Langer, eds., *Structure, Method and Meaning: Essays in Honor of Henry M. Sheffer* (New York, 1951), pp. 25–34.
[1] Ruth C. Barcan, "A Functional Calculus of First Order Based on Strict Implication," *Journal of Symbolic Logic*, XII (March 1946), pp. 12–15.

of some adjoined metalogic or metalanguage, whereas the laws governing such properties are, for an intensional calculus, statable within the system itself.

However, the distinction between extension and intension is as important for the logic of terms as for the logic of propositions. In fact, these two notions were first applied to general terms and later extended to propositions because of an observed analogy, though without examination of the basis of this analogy. Let us first attempt to clarify, very briefly, intension and extension as two dimensions of the meaning of terms and then give attention to the analogy referred to.

The *extension* of an expression is the meaning of it in that sense in which what is meant is the actuality or actualities which can be indicated or referred to by using this expression. The *intension* of an expression is the meaning of it in that sense in which what it means is what one intends to assert or imply by using it in reference to anything.

The extension of a term is the class of existents to which the term applies. This extension may be zero (an empty class) or universal or neither. Unless the existents to which '*A*' is to apply are specified by exhaustive enumeration, the extension of '*A*' cannot be determined except by reference to an antecedent criterion of classification. But the extension depends also upon the question what things which satisfy this criterion exist. For any term '*A*,' there will be some property (usually complex) such that '*A*' applies to anything, *x*, just in case *x* has this property. We may call this property, essential to the correct application of '*A*,' the *signification* of the term '*A*.' The intension of a term is correlative with its signification, but clarity requires that the two be distinguished. The intension of '*A*' may be identified by the dictum that any other term '*B*' is contained in the intension of '*A*' if, and only if, from the premise that *x* is *A* it is deducible that *x* is *B*. The intension of '*A*' would be completely specified by the "and"-relation of all terms whose applicability is so entailed by the applicability of '*A*.' However, in any language containing the words 'and,' 'or,' and 'not,' complete enumeration of all terms so included in the intension of '*A*' would not be possible, and the intension of a term is completely and precisely specifiable only by definition. The defining relation is an equivalence of intension. The intension of a term is universal if, and only if, it is a self-inconsistent designation or predicate, like 'round and square.' This is the case because, from the premise "*A* is round and not-round," it is deducible that *A* is *Y* for any term '*Y*.' And the intension of '*A*' is zero just in case '*A*' is an analytic designation or predicate, like 'square or not-square.' "*A* is square or not-square" is deducible from "*A* is *Y*," for every predicate '*Y*.' As will thus be evident, an analytic designation or predicate has zero intension in the sense that application of it conveys no information about that to which it is applied. All terms which are neither self-inconsistent nor analytic have an intension which is neither zero nor universal.

The notions of extension and intension can be applied to propositions in a manner the basis for which I borrow from Professor Sheffer. As he has for many years explained to his classes, there is for every statement '*S*' that which '*S*' asserts, and which the interrogation "Is it the case that *S*?" inquires about, and the postulation "Let us assume that *S*" puts forward as hypothesis. What all three of these entertainments entertain, in their various ways, is the *proposition* in question. It can be identified, for any statement '*S*,' with the expression 'that *S*,' which is what '*S*' affirms. For convenience of reading, it can also be identified with the expression which results from replacing the verb in '*S*' by its participial form; thus the proposition asserted by the statement "John is tall" is 'that John is tall' or 'John being tall.'

When so considered, a proposition turns out to be a kind of term. It signifies some "state of affairs" which must be discoverable in actuality if the corresponding statement is to be true. The intension of this propositional term includes all propositions which are deducible from it and would coincide with the conjunction ("and"-relation) of these. As for other terms, however, such a conjoint formulation of all entailed propositions would be interminable; and the intension of a proposition can be completely specified only by citing some equipollent proposition, having the same intension and entailing the same logical consequences.

The extension of a proposition—that to which it applies—is the actual world in case it is true and nothing in case it is false. Thus the extension of it is correlative with its truth-value. The actual world is that unique individual existent identified by the fact that all other existents are space-time parts of it. Propositions are thus singular terms. The state of affairs which a proposition *signifies*, however, is *not* a space-time part of the world, but a character or property which assertion of the proposition *attributes* to this actual world.[2]

The intension of any proposition, and any intensional function of

---

[2] This may seem incorrect; it may appear, for example, that "Christmas, 1950, is Monday" speaks of a state of affairs with temporal bounds. But Christmas, 1950, being Monday entails December 26, 1950, being Tuesday, and December 27, 1950, being Wednesday, etc.; and also entails December 24, 1950, being Sunday, etc. Thus the state of affairs, including all that this proposition entails and requires, is one which has no beginning or end. Something similar is true of every proposition referring to anything at a time.

one, is independent of the extensional property of truth or falsity, in the sense that, for any nonanalytic and noncontradictory proposition, what it entails, what it is consistent with, and what it is inconsistent with remain the same whether the proposition is true or is false. And the sense in which what a proposition means is the same whether it be true or false is the sense of intension.

Logic can assert no expression as true unless it is true by virtue of its intensional meaning, and it can assert no expression to be false except one which is contravalid by virtue of its intension. That there is such a thing as extensional logic is due to the fact that certain truth-functions are analytic by reason of the intensional meaning of the logical constants which figure in them and of their syntax.

To date, there exists no calculus symbolizing both extensional and intensional functions of terms, distinguishing these two and relating them. There is not even any calculus which is recognized as an intensional logic of terms. But expression of relations of intension is essential for a system which should be adequate even to the logic of ordinary discourse. For example, one would ordinarily say that unicorns have a horn in the middle of the forehead and that Zeus is a god, but not that unicorns eat sawdust or that Zeus is a fish. What one intends to assert is that being a unicorn entails having such a horn and that being Zeus entails being a god—affirmations for which no question of existence is pertinent. A similar intent characterizes many statements with terms whose denotation is non-empty, although it may there escape notice because assertion of the relation of intension implies the corresponding relation of extension.

However, although the above is correct, it would be incorrect to say that there is no calculus which is *interpretable* as a logic of terms in intension. The Boolean algebra is such a system. In that algebra, the element 0 ('zero') is the modulus of the operation $\times$, definable by the law that, for every element a, $a \times -a = 0$. And the element 1, being the modulus of the operation $+$, is definable by the equation $a + -a = 1$. But, assuming the interpretation of $\times$ as 'and,' of $+$ as 'or,' and of '$-a$' as 'not-a,' any expression of the form $a \times -a$ is not only a term whose extension is an empty class; it is also a contradiction in terms by virtue of its intension. And any term of the form $a + -a$ is not only one whose extension is universal; it is also an analytic designation or predicate of anything and everything, by its intension.

It requires only to impose the suggested reinterpretation on 0 and 1, taking '$a = 0$' to hold when, and only when, 'a' is a self-inconsistent designation or predicate, and '$a = 1$' to be true when, and only when, '*a*' is analytic (equivalent, for some *b*, to '*b* or not-*b*'), in order to impose a corresponding intensional interpretation on the algebra throughout, without affecting any formal law of the system. For example, the relation which, on the usual extensional interpretation, would be read as "The class *a* is contained in the class *b*" then becomes "The predication of *a* entails the predication of *b*"—a relation exemplified by "All mermaids live in the sea," but not by "All mermaids live in Southampton."

Incidentally, if Schröder had given attention to this possible interpretation, he might have observed that Boolean algebra can be interpreted also as a calculus of propositions, but *without* the additional postulate, "For every element *p*, either *p* = o or *p* = 1." As [M.] Wajsberg, [Paul] Henle, and [J. C. C.] McKinsey have shown, any system of strict implication (S2 to S5) is a Boolean algebra. And for any such interpretation of this algebra as an intensional logic of propositions, the additional postulate, above, is not only superfluous but contraindicated; it would require that all propositions be either analytic or self-contradictory. In this connection, we may remark that the Schröder "two-valued algebra," which includes the additional postulate, is equivalent to the calculus of propositions in *Principia Mathematica*, in the sense that the correct rendering in English (or German) of any law of either of these two systems is likewise a correct reading of some law of the other.

We may also observe that, as the existence of Dr. Barcan Marcus's functional calculus makes sufficiently evident, there must be some intensional calculus of terms which stands related to strict implication in the same general manner that the calculus of classes in *Principia Mathematica* stands related to the extensional logic of propositions.

However, the Boolean algebra is a rather unsatisfactory form for any calculus of logic and, in any case, is more usefully restricted to its usual extensional interpretation as a logic of classes. Moreover, the derivation from an intensional calculus of functions would be unnecessarily complex and open to objections on other grounds as well. The convenient basis for an intensional logic of terms can be developed much more simply—so simply that the general character and content of it can be indicated here, although it will not be possible to discuss all the technical questions arising in connection with it. An outline of this system, which I shall call the "calculus of predicates," is as follows.

PRIMITIVE IDEAS

(1) *Predicative Functions:* $\varphi\hat{x}$, $\psi\hat{x}$, and so on here represent paradigmatically any predicative function of a single variable *x*, the values

of x being restricted to singular terms whose applicability is to individuals. Predicative functions are here taken as functions the values of which are propositions, not statements. Let it also be noted that '$\varphi\hat{x}$' stands for the *function itself*—for expressions such as 'that x is a man,' 'that x runs fast'—not for singular propositions which would be values of the functions, like 'that Socrates is a man,' or 'that the leading horse runs fast.' And, as was explained earlier for propositions, we shall, for convenience of reading, take 'that x is red' as synonymous with 'x being red.'

(2) *Negation:* $\sim\varphi\hat{x}$. If $\varphi\hat{x}$ be 'that x is red,' $\sim\varphi\hat{x}$ will be 'that it is false that x is red' or 'it not being the case that x is red'; for brevity, 'not-$\varphi\hat{x}$' may be taken as the reading of '$\sim\varphi\hat{x}$.'

(3) *Compound Functions:* $\varphi\hat{x} \cdot \psi\hat{x}$. When $\varphi\hat{x}$ and $\psi\hat{x}$ are functions of x, $\varphi\hat{x} \cdot \psi\hat{x}$ is a function of x. Thus 'that x is red and that x feels damp' is synonymous with 'that x is red and x feels damp' and with 'that x is red and feels damp.'

(4) *Self-consistency:* $\Diamond\,\varphi\hat{x}$. If $\varphi\hat{x}$ be 'that x is red,' $\Diamond\,\varphi\hat{x}$ will be 'that x being red is consistent with x being red.'

(5) *Assertion:* $\vdash \cdot \varphi\hat{x}$. If $\varphi\hat{x}$ be a function, then $\vdash \cdot \varphi\hat{x}$ is the statement which asserts $\varphi\hat{x}$.

DEFINITIONS

11.01 $\quad \varphi\hat{x} \vee \psi\hat{x} . = . \sim(\sim\varphi\hat{x} . \sim\psi\hat{x})\ Df.$

11.02 $\quad \varphi\hat{x} < \psi\hat{x} . = . \sim\Diamond\,(\varphi\hat{x} . \sim\psi\hat{x})\ Df.$

11.03 $\quad \varphi\hat{x} \equiv \psi\hat{x} . = : \varphi\hat{x} < \psi\hat{x} . \psi\hat{x} < \varphi\hat{x}\ Df.$

14.01 $\quad \varphi\hat{x} \supset \psi\hat{x} . = . \sim\varphi\hat{x} \vee \psi\hat{x}\ Df.$

14.02 $\quad \varphi\hat{x} = \psi\hat{x} . = : \varphi\hat{x} \supset \psi\hat{x} . \psi\hat{x} \supset \varphi\hat{x}\ Df.$

17.01 $\quad \varphi\hat{x} \circ \psi\hat{x} . = . \sim(\varphi\hat{x} < \sim\psi\hat{x})\ Df.$

POSTULATES[3]

11.1 $\quad \vdash :. \varphi\hat{x} . \psi\hat{x} : < : \psi\hat{x} . \varphi\hat{x}$

11.2 $\quad \vdash :. \varphi\hat{x} . \psi\hat{x} : < . \varphi\hat{x}$

11.3 $\quad \vdash :. \varphi\hat{x} . < : \varphi\hat{x} . \varphi\hat{x}$

11.4 $\quad \vdash :: \varphi\hat{x} . \psi\hat{x} : \theta\hat{x} :. < :. \varphi\hat{x} : \psi\hat{x} . \theta\hat{x}$

11.5 $\quad \vdash : \varphi\hat{x} . < . \sim(\sim\varphi\hat{x})$

11.6 $\quad \vdash :. \varphi\hat{x} < \psi\hat{x} . \psi\hat{x} < \theta\hat{x} : < . \varphi\hat{x} < \theta\hat{x}$

11.7 $\quad \vdash :. \varphi\hat{x} . \varphi\hat{x} < \psi\hat{x} : < . \psi\hat{x}$

19.01 $\quad \vdash : \Diamond\,(\varphi\hat{x} . \psi\hat{x}) . < . \Diamond\,\varphi\hat{x}$

---

[3] McKinsey has shown that 11.5 is redundant, and [W. T.] Parry has shown that 11.2 can be derived when 19.01 is given.

OPERATIONS

The usual operations of proof are assumed, including that of conjunction—that is, when $\vdash . \varphi\hat{x}$ and $\vdash . \psi\hat{x}$, then $\vdash : \varphi\hat{x} . \psi\hat{x}$. Also, when $\vdash : \varphi\hat{x} \equiv \psi\hat{x}$, either of the two, $\varphi\hat{x}$ or $\psi\hat{x}$, may be substituted for the other.

The assumptions above are uniform throughout with those of S2. (We here give them the same numbers, for convenience of reference.) It follows immediately that, for every theorem of that system, there is a corresponding theorem of this calculus of predicates, provided the corresponding proof-operations are here valid, as assumed. On that point, however, the reader may have a doubt; in fact, he may have more than one. All of these doubts, I think, can be dispelled or obviated; the principal one only will be mentioned here.

When $\varphi\hat{x}$ and $\psi\hat{x}$ are functions, $\sim\varphi\hat{x}$, $\varphi\hat{x} . \psi\hat{x}$, and $\varphi\hat{x} \vee \psi\hat{x}$, which are extensional functions of $\varphi\hat{x}$ and $\psi\hat{x}$, are clearly functions and *not* propositions. But the case may appear to be different for the intensional functions of $\varphi\hat{x}$ and $\psi\hat{x}$; $\Diamond \varphi\hat{x}$, $\varphi\hat{x} \prec \psi\hat{x}$, and $\varphi\hat{x} \circ \psi\hat{x}$. For expressions of the form 'that x is so and so,' 'that x is such and such,' it will appear that an expression of the form 'that x being so and so is consistent with x being so and so,' or 'that x being so and so entails x being such and such,' or 'that x being so and so is consistent with x being such and such' is either true or false, without regard to any chosen value of the variable x. That is not quite correct, as will be shown below. But any *intensional* function of functions is such that any value of it is *either analytic or else false*. Hence, when it is true, it is analytic. And, although we are unaccustomed to recognize the fact, any propositional function which is analytic is *for that reason* assertable and is in fact a *true proposition*, although it still remains a function also, since it still has variable constituents and there are expressions which are values of it. Thus if any doubt should arise as to whether expressions of the form $\Diamond \varphi\hat{x}$ or $\varphi\hat{x} \prec \psi\hat{x}$ or $\varphi\hat{x} \circ \psi\hat{x}$ are, in proof-operations of this calculus, legitimately substitutable for $\varphi\hat{x}$ or $\psi\hat{x}$, the answer has two parts: first, that in this as in any calculus, what the simpler expression $\varphi\hat{x}$ or $\psi\hat{x}$ can stand for is a genus in which what any expression of more complex form, such as $\Diamond \varphi\hat{x}$ or $\varphi\hat{x} \prec \psi\hat{x}$, is an included species; and whatever holds for all members of the genus will hold for all members of any species. And second, as above, although intensional functions of functions are always such that any instance of them which is true is analytic, and hence a proposition, they are still functions.

Apart from any such technical question, it is of some importance to observe that, in any case, what postulates and theorems of this calculus express are facts which accord with our logical intuitions. Let us see what sort of facts these are, by interpreting some of the postulates. For this purpose, let us take the instances, for $\varphi\hat{x}$ 'that x is red,' for $\psi\hat{x}$ 'that x feels damp,' and for $\theta\hat{x}$ 'that x contains juice.' Let us also notice here that the postulates are *asserted*, and hence become statements, not propositions, for any chosen values of φ, ψ, and θ. (That simplifies the reading of them.) For our chosen values, what 11.1 states is: "That x is red and x feels damp entails that x feels damp and x is red." (In passing, let us note that this statement of an intensional relation of two compound functions nowhere requires any interior quotation marks. The same is true for every intensional function or relation.)

We may also observe that what 11.1 asserts is a relationship of any pair of chosen *predicates*, 'φ' in '$\varphi\hat{x}$' and 'ψ' in '$\psi\hat{x}$'; and that, in any case falling under it, retention of reference to the variable 'x' would be superfluous. Thus, for our example, what 11.1 says may be rendered more briefly: "Being red and feeling damp entails feeling damp and being red." The appropriateness of calling this system the calculus of predicates will thus become obvious.

In the same simplified form, what 11.6 asserts as holding of our chosen functions is: "That being red entails feeling damp, and feeling damp entails containing juice, entails that being red entails containing juice." Consonantly, 11.6 itself might be read: "That (the predicate) φ entails (the predicate) ψ, and ψ entails θ, entails that φ entails θ." Considerations of space forbid further examples, but the reader will easily supply them for himself.

Let us next remark that, although any intensional function and any intensional function of functions will be such that, for any instance in which it becomes true it will also become analytically true and assertable, nevertheless quantification of the variable 'x' in such a function can have meaning. For example, it is false that, for all values of x, that x is rectangular entails that x is square. But taking 'this equilateral on the board' as our value of x, we have the true proposition 'that this equilateral on the board being rectangular entails this equilateral on the board being square.' Hence it is true that, for some value of x, that x is rectangular entails that x is square.

It is a further important fact that the *assertion* of any intensional function, without quantification, is logically equivalent to assertion of the same function with the proper quantification. It will be intuitively clear that a function will itself be analytic if, and only if, all values of it are analytic. Thus, writing '$(Ax) \cdot \varphi x$' for "For all values of x, $\varphi\hat{x}$," and '$(Sx) . \varphi x$' for "For some value of x, φx," we shall have the following equipollences:

(1) $\vdash . \sim \Diamond \sim \varphi \hat{x}$ has the same logical force as $\vdash : (Ax) . \sim \Diamond \sim \varphi x$.

(2) $\vdash . \varphi \hat{x} < \psi \hat{x}$ has the same logical force as $\vdash : (Ax) . \varphi x < \psi \hat{x}$.

(3) $\vdash . \Diamond \varphi \hat{x}$ has the same logical force as $\vdash : (Sx) . \Diamond \varphi x$.

(4) $\vdash . \varphi \hat{x} \circ \psi \hat{x}$ has the same logical force as $\vdash : (Sx) . \varphi x \circ \psi x$.

It is (1) which formulates the principle enunciated; the others follow from that. The reader may have a doubt about (4), thinking that the consistency of two functions should be equipollent with the *joint truth* of them for some value of the variable or variables. Oftentimes, that would indeed be the only available method of *proving* consistency of functions; nevertheless, it is not what the statement of such consistency asserts. The functions 'that x is a prince of Denmark' and 'that x is melancholy' can be consistent (I will venture to assert that they are) regardless of the question whether any melancholy Danish prince exists, although *not* regardless of there being some value, c, of x for which 'that c is a prince of Denmark' and 'that c is melancholy,' whether true or not, are mutually compatible, neither of them entailing the falsity of the other. However, it is not (4) above but (1) and (2) which are particularly important. This is the case because, as we have seen, every postulate and theorem of S2, and hence of this calculus of predicates, is of the form $\sim \Diamond \sim A$ or reducible to that form, or of the form A, where $\sim \Diamond \sim A$ is also provable. In consequence, a complete calculus of propositional functions of one variable can be derived directly from the calculus of predicates by formalization of the principle (1) above, the additional primitive idea '$(Ax) . \varphi x$,' the definition of '$(Sx) . \varphi x$,' and a minimum of further assumptions which are analogues of theorems of the calculus of predicates, though not derivable from their analogues. The resultant calculus would, in general, be congruent with the functional calculus of Dr. Barcan Marcus.

For this development, it would be of prime importance that, although the calculus of predicates does not contain the distinguishing principle of S3,

$$\vdash : \varphi \hat{x} < \psi \hat{x} . < . \sim \Diamond \psi \hat{x} < \sim \Diamond \varphi \hat{x},$$

nevertheless the following proof-schema can be established as holding for that calculus: Given any theorem of the form $\vdash . \varphi \hat{x} < \psi \hat{x}$, the corresponding theorem of the form $\vdash . \sim \Diamond \sim \varphi \hat{x} < \sim \Diamond \sim \psi \hat{x}$ can be derived. (The reason why this can be established as holding, although the above principle of S3 cannot, is that every *theorem* which is of the form

$\varphi\hat{x} < \psi\hat{x}$ will be a formal tautology, whereas the *hypothesis* $\varphi\hat{x} < \psi\hat{x}$ will have values for which it is not formally analytic.)

It is also of some interest that, as is indicated by our earlier discussion of propositions, together with the complete parallelism between S2 and the calculus of predicates, the whole logic of propositions could be regarded as a special case of this calculus of predicates, for which the predicates φ, ψ, and so on become propositional terms signifying states of affairs. Thus the calculus of predicates could be taken as the basic branch of logic in general.

8. Some Suggestions Concerning Metaphysics of Logic

The suggestions which I should like to present concern small points, each having a bearing on a large topic. But each of them, though small, is too big to be covered adequately in a short compass: as here formulated, they are put forward knowing that you will supply the needed context and in the hope that they may serve as a basis for discussion.

The large question, which my suggestions all concern, is the relation between the conceptual and the existential. And the general thesis which these seem to me to support is that the conceptual and the existential are irreducibly different categories, both required for an adequate *theory* of logic, but that, within logic itself, there are only such truths as are certifiable from conception alone and are independent of existential fact.

Logic is the science which serves the purpose of finding out what can be determined by thinking without looking, and has no business with any fact the assurance of which requires sense experience. All empirical facts belong in the domain of some other and natural science. Logic is concerned with what is deducible from what, and hence with the distinction between suppositions which are self-consistent and those which are not, since Q is deducible from P if and only if the joint statement which asserts P and denies Q is self-contradictory. But it has no concern with the distinction, amongst statements which are both consistently affirmable and consistently deniable, between those which are actually true and those which in fact are false. All that logic can determine, in the case of such contingent statements, is what is deducible from them and what premises are sufficient for them; and these logical relationships of them are unaffected by their truth or falsity.

So much is commonplace. All statements belonging to logic and all statements certifiable by logic are analytic and deducible from any premise, including the premise which denies them. And from premises of logic alone, no contingent truth of existence or non-existence is derivable: they have no consequences save other statements which are likewise analytic. But that leaves it still desirable to identify something by reference to which logical truth expresses a kind of fact and logical

Read before the meeting of the Association for Symbolic Logic on December 28, 1949. Reprinted by permission from Sidney Hook, ed., *American Philosophers at Work* (New York, 1957), pp. 93–105.

falsehood does violence to fact: some ground on which what is logically true is distinguishable from the logically false, and is worth saying.

It is the prevailing practice at present to explain this character of statements of logic by reference to language. That procedure is both apt and economical. But I think that it will prove inadequate for the theory of logic unless certain simple and obvious facts about language are recognized and the implications of them adhered to. A first such fact is that linguistic entities are not physical objects or events but abstract things of which physical existents may be instances. If there are no universals, then there is no such thing as language. As a physical phenomenon, language is identifiable with sounds and marks. But a sound or a mark is not language unless there is a fixed meaning associated with and expressed by it. Furthermore, it is not the pile of ink on the page, or the noise occurring at 2:15 which is the linguistic entity. The same word or other expression must be able to occur at different times and places in order to be a linguistic entity; even the physical symbol is a universal, identifiable with the recurrent *pattern* of marks or of noises, of which a single physical existent can be an instance.

Second, the meaning associated with a symbol and essential to its being a linguistic entity must be a psychological or mental entity. I should be glad to avoid the metaphysical question of mind; and I have no full theory of the mental to offer. But we shall all agree that psychological happenings take place in those individuals called conscious and are not identifiable with marks on pages or with noises a phonograph may emit at certain times unheard by anybody. Whatever the nature of psychological phenomena, they are what is spoken of by common sense by referring to minds. Let me use this common-sense idiom—so far as possible without metaphysical prejudice. A meaning is something which is mind-dependent; no minds, no meanings. We speak of meanings as entertained, and the entertainment of a meaning is an occurrence: an event which is temporal if not spatial. But just as it is essential to a linguistic symbol that it be the same from page to page, and the pile of ink an instance of it only, so the meaning it conveys cannot be identified with the psychological occurrence called the entertainment of it: it must be the same meaning which is entertained when we read the same expression at different times, if the pile of ink is to exercise the function of expressing the same meaning on different occasions. This meaning as characterizing different psychological events, and the same for any occasion of its entertainment, is the concept. And a meaning as relative to such entertainments, I shall speak of as a conceptual meaning.

Third, most meanings, and correlatively most linguistic expressions, have reference to external existents or states of affairs, spoken of as something meant. In relation to such an objective actuality, the meaning entertained or linguistically expressed constitutes the criterion which operates to determine which or what, amongst actualities which may present themselves, are those so meant. And it so operates by determining some recognizable *character* of actualities as essential to their being accepted as what is meant. This character, even if there be no more than one actual entity instancing it, never extends to the whole nature of any individual thing but is, again, an abstract or universal entity: a property or attribute.

This last consideration will, of course, require some comment, lest it should seem to imply that individuals cannot be conceived and meant by language. I defer such comment to a later point.

Of these three abstract entities—first, the concept as psychologically instanced meaning; second, linguistic meaning as what patterns of sound or of marks convey, and as the meaning of such expressions in terms of other expressions; and third, the character or property of objective actualities which is essential to their satisfying the condition set by the concept and expressed in language—of these three, it is the first which is antecedent to the other two. We do not first have marks and sounds and then invent or try to discover concepts for them to convey, but devise language to convey what is conceptually entertained. If there should be any who announce that there are no such things as meanings, let us reply that their announcement is meaningless.

Given a meaning, it may be associated with a visual pattern or pattern of sound by a social convention or by individual declaration of intent. And given a meaning represented by one symbolism, another symbolism can be stipulated to have the same meaning. But conventions and stipulations are possible only with respect to the use of symbols. Given two meanings, the relation of them can in no wise be affected by any convention of language. Meanings and the relations of them are as they are and could not be otherwise; and the supposition that meanings arise from or can be altered by stipulations of language— if anybody should hold that supposition—would be ludicrous.

I have no intention of saying that concepts or that meanings exist. (That point we shall return to later.) Nevertheless I would suggest that they must be granted some manner of being, and that if any logician were to say, "There are no such things as conceptual meanings," he would be using Occam's razor to cut his own throat. Existence— I take it—refers to a relation between a conceptual meaning entertained and an actuality, empirically found or evidenced, which satisfies the intention of that conceptual entertainment. But in this connection, it is of some importance to observe that no empirical presentment could determine that "So and so exists," if the conception of 'so and so' as a meaning entertained did not function as a condition to be satisfied or not satisfied by what may be empirically disclosed. This is no more than to say what is obvious; we must know what we mean by 'so and so' before we can determine the existence of 'so and so,' since otherwise we should lack any manner of determining what empirical findings would be pertinent to this question of existence. The basic relation of empirical knowledge is this relation between a character mentally entertained as the concept of 'so and so,' and a perceptual finding of that which evidences this character essential to being 'so and so.'

Incidentally, perhaps this resolves the puzzle that 'existence is not a predicate.' In the statement "So and so exists," this seeming predicate 'exists' does not express any identifiable *character*, distinguishing one thing from another: the relevant character is expressed by 'so and so'; and there is no difference of conceived character between the silver dollar which I cannot find in my pocket and the silver dollar that I do find elsewhere. Strange as it may seem, the subject of "So and so exists" is the conceptually delineated so and so, not the empirically discovered so and so; if it were the latter, then the assertion of existence would be meaningful only when it is true, and we should have the ridiculous consequence that we could not think of or speak of anything which does not exist. What is *predicated* of this conceptually meant 'so and so' is a relation of correspondence of character between it and something empirically findable or evidenced by perception. And again incidentally, this shows that for the being of a *concept* or conceptual meaning, the ontological argument is perfectly good; whatever is mentionable must have this status as conceptual, whether it exists or not.

Empirical knowledge has thus two conditions: the condition of a conceptually entertained meaning and the condition of some relevant perceptual finding. But knowledge, the expression of which would be an analytic statement, has only one condition: the condition of a factual relationship of meanings as conceptually entertained. And this relationship is determined by these concepts themselves.

I have, so far, left the sense of 'meaning' which is here in question unduly vague, and attempted to characterize it principally by reference to its epistemological status and function. When we turn from the epistemological to the linguistic, and seek to delineate that meaning of the word 'meaning' which is here in point as a property of expressions, it becomes evident that conceptual meaning is not denotation or extension but is identifiable with or correlative to connotation or intension.

It is the intensional meaning of an expression which is the criterion of classification and sets a condition to be satisfied; the denotation of the expression is the class of actualities satisfying this antecedent condition. Due to the logically accidental limitations of what exists or is actually the case, a conceptual and intensional meaning is never determinable from, though it may be limited by, the class denoted. And for the same reason, the intensional meaning of an expression does not determine, but only limits, the denotation or extension of it. Denotation or extension is meaning as *ap*plication, coinciding with those actualities which instance the intension which operates as criterion of their selection from amongst things observed or things in general; the intensional meaning which so operates is meaning as *im*plication: as what is entailed and required to be the case *in order that* the expression should apply. Thus the question "What does the expression mean in the sense of denotation?" is the question "What thing or things does it single out as spoken of?" And the question "What does the expression mean in the sense of intension?" is the question "What is said about anything, or implied, by the application or predication of this expression?"

Since I have already done my best with respect to this topic of intensional and extensional meaning in another place, let me merely summarize here.

Linguistically, the intension of an expression '*A*' can be identified by the dictum that any other expression '*B*' is included in the intension of '*A*' if and only if from the premise that '*A*' applies to x it is deducible that '*B*' applies to x. Thus in linguistic terms, the intension of '*A*' would be constituted by the and-relation of all the predicates entailed by the predication of '*A*.' Intensional equivalence—reciprocal entailment of two expressions—is the relation of definition (though there are further and psychological or heuristic requirements of a practically satisfactory definition). It should be noted that entailment is not here a truth-value relation, since deducibility is not a truth-value relation.

However, 'linguistic intension,' as I here use that phrase, fails to cover something essential to meaning as condition of the applicability of an expression, because of the farfetched consideration that explicating one expression by means of others will never succeed of its intent unless *some* words used are already understood as rules of discrimination to be followed in applying them. On the side of that to which application is made, what is essential to such correct application is some character. This character or attribute which must be determined as present in determining correctness of the application of an expression, I will speak of as the *signification* of the expression. Thus there are three things here which are correlative: the concept which is the criterion or rule in mind; the character or attribute signified, which is in the *thing*; and the linguistic intension, which is a function exercised by the expression in relating the concept or rule of discrimination to objective entities which satisfy it. This linguistic intension may itself be expressed by reference to other expressions whose applicability is entailed by applicability of the expression in question.

The notions of intension and extension can be applied to propositions in a manner the basis for which is borrowed from my colleague Professor Henry Sheffer. For every statement '*S*,' there is a corresponding expression which '*S*' asserts, and which the interrogative sentence "Is it the case that *S*?" inquires about, and the postulation "Let us assume that *S*" puts forward as an hypothesis. What all three of these modes of entertainment entertain, in their various ways, is the proposition in question. It can be identified, for any given statement '*S*,' with the expression '*that S*,' which '*S*' affirms to be the case. (In passing, let us remark that in terms of propositions so expressed, the formulation of their relations of intension never requires quotation marks; and one superficial objection to the logic of intension thereby loses its superficial plausibility.)

When so considered, a proposition turns out to be a kind of term. It expresses a meaning which, as conceptually entertained, stands as the condition to be satisfied if something is to be recognized as being the case: the condition to be met if this propositional term is to apply to the actual. The intension as *linguistic* is the 'and'-relation of all propositions deducible from the one in question. And the signification of this propositional term is that state of affairs which must be found in what is actual if the proposition is to be accepted as true. For propositions, as for other terms, the conceptual meaning as entertained, the linguistic meaning as expressed, and the state of affairs signified are all correlative; and none of these three is strictly correlative with the extension of it. The denotation or extension of a proposition—the existent to which it applies—is the actual world in case it is true, and is nothing in case it is false. Its extension is thus correlative with its truth-value.

To anticipate points to which I shall revert shortly, the actual world is that unique individual existent identified by the fact that all other individual existents are space-time parts of it. Propositions are thus singular terms. But what a proposition signifies is some character or attribute of this individual, and *not* a part of it. The attempt to identify states of affairs with space-time parts of the world must fail—for several reasons, of which I shall mention only one. Whatever is true at some time and false at some other time, is not a proposition but a propositional function. Any proposition which has temporal reference requires, for the full expression of it, that this temporal reference be made explicit; and when that is done, it must be *always* true or else always false.

There are more considerations which cry out for attention than it is possible to discuss here. One of the most important is that there must be a conceptual meaning of the proposition, which is independent of its truth or falsity, because there must be a *criterion* of such truth or falsity—that is, a criterion of applicability of the proposition to what is actual—in order that such actual truth or falsity may be determined. This propositional concept is the same whether the assertion of the proposition—the statement—is true or is false; only on that condition would any truth or falsity be discoverable. Correlatively, the intensional meaning of any expression of the propositional concept entertained, and the signification of it—the state of affairs *supposed*—must remain the same, whether the proposition is actually true or actually false. And again correlatively, logic, which certifies no actual existence and depends on none, has nothing to do with the extensional relations of statements of fact, except hypothetically or—and this is the place to put the emphasis—so far as the extensional relations of propositions are deducible from their relations of intensional meaning. The logic which construes its basic categories as extensional and in terms of truth-values would seem to be strangely misconceiving itself as one of the natural and empirical sciences. Logic can certify no existential and empirical fact; and no empirical fact or set of such can certify any truth of logic. What logic can certify is the relation of intensional meanings amongst themselves: e.g., that whatever satisfies one condition must also satisfy another condition, that what satisfies one condition must fail to satisfy another condition, that what is requisite to satisfaction of one condition is the same as what is requisite to satisfaction of another, or that two conditions are mutually compatible but have none of the previous relations. None of these relationships can be empirically assured, with the exception of consistency; and consistency is, logically, a negative fact—the negative of a relation of deducibility.

I have so far spoken of individuals, of characters or attributes, of existence, and of an ontological status of conceptual meanings which is not that of existence, with no explanations. Adequacy in an implied metaphysics would take a book—one which I shall not attempt to write. Dogmatically and inadequately: only individuals exist. And I am satisfied to conceive individuals as continuous and bounded parts of the space-time whole. (The space-time whole itself is a Pickwickian individual, not being boundable.) One individual may be wholly contained in another, as the bottom board is included in a box. Two may overlap, as a dog and a hair that it sheds. Individuals having neither of these two relationships are distinct. The space-time attributes of a thing may serve as the 'principle of individuation' but cannot be exhaustive of its individuality; and space-time attributes themselves are specifiable only in relative terms. (In passing, please note that a pile of sand is an individual only if the pieces of air between the grains are parts of this individual pile: the *sand* in the pile is not a continuous boundable entity. This apparently trivial consideration might turn out to be important for clear distinction between individuals and characters.)

A character is an entity which can be instanced and is the same in all its instances. An instance of a character is an existent individual. Characters themselves do not exist, but they are real or unreal. A character is real if an instance of it exists.

Correlatively, neither concepts nor intensional meanings exist. But a concept is real if there is a psychological instance of its entertainment, or it is logically (and consistently) constructible from element-concepts which are entertained. (The notion of a concept never entertained may seem jejune; but we should remind ourselves that this is the only kind of reality which any but an infinitesimal fraction of the natural numbers have. In this connection also, we should observe the necessity of distinguishing a concept the expression of which would be of the form 'logically constructible from elements such and such by operations so and so' from any concept so constructed.) Similarly, an intensional meaning as a linguistic entity may have the kind of reality characteristic of expressions; that is, it is real if there is some pattern of sounds or of marks having an instance—some noise on some occasion or a pile of ink somewhere—which conveys this conceptually determinate meaning, or if it is consistently constructible by the rules of language from elementary expressions which are instanced.

As between the concept, or the intensional meaning, on the one side, and the corresponding character in an object or objects, on the other, the reality of the concept or the meaning does not entail the reality of the character as instanced in some existent. (It is by this fact that we are able to think of, and speak of, what does not exist. And if we could not so think, we could not act deliberately, since that requires us to choose amongst considered alternatives only one of which will ever be realized.) Also, the reality of the character, as instanced in some individual, does not entail the reality of the concept, or of the intensional meaning as a linguistic entity.

Meanings as concepts, meanings as linguistic intensions, and characters as instanced in existents are all three of them abstract entities or universals. Concepts and linguistic entities are—I have suggested—mind-dependent. Whether characters or attributes, as abstractable aspects of individual existents, are mind-dependent is a final question which lies between a metaphysics which is consistent with nominalism and one consistent with conceptualism. I shall attempt merely to indicate the locus of this somewhat tenuous issue. The conceptualist repudiates nominalism, for one reason because it reduces logic to a game played with fictions, having a psychological explanation but no validity. And for another because it reduces the basis of the intelligibility of things to a similar fiction. But he refuses the Platonic reification of abstractions, and he may also repudiate the basic argument of absolute idealism: to be real is to be intelligible, and to be intelligible is to be mind-related; hence no object out of relation to a subject. He may consider the logocentric predicament (Professor Sheffer's phrase) of a rationalizing mind which must think and speak in terms of universals no better argument for absolute idealism than the egocentric predicament is for personalistic idealism. If so, then he is left with a conception I can only suggest crudely by saying that the conception of a world of individual existents, none of them conscious, is a meaningful supposition, but that, in such a world, there would be no abstract entities, there would be classifiable things but no classes, there would be stars in the heavens but no constellations.

What suggests this manner of conception, and is at once less simple-minded than my crudely put suggestion and more pertinent to logic, is the fact that nothing can be literally apprehended by a mind except some abstraction or universal. Individuals can neither be thought of nor identified except through their inherent characters. The nominalistic conception that individuals are the first knowables and the logically primitive entities, and that individuals are primitively determinable by ostensive reference, is, I think, epistemologically untenable. It is plausible only when a genetic account of psychological origins is substituted for the required epistemological investigation of validities. No one can literally be shown what is meant by means of ostensive indications unless these are supplemented by some manner of empathetic guess-work. In the first place, characters can be pointed to, as well as individuals: it requires that the intention to indicate an individual and not a character should be divined before such an intended identification can be ostensively conveyed. In the second place, whether it be an individual or a character which it is intended to identify as meant, no pointing and no succession of pointings can delimit *precisely* what is meant—this for a number of reasons some of which at least will be obvious. Successive pointings may progressively limit and hence inductively approximate to an intended meaning, but—be it noted—such approximation can only be in terms of recognizable characters presented or not presented for observation. And the meaning in question will not be strictly apprehended until the one who observes guesses correctly the *rule of discrimination* which the one who points is using in determining when to point and when not to point. That criterion is the concept.

The intention to identify an individual as meant can, in any case, succeed only on account of the logically accidental limitations of what exists. An individual is apprehendable only as *that which* satisfies certain conditions specifiable in terms of characters it incorporates. The specified characters must be finitely enumerable, but the individual, being subject to the law of the excluded middle, is infinitely specific. I can only suggest and not develop the important features of meaning as denoting or designating which follow from this fact. The mother whose child, now six, was kidnapped at the age of two, passionately intends to refer to just one child. But it is a part of her tragedy that her attempt to identify this child may be mistaken because she is unable to specify sufficiently the characters to be looked for.

I can only suggest and not develop correlative considerations for the logic of singular terms and singular statements. "Zeus is a god" and "Socrates is a man" have the same grammatical form. But they are not of the same form logically. The former means that, for any x, that x is Zeus entails that x is a god. No implication of existence or nonexistence is involved, and the statement is analytic, being certifiable from the definitive meaning of 'Zeus.' "Socrates is a man" would satisfy the same paradigm, but it presumably intends the further implication that a unique individual exists satisfying the condition 'x is Socrates.' Although we know from the meaning of 'Socrates' that no nonhuman individual satisfies this condition, we have inductive assurance only of the existence and uniqueness of an object satisfying it; and the statement "Socrates is a man" is nonanalytic, like every assertion of existence.

One important point of distinction between individuals and characters must at least be mentioned since, without it, the distinction itself could be unclear. For every predicable relation of an individual to a character, there is the converse relation of that character to that individual. Individuals instance just those characters which they do; and conversely, characters are instanced in just those individuals in which they are. The difference is that every character instanced by an individual is essential to that individual's being just the individual that it is. That is implied by the infinite specificity of what is individual. A character, however, is just that character which it is regardless of what individuals exist and are instances of it. In other words, the relation between an individual and a character it instances is essential to the individual, inessential to the character. That is a basic difference between the two categories.

One corollary of this is the fact that any attempt to identify a universal or a character by reference to the class of individuals of which this character is predicable is doomed to failure. Any given predicate, taken as condition, delimits uniquely a classification of existents (which may be null) ; but no class of existents determines a unique predicate as that which all its members satisfy. Owing to the logically accidental limitations of what exists, as well as on account of the infinite specificity of each and every individual, there are always, for any given class of existents, at least two predicates (two which are not equivalent in intension) which are common to all and only those individuals which are members of this class. The predicates 'human,' 'featherless biped,' and 'animal that laughs' constitute a familiar though not too good example.

There are, I think, many other implications here involved, the investigation of which would be interesting and logically profitable. But time does not permit even the suggestion of them. In conclusion, let me mention one such consideration only: one with respect to which you may well think I have a prepossession.

The denotation or extension of any expression is always logically accidental: logic can never certify what it denotes or whether it denotes anything, except in those cases in which it is determinable, from its intensional meaning, that it has universal extension or that its extension is null. The statements belonging to any correct logic are those and those only whose truth is certifiable by reference to the intensional meanings of the logical constants of the system (including those conveyed by the syntactic significance of the order of writing). A logic in which the constants are confined to extensional functions symbolizes no element-relation such that whenever it obtains it is logically certifiable. The extensional logic of propositions, for example, instead of symbolizing and asserting that relation which obtains between *p* and *q* when and only when *q* is deducible from *p*, asserts a relation such that if two sentences be chosen at random from the morning paper, it is certain in advance that this relation will hold between one or other of them as antecedent and the remaining one as consequent. But it asserts this relation *only in those instances* in which the quite different relation which is the converse of 'is deducible from' also obtains. It thus uses tacitly, as criterion of assertion in logic, a relation which is not expressible in the vocabulary it provides; and what it asserts is logically certifiable for that reason only. I think it is desirable in logic that the logical criteria of logical certifiability should be expressed.

Index